Emotionalizing Fashion Retail

Jochen Strähle (Ed.)

Emotionalizing Fashion Retail

Bibliografische Information der Deutschen Nationalbibliothek:
Die Deutsche Nationalbibliothek verzeichnet diese Publikation in der Deutschen Nationalbibliografie; detaillierte bibliografische Daten sind im Internet über http://dnb.dnb.de abrufbar.

© 2015 Jochen Strähle

Illustration: **Reutlingen University**

Herstellung und Verlag: BoD – Books on Demand, Norderstedt

ISBN: 978-3-7347-5821-8

List of Contents

List of Tables 18

List of Figures 19

Emotionalizing the Fashion Retail **23**

1   The Landscape for Fashion Retailers 23

2   Emotionalizing the Fashion Retail- A Journey of Opportunities 25

The Fashion Retail Environment **29**

Emotions in the Fashion Retail – A Literature Review **30**

Abstract 30

1   Today's Hypercompetitive Mass Market 31

2   Emotions in the Fashion Retail 32

2.1   Costumer Research and its Classification in Behavioural Science 32

2.2   Costumer Emotions and their Origin 32

2.2.1   Analysing the Evolution of Emotion Research 32

2.2.2   Analysing the State of the Art of Emotion Research 35

2.3   Costumer Shopping Experience under the Influence of Emotions 44

2.3.1 Emotion's Dependency on Moderators 44

2.3.2 Emotion's Generation through Stimulus 48

2.3.3 Emotion's Influence on the Organism 51

2.3.4 Emotion's Influence on the Response Outcome 52

3 Discussion of Emotions in the Fashion Retail 56

4 Emotions as an Enhancement of the Unique Selling Proposition? 58

Omni-Channeling in the Fashion Industry - A Prerequisite for Emotional Shopping Experience? 61

Abstract 61

5 Introduction 62

6 Literature Review and Definitions 63

6.1 Omni-Channeling 63

6.2 Emotional Shopping Experience 65

6.3 Customer Segments 67

6.4 Changes in Technology, Consumer Behavior and Retail Environment 69

6.4.1 Technological Developments 69

6.4.2 Changes in Consumer Behavior 70

6.4.3 Shifts in Retailing 73

6.5 Chances to increase Shopping Experiences through Omni-Channeling 75

6.5.1	Incentives to get the Internet-Customer into the Physical Store	77
6.5.2	Incentives to increase Shopping Experience in the Store with Digitalization	79
6.6	Challenges in Omni-Channeling	81
7	Discussion	83
8	Conclusion	85

The Pre-Purchase Phase - How to Attract Customers 87

The Ethical Side of Emotional Fashion Advertising 88

Abstract 88

9	Introduction	89
10	Ethics in a Management Context	90
10.1	Ethics – A Definition and Its Relevance in Management	90
10.2	Ethics – A Part of Corporate Social Responsibility	92
10.3	Ethics in Marketing	95
11	Emotional Fashion Advertising	96
11.1	Advertising - Definition and Theoretical Approaches	96
11.2	Emotions in Advertising	97
11.3	Characteristics of Fashion Advertising	100

11.4	The Customer's Perception of Emotional Fashion Advertising	102
11.5	The Image of Physical Appearance and Attractiveness in Emotional Fashion Advertising	104
12	The Ethical Dimensions of Emotional Fashion Advertising	106
12.1	The Ethical Side of Managing Emotions	106
12.2	The Ethical Side of Influencing Customers	108
12.3	The Ethical Side of Using Idealized Images of Physical Appearance and Attractiveness	110
13	Discussion and Implications for Emotional Fashion Advertising	113
13.1	Ethical Responsibilities of Companies Using Emotional Fashion Advertising	113
13.2	Managerial Implications for Companies Using Emotional Fashion Advertising	114
14	Conclusion, Limitations and Further Research	116

Gaining New Customers with Social Media Campaigns **118**

Abstract		118
1	Introduction	119
1.1	Increased Importance of Social Media Engagement	119
1.2	Research Question	120
2	Literature Review	120
2.1	Corporate View	120

2.2	Digital Strategy	121
2.2.1	Strategy Development	122
2.3	Digital Marketing	124
2.3.1	Definition	125
2.3.2	Strategy Development	126
2.4	Social Media Marketing	134
2.4.1	Definition	135
2.4.2	Social Media Tools	136
2.4.3	Strategy Development	140
2.5	Social Media Campaigns	147
2.5.1	Measuring a Return on Social Media	148
3	Discussion	150
4	Conclusion	152

Enhancing Emotional Involvement with Video-Marketing 153

Abstract		153
1	Introduction	154
2	Literatur Review	155
2.1	Marketing communication	155
2.1.1	Define Marketing communication	155

2.1.2	Marketing communication in the 21th century	157
2.1.3	Video marketing as communication medium	160
2.2	Emotions and Involvement in Marketing	164
2.2.1	Emotions	164
2.2.2	Psychological processes within consumption behavior	166
2.2.3	Emotions affect sales	170
3	Discussion	172
3.1	Video marketing enhance emotional involvement	172
3.2	Trends to enhance emotional involvement with video marketing	174
4	Conclusion	177

The Purchase Phase - Converting Customers into Shoppers 179

Impact of Payment Methods on the Buying Decision- How does the Degree of Transparency of a Payment Method influence the Buying Decision in Fashion Business? 180

Abstract		180
1	Introduction	181
2	Fashion Consumption and the Decision-Making Process in Fashion Business	181
2.1	Fashion Consumption	182

| 2.2 | Decision-Making | 183 |

| 3 | Overview of Payment Methods used in Fashion Business | 190 |

| 3.1 | Cash | 190 |

| 3.2 | Cashless Payment Systems | 190 |

| 3.2.1 | Payment Systems in E-Commerce | 193 |

| 3.2.2 | Mobile Payment Systems based on NFC Technology | 194 |

| 4 | Transparency of a Payment Method and its Impact on the Buying Decision | 195 |

| 4.1 | What is Transparency of a Payment Method? | 197 |

| 4.2 | Classification of Payment Methods in the Degree of Transparency and Utilization | 198 |

| 4.2.1 | Cash | 198 |

| 4.2.2 | Debit Card | 199 |

| 4.2.3 | Credit Card | 200 |

| 4.2.4 | Purchase on account | 200 |

| 4.2.5 | PayPal | 201 |

| 4.2.6 | Mobile Payment based on NFC technology | 202 |

| 4.3 | Impact of Transparency of a Payment Method on Consumer Behavior and the Buying Decision | 202 |

| 5 | Implications for the Fashion Business | 207 |

Driving Excitement through Click and Collect 210

Abstract 210

1 Introduction 211

2 The New Retail Environment 213

2.1 Difference between Multichannel and Omnichannel Retailing 213

2.2 Click and Collect as an Integral Part of Omnichannel Retailing 214

3 Buying Behavior 216

3.1 The Buying Decision-Making Process.. 216

3.2 Customers' Behavior in a Multichannel Environment 217

4 Emotions in Fashion Retail 219

4.1 Influencing Customers' Emotions via Store Environment............................. 219

4.2 The Influence of Music And Scents 222

4.3 The Influence of Sales Personnel 222

4.4 Emotions in The Online Environment 223

5 Discussion 224

6 Conclusion 228

7 Limitations and Further Research 229

The Post-Purchase Phase - Transforming Shoppers to Lovers 231

Loyalty Programs for Fashion Retailers- An emotional perspective 232

Abstract 232

1 Introduction 233

1.1 Research question and purpose 234

1.2 Literature Review 236

2 Theoretical background to loyalty programs 236

2.1 Customer Satisfaction 236

2.2 Customer Loyalty 237

2.3 Creating customer experience 238

2.4 Loyalty Programs 238

2.4.1 Differentiation between loyalty programs 239

2.4.2 Perceived Benefits of Loyalty Programs 240

2.4.3 Program Loyalty 242

2.4.4 Examples for successful loyalty programs 242

3 Trends and Developments in Consumer Behaviour 244

3.1 Emotional components in Consumer Behaviour 245

3.2 Shopping Motivations for Consumers 245

3.3 Individual and Group Influences on Consumer Behaviour 245

3.4	The buying decision process	247
3.4.1	Problem Recognition	247
3.4.2	Information Search	247
3.4.3	Evaluation of Alternatives	248
3.4.4	Purchase decision	248
3.4.5	Post-purchase behaviour	248
3.5	S-O-R - Theoretical model of consumer behaviour	249
3.6	Stimuli and characteristics affecting consumer behaviour	250
4	Implication and recommendation	251
4.1	Interactive experience	252
4.2	Multi-partner program	253
4.3	Status	253
4.4	Communication	253
5	Conclusion and Limitation	254

Integrated Marketing Communication in Fashion: Converting Customers into Promoters? 256

Abstract		256
1	The Customer as Promoter an Introduction	257
2	Status Quo in Literature	258

2.1	The Power of Word-of-Mouth Communication	258
2.1.1	Methodology	258
2.2	Evolution from WOM to eWOM	260
2.3	Underlying Motives for Word-of-Mouth Communication	263
2.3.1	Customer Satisfaction, Trust and Commitment	263
2.3.2	Involvement Construct	264
2.4	Word-of-Mouth in the Fashion Context	268
2.5	Modern Communication Disciplines	269
2.5.1	Viral Marketing	269
2.5.2	Consumer Generated Media	276
2.6	Effectiveness and Efficiency of Word-of-Mouth	281
2.6.1	Quantitative and Qualitative Measurement	281
3	Discussion and Practical Implications in the Fashion Context	284
3.1	The Customer as Focal Point	286
3.2	Company Internal Redefinition of Strategies	286
3.3	Design and Operational Implementation of Marketing Communication	287
4	Conclusion and Limitations	288

Special Issues for the Sustainable Customer ... 291

The Sustainable Fashion Oxymoron- Want vs Act! ... 292

Abstract ... 292

1 Introduction ... 293

2 Literature Review ... 293

2.1 The Sustainable Fashion ... 293

2.2 Sustainable Fashion is an Oxymoron ... 297

2.3 Consumer's behavior ... 298

2.4 The change of the attitude towards life ... 299

2.5 Consumer's conflict of buying ... 300

2.6 Demand and supply of sustainable fashion ... 303

3 Discussion ... 307

4 Conclusion ... 309

Information Demand of the Sustainable Consumer ... 312

Abstract ... 312

1 The Importance of Information within Sustainable Fashion ... 313

2 Literature Review ... 315

2.1 The Definition of Sustainable Development ... 315

2.2 The Theory of Communication and Information Processing 316

2.2.1 Communication 316

2.2.2 Information Processing 318

2.3 The Information Demand of the Sustainable Consumer 321

2.3.1 The Sustainable Consumer 321

2.3.2 The Information Content 325

2.3.3 The Information Frame 329

3 Discussion 333

3.1 Consistency of results 333

4 Validity of Definition of the Sustainable Customer 334

4.1 Validity of Assessed Information Content 335

4.2 Validity of the Assessed Information Frame 336

4.3 Assessed Impact of Information on Sustainable Consumer Behavior 337

5 Conclusion, Limitations and Further Research 338

5.1 Conclusion 338

5.2 Limitations 339

5.3 Further Research 339

List of References 341

List of Tables

Table 1: Izard - Differential Emotional Scale 37

Table 2: Customer segments in multi-channeling 68

Table 3: Technological and consumer behavior changes 70

Table 4 Advantages of online and physical stores 76

Table 5: Tangible and intangible benefits from digital marketing 127

Table 6: Human needs that explain social behavior 141

Table 7 Traditional and new marketing communication 159

Table 8: Concerns of Green Consumers 327

Table 9: Communication Characteristics and Involvement 332

List of Figures

Figure 1: S-R Model 34

Figure 2: S-O-R Model 34

Figure 3: S-O-R Model including Cognition and Affect 34

Figure 4: Russell - Circumplex Model of Affect 39

Figure 5: Plutchik – Circumplex Model of the Basic Eight Emotions 40

Figure 6: S-O-R Model including Moderators 45

Figure 7: Limbic Model of Costumer Classification 46

Figure 8: Maslow - Hierarchy of Needs 47

Figure 9: Moderators of Costumer Shopping Experience 48

Figure 10: S-O-R Model, Triple C-Model, Stimuli: Content 49

Figure 11: S-O-R Model, Triple C-Model, Organism: Condition and Cause 52

Figure 12: Costumer Expectations – Tolerance and Indifference Zones 54

Figure 13: Costumer View - Perceptual Shopping Experience Process 56

Figure 14: Differentiation between multi-channeling, cross-channeling, omni-channeling 64

Figure 15: Modell of shopping experience 66

Figure 16: Information search in a sales channel before the purchase in a different sales channel, 103≤n≤699 71

Figure 17: Virtual Footwear Wall 74

Figure 18: Differentiation potentials for Omni-Channel Retailer 85

Figure 19: CSR Pyramid by Caroll, 1991 93

Figure 20: Number of diagnosed cases of anorexia in Germany from 2000 to 2012 111

Figure 21: "Which of the following devices do you own?" 125

Figure 22: Key digital media channels 130

Figure 23: "Thinking about devices, do you ever use them whilst consuming…?" 135

Figure 24: Popularity of Social Media Platforms 138

Figure 25: Social Media is time-consuming 139

Figure 26: „Please tell us why you joined a brand community. " 142

Figure 27: Social Media Strategy aims of companies 146

Figure 28: Communication model 156

Figure 29: Spread of advertising spending in Germany 2013 160

Figure 30: Emotional system of the Limbic model 165

Figure 31: Stimulus-Organism-Response Model 167

Figure 32: FCB grid 168

Figure 33: EDEKA Cash desk sinfonia 175

Figure 34: H&M Magical Holidays 176

Figure 35 Vaude Freeski 176

Figure 36: Classification of Fashion Purchases in the Buying Type Model 186

Figure 37: Steps in Consumer Decision-Making 187

Figure 38: Payment Service Providers 191

Figure 39: NFC Symbols 195

Figure 40: Classification of Payment Methods 198

Figure 41: Impact of Transparency on Consumption Behavior 204

Figure 42: Hedonic Approach - Impact of Transparency on Fashion Consumption 209

Figure 43: The Mehrabian Russell Model 220

Figure 44: Definition of Customer Loyalty Programs 239

Figure 45: The buying decision process model 247

Figure 46: An S-O-R model of consumer response to loyalty programs 249

Figure 47: An S-O-R model adapted by Kotler 251

Figure 48: Structure of Research Paper 259

Figure 49: Chronology of Literature 260

Figure 50: Factors Influencing the Customer in Nowadays Marketing Environment 262

Figure 51: Antecedents Affecting Traditional WOM Communication 268

Figure 52: Multiplier Effect in the Transmission of Viral Marketing Campaigns 272

Figure 53: Marketing Evolution 276

Figure 54: Participative Marketing Communication 279

Figure 55: Situational Related CGM-Management 280

Figure 56: Performance Measurement on Operational Level 282

Figure 57: Net Promoter Score in Customer Purchase Decision Making
          Process 283

Figure 58: GOTS 302

Figure 59: Growing Demand for Fair Trade Labelled Textiles in Germany 313

Figure 60: The Triple Bottom Line 316

Figure 61: Communication Process 317

Figure 62: Stimulus-Object-Response-Paradigm 318

Figure 63: Purchase Decision Making Process 324

Emotionalizing the Fashion Retail

Jochen Strähle

1 The Landscape for Fashion Retailers

The international fashion retailing scene has faced deep changes during the last decades. It is not only that new formats entered the market but also the way of distribution changed severely (Buvari, Dosé, & Vonstad, 2014) in the wake of the digitalization. From 2007 the sales volume for the German fashion online market has tripled from 12 Bill. € to 38 Bill. € (ECC Köln & hybris GmbH, 2014a). The unstoppable trend to the integration of the smartphone in the daily life will change the information and consumption patterns even more, as now the digital world will enter also the brick&mortar world (Bruce, 2012a; Daurer, Molitor, & Spann, 2012a). This reshaping of the market will set new challenges for every brand or fashion chain (Aubrey & Judge, 2012a). As more shares are transferred to a digital channel companies will have to react with a holistic new approach. This new approach will have to set its focus on several elements.

The first key element might be the distribution side of retailing. Starting from a single channel approach the idea of gaining new consumers through the use of multiple yet independent channels (Rittinger, 2014) was seen as one of the key growth possibilities. However, the fact that these channels have been focusing on different consumers groups (the online-shopper vs. the offline shopper), synergies were not the key idea behind it (Wilding, 2013). As these strategies have been developed in the pre-e-business era (Buvari et al., 2014) they obviously fail in an digital environment. Described as the channel-hopping phenomena (Hsiao, Ju Rebecca Yen, & Li, 2012; Schoenbachler & Gordon, 2002; Verhoef, Neslin, & Vroomen, 2007) companies started to react and hence went onto the idea of a no-line or omni-channel approach which aims to seamlessly integrate the channels together (Wilding, 2013). As this came most of the time from the internal requirements of a company, the current requirements will be to consider omni-channeling from a consumer's perspective, so to speak a consumer omni-channeling (Strang, 2013). In this context the consumer recognizes a brand more as a cloudy construct and is probably not aware of when an where he is contact with a brand. It just needs to be convenient at any time and any place (Ferguson, 2008a). However the distribution channels are used the basic buying process is not likey to be changed. So consumer processes still can be put down to a pre-purchase, a purchase, and a post-purchase phase (Kotler & Armstrong, 2014), knowing that of course this is not considered to be a linear system as consumer's will depending on the product jump back and forth within the individual steps (Solomon & Rabolt, 2004a). It will be critical for companies to elaborate each individual steps under the guidance of new technological innovations and their adaptions by the consumers. Therefor an in-depth discussion and a sorrow understanding about this process is the determinant for any marketing management activity.

The second key element will be the integration of emotions in all-single steps for this buying process while taking into considerations of the digital opportunities. It is agreed that all buying decisions are rooted in emotional and psychological motivations (Jiyun Kang & Haesun Park-Poaps, 2010). They therefor are known as a considerable criteria when it comes down to understand and manage the purchase decision of consumers (Eun Joo Park, Eun Young Kim, & Judith Cardona Forney, 2006). Most of the academic discussion are based on several derivates of the Stimulus-Organism-Response (S-O-R) paradmigm (Vieira, 2013) which mainly Mehrabian & Russel (1974) and Donovan & Rossiter (1982) brought to large attention. It is clear that the creation of a stimulus such as the ambient factors of a retailer (Baker, Parasuraman, Grewal, & Voss, 2002), such as music (Koo & Kim, 2013) or in general the allover store environment (Doucé & Janssens, 2013) are among the daily business of fashion retailers. They try to create an environment, which drives sales. However to create this particular ambience without understand other influencing factors like social factors (Changjo Yoo, Jonghee Park, & MacInnis, 1998) will not reach very far. Even more, the understanding of the black box (Sigg, 2009), i.e. what happens with a given stimulus inside an organism is still very limited. As a consequence the response, which will be the consumer's action, can only be something observed but which cannot be strategically managed. But if the aim for a positive experience as an emotional state is the driver behind every buying decision, marketers should closely investigate the external and internal process in order to create shopping channels or communication campaigns, which are productive.

The third key element will be the consideration of sustainable development within the fashion retailing. The industry has often been criticized for exploitation of human rughts, child labour issues and the overall non-ecological approach of its fast-fashion orientated supply chain management (Winge, 2008). The upcoming green fashion idea (Shrum, McCarty, & Lowrey, 1995) is hence covering these aspects. The three pillars environment, society, and economy have shaped the discussion about sustainability also in the fashion industry (Grober, 2013). Still the fashion landscape is dominated by a fast-fashion thinking with ever changing products at an ever-faster speed. But if more and more consumers start questioning the consequences of their own behavior and are willing to pay more for sustainable products (Dong, Richards, & Feng, 2014), fashion retailers will have to reshape not only their product structure or store layouts, but especially their communication towards their new green consumers, which might lead to full transparency of their supply chain. As mentioned before, the use of digital tools by the consumers will provide them an ever information base. To put it in a nutshell: Consumers want to have a good feeling when buying fashion. This will inevitably include not only the inner self-satisfaction of their egos but will also integrate their values towards a sustainable lifestyle. Therefor, a successful fashion retailer must also take into consideration the special requirements of a sustainable consumer in the digital age under the emotional perspective.

2 Emotionalizing the Fashion Retail- A Journey of Opportunities

What are now the key levers for fashion marketers? The following articles cover the most relevant topics in the digital era of fashion marketing. The aim is to provide both theoretical and practical insight into the idea of an emotional customer management (ECM), which aims to understand the mechanism of external stimuli provided by companies and the consumers' reaction. The better managers are able to understand the various facettes of decision making, the better they will provided real benefits to their target groups. The book follows a simple structure: What is our current situation? How then do we as marketers attract customers, convert them into shoppers and turn them into lovers?

The book is structured in five chapters. Each of these chapters focuses on the state of the art research on the buying process of fashion products. Based on distinct research questions, the reader will be able to dig deep into the individual levers for all main elements of a buying decision. It thus can provide a solide understanding on how to deal with consumer's preferences not only today but much more for the future.

Chapter 1 – The Fashion Retail Environment- is serving as an introduction to develop a solid understanding about the current situation of the fashion industry. This includes tow parts. The first one deals with „Emotions in the Fashion Retail" and covers a discussion about the term emotions, which is in ongoing use in the daily life, however finding a common sense proves to be pretty difficult. The most used theoretical frameworks are discussed in this context to understand the key mechansim in the buying process from a consumer's perspective. Second, the article „Omnichanneling in the Fashion Industry" features an analysis of the latest trend in the fashion retail. The idea of merging the various distribution channels together has challenged the practitioners in the past already, but the digital evolution has brought it to a new lever. Under this context the authors discuss, whether it is an unevitable must to provide this fullchannel experience in ordert o increase the emotional involvment.

The journey through the buying process starts in chapter 2 – The Pre-Purchase Phase. The focus lies on the question how to attract customers. The ethical side of emotional fashion advertising is discussed, as is the question of how to gain new consumers with social media campaigns. As rich-media marketing is on the rise, especially the role of videomarketing will change in the future. Under the light of the emotional framework, the authors provide a solid base for further developments of this field.

Chapter 3 – The Purchase Phase – questions how to convert the customers then into shoppers. As in everytrade the exchange of values is the essential part of any transaction so the authors put their eye on the payment process. In this book, this is examined under the perspective of the emotional status of a consumer. It shows clearly how the risk perception drives the final purchase both online and offline. As under the prerequisite of omni-channeling, click&collect stores are considered to become an essential element of future retail stores. The author hence examine, how and when a click&collect service offers real benefits. They also show clearly the current mishaps in the understanding of this service and provide new ideas to develop this to a successful concept.

Chapter 4 – The Post-Purchase Phase- deals with the question how to transform shoppers to lovers. Well discussed in literature under the terms of retail patronage or loyalty, the authors consider other explication models from the emotional customer side and turn them into recommendations for an emotion based loyalty program. Secondly they develop in the following article a framework on how to use customers as a promoter, which will truly become a necessity in a more social and digital world.

The last chapter concludes with „Special Issues for the Sustainable Customer". As the demand for sustainable products are on the rise in almost any industry, this will be a very relevant topic for future success. The authors however are critical in that way as they investigate first on the discrepancies between wanting vs. acting. They raise the demand of a clear definition of a sustainable customer first. They also discuss the special needs of communication and ask, what sources and elements are needed within the buying process to deliver the necessary amount of security for potential consumers.

The Fashion Retail Environment

Emotions in the Fashion Retail – A Literature Review

Madeleine Eller/Jochen Strähle

Abstract

Purpose – Emotions play a central role in approach- avoidance costumer conflicts in retailing. The purpose of this paper is to assess the influence of emotions in the fashion retail environment, in particular to investigate how emotions can be best defined and clustered as well as how emotions affect the costumer behaviour.

Design/methodology/approach – This paper offers a critical literature review to answer the two research questions and to present a thorough understanding of the state of the art. Thereby emphasis is put on secondary and tertiary literature.

Findings – The conceptual paper reveals a framework explaining diverse theories of emotional models existing in literature. Moreover, the stimulus- organism- response model is applied to costumer behaviour in the fashion retail to explain the shopping experience under the influence of cognitive and affective emotional processes. Finally, it is concluded that point of sales have to be turned into point of emotions in order retailers are able to develop sustainable relationships with their customers.

Research limitations/implications – The conceptual paper does not provide empirical testing of the proposed framework. However, it suggests practical implications and directions for future research.

Keywords – Emotions, emotional models, costumer behaviour, shopping experience, fashion retailing

Paper type – Conceptual paper

1 Today's Hypercompetitive Mass Market

Globalisation, low cost technologies and saturated markets makes products and services in the retail environment barely distinguishable, hence interchangeable. Perceived risk and costumer involvement during the costumer shopping experience decrease. It is no longer the product but the price point that is major decision criterion during the purchasing lifecycle. As a result, the retail environment has shifted from production to consumption prevalence, from needs to wants, from objective to subjective decision power. As homogenous offers flood the market, retailers are forced to change strategies. New strategies need to be developed that are designed of strong and innovative concepts in order to be able to win the market place. Strategies that explicitly focalise the individual costumer, the most important external variable the retail business is dependent on. "When dealing with people, let us remember we are not dealing with creatures of logic. We are dealing with creatures of emotions" (Sloboda, 2014). Emotions are a crucial factor during the entire costumer shopping experience. Emotions drive desire, needs, and wants as well as decisions and actions. Therefore, retailers have to tap into the deepest subconscious emotions of costumers to trigger sustainable interest as well as relationship towards their brand respectively their products or services.

To better understand the influence of emotions in the fashion retail environment this paper aims to answer the following research questions:

- How can emotions be best defined and clustered?
- How do emotions influence costumer behaviour in the fashion retail?

A critical literature review is given to answer the two research questions and to develop a thorough understanding of the state of the art. Thereby, the most important theoretical basic structures of diverse emotional models are investigated and the current status of research is reviewed. Based on these findings, it is analysed how the costumer shopping behaviour in the fashion retail is influenced by emotions. Goal of the paper at hand is to present an elaborate evaluation of the literature given that offers a framework for researchers and retailers to better review, understand and deploy emotions in the fashion retail.

2 Emotions in the Fashion Retail

2.1 Costumer Research and its Classification in Behavioural Science

The following literature review of emotions in the fashion retail is divided into three parts: a classification of emotions in the scientific research field is given, followed by an overview of the most important models of emotions. Based on the state of the art in literature, it is investigated how emotions influence the costumer shopping experience in the fashion retail environment in particular.

Emotions are an integrative part of the field of research of behavioural science. Hereby, the human and its behaviour is central point of concern. The field of research includes the following disciplines: anthropology, psychology and sociology. Costumer behaviour, one application of behavioural science is of central interest during the literature review of the paper at hand.

Costumer behaviour puts special attention on response patterns in purchase and consumption situations of economical goods and services. The branch of science is characterised by interdisciplinary, as it combines various factors of different behavioural sciences because singularly neither is able to explain the complex and multi-layered process of costumer behaviour. Among others sociology as well as psychology and social psychology are meld with biological or genetic processes such as brain activity. Outcomes of costumer behaviour research is applied in marketing that combines scientific and economic knowledge to smartly deploy costumers' actions as well as reactions of decision making with the goal of increasing positive economic outcome (Sigg, 2009, pp. 7–10).

2.2 Costumer Emotions and their Origin

2.2.1 Analysing the Evolution of Emotion Research

After the general classification of costumer behaviour in science, the following is analysing in which way emotions are incorporated in the field of research over time. The reasons for human behaviour are discussed widely. It was already in the ancient philosophy that nous was part of theories established by known philosophers and researchers. One of the first studying the field of emotions was Platon, in 400 before Christ. He declared emotions as factors strongly influencing and dominating rational thinking- factors, which are describing human affective behaviour. Only one hundred years later, a second influencing philosopher, Aristoteles, analysed these affects in greater detail and reasoned that emotions may be used as rhetorical methods influencing people to act or think in a certain manner. It is until today that the described finding is applied in marketing and retail. Some decades later, in the sixteenths century, Rene Descartes, started to question the given affective orientated theories of emotions. The modern philosopher was the first separating the rational consciousness from emotional states. In his theory, emotions are defined as an interaction between body and intellect. *I think, therefore I am* - Descartes's maxim described the dualism of affect and rational consciousness. This is a dualism that puts emotions as uncontrollable behavioural outcomes, driven by body arousal and generated by internal and external stimulus. According to Descartes's concept, emotions respect. arousal are not influenceable. The human intellect is merely able to prevent the realisation of visible arousal (Sigg, 2009). A further key milestone in behavioural research concerning emotion has been the findings of Charles Darwin in the 19th century. Focusing on studying emotional expressive behaviour, the researcher characterised inherent basic emotions that similarly exist across cultures and only differentiate in facial expression. Among others are joy, anger and surprise. Furthermore, Darwin argued that general emotional expressions are evolving over time and are highly adaptive to experiences (Ekman, 2006, pp. 12 -14).

The 20th century is marked by a perception change in the theory of emotions. Psychology is now separately seen from philosophy and neo- behaviourism, a further development of the behaviourism theory, evolved. Science was no longer in favour of Descartes reasoning and argued that scientific theories have to be based on measurable as well as observable variables. Therefore, neo- behaviourism strongly included natural science into explaining human behaviour. Contrary to the already existing S-R Model, a stimulus provokes a response, the S-O-R concept of the 20th century was extended by a third variable, the organism. Neo- behaviourist argued that is not the stimulus but internal, individual intervening variables, the organism, that process information to trigger the outcome of responsive behaviour. Still, stimulus plays a central role in information acquiring ("S-O-R Modell," 2014, p. -).

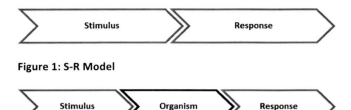

Figure 1: S-R Model

Figure 2: S-O-R Model

It was in 1929 that Robert S. Woodworth came up with the theory of the Stimulus-Organism – Response (SOR) Model. Conform to the neo- behaviourism approach, the psychologist defined the model based on observations of human behaviour. According to Woodworth, operations in the organism, the processing of internal and external information, are most notably shaped by either one of the two different procedures, cognition or affect, and result in the emerging of emotions. Cognition is described by subjective, inherent or semiskilled knowledge, stored in different neuronal cells of the brain. It is a complex and experience related construct that reacts subconsciously to certain stimuli according to already known categorisation and recognition. In other words, stimuli are processed dependent on judgements of old experiences saved in memory. The second approach takes into consideration that in absence of cognitive processes, neuronal activities responding to stimuli are emerging as well. Affect is subconsciously driven, also in form of emotions, developing new patterns of experience that are interpreted and stored by cognitive processes. Consequently, affect and cognition do not occur in concurrence but in interrelationship and interdependence (Sigg, 2009).

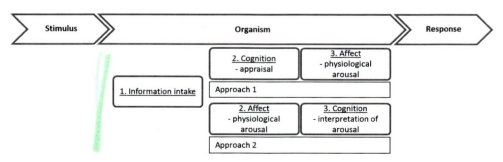

Figure 3: S-O-R Model including Cognition and Affect
Adapted from: (Sigg, 2009)

Of all decisions taken by a human, about 80 to 95 % are subconsciously emerging and may not be rationally reasoned. Awareness and processing of stimuli is strongly dependent on neuronal selection, based on motives of already experienced procedures (Bernecker, 2014, p.5).

2.2.2 Analysing the State of the Art of Emotion Research

Definition of Emotion

Emotions are a highly discussed topic in research over time. The behaviourist approach defined emotions as human uncontrollable outcomes of arousal influenced by external and internal stimuli. A further development of the S-R Model included the organism as central point of information processing. Neo- behaviourists established the S-O-R Model and divided between cognitive and affective resources of emotional responsive behaviour.

As emotions are widely investigated, the question arises how emotions can be best defined. Researchers from various branches are highly discussing this crucial topic with the result of disagreement as no common sense about influencing or information processing factors of emotions are able to be found. Definitions are rather made according to specific research area (Gallois, 1993). However, it is clearly set that emotions arise, when occurrences are of significance individual implication. This process is known as appraisal, in other words an evaluation of stimulus towards the own well-being. Emotions are intensified or diminished during this process and result in feelings. Feelings are subjective experiences of emotions. Constant experiences over a longer time frame and less intensive as feeling or emotions, are defined as mood. Yet, mood is not concretising a certain object of arousal but clustering several emotional experiences (Oliver, 2010, p.315). Caused by specific thoughts, feelings or moods; affect is subsuming only emotional batches (Nadler & Rennhak, 2009, p.13).

Even though no unique definition of human emotion exits in literature, researchers agree on that emotions are clearly have to be separated from emotional outcomes such as feelings, mood or affect. Furthermore, general compliance is made that human develop their response to emotions in the second step of the S-O-R Model, the organism. The response being made on basis of processes in the organism is shaped by cognition and affect. Besides, literature argues that emotions are object and situation related. Thus, emotions are subjective and personal related. Strongly interwoven and interdependent with emotional arousal are motives, attitudes, values and personality traits. In order to clarify the mentioned connection, the following is shortly defining the influencing variables. Motives perceived as rational wants and needs driven by obvious cognition. Attitudes are arising due to already experienced judgments based on past response patterns. Normally, attitudes are permanent structural behaviour; people are aware of and able to control in reactional outcome. The basis dimension of motive and attitude does form value perception. Values are desires and wishful thinking specified by a distinct social group. Usually, values are not easily influenceable by external forces, e.g. retailer's marketing, and are generally relevant to various objects of contemplation. Lastly, emotions are interdependent with personality traits. Hereby, the individual person is genetically but also socially shaped (Sigg, 2009).

As already said human responsive behaviour is mediator between the organism and its environment according to subjective states of feelings influenced by stimuli. Not only processes in the organism that originate in emotions but also physical human expressions are pushed by subjective individual, physiological and biological personality factors. Responsive expression can be classified into vocal, facial and body expressions. Hereby, besides from subjective states of mind, cultural backgrounds do play an important role in shaping, too. Culture is defined as "being a learned, shared, compelling, interrelated set of symbols whose meaning provide a set of orientation for members of society" (Strähle, 2013, p.90). In other words, culture is a heritage internalised by a group of people sharing certain norms and customs. Emotional driven human expressions are based on cultural learning as well as expectations and therefore are different in the world's hemispheres. For instance, some cultures blend similar emotional outcomes while others do not. Moreover, different rules and norms across cultures are showing how hard it is to define one universal emotion. Japan, as an example, ruled against the public display of expressions such as horror or shock, whereas the United States does not (Gallois, 1993). However, Öhmann proved that humans are genetically trained to register emotions coming from others. The researcher discovered that people are unconsciously and automatically reacting towards other people's expression by activating the neuronal network. Hereby, also different cross cultural expression can be classified, processed and reacted against (Tryon, 2014).

In summary, emotions are reactions to objects or occurrences with the result of mental and somatic changes and the outcome of expressive behaviour. Emotions are subjective perceived and shaped by cultural and social backgrounds. Contrary to attitude or mood, emotions are less deliberate with a shorter length of lifetime (Sabini & Silver, 2005). Since no universal definition of emotions is existing, several researchers tried to simplify the given complexity by developing models that put together commonalities into similar categorized sets. The following subchapter is investigating some of these important classical state of the art models.

Classical Models of Emotions

Carroll Izard was among the first researches developing an emotional model to cluster emotions into categories in the 20th century. The researcher followed an approach based on evolutionary and biological arguments. Ten discrete emotions, each reflecting a unique pattern of subjective experience was the outcome of his study. The relationship in between these emotions is described as unipolar or independent giving the fact of unlikeliness that the clustered emotions are occurring the same time. Izard's defines in his Differential Emotional Scale, emotions as primary inherent and as a basis for superposition when further emotions are revealed. According to his theory, emotions are alterable towards cultural differences. Clustered in pairs of two to reflect the differences in intensity from low to high, Izard displays his ten basic emotions (Oliver, 2010) as the following table shows:

Table 1: Izard - Differential Emotional Scale

Intensity	Low	High
1.	Interest	Excitement
2.	Joy	Elation
3.	Surprise	Astonishment
4.	Sadness	Grief
5.	Anger	Rage
6.	Disgust	Revulsion
7.	Fear	Terror
8.	Contempt	Scorn
9.	Shame	Shyness
10.	Guilt	Remorse

Adapted from: (Oliver, 2010, p.318)

Critics of Izard's Differential Emotional Scale say that the researcher is overemphasising negative feelings as only one out of ten pairs of emotions is having a positive affect (nr. two) and two an neutral arousal affect (nr. one and three) (Mano & Oliver, 1993).

Further important researchers in the field of emotion classification are Mehrabian and Russell. Their pioneering findings are summarised in the Pleasure – Arousal – Dominance (PAD) Model, 1974. Three dimensional in setup, the PAD Model is evaluating the activity level of emotional states in nonverbal communication including facial, body and vocal expression as well as social, cultural and subjective cues. Each of the three scales is used to measure a different outcome. The pleasure – displeasure dimensions takes into consideration how pleasant an emotion may be. For instance excitement or tranquillity is measured towards boredom. Normally, the scale uses 16 specific values in comparison. The intensity of an emotion is measured via the arousal – nonarousal dimension. Hereby, usually nine specific values are used. The last of the three dimensions, dominance – submissiveness, is displaying the controlling character of a certain emotion. Normally restricted to nine specific values, the influence of and on the environment is taken into consideration (Mehrabian, 1996). Because of the three dimensional mode, in total about 151 different emotions may be analysed across the explained dimensions (Sigg, 2009). As Shaver states, the PAD Model oversees a great room for evaluation. Therefore, it is strongly informative in assessment, especially in costumer behaviour studies (Mehrabian, 1996). However, Reisenzein argues that the PAD is instable in scaling solutions. It is because of that reason, the three dimensional model was later reduced to the two-dimensional model PAT, leaving out the dimension dominance - submissiveness. Still, Russell and Mehrabian's PAD Model is used widely in today's marketing evaluation (Oliver, 2010, p. 343)

A further classical model of emotions is the Circumplex Model of affect developed by James Russell. Russell came up with this concept as he was of the opinion that a dimensionality greater than two is unstable across various examined situations (Oliver, 2010, p.318). In Russell's two-dimensional circular space the axes arousal and pleasure are evaluated against each other. Hereby, pleasure and displeasure are negatively correlated whereas arousal and quietude are positively correlated.

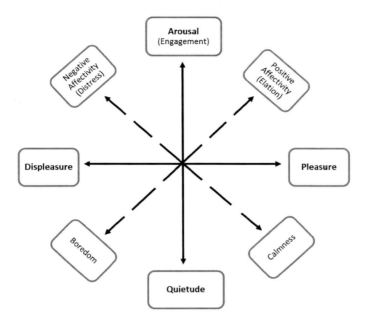

Figure 4: Russell - Circumplex Model of Affect
Adapted from: (Oliver, 2010, p.319)

Russell's Circumplex Model does redefine dimensions but does not reconfiguration affects (Mano & Oliver, 1993). With the given model, one is able to localise up to 28 different emotions. After Oliver, researchers are now able "to consider the possibility that low arousal sates (e.g. calmness (..)) are also basic" (Oliver, 2010, p. 319). Furthermore, the Circumplex Model assigns positive emotions greater interest.

Other researchers also use the Circumplex Model of affect. Though, they rotate the circumplex by 45 degree to make positive and negative affectivity to primary dimensions of the circumplex. The configuration of the axes is not changed; merely they are redefined in message. The mentioned change mechanism is displayed in Figure 4 and marked by the dashed axes. Engagement is positively correlated with positive and negative affectivity. Pleasure and displeasure are negatively correlated whereas positive affectivity and negative affectivity are orthogonal. Both, the just described as well as Russell's Circumplex Model are used in human behavioural studies. It is because of that reason, one has to clearly distinguish which model is applied in research as outcome is dependent on definition of the axes used (Oliver, 2010, p.319).

A last classical model of emotions presented in the paper at hand is Robert Plutchik's eight basic emotions. The researcher defined those eight as basic as they are of strong importance during the evolutionary survival (Tryon, 2014). Plutchik juxtaposes the listed eight basic emotions in a circle according to a circumplex structure illustrating bipolar emotions as for instance joy vs. sadness or anger vs. fear opposite to each other. Depending on the intensity of arousal and on combination possibilities second tier emotions are emerging out of the basic eight. For instance, high fear results in terror whereas low fear results in apprehension. Plutchik orientated his Circumplex Model after the colour wheel since colours also differentiate in intensity and mixture (Oliver, 2010, p.320).

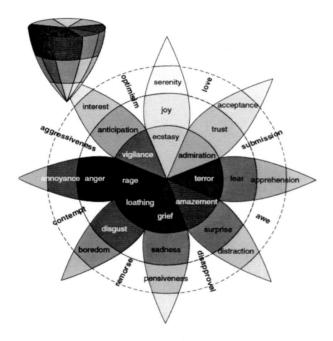

Figure 5: Plutchik – Circumplex Model of the Basic Eight Emotions
Adapted from: (Zurawicki, 2010, p.39)

Plutchik's theoretical background definition resulted in the Emotions Profile Index EPI, a questionnaire used to detected personal states of feeling. Easy to use, a clear graphical presentation of research outcome are advantages hereby. However, the EPI dimension definition is not completely correlated towards Plutchik's index of emotions. Hence, the two models are not 100% comparable (Bucik, Brenk, & Vodopivec, n.d.).

As the investigation of the given classical models of emotions in literature is revealing, several different dimensions of clustering and definition exist. Consequently, how emotions are originating and influenced is marked by a great complexity and is even made more complex as different opinions in literature exist about each model in terms of application, disadvantages and advantages. Izard's ten basic emotions are biologically seen primitive and result in the Differential Emotions Scale which quantifies each emotions at the same level of structural generality (Oliver, 2010, p.341). The three dimensional model, PAD, extends the concept of basic emotions to bipolar basic dimension which are especially useful for consumption experience evaluations that reason in emotional costumer profiles. After Havlena and Holbrook, the PAD model captures a greater field of emotional classification than Plutchik's eight basic emotions (Havlena & Holbrook, 1986). Contrary, Machleit and Eroglu are arguing that Plutchik as well as Izard are outperforming the Mehrabian and Russell model since a richer assessment of emotional responses to the shopping environment is given. Yet, PAD is a clearly sufficient model to use in primary domains as residential or work places, however its usability in the shopping environment is still highly discussed (Machleit & Eroglu, 2000). The last model discussed, the Circumplex Model in its two different implementations is capturing basic dimensions that ensure due to their two dimensionality, a strong stability across various situations (Oliver, 2010, p.341). Generally, as the models are clustering emotional states, one has to be aware that important information and correlations might get lost. Notwithstanding, the just described models offer a great advantage, the facilitated data analysis due to already established frameworks (Machleit & Eroglu, 2000).

Retail Models of Emotions

The given overview of classical models of emotions shows that a great divergence in the study of emotional content exists. As each model focuses different emotions as well as different scaling for measurement one has to decide on which model to choose when investigating a certain object or situation dependent on the research approach and whether the marketing or retail background is taken as a basis. Especially in the marketing context Izard as well as Russell and Mehrabian's model are commonly used to measure adequacy and appropriateness of the given strategy outcome. Talking about the retail environment, which is central point of interest during the literature review in this paper, various approaches are existing. When Hui and Batson investigated the shopping environment in the context of crowding in retail service settings in 1991, only the pleasure – displeasure dimension of the PAD scale was included. In 1993, Manon and Oliver evaluated the post purchase evaluation of feelings and satisfaction response taking utilitarian and hedonic appraisal as a two-dimensional construct. Hereby, they directly referred to Russell's Circumplex Model and the affective dimensions of pleasantness and arousal (Walsh, Shiu, Hassan, Michaelidou, & Beatty, 2011). These two examples illustrate that the retail environment, in particular costumer shopping behaviour, is offering massive space for research. Diverse variables, discussed in chapter 2.3.2., may be set in correlation to each other and studied based on a single classical concept of emotion or on a composition of various aspects of models. Yet, a distinct investigation of research done to develop retail models of emotions is out of scope of this paper, as various theories but no unique solution exist.

Neuromarketing of Emotions

Researchers in the field of retailing are particularly interested in revealing information of emotional states during the different steps of the S-O-R Model, in specific of the organism and response process part. Classical, marketing and retail models are of great help in evaluating classification of emotional responses to marketer's activities. Yet, these emotional responses first have to be detected and made visible. Hereby, several methods exist. One common method called self-report, a survey or interview, is asking directly after emotional states of the specific subject group related to consumption situations. Since emotions are often perceived unconsciously, self- reports hardly detect emotions entirely truthfully. A further method, observation, is monitoring the subject group, for instance during the purchasing process. Still information is barely given concerning prior internal organism processes. Both methods unites the fact that behaviour determinations of intuitive organism processes stay undetected (Sigg, 2009). However, it is of great interest to retailers to disclose what really drives costumers purchasing decisions.

Neuroscience, a relatively new area of research is adding a path of deeper truth to people's intuitive reactions. It was only in recent years, the field of research has grown to significant importance and contributed to a better understanding of costumer behaviour. Neuroscience, a fusion of various scientific disciplines such as biology, neurology or cognitive science, is the science of structure and function of the human nervous system. The nervous system, as the body's major communication and controlling system, is composed of the brain, spinal cord, nerves and ganglia. Hereby, receptors are touch points with external and internal environment. The brain, initial point of muscular, internal and external behavioural patterns, contains the cerebrum respect. limbic system which is above all involved in processing emotions (Zurawicki, 2010). Neuroscience makes it possible to reveal the interaction processes in the human brain with the Functional Magnetic Resonance Imaging (fMRI) research tool. It allows scanning emotional resonance and cognition by magnetic fields and radio waves. A colour coded image of the brain is produced by a scanner and a person's unconscious feeling about an object is made visible. fMRI makes it possible to objectively dig deeper in human emotional states. Moreover, it allows a continuous tracking of a person's brain activity respect. emotional state during the performance of different mental tasks such as product selection or orientation in brick and mortar stores (Jobber, 2010, p.126). Neuromarketing makes use of neurosciences, the application to analyse human behaviour, and sets it in relation to market places in order to understand what exactly determines costumer behaviour. With neuromarketing the classical communication model between retailers and costumers is shifted. It is no longer the costumer that is informed by the retailer about products and services but the marketer that is dependent on costumer insights in order to be able to promote efficiently (Ciprian-Marcel, Lăcrămioara, Ioana, & Maria, 2009). To be able to get the right information, neuroscience tools have to be chosen according to desired research outcome. For instance, eye tracking may be used to monitor people's eyes movement to get an understanding of the navigation on websites whereas automated facial coding may continuously record peoples' faces in order to track emotional response to visual merchandising in windows (Page, 2012).

Critics of neuromarketing say that conducted neuroscience studies are still exploratory, meaning no specific insights of how the brain regions are really working is given but summaries of brain activities are simply interpreted according to given observations (Garcia & Saad, 2008). Moreover, it is still questionable how and where the pure emotion originates (Oliver, 2010, p.317). Of course there is also the other side of the coin. Proponents are arguing that neuromarketing makes clear what really drives people's shopping behaviour as its methods are revealing emotional states during the different stages of costumer experience. Hence, retailers are able to add value to products and services in order to drive sustainable profit (Adhami, 2013). Sustainable profit means in the context of the paper at hand, to understand as well as to strengthen emotional attachment towards a brand or product. Retailers have to detect those important emotional connections and push costumer engagement in order desired results such as increased purchasing or deeper cross- selling are arising (Robison, 2006).

2.3 Costumer Shopping Experience under the Influence of Emotions

2.3.1 Emotion's Dependency on Moderators

For a long time it was perceived that the human being is taking decisions largely on a rational basis dependent on utilitarian needs and desires as well as product or brand attributes. Emotions and intuitive reaction were unpredictable and unfamiliar in originating, therefore despised. With the research breakthrough of the S-O-R Model - a stimulus is influences the organism which in turn processes information and emotions with the outcome of a response – the previously called black box, the organism, was in its early stages of development. The change of paradigm of the human and its behaviour, is now taking neuronal activities related to emotions into consideration. Hence, researchers are now able not only to get insights into cognitive as but also emotional resonance. As the human black box is understood step by step, marketers have to accept that costumers are no homo oeconomicus but homo neurobiologicus that do not take decision on utility and rational level but on emotional and subconsciously level (Sigg, 2009).

As already mentioned, the paper is examining human emotions in the fashion retail environment. Therefore, the costumer, a "individual() who buy(s) products or services for personal consumption" (Jobber, 2010, p.109) is main point of attention. To drive profit, retailers need to understand their costumers and how they shop. Hereby, special attention should be put on the study of commonalities of various arising emotions during the buying process and how these emotions can be best addressed. To get an understanding of the different steps of the costumer shopping behaviour, the following chapter is investigating the three parts of the S-O-R Model in detail with keeping in mind external and internal influencing moderator factors.

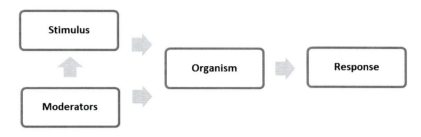

Figure 6: S-O-R Model including Moderators

Firstly, external and internal moderating factors influencing the processing of stimuli in the organism are analysed. In literature the thematic of moderators is discussed divergently. In fact, the topic is receiving only little attention. Partly, researchers are leaving the influence of moderators on costumer behaviour completely out of scope. Some others only investigate several distinct moderators relevant to the conducted study (Bohl, 2012, p.2). Actually, the topic of emotional affect due to subjective perceived environments is often overlooked due to the strong weighting of cognitive influencing factors such as information processing or storage (Donovan & Rossiter, 1982). However, retailers are forced to also consider the costumers' real driving forces, their emotions as these are stronger in activation of reactions than cognitive processes (Nadler & Rennhak, 2009).

Generally, moderators influencing costumer behaviour can be distinguished into three categories: personal moderators, situational factors and shopping motivation (Bohl, 2012, p.10). To start with, personal moderators are presented. Personality as "the inner psychological characteristics of individuals that lead to consistent responses to their environment" (Jobber, 2010, p.127) is shaped by demographic factors such as age or gender. Moreover, social factors as culture, reference groups, class consciousness or lifestyle are influencing the buying process (Jobber, 2010, p. 121). Retailers are advised to segment, target and position their costumers into homogenous groups sharing the same characteristics. With the help of a clear potential target market positioning strategy, marketers are then able to create perceived value propositions including costumer emotional systems. The Limbic Model is a helpful tool in establishing costumer profiles as it clusters costumers into seven different profiles.

Figure 7: Limbic Model of Costumer Classification
Adapted from: (Häusel, 2009)

The Limbic Model is taking into consideration valences of costumer balance systems (e.g. risk avoidance), dominance systems (e.g. autonomy) and stimuli system (e.g. reward) (Häusel, 2013, p.77 - 94). Besides, the Limbic system includes long-term, stable personal traits as well as instantaneous states of mood dependent on current situation and experience (Häusel, 2009, p.37). This differentiation of mood management is also essential during a further category of moderators, the situational factors. Hereby, the three stages of consumption are of central interest. Pre- consumption, consumption and post- consumption costumer actions are experienced differently due to various emotional outcomes, in particular due to pre-existing moods and on to moods emerging during the consumption process itself (Oliver, 2010, p.327 - 333). Besides, it is important to differentiate between first time consumers and repeated purchase consumers as they perceive environmental factors such as time pressure, motivation and knowledge of environment differently (Fiore & Kim, 2007). Together with the third tier of moderators, the shopping motivation, situational factors is taking into consideration whether the goal of purchasing is product, utilitarian or hedonic motivated (Bohl, 2012, p.10). Most important determination of shopping motivation is the relationship between need, desires and goals, respect. the attained step in Maslow's hierarchy of needs (J. B. Kim, Koo, & Chang, 2009).

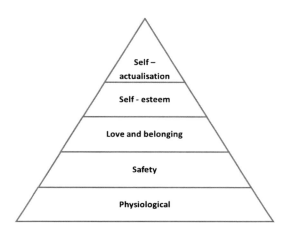

Figure 8: Maslow - Hierarchy of Needs
Adapted from: (J. B. Kim et al., 2009)

Regarding the step reached on Maslow's hierarchy of needs, the degree of costumer involvement is determined. Costumer involvement distinguishes between high and low involvement, hence between the intensity how costumers consciously assess products or brands. Higher involvement arises when high information content is needed to satisfy strongly relevant and important needs that affect for example self-image or perceived risk. On the other hand, low involvement costumers are looking for more elementary product or service alternatives that are passively experienced (Jobber, 2010, p.116).

The following figure, figure 9 is displaying all that has been said about internal and external moderating factors influencing the costumer shopping experience, respect. the stimuli and organism in the S-O-R Model. Recapitulating, the mentioned mediator variables may not be left aside when analysing costumer behaviour in the fashion retail environment, as they are stored in neuronal connections in the human brain.

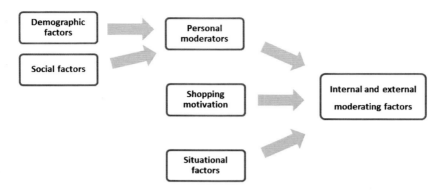

Figure 9: Moderators of Costumer Shopping Experience

2.3.2 Emotion's Generation through Stimulus

The costumer shopping experience in the retail environment is influenced by emotions in various process steps of the S-O-R Model. In the following subchapter, the emotional side of stimuli variables is examined. The content of stimuli is generated by retailers to strategically influence, create or alliterate neuronal activities in the costumer's organism. Central point of concern to marketers is to establish costumer benefits that strongly differentiate from those of the concurrence in order to be able to connect successfully and sustainable with customers. Goal of applied stimuli is to activate specific behavioural and emotional perspectives in the organism of the potential consumer to enrich buying experience and enhance final purchasing probability. Success outcome of the applied stimuli is depending on content and individual moderating influencing factors described in the subchapter above (Sigg, 2009, p.61 - 67).

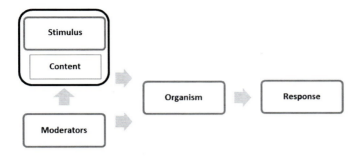

Figure 10: S-O-R Model, Triple C-Model, Stimuli: Content
Adapted from: (Sigg, 2009, p.59)

Contact points between stimuli and organism may be generated through various possibilities but differ especially between content of message deployed in either brick and mortar stores, e-commerce or m-commerce (Fiore & Kim, 2007). It is through human senses, costumers receive stimuli respect. external as well as internal information. Functioning as receptors, the five senses – vision, hearing, smelling, taste and touch - transfer environmental stimuli to the brain where signals are screened, clustered and transformed (Zurawicki, 2010, p.12).

As the send stimuli vary significantly from retailer to retailer and from channel to channel (Machleit & Eroglu, 2000), no best practice of application is given. Moreover, stimuli content concepts strongly depend on advertised product group, market positioning as well as target market. Hence, retailers need to individually develop stimulus strategies matching brand messages as well as emotional loaded shopping environment. Several authors have suggested universal categories that hereby need to be considered. One of those, is the classification into ambient, design and social factors. Talking about ambient factors, one has to consider shopping environment conditions that are beyond immediate awareness such as noise, air quality or scent (Bohl, 2012, p.9). For instance, noise is being perceived by the sense hearing. In inspirational shopping environments of brick and mortar stores, e.g. Zara, en vogue music may influence the costumer's emotional state to feel young, animated, fashionable and trend setting (Bruhn & Köhler, 2011, p.293 - 299). Together with the activated sense of smelling which is able to push profit up to 25 % if applied rightly, hearing is dominate factor when costumers subconsciously build prejudices that in turn influence length of stay and money spend (Häusel, 2009). Furthermore, design factors are a possibility for retailers to apply strongly shaping stimuli. Design factors in turn can be separated into aesthetic and functional factors. Functional aspects concern layout, comfort or signage, among others (Bohl, 2012, p.9). In online shops of controlled shopping environments, as for example Uniqlo, it is of great importance that negative effects arising from complicated navigation or unclear product or FAQ description do not lead to stressful perceived situations that destroy the desire to shop or the brand message of simplicity, quality and trust (Strähle, 2013, p.260). Aesthetic factors on the other hand consider physical cues influencing the customer such as architecture, materials or colours used (Bohl, 2012, p.9). 80 % of human sensory perceptions are processed by the sense vision. Thus, professionalism is crucial when developing visible stimuli. Especially in exclusive shopping environments such as Porsche Design, it is essential to implement a storyline consistent in product and service presentation, store architecture and also in the setup of online channels. Less is more and cognitive overloaded stimuli should be avoided in costumer hunting and selection of goods (Bruhn & Köhler, 2011, p.293 - 299). Lastly, social factors are including human influence stimuli on the shopping environment. On the one hand, social factors are strongly dependent on the number and behaviour of other costumers. A rather negative example hereby is retail crowding which may lead to unpleasant and unsatisfying shopping experiences (Machleit & Eroglu, 2000). On the other hand, service personal is shaping social stimuli. As one of the variables retailers have great influence on, service personal may be controlled and trained to correspond to brand message and shopping environment. For instance in experimental shopping setups as in the brick and mortar stores of Globetrotter, the outer experience and behaviour of sales personal has to match the outdoor character of the brand. Moreover, a pleasant number of service personal has to be employed on the shop floor that is also educated in product knowledge and usage of interactive features such as rain and high attitude cold chambers, canoe pools or climbing tunnels (Bruhn & Köhler, 2011, p.293 -299).

The degree of emotions response to introduced stimuli content may be differently experienced in intensity and frequency. When stimuli covering the same message, are arising during multiple occasions in multifaceted ways as well as when several different stimuli with the same content are experience together (Oliver, 2010, p. 326), costumers are addressed in a multidimensional way. This simultaneous communication of coherent information through different stimuli, called multisensory enhancement, is leading to a reinforcement of content impact on costumer behaviour as a greater number of neuronal processes are activated. Hence, a more intense and concrete manifestation of content is emerging (Häusel, 2013, p.15). As various possibilities of stimuli combination are existing, researchers tried to find potential relationships between individual stimuli. For instance, Ergolu studied in 2005 the effect of music tempo in relation to retail density. However, effects arising due to the merging of various stimuli in fashion retail settings is outside the scope of the paper (Fiore & Kim, 2007).

Sensual perception is of great importance to costumers when evaluating experiences. According to Bonner and Stanton, emotional influenced costumer behaviour in the retail setting is the result of interactions of channel environment stimuli and psychological environment moderators (Paunksnienė & Banytė, 2012). As stimuli strategies generated by retailers are the driving key success factors in costumer purchasing behaviour, stimuli have to match certain characteristics: consistency, clarity and concentration in message content to brand image, creativity and competence in configuration and across channel cooperation in implementation (Weber, 2012, p.39).

2.3.3 Emotion's Influence on the Organism

"Through the senses, the body perceives all information arriving from () (moderators and stimuli); the brain interprets this information and produces chemical and physical responses which are translated into thoughts and behaviours" (Zurawicki, 2010, p.12). In the S-O-R Model, it is the organism that is responsible for the described process. This process is two parted as awareness and reprocessing of influencing factors that result in emotions, are timely separated. Condition summarises the psychological state of mind due to physical occurrences based on emotions whereas Cause is using Condition to establish the response outcome, in particular behaviour (Sigg, 2009).

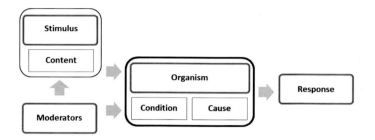

Figure 11: S-O-R Model, Triple C-Model, Organism: Condition and Cause
Adapted from: (Sigg, 2009)

In other words, the organism is balancing between mediators, stimuli and response. As already said, the costumer is perceiving stimuli and mediators through physical processes. Generally, the awareness of those Conditions is not compulsory connected to consciousness attention (Sigg, 2009). It is only during the Triple C Model process step Cause, that the costumer is dividing external and internal stimuli into conscious and affective behaviour. Hedonic approached, the cognition- affect- behaviour (CAB) model is an information processing approach incorporating current experienced stimuli that are affectively reacted on. Results are physical arousal and behaviour. Contrary, the consciousness- emotion- value (CEV) model, developed by Holbrook in 1986, is not only including cognition but also draws on already experienced and stored mental schemata in the human memory based on subjectively perceived moderators when judging on actual stimuli. Emotion go beyond affect with also including long term value perceptions (Ci, 2008, p.50 - 51).

2.3.4 Emotion's Influence on the Response Outcome

The final result of the intertwined processes of mediator, stimuli and organism, is costumer response. Costumer response as the last step of the S-O-R Model includes psychological outcomes such as attitude or expressive behaviour. Reactions towards desired product or service can either be classified into approach or avoidance. As costumer emotions are the mediating factor during the entire costumer consumption process, degree, direction, quality and consciousness of emotional arousal are highly determining factors (Sherman, Mathur, & Smith, 1997). In order retailers gain desired costumer responses, they are forced to build relationship between brand and channel atmosphere, product as well as costumer (Paunksnienė & Banytė, 2012). The following is broadly summarising important factors retailers have to consider when building up those relationships.

Negative vs. Positive Costumer Response

Why do costumers purchase? Costumers purchase to satisfy needs, to fulfil desires and to enhance the value perception of life. The overall goal of need fulfilment is arising from the step reached on Maslow's hierarchy of needs (compare chapter 2.3.1.). How does costumer decision behaviour function? In which way do emotions influence the purchasing decision? In order retailers fully understand the behaviouristics of their customers, emotional brain activities have to be taken into consideration. The limbic system as collective term for neuronal processes responsible for emotional processing is made partly visible by the findings of neuromarketing. It was a key milestone in understanding that the emerging of emotions by subjectively perceived moderators and stimuli is a crucial influence on human behaviour and particular on costumer purchasing behaviour. The more emotions are positively and less negatively perceived, the more products and services are seen as valuably and as an enriching factor in life. Hence, costumers are purchasing and are willing to spend more money. As emotional appraisal is happening mostly on a subconscious basis, retailers have to be on the watch on details as the buy button in the human brain is pressed only when content and condition fit and when enough neuronal synapses are activated (Häusel, 2009).

Expected vs. Experienced Costumer Response

Expectation is defined as "a prediction, sometimes stated as a probability or likelihood, of attribute or product performance at a specific performance level" (Oliver, 2010, p.21). Strongly correlated with expectations are anticipation, a positive costumer response respect. approach, and apprehension, a negative costumer response respect. avoidance. Meaning, shopping experience is connected to valence of emotional states that are either positive or negative in outcome (Machleit & Eroglu, 2000). These emotional states are emerging due to costumer expectations in consumption. Costumers go shopping with a defined intention and engagement. For instance, costumers might look for a certain product at a desired price level or expect a specific service level of an already known brand. Either the retailer is able to fulfil those levels of desire or not. Depending on if the costumer's actual experience meets the preceding expectation, anticipation or apprehension is arising. The following figure 12 is visualising the range of both levels by dividing descriptive ranges into tolerance and indifference zones. The zones are clustered into ranges of minimal and maximal acceptable level. Ranges do overlap but levels outside of accepted tolerance are situations costumers generally like to avoid. On the left hand side of figure 12 it is displayed that costumers usually have a higher degree of desired outcome than a realistic and objective degree of predicted outcome (Oliver, 2010, p.63 - 68).

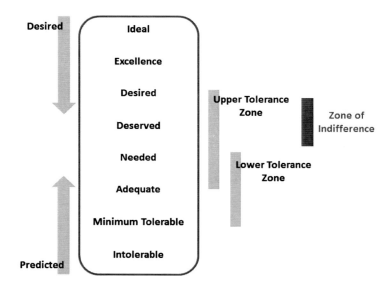

Figure 12: Costumer Expectations – Tolerance and Indifference Zones
Adapted from: (Oliver, 2010, p.68)

As also multiple expectations sets may be desired by costumers as well as several influencing factors may influence one emotional response, a distinct and unique measurement tool is not developable for analysing costumer expectations versus experiences (Oliver, 2010, p.84).

Long Term vs. Time Limited Costumer Response

Generally, retailers seek to develop long-term relationships with their costumers as therewith costs of continuously accruing new potential customers are eliminated and a sustainable profit level is guaranteed. Emotional relationship between retailers and costumers can be compared to inter human relationships as wrongly deployed stimuli initiated by retailers may lead to costumer disappointment or frustration. Consequently, continuous relationships between retailers and costumers may be destroyed (Nadler & Rennhak, 2009). It is called customer emotional attachment that describes the strength of bond costumers have with a certain retailer brand. Hereby, brand knowledge, connection, affection, trust and love play a shaping role (Theng So, Grant Parsons, & Yap, 2013). Neuroscience discovered that when costumers already developed neuronal synapses in connection to a certain brand, actual experiences relating to same topics are analysed and processed with a lower energy levels. Prove that brands may successfully exploit costumer behaviour emotionally (Nufer & Wallmeier, 2010, p.19). If retailers invest in strategies to enhance emotional branding, success may be guaranteed as a clear identification towards the brand is created that clearly differentiates towards competitors. Emotional branding may help to build emotional brand pillars, costumers relate to positive neuronal brand connections. With the help of these stored pillars in people's brains, recall is made easy and finally brands turn into lovers and relationships into a long term passion (Nadler & Rennhak, 2009). Brand loyalty which is "a deeply held psychological commitment to repurchase a product or patronize a service in the future despite obstacles or disincentives to achieve the consumption goal" (Oliver, 2010, p.23) is the higher level of emotional costumer attachment and dependency towards a brand. Clearly distinctive is brand loyalty from repeated purchasing which is rather emotional constrained and associated with random repetitive behaviour (Theng So et al., 2013). In order to reach the level of costumers developing brand loyalty, retailers have to analyse their costumers' post consumption experiences and react accordingly. Post consumption can be differentiated into product evaluation, created affect and satisfaction. During the post consumption experience satisfaction summarises all emerging emotions and is therefore strongly linked to the development of brand loyalty (Mano & Oliver, 1993). Given the costumer perspective, satisfaction is strongly linked to an individual desire or goal that should be attained by consuming products or services. Ideally costumer responses are positive and according to expected outcome in order decision making is reaffirmed in a satisfactorily way (Oliver, 2010, p.4).

To summarise, emotions in the fashion retail exist along the entire costumer purchase process. Influenced by mediators and stimuli, different emotional states juxtapose in the organism, the human brain. Desired goal by retailers is to win a positive costumer response that is marked by post consumption satisfaction and eventually results in brand loyalty. To conclude the chapter of costumer shopping experience under the influence of emotions, the figure below is resuming the entire costumer's perceptual process that is interwoven within the S-O-R Model and it is determinative of costumer shopping experience in the fashion retail.

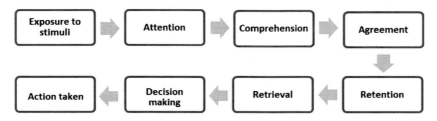

Figure 13: Costumer View - Perceptual Shopping Experience Process
Adapted from: (Weber, 2012, p.11)

3 Discussion of Emotions in the Fashion Retail

Given the critical literature review of emotions in the fashion retail, the questions arises how the state of the art classical models of emotions may be set in relation to the analysed steps of the S-O-R Model. As mentioned in the chapter above, no unique definition of emotions exits because of their emergences based on various different internal and external influencing factors. To facilitate this complexity, researchers developed models uniting emotional commonalities into similar clusters. Nonetheless, each model of clustered emotions has is strength and weaknesses as well as possible field of application in measurement. In fact, the research of fashion retail mingles and adapts the classical models again to make them compatible to the topic of concern and goal of adequate, reliable and comprehensive measurement. The adapted models of emotions applied in retail are characterised by a low lifespan as fast rhythmic of seasonality as well as innovative marketing trends and possibilities frequently shape costumers' desires and wants in different directions. Moreover, costumer-shopping behaviour is influenced by individual and subjectively perceived costumer variables as well as retailer initiated stimuli corresponding to brand message or product value proposition. The complexity is even extended as retailers do not only use one channel to deploy the content of stimuli but several, either in dependency or autonomy. As costumer response towards the retailer's marketing is never stable across costumers and channel, retailers are not advised to use one single solution for emotional measurement. Rather companies should gain a deep understanding of how the costumer's brain works to be able to comprehend how decisions are made and why actions are taken. It was because of this reason, the paper hat hand set the S-O-R Model in the context of fashion retail to broadly examine how emotions influence the different steps of costumer shopping experience. As the investigation shows, emotions are main driver of the entire process. Thus, the point of sale has to be turned into point of interest and more specifically into point of emotions. Thereby, retailers may develop sustainable relationships with their customers by making stimuli content respect. unique selling proposition unique, appealing and wanted. With understanding the emotional side of costumer behaviour that is able to be measured by models of emotions, retailers are moving towards the fulfilment of objective to turn customers into fans- Fans that are connected to a brand with a deep routed identification as well as with an authentic belonging.

The critical literature review with its investigation of emotional models in general and costumer-shopping experience under the influence of emotions in the fashion retail in particular, offers a framework useful for both academia and industry. Academia may use the overview of already existing theories in literature to develop empirical studies examining new fields of research. Industry may use the given framework to push on with enhancing their shopping environments to success by considering the complexity of relationships between variables creating emotional shopping experiences.

4 Emotions as an Enhancement of the Unique Selling Proposition?

To be able to win today's flooded and hypercompetitive mass market, retailers have to understand the real drivers of customer shopping behaviour, the human emotions. It was already stated in the introduction and proved by the literature review that emotions are a fundamental factor in shaping the costumer shopping behaviour and experience in the fashion retail. Thus, tailoring retail strategies to emotional costumer expectations is vital when creating a sustainable unique selling proposition and point of differentiation towards competition.

The phenomena of emotions and their influence on human behaviour was already a highly discussed topic of research in the ancient world. Initially seen as a treat to rational thinking, Aristoteles added that emotions may be used as rhetorical models influencing people's thinking. It was in the modern period, Descartes argued that emotions may be driven either by rationality or affect. Still, until the 20th century emotions were perceived to be rationally dominated. Moreover, economy was separated from psychology and retailers orientated their strategies towards the guiding principle of the homo oeconmicus. With the introduction of the stimulus- organism-response model, emotional driven behaviour was integrated in scientific research and also in economic theories. Meaning, cognitive as well as affective emotional processes occurring in the human brain, the organism, were included in the explanation of behaviour. Yet, detailed explanations of emotional origin stay undiscovered. Researchers in the field of customer behaviour were unable to agree on a unique definition of emotion. Therefore, basic dimension of emotions were determined to simplify the complex field of research and resulted in several different models of emotions. The presented classical models of emotions in the paper at hand, distinguish themselves above all in measurement scale. Izard based his ten basic emotion on a one dimensional level, Russell, Plutchik as well as other researcher on the Circumplex Model, in other words on a two dimensional level and Mehrabian and Russell' PAD Model on a three dimensional level. As each model focuses different emotions, the field of application various tremendously. Thus, models of emotions in retail are the result of adaptions and combinations. Neuromarkting, a branch of research that has grown to significant importance in last century, contributed to a better understanding of emotions influencing costumer behaviour in the fashion retail. Through magnetic fields and radio waves, neuromarketing makes it possible to more deeply discover the human nervous system and unconscious emotional states. Thanks to neuromarketing, retailers are now able to more specifically detect emotional connections towards brands or products and push those accordingly to increase purchasing behaviour.

As fashion retailers are hunting after sustainable profit, costumer behaviour as one of the most important external variables has to be understood. Emotions play a vital mediating role in retail settings, hence emotions configure the entire shopping experience. Especially in the fashion retail environment costumer behaviour is determined by personal and situational influencing factors and driven by shopping motivation. Generally, emotions are subjectively perceived, visually expressed and shaped by neuronal activities in the human brain that are influenced by cultural learnings and inherent knowledge. Consequently, costumer behaviour influenced by internal and external moderating factors is strongly divergent from human to human. Still, retailer initiated stimuli are able to affect, enrich and enhance shopping experience in evaluation, attitude and response formation. As the send stimuli vary significantly between brand and product message content as well as used channel, no best practice of application is given. However, the presented stimuli classification into ambient, design and social factors might help to develop a strategy that attacks the human senses in a successful way. The S-O-R Model defines the organism respect. neuronal activities in the human brain as processor of all influencing factors. It is during this step, given experiences are interpreted and physical responses are developed. Costumer response is classified into approach and avoidance. Either experiences match costumer pre developed expectations, thus emotions are positive, or the minimal tolerance zone is not met. Hence, costumers are emotionally seen disappointed and may purchase less until nothing. Level of activation, quality and direction of emotions shape the creation of emotional bonds between retailers and their customers. Notably, the post consumption evaluation is sign post of whether satisfied costumers turn into loyal lovers.

The critical literature review offers a framework for researchers and retailers to better review, understand and deploy emotions in the fashion retail as it is inevitable to include emotions into retail strategies in today's hypercompetitive market place. Strategies should emotionally tie costumers to brands, products or concepts and enable retailers to enhance their unique selling proposition with a point of emotions. In doing so, applications to create emotions have not only to be icluded in long term strategies but also in realisations of stimuli at the point of sale.

The conceptual paper at hand does not provide an empirical testing of the proposed framework due to the limited scope of time. However, the opportunity driven findings of the conceptual paper are motivation to continue working on investigating emotions in the fashion retail. Approaches for further research may be to deeper analyse the role of moderators on costumer behaviour and the interrelations between emotional components arising through different stimuli in diverse channels. Furthermore, the given framework may be analysed empirically.

Omni-Channeling in the Fashion Industry - A Prerequisite for Emotional Shopping Experience?

Christina Laake/Jochen Strähle

Abstract

Purpose – The purpose of this paper is to analyze if omni-channeling is a prerequisite for physical stores to create an emotional shopping experience.

Design/methodology/approach – The decision was taken to use a qualitative method in form of a literature review. A systematic and method-based approach will ensure to either prove or refute various literature findings in order to analyze results.

Findings – Due to the technological developments and changes in consumer behavior, the retailer needs to adapt digital tools and to offer services that link on- and offline channels ensuring an emotional shopping experience. Multi-channel retailers need to integrate their channels to satisfy the customer.

Research limitations/implications – The paper focused on omni-channeling only with regard to consumer behavior and shopping experiences. Managerial and organizational necessities for the integration of multiple channels were not taken into consideration.

Keywords – multi-channel, omni-channel, emotional shopping experience, consumer behavior, retailing

Paper type – Research paper

1 Introduction

Presently, omni-channeling attracts as much attention as only a few managerial practices have experienced before. An increasing use of the Internet and the rapid expansion of the mobile Web lead to a digital revolution in the fashion retail industry. Multi-channel retailer and the E-commerce gain more and more market share at the expense of traditional local retailers. Due to the progressive mobilization, which may be attributed to the increasing use of smartphones and tablets, the customer can shop anywhere and anytime. The increasing transparency of services and prizes forces retailers to develop differentiated value propositions and to focus on the customer. As a result, the customer expectations have increased in all channels and high service and convenience levels are taken for granted. Driven by these developments, new chances and challenges emerge: With a smart channel linkage like the use of tablets, information terminals, QR Codes or augmented reality, the customer can profit from typical online advantages (bigger product range, product information, customer advises etc.) in physical stores. Though customers receive an integrated, seamless omni-channel experience. However, omni-channeling in the fashion retail industry is still in the development stage. There are different challenges a retailer has to face when outlaying his multi-channel strategy into a omni-channel one.

To gain a profound understanding of omni-channeling and its relevance for emotional shopping experience, the paper addresses the specific research question:

Is omni-channeling a prerequisite for emotional shopping experiences in physical stores?

The decision was taken to use a qualitative method in form of a literature review. A systematic and method-based approach with a flexible view will moreover ensure to either prove or refute various literature findings in order to analyze results and to draw a final conclusion. The literature review of this paper is based on the results of perusing different sources ranging from books to online databases to find appropriate academic findings. Additionally, reference lists of eligible scientific research papers served as basis for studies in greater depth. A preliminary literature review in general resulted in the establishment of the paper outline, followed by a specified research for the individual chapters. The use of search key words helped to define the scope of the research question while reviewing the current breadth of professional and academic literature. Based on the literature findings, a critical reflection, discussion and evaluation of the results were conducted.

The paper commences with the definition of omni-channeling, emotional shopping experience and customer segments before actual changes in technology, consumer behavior and retail environment are explained. Next embedded in the paper is a part concerning the chances that arise by the implementation of omni-channeling for the shopping experience. Followed by a section dealing with occurring challenges. A subsequent discussion and evaluation refers back to the research question. Conclusions and foresights are offered to review all gained findings and to sum up the outcomes of this research paper.

2 Literature Review and Definitions

2.1 Omni-Channeling

The literature presents different definitions of omni-channeling (Schramm-Klein, 2012, p. 419). Especially an exact distinction between the terms multi-channeling, cross-channeling and omni-channeling is missing and often, those terms are used synonymously (Heinemann, 2013, p. 9). On closer inspection, they all describe the consistent and customer-oriented development of different sales channels differing in their strategic approaches (Schramm-Klein, Wagner, Neus, Swoboda, & Foscht, 2014a).

In most of the literature, multi-channel retailing stands for direct sales with simultaneous use of two or more distribution channels, i.e. via store, catalog and Internet (Heinemann, 2013b; L. G. Poloian, 2013). Multi-channel retailer try to harmonize the prices, as well as the promotion style, even though the channels and belonging systems are managed separately (Schwerdt, 2013). For the consumer, this means that the products are indeed across channels available, but enhanced services or complaints can only take place within a channel (Fost, 2014, p.41).

In order to meet the increasing importance of integrated multi-channel retailing systems in corporate practice, the term cross-channel retailing evolved (Schramm-Klein, 2012, p. 421; Zentes, Foscht, & Swoboda, 2012, p.53). This should emphasize the aspect of the sales channel link and delineate it from the traditional multi-channel retailing (Rittinger, 2013, p.21). In cross-channel retailing, the customer is able to change the channels during the buying process. An example could be an online purchase and a physical pick up at the POS (Fost, 2014, p.42). This process is called Click & Collect heine(Rittinger, 2014). A successful cross-channel management requires multiple integrated channels, which are technical and organizational separated (Greenwich Consulting Deutschland GmbH, 2012).

The evolution of cross-channeling is omni-channeling which represents the focus of this paper. Here, the individual sales channels merge into so called touch points in a joint purchasing environment of the consumer, who gets access to the entire range of products (Fost, 2014, p. 42). The lecturer in marketing, Subrat Kumar Panigrahi, declares that "all channels have converged to the point that they have become one unit" (Panigrahi, 2013). The consumer enjoys a location-independent, continuous consistent and personalized shopping experience (Fost, 2014, p. 42). On this basis, Heinemann stresses that omni-channeling especially represents a change/trend in consumer behavior (Heinemann, 2013, p.9). Peter Sachse underlines this by expressing that "the consumer can choose whatever channel she wants to interact with you on, any device that she'd like to do that with, and (still) get a very consistent (shopping) experience" (Panigrahi, 2013). All product and customer data is centrally stored and updated in real time, so that, for example, the sales stuff is informed about the customer and that he has recently ordered a piece in the online store (Fost, 2014, p. 42). According to IDC, omni-channel consumer have a higher brand loyalty and spend about 20% more money than multi-channel consumer would do (Pine & Gilmore, 2011; Wiehr, 2011). Tools in omni-channeling, that are explained in the further reading, are used to prevent the customer to leave the brand during the buying process (Fost, 2014, p.44).

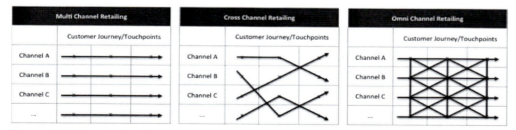

Figure 14: Differentiation between multi-channeling, cross-channeling, omni-channeling
Adapted from: (Schramm-Klein et al., 2014)

2.2 Emotional Shopping Experience

"Shopping environments can evoke emotional responses in consumers and (...) such emotions, in turn, influence shopping behaviors and outcomes" (Machleit & Eroglu, 2000). This quote demonstrates the importance of the shopping environment for the emotional shopping behavior, which will now be explained in greater detail.

The shopping process is linked with specific goals and constraints like recreation needs, limited budget, need to find a specific item or time pressure. Shoppers are confronted with emotional reactions as they work toward achieving the goal (Machleit & Eroglu, 2000). The consumers' shopping experience depends on his either utilitarian or hedonistic shopping motives (Babin et al, 1994) and consequently, his perception is depending on the shopping context (Barnes & Wright, 2012, p.58). They expect features for increased efficiency in shopping, for subjectively perceived purchasing advantages or subjectively experienced shopping fun. For emotional experiences, the shopping environment should activate and entertain the customers, stimulate them to browse and stroll and address their sensorial senses (Gröppel-Klein, 2012). Machleit and Mantel derived from different literatures: "Emotion experienced while shopping has been shown to affect a variety of responses such as approach behavior, spending levels, retail preference and choice, willingness to buy and shopping satisfaction" (Machleit & Mantel, 2001). Emotional shopping experience is described in several literature findings as entertainment. One example is given by Barnes and Wright who suggest that "literally every customer encounter represents an opportunity to impress and entertain, that customer experiences have the potential to become memorable and extraordinary" (Barnes & Wright, 2012). Kim et al. even describe it as "a sensation that occurs within an individual when a business intentionally and successfully uses services as a stage and good as props to connect a physical, emotional, intellectual and or spiritual level" (HaeJung Kim, Ahn, & Forney, 2014). To create experiences, Colin Shaw classifies in his book five imperatives: „1. Manage experience as theatre, 2. Use experience to build brand equity, 3. Balance control and spontaneity, 4. Manage conflict between creativity and business 5. Develop and use appropriate measures" (C. Shaw, 2007).

In retail settings, the atmosphere of a store plays an important role for a satisfying shopping experience and for achieving a favorable store image (Machleit & Eroglu, 2000; Machleit & Mantel, 2001). Factors, the retailer can actively control, are for example the lighting, music, scent, colors, a service-orientated stuff, displays, product demonstrations. The "Touch & Feel" experience is especially in the fashion industry of great importance. Contrary, situational factors like interactions with other shoppers or human crowding and individual factors like time pressure, mood or budget constraints are beyond the control of the retailer (Machleit & Mantel, 2001). The individual perception of the shopping experience is therefore influenced by multiple factors that are illustrated in the following figure.

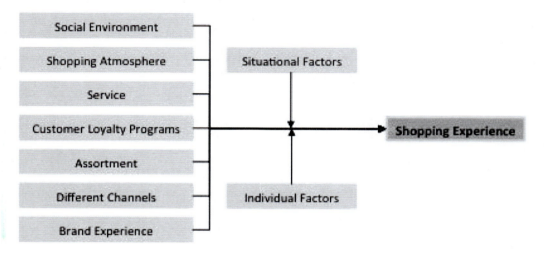

Figure 15: Modell of shopping experience
Adapted from: (Toth, 2014, p.50)

In the context of the multi-channel environment, a positive shopping experience can be provided when the customer experiences the same brand image and consistency across all channels. Zentes et al. state: "If a retailer employs different retail channels, coherence between store atmospheres in all channels is important. Similarity within the appearance of a multi-channel retailer has been found to have a positive influence on consumer attitudes towards the retailer" (Zentes, Morschett & Schramm-Klein, 2011a, p.284). Nevertheless, the retailer must highlight the strengths of the different channels clearly so that the customer can select the channel depending on the situation, but overall has the option of a 360° experience (J. Strähle, Von der Forst, Micarelli, & Schmidt, 2014).

2.3 Customer Segments

Both omni-channeling as well as the design of the shopping experience can be considered as measures for optimal satisfaction of customer needs. An understanding of different customer segments is essential. According to Neslin & Shankar, "customers differ in intrinsic preferences for channels in their response to marketing activities by channel; and by component of sales and profits (e.g., purchase quantity, timing, returns, and margin). There is also evidence that customers vary in how much inertia affects their channel choices" (Neslin & Shankar, 2009, p.71). One customer segmentation is made by Keen at al. identifying "generalists", "formatters", "price sensitives" and "experiencers" in a study of US multi-channel shoppers. For "generalists", channel choice is an element of their shopping experience, whereas "formatters" only buy in physical stores. "Price sensitives" choose the channel based on the cheapest offer and "experiencers" stick to the channel they already had good experiences with (Keen, Wetzels, de Ruyter, & Feinberg, 2004). Konus, Verhoef, and Neslin (2008) classify three multi-channel segments: "Uninvolved Shoppers" have a low purchase involvement and do not prefer a specific distribution channel; "Multi-channel Enthusiasts" are characterized by a high degree of innovation and a positive attitude towards all distribution channels and "Store-focused Consumers" prefer the stationary business over other distribution channels. In this context, the most recent study is made by Roland Berger Consultants and ECE who determine based on a survey of almost 42.000 people seven different customer segments differentiating in shopping behavior and demographics (Bloching et al., 2013). Their characteristics are shown in Table 2.

All customer segmentations have in common that at least one consumer group prefers the physical stores ("Formatters", "Store-Focused Consumers" and "Mainstream Offline Shoppers and Traditional Senior Shoppers"). This can be seen as an indicator for the remaining relevance of physical stores. While Konus et al. only focus on the consumer's attitude toward channels, the study of Roland Berger Consultants and ECE also integrates demographic aspects of the consumer groups.

In the context of digitalization and new technologies, an often referred to consumer group are the digital/smart natives. They are classified as the generation that grew up with new digital technologies (Gründerszene, 2014): Being between 16 and 25 years, owning a smartphone and using it daily. As "early adopters" they often represent the future behavior of the population (ECC Köln & hybris GmbH, 2014b). Opponent to digital/smart natives are "digital immigrants". Those are people that first got to know the technology when they were grown-ups. Fost argues that the "tsunami" of the digital natives and their purchase order is still to come and that it will speed up the channel shift significantly (Fost, 2014, p. 15).

Table 2: Customer segments in multi-channeling

Name	Description	House-hold size	House-hold income	Ø age	% of sales	Segment size
Mainstream Offline shoppers	Surf daily in the Internet, but prefer buying in physical stores together with friends, place great emphasis on fun, watch their money	3,1	2.219€	28,4	23%	25%
Traditional Senior Shoppers	Service-oriented seniors who like spending time for shopping in local stores	1,9	1.957€	64,1	27%	28%
Simplistic Shopping Minimalists	Minimalists that do not like shopping. Want a simple and stress-free shopping process with low prices	2,5	2.427€	46	10%	11%
Joy-Seeking Multi-channel Natives	Primary students that spend much time in the internet. They buy in both channels when money available	2,6	1.242€	24,5	8%	9%
Well-Off Shopping Enthusiasts	Economically established segment with the highest household income. Buy gladly and often offline as well as online. the demands on the quality are high, the price is less important.	2,9	3.510€	45,6	13%	10%
Efficient Multi-channel Shoppers	The Internet is often used because it enables 24h shopping and fits better into their hectic everyday. When is it faster or more convenient, they also buy stationary	2,9	3.009€	32,6	10%	8%
Non-Urban Shopping Pragmatists	Have long ways to arrive at a shopping center, planned purchases are conducted online, if they are already in a shopping environment, they are likely to make impulse purchases	2,9	2.743€	33,6	9%	9%

Adapted from: (Bloching et al., 2013)

2.4 Changes in Technology, Consumer Behavior and Retail Environment

2.4.1 Technological Developments

The digital revolution has arrived in the retail environment. Two-thirds of the German population use the Internet, more than half of it is buying online. Since 2007 the sales volume of the Internet retailers has tripled from 12 Billion Euro to 38 Billion Euro in 2013. According to forecasts will the online sales volume reach 55 billion Euro in 2017, growing an average of 11 Percent p.a. (ECC Köln & hybris GmbH, 2014b). The parallel use of different sales and information channels (omni-channeling) is especially enhanced by the mobile Internet (Heinemann, 2014, p.9). Smartphones or tablet-pc can be used at physical stores and enable a direct access to Internet contents (Bruce, 2012b; Daurer, Molitor, & Spann, 2012b; Zentes, Morschett, & Schramm-Klein, 2011b). Recent studies show, that 65% of smartphone owners make use of it at the POS (Eckstein, 2013). As a result, customers are able to increase their level of information, for example about the price or functionality of the product. The mobile web will most likely soon replace notebooks and pc as primary device for Internet usage. The investment bank Morgan Stanley has predicted that there are more mobile Internet users than desktop Internet users in 2014. The majority of the mobile Internet services is used for pre-purchase activities of products (Accenture & GfK, 2010; Eckstein, 2013). A therefore often used acronym is ROPO which stands for Research-Online and Purchase-Offline (Heinemann, 2012, p. 33; Sommer, 2013). A "realtime" integration of the sales channels becomes an urgent requirement (Schramm-Klein, 2012). Schröder and Zaharia state that "the combination of new retailing formats, new products, new information and communication technologies, and changing conditions in peoples' personal environment, has contributed to a profound change in customer behavior" (Schröder & Zaharia, 2008). Technology has a huge impact on the development of multi-channel strategies and a shift in consumer behavior is underlined in the following table.

Table 3: Technological and consumer behavior changes

Author	Statement
(Kollmann & Häsel, 2006, p.216)	Technological advances and changes in consumer behavior imply that cross-channel concepts will become a driving force in many industries
(U. M. Dholakia et al., 2010)	(…) as technology advances, consumers are increasingly shopping across a variety of channels and communication media
(Van Bruggen, Antia, Jap, Reinartz, & Pallas, 2010, p.338)	The challenges of designing channels for today's customers are the need for flexibility and adaptability, thus allowing customers to navigate across channels in a seamless manner
(J. Zhang et al., 2010a)	Consumers prefer to interact with a retailer anytime, anywhere through multiple, seamless interfaces
(Shankar, Inman, Mantrala, Kelley, & Rizley, 2011, p.33)	As technology enables shoppers to increasingly use and engage with multiple channels of a retailer, they are also looking for consistent information and seamless experience across these channels. To satisfy and retain shoppers, retailers may need to provide the same information in the same style and tone across the channels

Adapted from: (Rittinger, 2014)

2.4.2 Changes in Consumer Behavior

The consumer behavior has changed over the last decades from a constant over a hybrid to a multi optional behavior (Heinemann, 2012, p. 29; Wirtz, 2008, p. 45). Consumer show a complex and sometimes contradictory purchase behavior (Schramm-Klein, 2003, p.39; Wirtz, 2008, p.47).

There are different motives leading to multi optional behavior, such as variety seeking, smart shopping or convenience shopping. As special format of variety seeking constitutes Müller-Lankenau the so called channel-hopping (Müller-Lankenau, 2007, p.47). In turn, Heinemann explains the channel-hopping as a result of the increasing desire of the customers for convenience (Heinemann, 2008, p.48). It describes the behavior of a customer who switches during the buying process across different sales channels of one retailer (Heinemann, 2012, p.30). A study of ECC Köln in cooperation with hybris software determined the increasing interactions between the different sales channels (ECC Köln & hybris software, 2013).

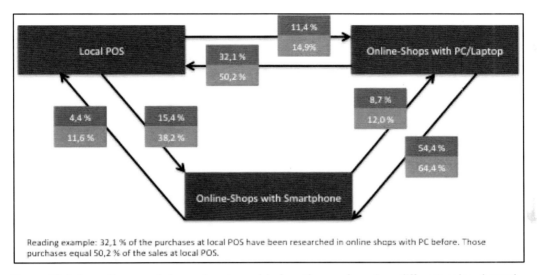

Figure 16: Information search in a sales channel before the purchase in a different sales channel, 103≤n≤699
Adapted from:(ECC Köln & hybris software, 2013)

The increasing omni-channel usage and the unlimited ability to get products on the Internet lead to a shift of the individual phases of the purchase decision process. Consequently, the point of decision has detached from the point of sale (Boersma, 2010, p. 25) and each consumer goes through his individual customer journey. A possible new buying process might be, that the customer first choses a product that fits his needs in the Internet. Supported by price search engines, online marketplaces, social shopping services, social networks or communities he receives information about interesting products. At the physical store, he can try on his chosen items, because he checked online the ability of the piece or because he picked „Click & Collect" and the fashion item has been delivered to the local POS. He decides whether he buys the item at the store or later at the online-shop (Dorman, 2013). According to Heinemann, does finding the right information offer

the most value for the customer and hence becomes the most valuable part of the buying process (Heinemann, 2013a, p.11). The modern customer journey is like a cycle with multiple feedbacks to the customer testimonials and recommendations from other participants (Haug, 2013). The already mentioned channel-hopping and the ROPO effect can be seen as good examples for that. Verhoef et al. discovered in their research three arguments for this kind of behavior: "attribute-based decision making", "lack of channel lock-in" and "cross-channel synergy" (Verhoef, Neslin, & Vroomen, 2007). "Attribute-based decision-making" is based on the consideration that distribution channels have specific advantages and disadvantages that make them differently attractive for the various phases of the purchasing process. "For instance, the Internet is often considered convenient for gathering information, while it is also considered to be risky to purchase because of security factors or the inability to physically touch and test the product" (Verhoef, Neslin, & Vroomen, 2007, p.132). "Lack of channel lock-in" refers to the failure to permanently retain customers in a single sales channel. The last reason, "cross-channel synergies", explains that the sales channels complement each other and thus enable the customer to achieve a higher shopping experience.

In the upcoming years, this behavior will intensify since digital and smart natives proliferate and request a different targeting (Heinemann, 2014b, p.2). Their natural handling with new technological items and their Internet based information searching and purchasing lead to different expectations. A study of the ECC Köln in cooperation with hybris software conducted a survey about smart natives and their expectations and behavior across multiple channels (ECC Köln & hybris GmbH, 2014b). They unveiled that their buying behavior is marked by five characteristics. First, their smartphone is essential for living. Second, online buying is a matter of course and for one quarter of the smart natives, it is the preferred way to purchase items. However, two thirds cannot imagine that online-shops will replace physical stores. Especially interesting for our research question is the aspect, that smart natives postulate omni-channeling. Their tolerance for not integrated multi-channel retail systems is very low and they do not differentiate between the multiple sales channels. As last finding it is stated that smartphones serve as the ultimate shopping-assistant, not only as information provider but also as a way to pay for the products (ECC Köln & hybris GmbH, 2014b).

The costumer of the future will hardly even be aware of whether he purchases online, offline or mobile (Heinemann, 2013a, p.9). Already now, he requests a seamless integration of the sales channels. Thus, the increased customer demand represents new challenges for the retailer, but also offers opportunities to increase customer loyalty through the use of new technologies and integrated channels (Wirtz, 2008, p.72). „The new business model requires understanding the informed and empowered consumer and focusing on him rather than the old retail-channel focused one" (Schoenbachler & Gordon, 2002).

2.4.3 Shifts in Retailing

As online purchases increase in importance, an online presence for retailers is attractive. This development will increase in the next years, to the expense of pure offline retailers (Heinemann, 2014a, p.19).

The decline in the shopping frequency is one of the impacts that are already measurable. In a survey of the ECC Köln, 60% of the respondents reported to already notice a decline in frequency at shopping areas (ECC Köln, 2014). To counteract this movement, physical retailers try to focus on their service ability and the shopping experience. (M. Brown, Mendoza-Pena, & Moriarty, 2014) highlight: "Stores provide consumers with a sensory experience that allows them to touch and feel products, immerse in brand experiences, and engage with sales associates who provide tips and reaffirm shopper enthusiasm for their new purchases". However, the mobile Internet enables the consumer to be more informed about the product than ever before. This makes it difficult for the sales personal to keep up with the emancipated and informed customer and it will lead to a change in the role of the seller. Due to the increasing blur of the different channels, the urge to fulfill a transaction intensifies. Unsure customers do not have to come back to the physical store but can easily decide to purchase their chosen product via online channel, but there, he will choose the best offer regardless of which retailer (Heinemann, 2014a, p.18).

The upcoming question is what will happen to the physical retail stores? Already now, the German retail sector has by far the largest retail space per capita but generates the lowest revenue per square meter in Europe (Graf, 2012). In a presentation about digitalization in the fashion retail sector, Dr. Haar underlines upcoming and necessary changes of the fashion and lifestyle presentation in retail. According to him, individual multilabel areas and digital brand centers with less stock and better staging will replace the nowadays everywhere present monolabel shops and areas (Haar, 2014). Physical retail can use the potential of new technologies to change the shopping experience and offer a value-add for the shopper. One possibility therefore is tested by Adidas. The brand established a "Virtual Footwear Wall" to supplement the existing assortment with online footwear models (Schramm-Klein et al., 2014).

Figure 17: Virtual Footwear Wall
Adapted from: (Lucas, 2012)

Consequently, the physical stores will develop more and more to showrooms, where the whole product range is demonstrated, customers can touch and feel, but the product will then be ordered online resulting in less needed space.

In contrast to that, pure online player like eBay or Amazon try to transfer the shopping experience back to physical stores. Amazon has already opened pop-up stores in San Francisco and Sacramanto in addition to a retail store in New York. According to Lee Yohn "Amazon's primary reason for opening physical stores is to market the Amazon brand. An instore experience is the best way to make the brand seem more human. In person, Amazon can best demonstrate its brand personality and create a more emotional connection by appealing to the five human senses" (Lee Yohn,

2014). With the so called „online to offline approach", pure players can use all their customer data to reach optimal alignment to the customer, for example in form of analyzing the best geographic location (Fost, 2014, p. 38).

Even though there are already good approaches to omni-channeling systems in Germany, they are still in their initial phase (Haug, 2013, p.36). Especially the fashion industry has a great backlog in terms of channel crossing services (Heinemann, 2012, p.229) As result, the multi-channel offering of the 100 biggest German fashion retailers is modest. According to research of the online agency Shopmacher, the top brands offer to three quarters of its 127 online-shops a multi-channel approach, but only every fifth web-store offers the service to return online ordered goods in the physical store. Sebastian Wohlrapp, CEO of dmc Commerce Consultants in Stuttgart, criticizes that multiple retailers are still organized in silos, which means, that the individual channels are not affiliated (Rösch, 2014). Nevertheless, as it became evident in the previous part, more and more retailers develop their multi-channel-system towards more channel integration in form of omni-channel systems. In the future, it can therefore be expected that the integration of multiple channels for the parallel usage will increasingly take place (Schramm-Klein et al., 2014).

2.5 Chances to increase Shopping Experiences through Omni-Channeling

The customer requirements have intensified, pure online player extend their online presence and open up physical stores. Further, the customer frequency does decrease continuously in shopping. Therefore the question arises how the retailers will counteract these developments?

Many manufacturer brands as well as multibrand retailers have an online-shop besides their physical stores. This enables them to profit of the advantages from both, physical and online presence. Those are demonstrated in the following table.

Table 4 Advantages of online and physical stores

Advantages Online Retail	Advantages Physical Retail
- Widest range	- Selected range
- Shopping at any time, any place	- Take-away immediate
- High price transparency	- Return comfortable in the store
- Swarm intelligence through customer reviews	- Provided by sales
- Detailed product information	- Customer can test and try
- Integration of social media	- Shopping as an event
- Communities and advice about the products	- All the senses are satisfied

Adapted from: (Fost, 2014, p.38)

In the past, most of the retailers managed those channels individually and separately, but channel integration is an unstoppable and necessary step in response to the increasing customer needs (Heinemann, 2013b; Zentes et al., 2011b). The opportunity lies in the use of synergies that "can be created through cross-channel promotion, communication, information sharing, digitalization, and sharing of common assets" (J. Zhang et al., 2010a). The Boston Consulting Group emphasizes the increasing importance by saying: „To make good on the multi channel promise, you need to shift from thinking in terms of separate channels that offer various sales and services to developing a business model in which sales and services are seamlessly integrated across channels." (DasGupta, Journo, Loftus, & Tardy, 2009).

Empirical studies could show that integrated distribution channel structures could lead to an increased customer satisfaction and a better perception towards retailers (Bauer & Eckhardt, 2010; Schramm-Klein, Wagner, Steinmann, & Morschett, 2011). The increased customer satisfaction stems from the luxury of being able to select the optimal distribution channel according to current needs and purchasing situation as well as changing these at any time and without any risk. This has also a positive influence on the customer loyalty (Heinemann, 2013b, p.223). Rittinger (2014, p.20) examines based on the VRIO concept, if omni-channeling can lead to a competitive advantage. His conclusion is that the required criteria "Valuable", "Rareness", "Non-imitability" and "Organization Specifity" can be fulfilled and that omni-channeling is able to offer a value-add to the customers and a chance to differentiate from competitors.

The customer profits from the following advantages (Heinemann, 2013b, p.20):

- **Flexibility:** The customer can for example choose the product in the Internet. Consequently, it will be delivered to the store, where he can try it on (Click & Collect) (Schramm-Klein, Wagner, Neus, Swoboda, & Foscht, 2014, p.175)
- **Experience:** The costumer can make a photo in an interactive mirror at the Adidas Neo Store in Stuttgart, post it on Facebook and integrate his friends in his buying decision
- **Simplicity:** The shopper is not limited by the information on the price tags or labels, but can query all necessary information with a smartphone online

As Galliano and Moreno pointed out: "customers increasingly demand thorough and effortless inventory access, simple and quick payment, convenience, flexibility, and immediacy in pickup and delivery"(Gallino, Moreno, & Stamatopoulos, 2014, p.1). Technological progresses enable retailers in many ways to optimize the shopping experience for the customer. A primary goal is to prevent the customer during his customer journey to switch to another brand. Some of the most discussed strategies in the fashion industry are presented in the following.

2.5.1 Incentives to get the Internet-Customer into the Physical Store

In the following, activities are described that help a retailer to get the customers from the web or in this case his online website to his physical store. This includes ROPO, Store-Locator, Click & Collect or Click & Reserve.

ROPO, the already mentioned Research-Online, Purchase-Offline effect, leads to many offline purchases even though the purchasing decision was made in the Internet. This means, that a lot of offline purchases were influences by online marketing measures. The ROPO effect will presumably increase in the next years due to the enormous growth of the mobile Internet.

Store-Locators are nowadays almost a basic feature of an app, since they are an immense help to direct the consumer into the store. Via GPS, the location of the customer can be determined by the position of its smartphones. Through graphical presentations can a retailer indicate the closest shop (Heinemann, 2013b, p.39). Global players like Zara or H&M already make use of this technology. When customers are already in the vicinity of the store, it makes sense to use the **geo-fencing** activation method and address them via SMS, email or voice message with a personalized offer. This can contain for example a discount on a matching product category. Due to the immediate availability and proximity, it is likely that many customers will visit the store. However, this method requires an opt-in process, in which the customer has previously released its data for the mobile contact (Haug, 2013, p.48).

Click & Collect as well as **Check & Reserve** are both methods where the customer can choose a product or check its availability in the Internet and tries it on at the physical store.

At **Click & Collect**, online shoppers have the opportunity to pick up the online ordered goods in a physical store. Concerning the delivery time, the amount of shipping costs or payment options, the retailers have different frameworks. Benefits that accrue to the customer include increased flexibility, no shipping costs, as well as the trying of the goods on the spot (Zaharia, 2013, p.130). So far, Germans uses, according to a survey, with 21% least the Click & Collect concept in comparison to other European countries (Engleson & Ganesh, 2014). In countries like UK (56%) or France (60%), this concept is more offered and used (Schramm-Klein, Wagner, Neus, Swoboda, & Foscht, 2014, p.181). However, more and more German retailers started offering this service, for example C&A or Karstadt (Der Handel, 2012; Karstadt Warenhaus GmbH, 2012). By offering Click & Collect the retailer will profit of a high potential for cross selling and up selling and the customer frequency will increase. Indeed, Haupt argues, that this potential is often not used since the service personnel handles Click & Collect like a pick-up-station instead of offering personalized advises or recommendations (Haupt, 2014b).

Check & Reserve describes the possibility to check on the Internet the availability of a product in a specific store, to reserve it and pick it up. Click and Reserve accounts for 22% of Argos, an UK Multi-Channel retailer, sales, bypassing even classical online orders (Heinemann, 2013b, p.39). 56,1 % of the investigated digital natives consider this feature as essential for retailers and 65,2% would like the chance to check the availability of products in the physical stores (ECC Köln & hybris GmbH, 2014b).

Another approach to increase frequency and to simplify the buying process for the customer is to offer them the return of their online purchases at the local POS. A survey determined, that already 68,8% of the digital natives think this feature is necessary for the multi-channel-retailer (ECC Köln & hybris GmbH, 2014b).

2.5.2 Incentives to increase Shopping Experience in the Store with Digitalization

Contacting the customer via mobile devices and making the local assortments through online offline channel links available increase customer frequency in the stationary shop. However, those potentials can only be exploited when the provider fulfills the customer expectations at the POS in the best possible way. An inspiring multi-channel experience, which contents good consulting and uncomplicated processes, is necessary.

One of the biggest problems in the physical stores is the limited assortment selection due to the limited space capacity. By linking the online and offline channels, the retailer is able to enlarge his assortment in form of endless shelves (Haug, 2013,p.45). Customers can buy the articles that might not be available in the store in the right color or size in the online store. Therefore, terminals can be made available, or the seller can actively offer this service during the sales advice and order the item with the customer on a tablet (Heinemann, 2013b,p.45). It is important that the seller encourages the customer to this kind of service instead of trying to prevent it. Runners Point, a pioneer in omni-channeling, provides touchscreen terminals, enabling the customer to access the whole online assortment and even allowing him to order the product to his home or to the physical store (Kolbrück, 2014). However, Strähle criticizes that the implementation in many stores already fails because of various factors. For example, when a customer comes into the store and asks for an article he has seen at the online store. In many cases, the seller cannot provide any information, as they have no Internet connection in the store. This lack of information and incompetence lead to a negative brand perception by the customer (J. Strähle et al., 2014).

Another tool to integrate technology to stores is augmented reality. It is based on smartphone-technology that connects the real environment with virtual elements in real time (Heinemann, 2013b, p. 49). The integrated camera of the smartphone captures the environment and the smartphone-display is superimposed with virtual elements (Fost, 2014, p.45).

#In the stationary fashion retail, augmented reality can be used to present the product in a different way and thus, generate an additional factor for the shopping experience. Nevertheless, augmented reality is still in the development phase meaning, that the tool in the physical store is still a prototype. The same applies for virtual walls or mirrors, like the Adidas Virtual Footwear Wall or the Virtual Mirror in Adidas Neo Stores. They can provide a Unique Selling Proposition and enhance shopping experience (Schramm-Klein et al., 2014), but a prerequisite is that they function without troubles. Therefore, it will probably still take some time until those tools are a matter of course (J. Strähle et al., 2014). A trailblazer is the retailer Lengermann & Trieschmann in Osnabrück who designed the first shop windows with augmented reality in Germany. The customer was able to download the augmented reality app via scanning the QR-Code. Then, they could photograph the shop windows and play movie-sequences on the display of their smartphone. Models in jeans of G-Star, Maison Scoth, Levi's, Bluefire and other denim brands present the outfits while butterflies and birds fly around. At the end of the spot, customers see in which floor they find the presented jeans. The campaign "blue magic" which concentrates only on jeans is continued inside the store where jeans are wrapped around a real tree (Damm, 2014).

QR-Codes like the one that was used in the example above can serve for different aspects: Promotion of new products, offering coupons, comparing prices in other stores, direct online shopping, providing product information (Fost, 2014; Morschett, 2012; Schramm-Klein et al., 2014). In general, they are an easy chance for the retail to link his physical store with other sales channels. Similar to the process of barcode scanning, QR-Codes enable multiple usage possibilities with an appropriate scanner which is usually as a App in the smartphone integrated (Schramm-Klein et al., 2014). Since QR-codes are cheap in producing and versatile placeable, they are already often used in praxis. A research has developed, that already 18,6% of the smartphone users in Germany scan QR-Codes. The same study also revealed that in comparison to the year before the usage of QR-Codes increased about 96% in Europe (ComStore, 2014). It is very likely that QR codes will soon be an integral part of every store.

In the context of omni-channeling it is of increased importance to make simple payment methods across all channels possible. Therefore the integration of new and alternative paying methods plays a viral role, especially mobile payments are focused (Schramm-Klein et al., 2014). Multi-channel retailer can link the payment way of multiple channels and propose an extended service. If a customer has paid for example his online purchases always with paypal, he should be able to pay this way in the physical store as well. Mobile payment therefore serves as an approved interface to enable a seamless change between the channels (Schramm-Klein et al., 2014). Additionally, it contributes to a positive shop atmosphere when long might be a phenomena of the past.

2.6 Challenges in Omni-Channeling

Multiple retailers have difficulties integrating their online and offline channels. As reasons for this, seven general problem fields and challenges can be categorized: 1. Organizational challenges due to evolutionary grown structures, 2. Corporate culture challenges presented by department egoism and competition, 3. A cross-channel data integration for channel-specific IT-systems, 4. Increasing management complexity based on cross-channel strategy development and implementation, 5. Lack of strategic flexibility, 6. Too high complexity for logistic systems, 7. High investments in information technology. Particularly medium-sized companies do not have the financial resources and the know-how to integrate the distribution channels value-adding for the costumers (Rittinger, 2014).

With regard to the shopping experience, the retailer is faced with challenges in form of customer understanding, channel consistency, attitude of sales staff concerning omni-channeling and flexibility.

Consumers will demand increasingly customizing services regardless of location or time and select their channels situational. The task is therefore to create a holistic, cross-channel customer service and to ensure a seamless shopping experience across all touch points (Schramm-Klein et al., 2014). However, many retailers still have different assortments, inconsistent branding, and no channel crossing customer relationship management. If the customer is restricted in his channel-hopping possibilities, sustainable customer dissatisfaction is often hard to correct (Heinemann, 2008, p.189). A great danger is thus that the customer transfers the negative experience of one channel to the other channels of the brand. In addition, the inconsistency across the channels leads often to confusion of the customer. The channels cannot be connected to the same brand and an image of missing professionalism and coordination arises (Heinemann, 2008, p.189). Another treat is to loose the customer during channel-hopping to other brands (Fost, 2014).

An improved linkage of the different channels is often prevented by the sales stuff. Their attitude toward online-channel-sales is often critical since they fear a reduction in their own sales. This is often the case when the individual sales channels are managed as autonomous regions in terms of a profit center (Heinemann, 2008, p.185). In contrast to that are the interests of an omni-channel company in which it is only important, that the customer buys a product independent of the channel he chooses. Consequently, one important issue is to communicate and embed this thinking in the perception of the sales stuff because they are a key element for the customer's shopping experience and loyalty.

Due to the higher customer requirements the role of the service stuff has changed (Raithel, 2014, p.24-25). Since the customer has in most cases already achieved his requested information in the Internet, social-communicative competences has to be focused on (Schramm-Klein et al., 2014). Therefore, they serve as "touchpoints at the shop space" which need to emotionalize the customers and in the same time increase their boundaries to the online-shop. It means that online-activities should be promoted and the online assortment should be integrated into the advising activities. Because of expected 360° customer service, the sales people need to be informed about the online and offline assortment and be able to provide quick information to the customer. However, it is a change in the corporate culture and in practice, it is a lengthy, complex process that needs to be implemented step by step (Raithel, 2014, p.24-25).

Another relevant issue is the flexibility of a company. Schmidt argues that retailers become incapacitated when they try to solve all challenges at the same time. It is important to perform first best in every single channel. Only then, an integration of the different channels is useful and recommended (J. Strähle et al., 2014). However Heinemann underlines, that the less differentiation between the different channels is obvious, the more likely cannibalization occurs. To demonstrate the differences the advantages of the channels need to be accentuated (Heinemann, 2008, p.186).

3 Discussion

As literature and analyzes studies have demonstrated, the technological developments lead to a shift in consumer behavior and the retail environment. Mobile advices enable the consumer to shop location and time independent and his channel choice will be situational driven. It is very likely that the customer uses different channels simultaneously and has higher expectations from the retailer (Schramm-Klein et al., 2014). The traditional observation in which the purchase decision was associated with the channel does not fit anymore to the function and usage of multi-channel systems nowadays. The decision process is multi-level and the channels contribute in their combination to the company's success. That is why the retail environment tries to counteract the changing consumer behavior resulting in increased integration of their sales channels. However, the transition from an isolated multi-channel system to an omni-channel system contains multiple strategic, organizational and corporate cultural challenges (Rittinger, 2014). The multiplicity of the channels and the complexity in controlling the multi-channel-systems will increase, especially because of a growing number of electronic channels. Through increased mobile channel use, the consumer behavior will significantly change and claims for an intensified examination of integration.

It is therefore important for the retail industry to focus on the customer. Omni-channeling has the goal to enhance the relationship between consumer and brand. In most cases, an omni-channel retailer can offer his customers added value. However, before implementing such a strategy, the first question must be if multi channeling makes sense for the individual target group. Next step is to identify the buying motivation of the customers, whether they want to safe time, have experience shopping etc.. Resulting recommendations for action can then be derived (Bloching et al., 2013). In case the target group prefers to shop in the physical stores (see chapter 2.3 customer segments), the importance of omni-channeling has a minor relevance.

The different usages and examples for cross- and omni-channeling, like ROPO or Click & Collect, have demonstrated the key role of physical stores with regard to the positioning of multi-channel systems. The peculiarity lies in the fact that they allow the physical presence of products and people, the integration of direct, personal contacts and relationships, as well as a multimodal customer contact (Schramm-Klein et al., 2014). Especially when refocusing on the physical stores, the combination of traditional elements of the store design and new technologies and mobile channels play an important role. The physical store will always have the advantage of the sensory component allowing the customer to "touch & feel". Combining the given advantages with new technological chances, the shopping experience will increase qualitative and the efficiency of the buying process for the customer will enhance.

The expert discussions about multi-channel systems in retailing and the recent customer observations with regard to the shopping experience of the future, delivers the impression that retail will mostly be driven by electronic channels (Schramm-Klein et al., 2014). Often not taken into consideration is the fact that technological potentials can lead to new impulses in the physical stores as well. Technologies like QR Codes or augmented reality can also be implemented without an online store, like the show window of Lengermann & Trieschmann clarifies. The goal is to create a shopping experience that intensifies emotions and activates consumer's feelings.

Referring back to the research question: **"Is Omni-Channeling a prerequisite for physical stores to generate an emotional shopping experience?"**, a clear answer can be derived.

No, it is not a prerequisite because the need for omni-channeling is strongly depending on the retailers target group and emotional shopping experiences can also be provided without having multiple channels. Nevertheless, the greatest growth rates are expected by the multi-channel-providers, followed by the online players, at the expense of the pure offline player in form of the traditional retailer (Haug, 2013, p.34). However, for already existing multi-channel retailer is no way around an integration of the channels in the long run. As the chart below demonstrates, omni-channeling becomes more and more a necessity instead of a tool to differentiate from competitors (Heinemann, 2008, p.187). Noticeable is, however, that the implementation is a complex process that requires a clear strategy and requires a good performance of the single channels.

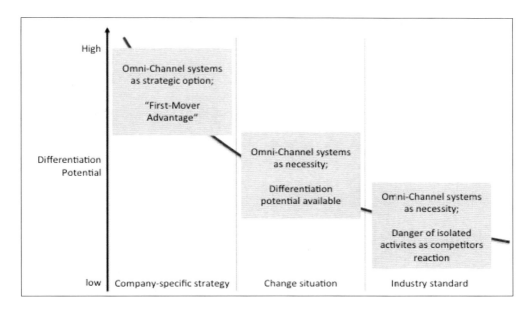

Figure 18: Differentiation potentials for Omni-Channel Retailer
Adapted from: (Heinemann, 2008, p.187)

4 Conclusion

Due to changes in the fashion industry, omni-channeling has grabbed center stage in the last few years. The aim of this paper was to critically reflect on the necessity of omni-channeling for emotional shopping experiences.

The outcomes of the literature review asserted that the management of multiple channels is strongly depending on their linkage and integration with the highest evolution form of the omni-channel retail. The perceived shopping experience varies with the shopping motives, the situation and the individual preferences. To understand those, in the literature are multiple customer segment schematics designed explaining different types of multi-channel consumers. It could be demonstrated, that developments in the technology, new customer behavior and retail formats bring chances as well as challenges for the retailer.

As chances, the higher customer satisfaction and increased shopping experience can be named. The retailer can use features like Click & Collect to get the shopper from the online-shop to his store. There, he can uses endless shelves, terminals or QR codes to increase the emotional shopping experience. The challenge in the development to more integration across the channels lies among other things in the consistency across the different sales channels and the professional training of the sales personal and their attitude towards omni-channeling.

Further investigation both in terms of literature reviews and practical analysis is always possible but within the dimensions of this paper not feasible. On a scientific level, future investigations could be directed toward further examinations of strategic and organizational challenges and prerequisites a retailer has to face for the integration. In this paper, factors such as lack of know-how and capital or high complexities were not researched in detail.

As a summary of results, the implementation of omni-channeling can be regarded as a roadmap to success if one understands what one's expectation from omni-channeling is. With regards to the prior set research question "Is Omni-Channeling a prerequisite for emotional shopping experience in the physical stores?" it can be considered that for multi-channel retailers, the step to channel integration is indispensable since the customer requests an optimal gearing and seamless channel-hopping across the channels. However, pure offline retailers can draw on technological innovations and provide an emotional shopping experience also without other existing channels. Future predictions include an increasing development of multi-channeling towards omni-channeling. The success of the omni-channel system will crucially depends on the retailer ability to know his target group and to provide a consistent brand image along all touch points. Emotional shopping experience is given if the retailer can offer customers added value.

The Pre-Purchase Phase - How to Attract Customers

The Ethical Side of Emotional Fashion Advertising

Theresa Höckner/Jochen Strähle

Abstract

Purpose – The purpose of this paper is to analyze if the practice of emotional fashion advertising has ethical dimensions, which must be considered by the companies using those advertising approaches in order to adhere to their general ethical and social responsibility.

Design/methodology/approach – A literature review was conducted using mainly peer-reviewed articles and books.

Findings – First it was shown that companies have a social and hence ethical responsibility toward the society they operate in and that this responsibility includes their marketing and advertising activities. Furthermore it was examined how emotional advertising works in order to analyze this practice from an ethical point of view. It was shown that an emotional advertising approach can have negative effects on consumers and therefore could jeopardize a company's ethical responsibility.

Research limitations/implications – Implications given are to identify and limit possible negative effects of a company's emotional fashion advertising. But the findings of this paper are limited, because they are based on research findings resulting from different studies using different approaches and research settings.

Keywords – emotional advertising, fashion advertising, ethical advertising, marketing ethics

Paper type – Research paper

1   Introduction

Emotionality in fashion businesses is a topic of increasing interest. Many fashion companies nowadays create emotional fashion advertising in order to promote their products and to gather customer's attention for the brand. New technologies and neuroscientific methods enable marketers to better understand and manage the customer's emotions (Fulmer & Barry, 2009). Academic literature increasingly explores this topic but little research is done on the ethical dimension of those advertising practices (Fulmer & Barry, 2009). This work is determined to find out if the practices of emotional fashion advertising have an ethical dimension and if the fashion company jeopardizes its general ethical and social responsibility by using this advertising approach. Therefore a literature review was conducted and the findings are presented in the following order. First – in chapter 2 - a definition of ethics in general and their relevance in business and management will be given to set the basis for the following description of CSR and a specific CSR model. Then a closer view of the relevance of ethics and CSR in advertising is given. The third chapter is dedicated to define and explain "emotional fashion advertising". Therefore advertising in general will be shortly defined in order to examine the ways and effects of using and arousing emotions in advertising. Thirdly the special characteristic of fashion advertisements are given and then it will be examined how the customers perceive those advertisements. And finally a closer look will be taken on the image of attractiveness and physical appearance displayed in fashion advertisement. In the following chapter each dimension of emotional fashion advertising will be approached from an ethical point of view. Therefore the ethical side of influencing emotions and the customers and promoting an idealized image of attractiveness and physical appearance will be discussed. To finally discuss if fashion companies harm their overall ethical responsibility when they are using emotional fashion advertising and how this harm can be prevented or limited by using different advertising practices. In the end of this paper a conclusion will be given and the limitations of this work will be pointed out in order to make suggestions for further research.

2 Ethics in a Management Context

2.1 Ethics – A Definition and Its Relevance in Management

Ethics are "moral principles that govern a person's or group's behavior" (*New Oxford American dictionary*, 2010). These principles also direct and define the moral correctness of conduct. Furthermore the "the branch of knowledge that deals with moral principles" is known as ethics as well. (Lindberg & Stevenson, 2010) A simplified interpretation of the ethics would be to define it as the ability to categorize behavior in right vs. wrong and to base the own decisions on this judgment. (Paulins, 2009)

It is argued that humanity itself is defined by ethics because the ability of human beings to base their decisions and behavior on moral principles and values distinct them from animals, which are guided by instincts (Paulins, 2009). Another determining factor of ethics are cultures, based on Czinkota's and Ronkainen's (2010) defintion cultures are a system of learned behaviour and hence influences a persons morals and values. But there is a great variety in cultures and consequently of ethical perspectives. (Paulins, 2009) In this paper the focus will be on western cultures and therefore different westerns philosophcial approachs on ethics will be examined shortly.

Western philosophy can be roughly divided in three schools of ethics: Aristotle's virtue approach, the princplied approach based on duty by Kant and Ultiliatriansim (Lindberg & Stevenson, 2010; Paulins, 2009). Further appraochs are the common good approach, the rights approach and the fairness (or justice) approach (Paulins, 2009). These and several other approaches try to define how an ethical choice - the "right" decision - can be made. Non of these approaches is the correct ethical guideline used by the western society to make ethical choice. They are different perspectives on ethics in general, ethical decision making and the "right" solution for ethical dilemma. An ethical dilemma often occurs in the process of decision making for example if the ethical choice is not the easiest, the financially most efficent, the one reached upon a consensus, etc. (Paulins, 2009).

Based on the definition above it can be stated that every person is confronted with ethical decision-making and hence ethical dilemmas. Especially managers who have to decide on various problems and questions on a daily basis often face ethical dilemma. Carroll (1991) categorized three types of management: the immoral, the amoral and the moral management, which are still valid today. In this categorization the terms ethics and morality are used synonymous. If a manager actively decides, acts and behaves against the "right" or ethical choice he/she is classified as an immoral manager. In immoral management ethical principles are negated. The main goal of an immoral manager is to increase a company's (financial) success. Hence legal restrictions and standards are impediments and should be overcome or avoided. Every opportunity should be exploited in the company's favor and customers are perceived as one of these opportunities and all marketing activities are based on this assumption. (Carroll, 1991) Amoral management does not take any kind of moral into account. It means to be neither immoral nor moral. An amoral manager is not aware that his/her decisions may affect other people in a negative way. They miss the ethical dimension of their work and actions. This includes the unintentional amoral manager, who is just careless and unmindful and the intentional amoral manager, who is aware of ethics but does not intent to acknowledge it in his/her business decisions. In amoral management the company does not consider the customer's perspective on ethics and the moral dimension of the firm's interaction with customers. (Carroll, 1991) The third category is the moral management. It means not simply acknowledge the ethical dimension of managerial activates but rather taking a position of high moral standards and exemplified ethical behavior in management. The company's goal is to be profitable and successful while abiding by high moral standards. Legal restrictions are seen as the minimal standard of moral behavior and the company tries to act above the mandate of law. In moral management the firm's relationship with the customer is seen as an equal transaction. The consumers must be treated fairly therefore they have to receive fair value, complete information and satisfaction at its best from the company in exchange for the money they pay. The rights of the customer are valued and may be extended above the legal standards by the company. (Carroll, 1991) Today all three kinds of management can be found whereupon the immoral and amoral kind of management is seen most frequently. When arguing that leadership by example is the best way to improve the ethics in management the leadership model of moral management sets this ideal standard of ethical management. (Carroll, 1991)

2.2 Ethics – A Part of Corporate Social Responsibility

Based on the definition every person or group is guided by ethics, develops own values and faces ethical dilemmas (Lindberg & Stevenson, 2010; Paulins, 2009). Hence companies have an ethical perspective, they employ people, who all have own ethics and in addition to that the company itself has ethics as an own group in society and companies interact with consumers, who also hold their own ethical values. So it is obvious that every company has an ethical dimension. In the beginning it was assumed that a company's only responsibility was to be profitable to provide jobs and realize the highest possible financial gain to shareholders (Carroll, 1991). Soon the law of the country the company was operating in dilated this responsibility. It was understood that companies have to abide by the national and later international laws while pursuing their company's interest. In the 1960's a third responsibility of companies was defined: the social responsibility. (Carroll, 1991) Later the term corporate social responsibility (CSR) was introduced and since than it is often used in academic literature, discussions and from various companies. Nowadays there are several definitions and interpretations of the term CSR. In general the term is used to describe any kind of social- and moral-motivated behavior and actions of companies' toward society and environment (Duong Dinh, 2011). It declares not just systems or governments accountable for vast responsibilities like a social responsibility and hand this responsibility partially over to individual corporations and managers (Kotler & Armstrong, 2014). It is suggested that companies have a social conscience (Kotler & Armstrong, 2014) and act beyond the company's immediate financial interest (Carroll, 1991). Furthermore CSR goes beyond the legal restrictions and standards. It is expected that companies voluntarily do more than what the system allows (Duong Dinh, 2011; (Kotler & Armstrong, 2014), because it is still possible for a company to act within the legal framework but being from an ethical point of view highly negligent (Kotler & Armstrong, 2014). These are quintessential statements about CSR, which can be found in most CSR definitions but still cannot provide a concise understanding.

Therefore the CSR pyramid by Carroll (1991), which is often used and cited in academic literature (cf. Duong Dinh, 2011; Wehner & Gentile, 2012) will be explained in more detail and is subsequently used as the definition of CSR in this paper. Carroll (1991) suggested that there are four responsibilities in CSR: the economic, legal, ethical and philanthropic responsibilities.

Figure 19: CSR Pyramid by Caroll, 1991
Adapted from: (Carroll 1991, p.42)

In this CSR model a company's economic responsibility is the foundation. It represents the historic aim of any company to be profitable and to provide goods and services customers need and will pay for (Carroll, 1991). The next step is the legal responsibility. Every corporation has to obey the regional, national and international laws. The companies are expected to act within the legal framework. (Carroll, 1991) Both responsibilities are widely accepted and mentioned in many other CSR definitions. But as discussed earlier CSR also means to act beyond the existing legal restrictions. The third responsibility – the ethical responsibility – embraces these actions and concessions, which are not specified in law rather than expected from society. Some very basic ethical norms can already be found in the economic and legal dimension but this third responsibility goes beyond this obvious and severe restrictions or standards. Hence the ethical responsibility is not as clearly defined as the economic and legal responsibility and every corporation needs to examine its own ethical responsibility and morality. (Carroll, 1991) The philanthropic responsibility is the last responsibility in Carroll's pyramid. Nowadays the society expects companies to be good corporate citizens. Hence the companies are required to engage in activities, which will increase the social prosperity and goodwill. (Carroll, 1991) The latter responsibilities are describing voluntary activities of the companies but society today expects the companies to adhere to this responsibilities (Wehner & Gentile, 2012).

A separation of ethics and economics by companies is not an accepted position in society today. Companies that only value their economic responsibility and financial gain will experience criticism and resistance. (Wehner & Gentile, 2012) Acting in a social responsible way is the basis of a company's legitimation (Duong Dinh, 2011). Based on the stakeholder theory a company's success is also based on its relationships to the different stakeholders and their standing in society (Duong Dinh, 2011). To be profitable and respected by customers and other stakeholders companies have to perform acceptably in all four dimensions of this CSR model. This broad view of responsibilities affects every part of the company including the marketing (Polonsky & Hyman, 2007). In return it may help to satisfy customer needs beyond the product and service provided and will help building strong and trustful customer relationships (Kotler & Armstrong, 2014). Companies should "build profitable customer relationship by creating value for customers in order to capture value from customers in return" (Kotler & Armstrong, 2014).

2.3 Ethics in Marketing

The CSR Pyramid is applicable to every corporation and hence it is relevant for every department of a company. These responsibilities permeate all actions of the company including a company's marketing and more specific it's advertising. (Polonsky & Hyman, 2007) To ensure a social and ethical marketing a company should develop a corporate guideline, which ensures consistency in ethical behavior and must be obeyed by the employees and managers (Kotler & Armstrong, 2014). Especially the marketing department, which aims to build a strong relationship with the customers should apply a company's philosophy on societal responsibility and comply to the ethical standards and corporate conscience (Kotler & Armstrong, 2014). This understanding of marketing ethics should go beyond what is regulated by law, even so in past years "broader marketing and advertising regulations have been established nationally and globally" (Polonsky & Hyman, 2007, p. 7).

In order to develop ethical responsible advertising a marketing manager has to consider the interests of all stakeholders when developing an advertising strategy (Polonsky & Hyman, 2007). An unethical advertising activity will also affect the economic dimension of a company, because some stakeholders may see this advertisement as irresponsible. This may lead to harmful publicity for the company or damage their relationships to the customers. Even the company's long-term success and survival is jeopardized, when for example the company's image is hurt due to the criticized advertisement (Kotler & Armstrong, 2014; Polonsky & Hyman, 2007). The resulting damage on the company's success is therefore also a violation of its economic responsibility (Polonsky & Hyman, 2007). Any advertising, which results in "physical, financial, or emotional" injuries of a customer, is deemed as unethical (Polonsky & Hyman, 2007, p. 5). That there are advertisements, wich are critizied by stakeholders and may offend customers or other groups of stakeholders shows that some companies ignore of disobey their responsibilties (Polonsky & Hyman, 2007). In contrast to harmful advertisement and its impact on a firm's success, ethical responsible advertisement can be benifical for a company, e.g. by enhancing customer's value and the company's relationship with the customer (Polonsky & Hyman, 2007). Marketing managers should be focused on realizing a mutual gain and consider the long-term effects of their advertisement on the company (Kotler & Armstrong, 2014).

Because advertising has such a high impact on a company's perception and marketing systems are often accused of having a negative influence on society, e.g. pollute the cultural heritage or foster materialism (Kotler & Armstrong, 2014) it is inalienable for companies to consider the social responsibility and the ethical dimension of their advertising. Therefore the American Marketing Association, a global association of marketing managers and academics, published in 2014 a "Statement of Ethics", which provides the following ethical norms and values for marketers:

> 1. Do no harm. This means consciously avoiding harmful actions or omissions by embodying high ethical standards and adhering to all applicable laws and regulations in the choices we make.
>
> 2. Foster trust in the marketing system. This means striving for good faith and fair dealing so as to contribute toward the efficacy of the exchange process as well as avoiding deception in product design, pricing, communication, and delivery of distribution.
>
> 3. Embrace ethical values. This means building relationships and enhancing consumer confidence in the integrity of marketing by affirming these core values: honesty, responsibility, fairness, respect, transparency and citizenship. (American Marketing Association, 2014)

3 Emotional Fashion Advertising

3.1 Advertising - Definition and Theoretical Approaches

Advertising can easily be defined as „any paid form of nonpersonal presentation and promotion of ideas, goods and services by an identified sponsor" (Kotler & Armstrong, 2014). The basic advertising process can be defined by Shannon and Weavers (1950) communication model: The company is the sender and transmits its message respectively its advertisement to the targeted recipients. If the audience is able to decode the received message correctly it can answer appropriately, e.g. by buying the promoted product. This process can be disrupted by noise, wich can be created by various stakeholders and may lead to an undesired or irresponsible reaction of the audience or other stakeholders. (Polonsky & Hyman, 2007) The ideal qualities of the message encoded in the advertisement are described by the AIDA model: the advertisement should trigger attention, than gather interest, awake the desire and finally lead to the required action (Kotler & Armstrong, 2014).

To create an ideal message that corresponds to the AIDA model marketers generally can decide if the message should have a rational, emotional or a moral appeal (Kotler & Armstrong, 2014). Rational appeals focus on the product features and their benefit for the customers. The recipient of the message is expected to act based on his/her self-interest (Kotler & Armstrong, 2014). By using emotional appeals marketers try to evoke positive or sometimes even negative emotions to influence the audience's reaction in their favor. It is argued that an emotional appeal attracts high attention and trust in the promoted brand, because consumers tend to feel before making a reasoned decision. (Kotler & Armstrong, 2014) Moral appeals are often use to induce the consumer to support a social cause or project. Hence moral appeals aim at the receipients ethical beliefs and morality. (Kotler & Armstrong, 2014) An emotional advertisement appeal is also known as the affective marketing approach. Advertising strategies can be devided in the cognitive approach and the affective approach. When companies build their advertisement on reasonable arguments and the products rational benefits it uses the cognitive approach (Panda, Panda, & Mishra, 2013). In this work the focus will be on emotional respectively affective appeals of advertising.

3.2 Emotions in Advertising

Advertisements are offering a good vehicle to provoke an emotional reaction. Emotions are defined as a specific example of feelings (Cohen and Areni, 1991 cited by (HyeShin Kim, 2000) or more precisely as an "instinctive or intuitive feeling as distinguished from reasoning or knowledge" (Lindberg & Stevenson, 2010).

Researches have shown that advertisements can cause the appearance or the change of emotions (Fulmer & Barry, 2009). These evoked emotions influence the customer's attitude towards the advertised product (Holbrook & Baltra, 1987 cited in Fulmer & Barry, 2009 and (HyeShin Kim, 2000)). The advertisements are external triggers that "can be managed intentionally to activate specific moods and emotions in others" (Fulmer & Barry, 2009, p. 159). Effective emotional advertisements are expected to build long-term consumer relationships and loyalty (Bülbül & Menon, 2010) and hence lead to a positive brand perception, which can result in higher purchase intentions (Panda et al., 2013). If an advertisement creates postive feelings, these emotions can be transferred to the brand and result in a postive brand perception (Panda et al., 2013). A positive brand perception can also be achived if the brand including its advertisement represents the values of the customer (Ko, Norum, & Hawley, 2010). To develop an favorable attitude towards a brand, brand knowledge is required (Panda et al., 2013). Advertising is also used to build this brand knowledge and recall. Brand recall is exceptionally important, because it guides the customer at the point of purchase. (Panda et al., 2013) Emotional advertising generates higher brand recall including not just the brand name but also the message transmitted by the advertisement, it is also better liked (HyeShin Kim, 2000); Stout & Leckenby, 1986). In general a strong emotional bond between customer and brand is benefical for the company, because research shows that customers, who are emotionally involved in a brand are less price-sensitive and willing to pay more (Panda et al., 2013). Advertising can help creating this emotional bondage. Creating emotions during the purchase or consumption process is beneficial for the company, because the customer's consumption process is influenced by emotions (Panda et al., 2013). Emotional advertisements have a higher influence on the customer's decision making process compared to rational appeals (Panda et al., 2013).

But the way customers react on an advertisement and the intensity of the aroused emotions vary significantly, hence it cannot be accurately predicted how an advertisement influence the individual attitude of a consumer toward a brand (D. J. Moore & Harris, 1996). The messages embedded in the emotional advertisement may not be decipherable by all receipients or cause different reactions (Fulmer & Barry, 2009). Even if an adverisment makes consumer generally experience positive emotions their impact on the consumption can vary as well (Panda et al., 2013). Using emotional appeals in advertising can also be disadvantageous for a brand when the customer feels offended by the advertsiment or is misled (Paulins, 2009). Arousing negative emotions with an advertisement can result in unfavorable attitudes toward the advertisement and hence the promoted brand (D. J. Moore & Harris, 1996).

The emotions created by advertisings are known as ad-evoked feelings (Huber, Meyer, & Weihrauch, 2011). As soon as an advertisement transfers an emotional content to the customers it has an substantial impact on the brand attitudes (Geuens, De Pelsmacker, & Tuan Pham, 2014). "Regardless of how creative or informative the respondents found the ads to be, the emotional content of these ads had a significant positive influence on consumers' attitudes toward the advertised brands" (Geuens et al., 2014). It is also insignificant if the advertsited product is a high- or a low-involvement product, the ad-evoked emotions will have a postitive influence on the brand attitudes either way (Geuens et al., 2014). The positive brand attidudes can be created because the advertisement has caused pleasant feelings in the customer's mind, which reults in favorable thoughts about the brand. The second way to create a positive brand attitude via an advertisement is creating a evaluative conditioning effect. This means the customer will pair the brand with the feelings aroused by its advertisement, hence these feelings are incorporated in the customer's evaluation of the brand. (Geuens et al., 2014) In general a higher impact of ad-evoked emotions can be seen for brands and products that are associated with fun and other hedonistic values rather than functionality (Geuens et al., 2014). Based on their reseach Geuens et al. (2014) advise marketers to develop advertisements that evoke postive feelings because these advertisements are better liked and will also create more positive brand attitudes.

In addition to the brand attitude which can be influcenced by emotional advertising there is also an advertising attitude. Advertisements create a stimulus to which the consumer responds either in a positive or negative way, this reaction is defined as the advertising attitude (Lutz, 1985 cited by (HyeShin Kim, 2000). To describe the state of feelings or emotions generated by an specific stimulus the term affect is used (Bakalash & Riemer, 2013; Fulmer & Barry, 2009, (HyeShin Kim, 2000). A customer's affective reaction to an advertisement is defined by the emotions this advertisement evokes, when the consumer sees it (Bakalash & Riemer, 2013). Various academics have shown that affect causes biases in the customer's perception, reaction and evaluation (Fulmer & Barry, 2009). This is done unconsciously to ease and streamline the ampleness of impressions and decisions in the everyday-life of every consumer (Fulmer & Barry, 2009). Research has also shown that the intensity of the effect has a direct impact on the emotional reaction (Larsen & Diener, 1987; (D. J. Moore & Harris, 1996). In general creating an affect causing positive emotions is better than trigger unfavorable emotions, because people prefer positive situations and are likely to avoid negative emotions (D. J. Moore & Harris, 1996). Thus emotion-based advertising aims to evoke strong positive affects (Panda et al., 2013). The intensity - strong vs. low - and the tendency - negative vs. positive - are just two ways to describe and differentiate affects or emotions. Another way to describe different states of feelings is concret vs. abstarct affect (Bülbül & Menon, 2010). Concret affect is short-term orientated and abstract affect has a long-term impact (Bülbül & Menon, 2010). Thus advertiser have to consider which orientation – short-term or long-term – corresponds to their advertising strategy or goal and select the emotional appeal accordingly (Bülbül & Menon, 2010). A brand could also use both appeals, e.g. by creating abstract affective appeals at the very beginning of a customer's decision making and a concret affective appeal again at the end, when the consumer does the actual purchasing (Bülbül & Menon, 2010). Affective appeals can also help a brand building a strong relationship to its customers and holding them over a long periode of time (Panda et al., 2013). Another significant impact of affective responses of consumers to an advertisement is the increased memorability, which is always desired when creating advertisings (Bakalash & Riemer, 2013). "Neuroscientific research indicates emotionally arousing stimuli engage specific neural mechanisms that enhance memory" (Bakalash & Riemer, 2013, p. 278). Furthermore it was proven that the memory of an advertisement can influence the judgment and "other behavioral responses" like the purchase intention (Bakalash & Riemer, 2013).

3.3 Characteristics of Fashion Advertising

An emotional or affective appeal of advertisement can be used for various product groups including fashion. Fashion is an unique product category, it belongs to the category of high involvement products, which are generally used by customers to express his/her self (Aagerup, 2011; Banister & Hogg, 2004). Another specific characteristic of fashion is, that it is generally "youth and female oriented" (HyeShin Kim, 2000). Therefore this work focuses on young females as it is usually done by literature and in practice. It is very attractive to marketers to use an emotional appeal in fashion advertising because it is hard to communicate the value and attributes of a fashion article by using rational or logical arguments (Panda et al., 2013). Hence fashion advertisements start using complexly composed and clourful images in order to generate strong emotional appeals (HyeShin Kim, 2000).

In fashion advertising physical attractiveness is highly important, therefore beauty stereotypes are often used (Caballero & Solomon, 1984). In addition to that illusionary product settings are created (HyeShin Kim, 2000). Both helps generating and communicating the desired emotional appeal. Generally the visual impression is extremly important in fashion advertisements to create the affective appeal (HyeShin Kim, 2000). Research has shown that the emotional appeal in fashion advertisement becomes increasingly important. During the 1970s until the 1990s a functional appeal dominated in fashion advertising but by the 2000s it became obvious that usage of emotional appeals increases. Nowadays most marketers use affective appeals to advertise fashion products. (Ko, Norum, & Hawley, 2010) Another trend that can be established is the consumers' tendency to pursue hedonic values and consumption rather than functional and utilitarian consumption ((HyeShin Kim, 2000); (Ko et al., 2010). Fashion products are hedonic products and they are generally consumed to achieve some kind of self-enhancement (Ko et al., 2010).

Happiness, attractiveness, elegance, freedom etc. are a few examples of emotions aroused by affective appeales of fashion advertisings (Ko et al., 2010). To measure the emotional states evoked by an advertisement with an affective appeal researchers often use the PAD – Pleasure-Arousal-Dominance – model, an emotional state model developed by (Mehrabian, 1996). Both (HyeShin Kim, 2000) and (Ko et al., 2010) applied this model to fashion advertisements. The study conducted by (Ko et al., 2010) shows that the feelings of "happiness, elegance, beauty, freedom and sentimentality belong to the pleasure dimension, and that the feelings of the exotic, fresh, daring, and sexy belong to the arousal dimension" (Ko et al., 2010) and that feelings of domination (e.g. control, submission, etc.) are hardly to find in fashion advertisements. Kim (2000) was able to show that the emotional dimensions of pleasure and arousal can lead to a positive advertisement attitude, which is desirable as disscussed beforehand. As already mentioned fashion advertismnents try to evoke emotions related to the customer's hedonic values and can be described as an characteristic of fashion advertisements. These emotions are also part of the pleasure and arousal dimension ((HyeShin Kim, 2000).

3.4 The Customer's Perception of Emotional Fashion Advertising

Fashion products are often bought and used by customers because they want to indulge in or pursue some kind of self-enhancement (Banister & Hogg, 2004; (Ko et al., 2010). This is even one of the top-priorities and motivations guiding consumers' behavior and purchase decisions (Banister & Hogg, 2004). Hence a fashion advertisement displays an image that is highly attractive in order to create an image or state many consumers can aspire to (Aagerup, 2011). An example is the use of highly attractive and skinny fashion models (Aagerup, 2011). Still the image should not be that attractive that it seems unattainable for the respondent (Aagerup, 2011). The balance in regard to the customer is described by the self-image congruence. A company creates an image of its brand – the brand personality – and of its perceived user with the advertisings. The perceived user is also known as the ideal user and "displays characteristics that a brand owner would like his or her brand to share to appear attractive" (Aagerup, 2011, p. 486). The customer evaluates the similarities and differences of the ideal user personality and herself. When this evaluation leads to a match between the consumer's personality and the brand's perceived personality this results in a favorable attitude toward the brand and may influence the customer's purchase decision (Aagerup, 2011; Sirgy, 1982). This is known as self-image congruence and can also positively influence the customers preference (Sirgy, 1982) and brand loyalty (Aagerup, 2011). This enhancement of a brand evaluation can be advertisement-based (Aagerup, 2011). But in order to utilize the positive effect of the self-image congruence the advertisement and its model has to fit the product type and suit the desired image (Aagerup, 2011). If the advertisement does so and presents the customer's ideal image of a woman it will provoke a strong positive reaction (Feiereisen, Broderick, & Douglas, 2009). The perceived similarity between the customer and the ideal fashion user is also important and does not necessarily reflect actual similarities. Research has shown for example that women prefer and identify with younger models in fashion advertisements (Aagerup, 2011), if the difference is not too extreme (Chang, 2008). Customers who perceive a similarity tend to rate models more attractive and their clothing more fashionable and also develop a purchase intention (Aagerup, 2011; Kozar & Damhorst, 2008).

On the one hand highly attractive and thin models increase the customer's tendency to develop a favorable attitude toward an advertisement and respectively the brand (Aagerup, 2011). On the other hand especially young women are influenced by these idealized pictures, which can lead to "negative effects on women's health and self-esteem" and even cause deseases like "anorexia, bulimia, and depression" (Aagerup, 2011, p. 487). But advertisements do not necessarily have to present thin models, if an advertisement shows average-size women it can be equally effective in regard to the customers attitude towards advertisement, brand and purchase intention (Halliwell & Dittmar, 2004). However using overweight models in a fashion advertisement has negative effect on the brand. Research has shown that consumers perceive the brand as unsophisticated, rough and dull if its advertisement features an overweight model. This attributes are generally undesirable or harmful to an fashion brand. (Aagerup, 2011)

The models used in fashion advertisement have a big impact of the customer's perception of the advertisement itself and the brand. As already mentioned some features of a model like weight and physical attractiveness have a positive or negative influence. (Chang, 2008) To avoid a negative effect fashion brands generally choose highly attractive models to represent their brand and create their brand personality. That highly attractive models are expected to be more effective can be explained by the halo effect, which is a cognitive bias. People tend to be influenced in their opinion about a thing, person or area by the impressions created in another area, this is known as halo effect (Lindberg & Stevenson, 2010). Many academics have shown that physical attractiveness and the expected success, personality, positive life, etc. of a person are related due to the halo effect. Bower and Landreth (2001, p. 2) sum up the various findings of researchers by stating "beautiful people are believed to have more positive life outcomes (e.g., more successful careers, better marriages) and not suffer from the problems of 'normal' people". The halo effect only occurs, when it is linked to social desirability aspects (Wade, Fuller, Bresnan, Schaefer, & Mlynarski, 2007, p. 318) and is hence often also shortly defined with the term "what is beautiful is good" (or vice versa) (Englis, Solomon, & Ashmore, 1994; Tiggemann & Polivy, 2010; (Y. Zhang, Kong, Zhong, & Kou, 2014). The use of very thin models in fashion advertisements can also be explained by the halo effect "women are considered more attractive, better mate choices, and more positively, in general, if they are thin" (Wade et al., 2007).

The physical attractiveness of a model does influence the customer's perception because attractiveness is a basis of social stereotypes, which help consumers to ease the information processing and guiding many reactions in the everyday life (Caballero & Solomon, 1984). There are positive and negative sterotypes in regard to this topic. Examples are the weight – thiness is linked with more positive stereotype than heaviness – and the age – youth is more favorable than advanced age (Jackson & Ross, 1997). The study conducted by Jackson and Ross (1997) has also shown that Caucasian and African-American models are rated more often attractive than other models. Even though Jackson and Ross (1997) rate the weight and body type of a model as the most important factor, when consumers – other women – judge their attractiveness. To describe different body types three somatotypes are used: the endomorph, ectomorph and mesomorph body types (Jackson & Ross, 1997). Research has shown that certain stereotypes are linked to each somatotype. Endomorph body types for example are rated old fashioned, less attractive and older and ectomorph body types are rated thinner and younger (Wells & Siegel, 1961 cited by Jackson & Ross, 1997).

Based on these research results fashion brands use highly attractive, thin, ectomorph models in order to create appealing advertisements. In turn consumer compare themselves with the idealized models in the advertisements (Aagerup, 2011), which can affect the customer's self-concept and feelings (Richins, 1991). This can lead to dissatisfaction when there is an incongruity between the consumer's self - the actual level - and the model – the ideal level - regarding an attribute that is important to the consumer (Richins, 1991). Findings of Richins (1991) study have shown that women compare themselves to models in advertisements and envy their beauty. If there is one body part the woman is especially dissatisfied with she will also compare this specific body part with the model. 33.8% of the participating women of Richins' (1991) study stated that fashion advertisements make them feel dissatisfied with the way they look. Though one interpretation of the findings is that customer's comparison leads to their dissatisfaction (Richins, 1991). This dissatisfaction may lead to negative feelings like frustration and anxiety, which can make an advertisement less successful (Bower, 2001) because this can lower the customer's purchase intention.

3.5 The Image of Physical Appearance and Attractiveness in Emotional Fashion Advertising

Using human models in advertising is a very common approach. In 2008 about 60% of all advertisement displayed human models (Chang, 2008) and in Germany a survey from 2010 showed that 66% of the consumers think that it is important for an advertisement to shown likeable people and even 31% stated that attractive models are important in advertisements (Innofact AG, 2010). Especially in print advertising the customer's judgement of the model can only be based on his/her physical appearance. Therefore highly attracttive and thin models are used particularly in fashion advertisements because they are expected to have better and more desirable lifes due to the halo effect, which is explained in chapter 3.4 in more detail (Bower & Landreth, 2001; Englis, Solomon, & Ashmore, 1994). The effectiveness of the halo effect in advertsing has been shown by research, which resulted in the conclusion that attractiveness-relevant or enhancing products like fashion articles should be advertisesed by highly attractive and thin models (Bower & Landreth, 2001; Kahle & Homer, 1985; Kamins, 1990) because they are suited best for communicating competence (Aagerup, 2011).

In fashion advertising the models have a highly important role because they act as a medium between the customers and the promoted product. The fashion model represents a desirable image, which should make the customers try to attain that ideal image by buying the advertised product (Jackson & Ross, 1997). In order to create this desiarble image the model has to be highly attractive and thin as already mentioned. Advertisers have started to create this ideal image by manipulating "the appearance of the fashion model so that she embodies an appearance, which meets the prescribed social preferences for physical attractiveness" (Jackson & Ross, 1997, p. 324). The goal of this manipulation is to create the epitome of physical attractiveness in terms of age, weight, ethnics, facial features etc. to present the most effective model based on the general social preference to the customers in the advertisement (Jackson & Ross, 1997). But the fashion industry is also criticized by the consumers and other stakeholders for displaying this manipulated images of models because it is unrealistic and not actually attainable by the customer (de Luce, 2001; Kozar & Damhorst, 2008; Richins, 1991). A study conducted by Fay and Price (1994) has shown that the body shape in fashion advertisement has shifted over the years to a less curvaceous and lighter ideal compared to the 1950s and would now "be achievable only by risk to health and/or surgical intervention" (Fay & Price, 1994, p. 15). Although the ideal is a manipulated image and therefore generally impossible to achieve many women internalize this image and try to attain it, which can result in dissatisfaction with the own body and attractiveness and even illnesses and eating disorders like anorexia and bulimia (Paulins, 2009; Tiggemann & Polivy, 2010). Even though a study conducted by Aagerup (2011) has shown that it is still advisable for fashion brands to present thin models in their advertisements and that it might be even harmful to a fashion brand to show an overweight model. In terms of facial attractiveness it has been stated that classic beauty and a sensual or exotic look are best fitted and effective to promote fashion products (Englis et al., 1994). Due to the increasing cultural diversity in many western countries an ethnical mix is increasingly perceived as beautiful not just Caucasian features (Englis et al., 1994). But still a majority of fashion models has Caucasian features like blond hair and blue eyes. This idealization of the Caucasian beauty ideal is often criticized by different stakeholders some of them even consider it to be racist (Paulins, 2009).

4 The Ethical Dimensions of Emotional Fashion Advertising

4.1 The Ethical Side of Managing Emotions

As already discussed in chapter 3.2 advertisers try to influence the customer's brand perception, attitude and purchase intention by creating emotional advertisements. Advertisements can arouse positive or negative emotions and hence may influence the decision-making process (Fulmer & Barry, 2009). Strong emotional appeals are increasingly important to advertisers because it gets harder to get the customer's attention and they are "generally inattentive to ads in the first place" (Hyman & Tansey, 1990, p. 106). But consumers are not always aware that they are influenced by an advertisement and even if they are aware it is "unclear to what extent people are able to control the effects that their affective experiences have on their cognitive processes" (Fulmer & Barry, 2009, p. 169). So it cannot be assured that consumers who are aware of and want to avoid these influences can counteract the effects of advertisements (Fulmer & Barry, 2009). It was even argued that they are unable to do so (Shapiro & Spence, 2005). The ability of advertisement to subliminally influence consumer's thoughts and actions create an ethical dilemma (Gratz, 1984). Gratz (1984) argues that by using advertisings with affective appeals an invasion of the consumer's privacy takes place without permission and is hence ethically risky. Because emotional management through advertising is effective and often takes places without the awareness of the influenced person "attempts at emotion management through advertising risk violating basic notions of autonomy and of respect for persons as ends themselves" (Fulmer & Barry, 2009, p. 176).

The practice of influencing consumers' emotions through advertising may be ethically inappropriate, especially if it is done "with the intention or effect of altering their mental processes in ways that may elicit outcomes different from those that would otherwise occur" (Fulmer & Barry, 2009, p. 171). Emotional advertising often has this intention. The advertisers use their knowledge of the human reaction to affective appeal and hence can easily manipulate the consumer's emotions in order to increase the favorability of their brand and the purchase intention (Fulmer & Barry, 2009). One way to decide whether an advertisement is ethical or unethical is presented by Santilli (1983), who argues that advertisement, which are informational and completely truthful are always ethical and persuasive advertising like advertisements with an affective appeal are always unethical and immoral. Drumwright and Murphy (2004) argued that people responsible for advertising often exhibit "'moral myopia', a distortion of moral vision that prevents moral issues from coming into focus, and 'moral muteness', meaning that they rarely talk about ethical issues" (p. 7). Many advertisers find those moral principles most attractive, which are low on ethics and offer wide discretion, which means generally using just the legal framework as ethical standard because there are little legal sanctions to emotional influences trough advertisements (Mujtaba & Jue, 2005 cited by Fulmer & Barry, 2009).

Technical and innovative developments make the emotional influence of consumers more and more easy for advertisers. New and more effective methods like neuromarketing are already deployed and these new "neuroscientific methods will likely enable marketers to become even better at managing the emotions, and consequently the cognitions and behaviors, of consumers" (Fulmer & Barry, 2009, p. 177). Therefore it gets increasingly important to discuss the ethical side of this emotion management, which is not done to a high extent in the contemporary scholarship of business ethics (Fulmer & Barry, 2009).

But consumers are not solely influenced by companies' advertisement; some NGOs (non-governmental organizations), environmental or social organizations and other stakeholders are creating emotional campaigns to make customers engage in more ethical behavior and consumption. There are negative campaigns pointing out unethical and unsustainable business practices of certain companies and green advertising promoting a more environmental friendly consumption. Cervellon's study (2012) indicates that campaigns targeting brands and exposing their unethical behavior can negatively affect consumers' brand attitude and purchase intention, especially when the customer has a high eco-purchase involvement and a low product or fashion involvement. Fashion companies particularly engaging in ethical and sustainable business practices can also use this effect by positively promoting their efforts and hence guide the ethical decision-making process and purchase intention of the customers (Fulmer & Barry, 2009).

4.2 The Ethical Side of Influencing Customers

Advertisement generally display an unrealistic and idealized image because this is known on having a positive effect on the way consumers perceive the advertisement due to the halo effect and other unconscious reactions discussed in more detail in chapter 3.4. Consumers compare themselves to these idealized and often manipulated images, which are highly unrealistic and may be impossible to achieve (Richins, 1991). If the discrepancy between the idealized image and the real mediocre state of consumer is to big this comparison can lead to anxieties, unhappiness, depression, shame and even illnesses (Bower, 2001; Jalees & Majid, 2009; Richins, 1991). Research has shown that the comparison to the idealized models in advertisements leads to lower satisfaction with the own appearance (Jalees & Majid, 2009) and also results in a lower rating of an average woman's attractiveness (Richins, 1991). Women who compare themselves with the idealized model in advertisement generally see the necessity of self-evaluation, -improvement and – enhancement (Jalees & Majid, 2009). It was shown that self-evaluation is the motive of young females to compare themselves to models in advertisements and that this comparison temporarily lowers the self-perception and self-esteem of these women (Martin & Gentry, 1997). Especially pre-adolescent and adolescent females are influenced by these images and the effect of comparison (Martin & Gentry, 1997). The idealized images in advertisements convey unrealistic guidelines in terms of attractiveness to those girls (Jalees & Majid, 2009). They make the young females focus on their physical appearance and let them see their bodies as objects, which ought to be improved and are the basis for the judgment of their personal value (Jalees & Majid, 2009; Martin & Gentry, 1997). Even though advertiser strategically place such advertisement where it is ensured that young females notice them, e.g. about the half of the space in the best selling magazines for girls and female teens displays advertisements (Evans, Rutberg, Sather, & Turner, 1991).

In addition to that the comparison and the resulting dissatisfaction with the consumer's own appearance creates a negative mood (Tiggemann & Polivy, 2010). Tiggemann and Polivy (2010) have also shown that once a comparison to a model takes place it always takes the physical appearance and attractiveness into account even though another dimension for the comparison was given. The self-esteem only can be protected when the viewer sees an idealized model in an advertisement and realizes that the model's appearance is manipulated and unrealistic and thus try to avoid the comparison to the model and the resulting effects (Martin & Gentry, 1997). Especially for overweight consumer's it is diffcullt to avoid negative emotions and lowering of self-esteem when looking at a fashion advertisement, because comparisions have a similarity and dissimilarty focus. Thus overweight women would generally identify themselves with overweight models and disassociate from thin models but fashion advertisements show thin models and emphasize the dissimilarity in comparison for overweight women. Hence these women feel worse while very thin women may even feel better, because they identified a similarity to the model. (Aagerup, 2011)

Research has shown that the idealized, highly attractive and thin models in advertisements and negative effects on the consumer's side like depression, low self-esteem, anxieties etc. are correlated. These findings have led to a controversy and make different stakeholders claim that these images are unethical (Aagerup, 2011). The advertisements and the companies developing and using them are accused of creating inferiority complexes, negative feelings and are also cultivating and help maintaining a stereotypical image of women that declare women to be sex objects and inferior to men (Jalees & Majid, 2009). In fact it cannot be guaranteed that the consumers and particularly adolescent and pre-adolescent females - which are extremely influenced by the advertising images (Aagerup, 2011) - are aware that the fashion models they see in advertisements are idealized and manipulated and also be conscious about the effects of those images on their self-evaluation, self-esteem, health and mind. Hence the same ethical arguments against influencing the customer's emotions without their knowledge presented in chapter 4.1 are also valid for unconsciously or consciously influencing customers through images in advertising. When consumers are not aware that there are influenced and manipulated or do not know how to avoid such effects these practices have to be take in ethical consideration and may be found to be immoral (Fulmer & Barry, 2009). The idealized images in advertisements exclude some groups of customers e.g. overweight or old women feel neglected by fashion advertisements (Aagerup, 2011; Kozar &

Damhorst, 2008). But consumers can also be influenced by campaigns against the common advertising practice and proclaiming a more ethical advertisement images (Cervellon, 2012). If they got aware of the advertising practices and the negative influences on themselves, consumers may even engage in actions exposing these effects and damaging the reputation of a company using these practices. This is most likely if the topic or company's behavior is of personal relevance for the consumer. (Cervellon, 2012)

4.3 The Ethical Side of Using Idealized Images of Physical Appearance and Attractiveness

Fashion advertisements display a certain ideal of attractiveness and physical appearance of women, which is not realistically attainable. There is a more detail description of the images the fashion industry is creating through their advertisements and how they differ from real women in chapter 3.5. However the goal of fashion advertisements is to create the ideal women and the female viewers of this advertisement will compare themselves to this ideal, which results in serious social consequences (Jalees & Majid, 2009). Some of them were already discussed in chapter 4.2 beforehand and include lowering women's self-esteem, causing eating disorders like anorexia and bulimia and influencing especially adolescent and pre-adolescent females in the way they see and evaluate their body and attractiveness (Aagerup, 2011; Bower, 2001; Jalees & Majid, 2009; Martin & Gentry, 1997; Richins, 1991). Advertisers are not only using highly attractive and thin models they are also manipulating the images and therefore create an artificial ideal usually unattainable by healthy means (de Luce, 2001; Fay & Price, 1994; Jackson & Ross, 1997; Kozar & Damhorst, 2008; Richins, 1991). In western society the physical appearance is very important and basis of most women's self-esteem and self-concept especially for adolescent females (Bower, 2001) and attractiveness and thiness are social desirable (Aagerup, 2011; Jackson & Ross, 1997; (Wade et al., 2007). Fashion advertisements use this desired image and even enhance it and are therefore accused to aggrandize the role of physical appearance in society, help promoting the image of females as sex objects, limiting their relevance to their physical appearance (Jalees & Majid, 2009) and telling them that "some types of beauty are more highly valued than others" (Englis et al., 1994). Especially young women do frequently compare their own appearance to models shown in fashion advertisements and do report that this comparison creates a feeling of dissatisfaction (Bower, 2001; Richins, 1991). But women who become aware of the effects of fashion advertisements to their own feelings, health and minds are developing negative reactions toward highly attractive models and cumulatively complaining about the use of these idealized images in advertising (Bower, 2001).

Fashion advertisements are mainly claimed unethical because their advertising image is so extreme e.g. due to very thin fashion models that it encourages especially adolescent and pre-adolescent females to indulge in unhealthy eating disorders and even lead to serious illnesses like depression, anorexia, bulimia (Aagerup, 2011; Richins, 1991). Researchers were able to show a correlation between the exposure to fashion images and the occurrence of body dissatisfaction, desire to be thin and eating disorders (Tiggemann & Polivy, 2010). In addition to that there are the negative psychological impacts on the women like lowering the self-esteem and creating negative feelings (Aagerup, 2011; Martin & Gentry, 1997). A "pervasiveness of dieting and dissatisfaction with body-shape among young women and adolescent girls" can be seen in western, wealthy societies (Fay & Price, 1994, p. 5) the occurrence of for example anorexia has increased in those societies over the last decades (Fay & Price, 1994) as shown in figure 2 for Germany (Statistisches Bundesamt, 2014).

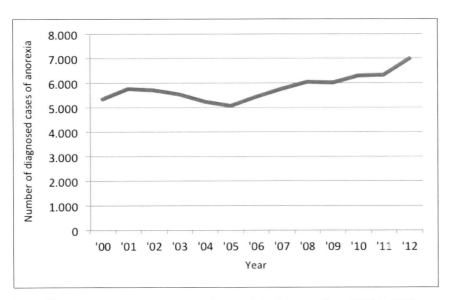

Figure 20: Number of diagnosed cases of anorexia in Germany from 2000 to 2012
Adapted from: (Statistisches Bundesamt, 2014)

Anorexia appears often among young females of upper socio-economic groups and often is linked to images of thin models presented in fashion advertising because "it can be said that advertisements legitimize and confirm societal pressure to be thin" and encourages attempts to attain this ideal (Fay & Price, 1994, p. 6). This is especially critical for adolescent and pre-adolescent females because they tend to see their body as an object (Martin & Gentry, 1997) that can be improved by dieting in order to achieve the ideal shown in advertising (Fay & Price, 1994; Jalees & Majid, 2009). The images in advertisement encourage these women to "improve" their physical appearance and attractiveness, which are the basis of their self-concept (Fay & Price, 1994; Jalees & Majid, 2009). But from an ethical perspective advertisers should try to avoid presenting images, which make their female viewers to conduct negative, unhealthy actions (Peterson, 1987). Encouraging eating disorders is agreed to be immoral and seeing images of thin models in advertisements induces women, who have an eating disorder to continue their dangerous and unhealthy practices (Peterson, 1987). Peterson's (1987) research has also shown that reducing allusively promoting a thin ideal through fashion advertising might help preventing eating disorders like anorexia and bulimia. Aagerup (2011) agrees with this hypothesis and is arguing that women with eating disorders can be helped to lower their anxieties by showing average rather than thin models in fashion advertisements. This makes the assignment of real, average sized women in fashion advertising an ethical argument or even obligation (Aagerup, 2011). Advertisers creating these idealized images in fashion advertisements are also claimed to be immoral because not the advertised fashion brand but the young women seeing the advertisements pay the negative, psychological cost of those marketing practices (Jalees & Majid, 2009). The features – attractiveness, youth, thinness - of a desirable women emphazied in fashion advertising are not attainable for most women to the presented degree but "advertisers, while portraying an ideal look, are suggesting that women who are not at par with models being portrayed must improve on their looks" (Jalees & Majid, 2009, p. 12). So this must consequently lead to the customer's dissatisfaction with his/her own body and attractiveness (Richins, 1991). Customer's and other stakeholders become increasingly aware of those advertising practices and opposing those images and condemn them to be unethical (Aagerup, 2011).

5 Discussion and Implications for Emotional Fashion Advertising

5.1 Ethical Responsibilities of Companies Using Emotional Fashion Advertising

This literature review has shown that a company's social responsibility also comprises their advertising practices. Fashion companies are facing special ethical issues due to the nature of their advertisements. Additional ethical considerations occur when fashion advertisements have an emotional appeal. Emotional fashion advertisement are deemed to be unethical by an increasing number of stakeholders and especially consumers (Aagerup, 2011; Paulins, 2009) because they promote an idealized, unrealistic and often unhealthy image of beauty and thinness, which aims to create the need in the customers' minds to enhance their physical appearance by buying the advertised product (Aagerup, 2011; Bower, 2001; Jalees & Majid, 2009; Martin & Gentry, 1997; Richins, 1991; Tiggemann & Polivy, 2010). But the big divergence of the ideal image in advertising and the reality makes women and particularly adolescent and pre-adolescent females feel dissatisfied, concerned and ashamed of their own physical appearance, which can finally lead to serious illnesses like anorexia, bulimia and depression (Aagerup, 2011; Bower, 2001; Martin & Gentry, 1997; Tiggemann & Polivy, 2010). Consciously creating and using those negative effects through advertisements is immoral and a violation of a company's ethical responsibility, because it is unfair to manipulate a consumer's emotion and perception of physical attractiveness without his/her awareness and hence without the chance to avoid this potentially unwanted influence (Fulmer & Barry, 2009; Gratz, 1984). This advertising practices can also be harmful to women, especially adolescent and pre-adolescent females, who are influenced by the idealized images to that extent that their resulting dissatisfaction with their own body makes them develop illnesses like eating disorders and depressions (Aagerup, 2011; Bower, 2001; Martin & Gentry, 1997; Tiggemann & Polivy, 2010). Therefore those practices can be deemed to be unethical on the basis of the marketing ethics developed by the American Marketing Association (2014) and the definition of ethical responsibilty of coporations by Carroll (1991). Even though the company using such practices may fulfill other dimension of their CSR e.g. their legal responsibility by obeying the legal restrictions (Carroll, 1991). But using just the law, as an ethical benchmark for advertising is not enough from a moral perspective (Duong Dinh, 2011; (Kotler & Armstrong, 2014), which can be shown by the increasing criticism and rejection of these advertising practices and images by various stakeholders and especially customers (Aagerup, 2011; Bower, 2001; Martin & Gentry, 1997; Paulins, 2009), even though the criticized company is not necessarily disobeying a law. A fashion company can even violate the very basic economic responsibility to be profitable (Carroll, 1991), when its advertisement displeases customers and other stakeholders to that extent, that the customers relationships, sales and long-term success of the company are harmed (Kotler & Armstrong, 2014); Polonsky & Hyman, 2007).

It is understood that companies have an ethical obligation toward society in general and their customers and that their advertising strategies have to align to these obligations (Hyman & Tansey, 1990). This is especially crucial, when they employ advertising practices that have psychological, affective effects on customers and may be even harmful for some of them (Hyman & Tansey, 1990). Even though is was indicated that advertisers often show moral myopia and moral muteness, which compromises or even prohibit an ethical approach in advertising (Drumwright & Murphy, 2004). Hence a company's management is urged to encourage and assure ethical advertising.

5.2 Managerial Implications for Companies Using Emotional Fashion Advertising

The ethical challenges and controversies emotional fashion advertising creates with its idealized images must make managers and advertisers start thinking about alternatives to the common practices. One example would be the use of realistically proportioned women instead of very thin models in advertising campaigns. The most famous example of such an advertising campaign is from the cosmetic brand Dove (Bissell & Rask, 2010; Paulins, 2009). Though Aagerup's study (2011) has shown that overweight models are linked with negative attributes, which could be harmful for a fashion brand, the use of neither underweight nor overweight models rather than models with a realistic weight and physical appearance may have a positive effect on the women seeing and comparing to the advertisement as well as the brand showing such images (Bissell & Rask, 2010; Halliwell & Dittmar, 2004). Researchers have found that advertisements with average-sized women can be equally effective in terms of the consumer's brand perception and purchase intention compared to an advertisement with a thin model (Halliwell & Dittmar, 2004). In addition to that results the exposure to average-sized or plus-sized models in advertising not in significant dissatisfaction or negative attitudes of women with or toward their own bodies (Bissell & Rask, 2010). Due to the negative and immoral effects of the common idealized fashion advertisement and the proven positive or at least not harmful effects of advertisements featuring average-sized models, well-known fashion brands like Calvin Klein, H&M and Ralph Lauren have started using average-sized models in their advertising campaigns (Cochrane, 2014). Those strategies could make brands perceived as special and likeable (Aagerup, 2011), because it is likely "that changing social values could lead to a positive outcome from using models whose weight is a little closer to the norm" (Fay & Price, 1994, p. 16).

In common fashion advertisement peripheral groups are underrepesented (Jackson & Ross, 1997) for example overweight models like already discussed beforehand and also older models. But when the discrepancy between the idealized image and the reality is too big, the "real" women do not feel addressed by the advertisement because they cannot identify themselves with it (Chang, 2008; Jackson & Ross, 1997). "Such underrepresentations may be harmful to fashion advertisers because those who fall within peripheral categories often represent large and potentially lucrative markets of consumers "(Jackson & Ross, 1997, p. 329).

Adolescent and pre-adolescent females are often influenced by the idealized images of fashion advertisement prone to develop eating disorders like anorexia and bulimia (Aagerup, 2011; Bower, 2001; Martin & Gentry, 1997; Tiggemann & Polivy, 2010). Women who already suffer from eating disorders show to be influenced even more by fashion advertisements (Peterson, 1987). Peterson (1987) argues that creating advertisements that are less suggestive and do not promote an unhealthy thin ideal might help reducing eating disorders of young females and consequently would be more ethical. Another approach to a more ethical fashion advertising would be to first identify if there are people who could be upset or harmed by the images shown in the advertisement – in this case this would be young females who could develop or intensify an eating disorder – and secondly give them the chance to avoid the advertisements and respectively their negative effects on them (Hyman & Tansey, 1990). Identifying the images shown in advertisements as manipulated and unrealistic might for example limit the negative effects arising from the comparison. A woman's body-dissatisfaction could also be prevented when fashion advertisements induce women to compare themselves with the advertising images on the basis of a characteristic they are valuing in themselves like e.g. their intelligence (Tiggemann & Polivy, 2010).

Kotler and Armstrong (2014) define two approaches for companies to a more ethical marketing. When engaging in consumer-oriented marketing the marketer will organize the marketing activities always from the customer's point of view, so any marketing activity that would be harmful to the consumer can be identified. The second approach is the societal marketing, which makes the marketers consider "consumer's wants, the company's requirments, consumer's long-run interests, and society's long-run interests" (Kotler & Armstrong, 2014) to ensure ethical behaviour from all three perspectives.

6 Conclusion, Limitations and Further Research

Companies in general have a social and ethical responsibility, which is usually described with the term corporate social responsibility. CSR incorporates every part of a company including its advertising. The companies must be aware that they have not just a financial responsibility to their business and shareholders and are restricted by law but that they have also a moral and social responsibility as part of the society within they are operating. The emotional advertising of a fashion company can compromise their ethical responsibility, because it may influence customer in an immoral way or even harm young women by encourage negative and unhealthy perceptions about their attractiveness and their physical appearance. Fashion companies need to be aware of the possible negative effects of their advertisements and their ethical dimensions in order to counteract arising problems and preserve their ethical integrity.

The findings of this work are limited because it is solely based on studies conducted by others. The presented results are based on a literature review and hence not specific research findings to support the thesis that fashion companies have an ethical responsibility due to their emotional fashion advertising rather than a combination of findings shown by other academics to support other hypothesis. Another limitation is the date of some used literature. Many academics have based their research on the topic on findings from the 1980s and 1990s or sometimes even older. Some studies are agreed to be fundamental and are hence cited till today. But the findings and their up-to-dateness were not questioned in the last years. So it might be reasonable to conduct new studies to investigate the influences of fashion advertising on women. Further research could also concentrate on other social groups to be studied for example elder women or men in contrast to young females, who are usually examined for studies on the topic. New technologies have made the customer's mind and emotional reaction more accessible and intelligible but there is little research conducted on the ethical dimension of those new advertising technics, even though there are already used in practice.

Gaining New Customers with Social Media Campaigns

Annika Sauerhöfer/Jochen Strähle

Abstract

Purpose –This research paper provides a general assessment and analysis of social media in a digital marketing context and highlights its current use, risks, but also its enormous potential for companies to extend their customer reach by using such new channels, which has not been broadly established yet.

Design/methodology/approach –Desk research

Findings – Key findings demonstrate the importance of social media engagement for companies and present respective difficulties in designing a social media strategy. Since marketers are under constant pressure to justify social media spending, measurement methods need to be established. Expressing the return on social media spending in actual numbers has so far represented a major obstacle for firms.

Research limitations/implications –The paper represents a rather general assessment of social media. Hence, country or culture specific use or reach of social media is not analyzed. Today's fast changing environment requires an adoption of social media strategies to the ever-changing digital, social and cultural environment of the respective target group.

Keywords – Digital strategy, social media marketing, social media strategy, return on social media determination, social media measurement

Paper type –Research paper

1 Introduction

1.1 Increased Importance of Social Media Engagement

As the world is increasingly going mobile, social media represents more and more an integral part of many users' everyday life. Companies want to make use of these new ways of communication by developing innovative marketing channels and aiming at converting online users into customers, which eventually should translate into increased sales. Ultimately, however, consumers are worth much more than their actual purchase. Positive word of mouth and recommendations on social media portals can foster a brand's reputation and increase its reach.

The current hype around social media marketing as part of a company's digital marketing strategy makes it nearly impossible for firms to survive without a convincing online presence. Facebook, Twitter and other online tools facilitate direct communication between companies and its customers and have the potential to create strong customer ties, as well as new capabilities for marketing and innovations in product development. The constantly rising number of new social media platforms and tools make it however difficult for companies not only to keep up but even to be ahead of developments. Suitability and relevance of social media channels to a company therefore need to be carefully assessed and chosen according to a firm's digital marketing aims. Rushed reactions to the fast-evolving environment pose just one of many risks, potentially damaging a firm's reputation instead of fostering it. Hence, a precisely formulated strategy is needed.

Due to a tightening economy and cuts in many companies' marketing budgets, marketers feel the need for ensuring that investments are worth the spending. This in turn requires the invention of measurement tools in order to determine a return on social media. Many tools have been invented already, but a precise measurement expressed in numbers remains difficult.

Given the above-mentioned factors, social media is one of the key management challenges in digital marketing and needs to be managed properly. This paper focuses on how to gain new customers through social media and increase a company's favorability.

1.2 Research Question

The question: "Do Social Media Campaigns have a significant impact on gaining new customers?" will be answered in this paper. The focus will be laid on:

(1) Relevance of Social Media to companies?
To what extend apply the current developments in social media to various companies and how big is their potential for increased sales by tapping these new marketing channels.
(2) How to set up an appropriate strategy?
Which factors need to be considered and how should the process be managed?
(3) How to analyze impact?
This section focuses on whether there exists an appropriate tool for a return on social media determination and names respective challenges.

2 Literature Review

2.1 Corporate View

"Digital is fundamentally shifting the competitive landscape in many sectors"
Paul Willmott, McKinsey London, May 2014
(Willmott & McIntosh, 2014)

The recent digitalization hype has not only created a new competing environment for companies, but has also led firms to act overhasty. In order to respond appropriately to a constantly increasing digital world, a strategy is needed to understand and define company's value from digitalization. Customer behavior on how to gather information has changed with this trend as well. While in the past the main information flow was reached through TV, radio, newspapers and magazines, in today's time a great diversity of online platforms and channels are available for getting information. These information are increasingly used for purchase decisions and make new approaches inevitable (Willmott & McIntosh, 2014). In addition to that, technological development made it possible for stakeholders to increase their power over corporations (Argenti & Barnes, 2009, p. 62). A strategy is needed in order to give a roadmap to all these issues, since the emergence of new tools and technologies have the potential to enable a larger interactivity between firms and their customers (Sashi, 2012, p. 255).

2.2 Digital Strategy

While 'Digital' can be seen as an umbrella term to summarize all electronic connected media activities, technologies and channels, 'Digital Strategies' "provide measureable direction on how [to] use digital to achieve a vision and its specific business, brand and/or marketing objectives" (Dillon-Schalk, 2011, f. 3).

A digital strategy requires a synchronization of the IT infrastructure with the traditional business strategy, elucidating how investments in IT foster a specific objective. Ideally, technology should be seen as a strategic asset to maintain a competitive advantage or gain new competencies (Mithas & Lucas, 2010, p. 4).

A digital strategy has therefore not only an influence on a company's success, but also an impact on many functional areas, such as:

- Sourcing, e.g. Omission of an Intermediary
- Production, e.g. improved Customer Insights
- Logistics, e.g. Radio Frequency Identification
- Human Resources, e.g. Acquisition of new Employees
- Financial Decisions, e.g. Investment and Funding Sources, Performance Criteria
- Marketing, e.g. Search Engine Optimization
(Gay, Charlesworth, & Esen, 2007, p. 58)

Since a digital strategy has an impact on most of the organization, the establishment needs to be consistent with a firm's overall corporate strategy (Willmott & McIntosh, 2014). It consequently needs to be communicated throughout the whole organization.

However, the main focus of a digital, or e-strategy, should be laid on a company's customers. It is vital, that technology is designed in a way to provide customer benefits. Technological issues, such as easy site navigation and ordering/ payment processing and a fast access to product information need to be addressed in order to facilitate a customer's digital experience. Transparent order tracking and effective distribution networks help to create additional value (Gay et al., 2007, p. 44ff). This example shows that there are various functional areas involved.

It is crucial to understand the true value that digital delivers from scratch and its potential in the medium term, since efficiency will only then be visible (Willmott & McIntosh, 2014)

The technological issues addressed above should always be considered when developing a digital strategy. Objectives, strategies and tactics will however depend on a firm's level of Internet maturity. In the most sophisticated stage a company transforms "the entire enterprise through seamlessly integrating all processes through end-to-end web-based interactions with customers and business partners" (Gay et al., 2007, p. 46). Hence, a detailed plan is needed to reach this goal.

2.2.1 Strategy Development

This path can be determined with the help of common analytic frameworks, such as SWOT Analysis, Porter's five forces and the Ansoff Matrix, which is illustrated below:

- Market Penetration, e.g. exceptional online customer service
- Product Development, e.g. new online B2B marketplaces in existing markets
- Market Development, e.g. market entrance though online shop
- Diversification, e.g. customization of products with help of IT tools

As this example shows, it is crucial to take the competitive environment, e.g. impact of new market entrants, and the corporate view, e.g. potential change of processes, into consideration (Gay et al., 2007, p. 44).

It was already outlined, that IT plays nowadays a significant role in determining a company's success. Dysfunctional IT management can however jeopardize this effect, which means that top level managers of different departments must work closely together when setting up a strategy. As Mithas and Lucas expound, many firms are however still in an early stage to discover the potential of IT. The authors recommend corporations to invest in the so-called 'ITracy', deriving from IT and digital literacy. In their view, ITracy is a skill that all managers need in today's information economy. It is based on three pillars of synchronizing the business strategy with IT, the effective governance of IT as well as its management and implementation (Mithas & Lucas, 2010, p. 4ff).

Synchronization ("Where do we want to be?")

The competitive position of a company needs to be analyzed in order to develop an understanding of how to improve the situation. Harvard Business School Professor Porter shows three methods to achieve a competitive advantage through IT:

- Change of Industry Structure
  This approach suggests using IT to tilt the proportion of supplier and customer power, new and substitute products
- Outperformance of Competitors
  IT should be either used for cost differentiation or serving of a niche segment with better IT solutions and more cost-effective products
- Creation of New Business
  The establishment of a new business, that has already synchronized its corporate strategy with IT

When transforming the digital strategy, a company needs to take the tradeoff between serving existing customers and establishing a new customer-base into consideration. This can always lead to the potential threat of losing old customers, which are not using digital media.

Governance ("How do we get there?")

The governance of a digital strategy exceeds the synchronization of business and IT strategy. Key responsibilities that are related to IT decisions (what?, who?) should be clearly determined for each manager (Mithas & Lucas, 2010, p. 4ff). In addition to that, a digital plan needs to be established. This shows the digital roadmap with projects and the related budget (Dillon-Schalk, 2011, f. 6). These projects need to be prioritized and determined whether they should be kept in-house, being outsourced or rented. It also contains the key decision "whether to attack or [to] defend" (Willmott & McIntosh, 2014).

Management ("How to successfully complete?")

To manage successfully, a vision about how to manage legacy upgrade decisions and risk is needed (Mithas & Lucas, 2010, p. 5). A main obstacle in the constantly changing digital world is to keep pace with technological innovations(Gay et al., 2007, p. 44). This is the reason why the strategy must be updated regularly and a measurement plan to react appropriately is needed (Dillon-Schalk, 2011, f. 6).

It is of high importance to see all three pillars (Synchronization, Governance, and Management) examined above as being interconnected. Only then a digital strategy can be sustainably successful.

2.3 Digital Marketing

"The competitive advantage of large multinationals has become undermined in this new world, where individuals, small non-profits and groups of like-minded activists use e-advocacy tools to great effect."
(Argenti & Barnes, 2009, p. 6)

Since the evolution of the World Wide Web people are nowadays as closely connected as never before. The establishment of further digital technology platforms, such as interactive TV, IPTV (Internet Protocol Television) and mobile phones facilitate communication (Chaffey & Ellis-Chadwick, 2012, p. 10). This and the constant growing range of new media channels provide significant digital marketing opportunities. This is underlined by a survey ('Wave 7') conducted by Universal McCann in 2013, where over one billion people from 72 countries participated. Figure 21 illustrates that owning smart and mobile devices significantly increased from 2012 (Wave6) to 2013 (Wave7).

However, as the quote above shows, companies are experiencing a shift of power; they are increasingly losing control over their organization's reputation and messaging. These facts make it inevitable for marketers to redefine their communication strategies, which need to be carefully considered and integrated into the overall digital strategy (Argenti & Barnes, 2009, p. 62ff).

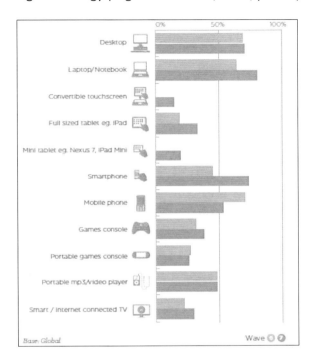

Figure 21: "Which of the following devices do you own?"
Adapted from: (Parker, 2013, p. 8)

2.3.1 Definition

The definition for digital marketing by Chaffey and Ellis-Chadwick (2012), "achieving marketing objectives through applying digital technologies" (Chaffey & Ellis-Chadwick, 2012, p. 10) illustrates that the adoption of technology is a prerequisite for successful marketing management. A shift from internet to digital marketing is needed in order to include all available technologies. It is for instance important that Social Media Campaigns also work properly on smartphones and tablets to generate an overall brand experience. The goals of digital marketing are to identify potential customers and establish a personal dialogue with each of them, the acquisition of new customers through understanding consumer wants and the satisfaction of existing customers. Simple website usage and exceptional customer usage are issues to be dealt with (Chaffey & Ellis-Chadwick, 2012, p. 15). Hence, digital marketing is an important tool for building a relationship between customers and brand. This concept, also known as Electronic Customer Relationship Management (E-CRM), reaches for the maximization of sales to existing customers through using digital communications. Certain techniques, such as databases and personalized web messages help to reach this aim (Chaffey & Ellis-Chadwick, 2012, p. 10).

2.3.2 Strategy Development

"A digital marketing strategy is needed to provide consistent direction for an organization's online marketing activities so that they integrate with its other marketing activities and support its overall business objective"
(Chaffey & Ellis-Chadwick, 2012, p. 190).

This quote demonstrates that a digital strategy has much in common with a traditional marketing approach and consequently contains four main steps: situation review, goal setting, strategy formulation, resource allocation and monitoring.

Situation Review

A situation analysis is needed to gather information about the external environment of a company and its internal resources and processes. It shows the effectiveness of a firm's current marketing activities. Information about the external environment includes micro-environmental factors (customer demand, activity of competitors, marketplace structure, buyer-supplier-relationship) and macro-economic factors, such as government regulations, taxation, legal, social and ethical issues and data protection. Internal resources and processes can be reviewed with the help of an audit. Topics included will be the business effectiveness on which extend marketing generated sales and profit, marketing effectiveness and resource analysis. Marketing effectiveness can be assessed by for instance leads and customer service and conversion and click-through rates. Resource analysis contains the assessment of financial, technology infrastructure and human resources to deliver a firm's digital services. A strengths and weakness analysis (SWOT-analysis) will be included as well (Chaffey & Ellis-Chadwick, 2012, p. 202ff).

Goal Setting

It is crucial to define clear corporate objectives for being able to set up a suitable strategy. This is the reason why goal setting is important and should therefore be considered well. The aims should also be consistent with other business objectives and complement them. If a market share in a specific target marked is wanted to be increased (business objective), the support of digital marketing should be a goal.

Chaffey and Ellis-Chadwick (2012) propose to start with thinking about potential digital media benefits. They are both tangible and intangible and can be converted into objectives. Table 5 presents such benefits (Chaffey & Ellis-Chadwick, 2012, p. 209ff).

It is also crucial to think about the relevance for customers first. There is a danger in just using channels, because of the digital media hype instead of focusing on how to serve customers best (North & Jason Oliver, 2014).

Table 5: Tangible and intangible benefits from digital marketing

Tangible benefits	Intangible benefits
Increased sales from new sales leads giving: - New customers, new markets - Existing customers (repeat- and cross-selling) Cost reduction from: - Reduced time in customer service - Online sales - Reduced printing and distribution costs of marketing communications	Corporate image communication rise due to increased revenue from: - Enhanced brand - More rapid, more responsive marketing communications including PR - Improved customer service - Learning for the future - Meeting customer expectations to have a website - Identifying new partners, supporting existing partners - Feedback from customer on products

Adapted from (Chaffey & Ellis-Chadwick, 2012, p. 211)

Strategy Formulation

A digital strategy is needed to ensure consistency in a firm's marketing activities across online and offline platforms (North & Jason Oliver, 2014, p. 3). Alternative strategies need to be selected, the merits defined and the best strategy evaluated. Key decisions include the choice of a company's target group, and the selection of channels that deliver value best to this group (Chaffey & Ellis-Chadwick, 2012, p. 218).

The emphasis of a digital strategy should be laid on continual customer engagement. The customer expects a regular content delivery. Therefore, a company needs to use a platform constantly, and not only when it suits the firm. This requires an investment plan that includes continual investments over a long period of time. Only then a company's customer will still be interested and engaged (North & Jason Oliver, 2014).

Customer journeys mostly shift between various forms of online presence, as consumers make use of different media to access product information, the actual purchase and the reception of customer support. It is therefore crucial for marketers to understand these touch points when developing a digital strategy. Three types of media channels need to be taken into consideration: Paid, Earned and Owned Media (Chaffey & Ellis-Chadwick, 2012, p. 11).

Paid Media

As already contained within the term, paid media refers to investments in different media. Site visitors, search engine reach and conversions, ads displayed and affiliate marketing belong to this type of channels as well as traditional media, such as direct mails, print and TV advertising

Earned Media

Earned media has the purpose to increase word-of-mouth and brand awareness. This can be reached through partnering with bloggers, publishers and other influencers on the one hand, and through online sharing of posts and conversations between companies and their customers on the other hand. Relevant channels are offline and online, mostly social networks, blogs and social media marketing.

Owned Media

This term comprises online and offline media channels which are owned by the brand. Typically, online forms are a brand's social presence (for instance on Facebook, Twitter, LinkedIn), mobile apps, websites and blogs owned by the brand. Offline includes retail stores and brochures.

Multi-channel marketing is needed to embrace all possible customer journeys (Chaffey & Ellis-Chadwick, 2012, p. 11).

The most significant media channels are shown in Figure 22.

Resource Allocation and Monitoring

In order to ensure to be on track, a feedback loop needs to be established. Problems need to be identified and actions undertaken to revise those. This is extremely important, since a lot of companies fail to keep focus which leads to strategic errors (North & Jason Oliver, 2014).

Challenges in developing and managing a digital marketing strategy may arise, if some of the aspects above are not considered. Unclear responsibilities, insufficient budget allocation, no object setting, inexperienced staff and poorly measured results from digital marketing are issues companies mostly face if marketers lose focus(Chaffey & Ellis-Chadwick, 2012, p. 23).

It is important to first establish an overall digital marketing strategy and only afterwards a campaign strategy to put emphasis on different channels and happenings. Therefore, a digital marketing strategy can also be seen as a channel marketing strategy, because defined objectives and followed actions should always be channel-related in order to take channel specifications into consideration. With this approach consumer touch points can be optimized (Chaffey & Ellis-Chadwick, 2012, p. 190). Key digital media channels are illustrated in Figure 22 below.

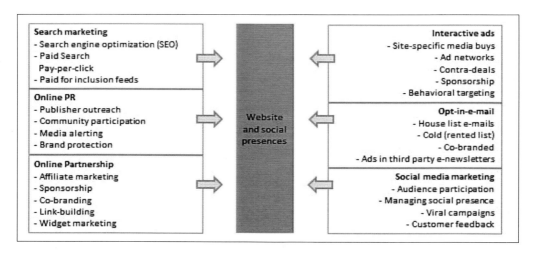

Figure 22: Key digital media channels
Adapted from: (Chaffey & Ellis-Chadwick, 2012, p. 30)

The most important digital media channels are:

- Search engine marketing
  With the help of search engine marketing the click-through rate to a company's website can be enhanced.
- Online PR
  The aim is to answer to negative mentions and to maximize favorable mentions of the firm, brand, product or website on a third-party website. This can include blogs, social networks, feeds and podcasts.
- Online Partnerships
  In order to promote a company's products and services on a long-time basis, partnerships with third-party website providers need to be established. There exist various forms of partnerships, among others affiliate marketing and price comparison sites.
- Display advertising
  Through use of banners and online ads in general the click-through rate and brand awareness can be increased.
- Opt-in e-mail marketing
  E-mail marketing includes the usage of in-house lists to activate consumers,

- as well as an ad placement in a third-party newsletter and the rent of an e-mail list.
- Social Media marketing
  Social networks, for instance Facebook or Twitter are used by a company to get in contact and participate in a communication with potential and existing customers. The concept of viral marketing plays an important role in social media marketing, because it implies the communication of messages between two users.

(Chaffey & Ellis-Chadwick, 2012, p. 29ff)

Shift from push to pull advertising

The classical push approach contains sending newsletters and emails directly to customers. Customer preferences and willingness to receive advertisement are not considered. In contrast to that, in pull advertising a customer determines what he is interested in and consequently about what he wants to be informed. When typing in a search term in a search engine, the company reacts by showing personalized advertisement. Since the consumer is already interested in this specific subject, pull advertisement is perceived as being positive and useful and therefore generates a higher conversion rate than the traditional approach which is often perceived as being irrelevant (Spriestersbach, 2014, pt. 1.4).
Furthermore, advertising wastage can be reduced when using pull strategies. However, this consequently brings a decrease of control over a company's communications, which makes both approaches equally relevant for marketers (Chaffey & Ellis-Chadwick, 2012, p. 432)
These facts need to be taken into consideration when choosing an appropriate digital media channel.

Gaining customers through digital marketing

Literature suggests using three different classifications depending on the purpose for gaining customers with digital marketing. These are: performance, relations and brand marketing.

Performance marketing

The term summarizes all marketers' activities that are measurable. Relevant channels are therefore Search Engine Optimization (SEO), Search Engine Advertisement (SEA) and E-mail marketing. The aim is to fulfill existing demand effectively through measurements and reactions and thus represents a reactive approach.

Relations marketing

The aim is to establish a communication with potential and existing customers to build a positive brand experience, where the performance can be built upon. The most important channel for relations marketing is Social Media, since it is suits best for increasing positive word-of-mouth and recommendations of a company's brand. Theme campaigns need to be consistent and authentic with corporate communication. Personalized E-mails are also suitable for relations marketing.

Brand marketing

Brand marketing is especially important for small companies and new launched products. If these products are not known yet, SEA and SEO can't be used. Brand marketing plays an important role for a clear differentiated positioning of the brand: recognition needs to be increased in order to enhance demand. Emotions are here very important for building trust and to increase relevance to consumers. The stronger the brand, the better the conversion rate from potential customers will be. Brand marketing should always be part of campaigns (Spriestersbach, 2014, pt. 10.2).

All classifications need to be combined in order to reach all potential customers. Relation marketing is probably the most relevant category, because it aims at building a positive brand experience. This is crucial to reach a high degree of customer loyalty. High brand recognition is important for a brand to be at the top end of a consumer's head. Blum even claims, that a human brain is only capable to recognize four to five brand names per category that immediately come to a consumers mind. It is therefore of high importance for a brand to be included into this list (Blum, 2014, p. 76).

Customer Journey Management

Next to branding to achieve reach and customer retention reasons, the most important aim for companies is to generate a high click-through-rate (CTR) from different media channels to an own company's website in order to facilitate higher conversions. This can be enhanced by customer's journey management.

A customer journey projects the way from brand awareness to the actual purchase and is similar to the AIDA-model, which will be explained in section 2.5. The customer journey happens before the actual purchase and it is therefore important for a firm to cover all phases of this journey.

- Awareness
  The aim is to create reach, which is important for a company's positioning. Social media marketing offers important touch points at this phase to generate attention and to get in contact with potential customers. Search engine advertisement and search engine optimization are also suitable for this phase.
- Favorability
  In order to establish favorability, the brand needs to transport emotions to potential customers. Recommendations of friends make brands more wanted. This can be achieved through social media marketing.
- Consideration
  A product has to transport value to a customer. The aim in this phase is to introduce the product to users, which can be either done through social media marketing or comparison portals.
- Intent to purchase
  Search engine optimization and search engine advertisement are the most suitable for this phase of a customer journey. Social media is only an adequate tool with constraints (Spriestersbach, 2014, pt. 1.5).

Firms often use customer journey management for analyzing consumers' habits and virtual ways in order to reduce the complexity that aroused by the diversity of digital media channels (Heinrich & Flocke, 2014, p. 826). Knowledge about customer preferences can have positive impacts on the value chain, an earlier demand forecast impacts for instance suppliers, as well as the innovation potential of companies (Woodcock, Green, & Starkey, 2011, p. 51).

2.4 Social Media Marketing

"Social media is where your actual and potential customers are interacting, and it shapes how they think."
(Fisher, 2009, p. 190)

As this quote demonstrates, social media can have a significant impact on a corporation's reputation. Considering the fact, that out of 7.280 billion people of the total world population, 2.060 billion people actively use a social media account ("We Are Social's Digital Statshot 003," 2014),this represents an enormous potential for companies. Wave 3 is a social media research study conducted by Universal McCann released in spring 2008 with 17000 participants from 29 countries. 34 % of Internet users stated, that they post opinions about company's products on their blog. 36% of users even think more positively about firms that run a blog (Fisher, 2009, p. 190). Figure 3 shows one finding of Wave 7, which was first published in 2013. More than one billion Internet users from 72 countries participated. The finding confirms an issue that we all quite knew already: the smartphone has become "an ever present companion" with all different types of media (Parker, 2013, p. 29). This means, that companies must be aware about the fact that social media is used everywhere at every time and that consumers expect companies to be up to date. Since a customer is far more worth than his pure purchases and social media can have an impact on future spending, a detailed strategy is needed (Fisher, 2009, p. 190). The use of social media can furthermore build a bridge between consumers and a company, meaning that if properly done, the possibility to get closer to a firm's customers will be improved. This can facilitate increased revenues, efficiencies and cost reductions (Heller Baird & Parasnis, 2011, p. 30).

Social media marketing is therefore the most significant part of digital marketing to acquire new customers and establish a long-term relationship with existing customers. An approach on how to establish a sufficient social media strategy will be introduced later in this chapter.

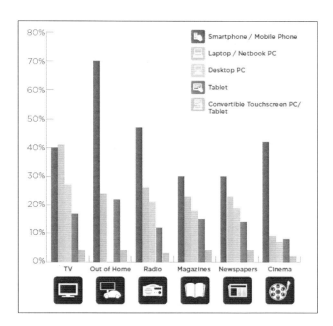

Figure 23: "Thinking about devices, do you ever use them whilst consuming...?"
Adapted from: (Parker, 2013, p. 29)

2.4.1 Definition

Social media mainly consists of conversations between consumers. Integrated technology helps users to share pictures, audios and videos on various platforms that are diversely designed. By doing so, social interaction can be established and shared meanings in communities build (Hettler, 2010, p. 14). Since conversations often take place without the interaction of a company, a marketing approach is needed.

Social media marketing aims at "monitoring and facilitating customer-customer interaction and participation throughout the web to encourage positive engagement with a company and its brands" (Chaffey & Ellis-Chadwick, 2012, p. 30). Interactions can occur in different channels, which will be introduced later in this chapter. Well established social media marketing will not be perceived as being plain advertisement – the goal is to give internet users added value and to establish a strong brand preference through doing so (Spriestersbach, 2014). Participation aims not only at getting in contact with existing and potential customers, but also at establishing a dialogue with a firm's critics (Fisher, 2009, p. 192). The main goal of social media marketing is therefore to improve a firm's reputation and to increase positive word-of-mouth communication. It is an important tool for relations marketing and important for gaining new customers, as discussed in 2.3.

Viral marketing is closely related to social media marketing, where a marketing message is communicated from one person to another. It includes platforms, such as social networks, blog sites, and e-mail communication. A distinctive attribute is the rapid, mostly real time, transmission of messages (Chaffey & Ellis-Chadwick, 2012, p. 29).

Another concept, which is closely linked to social media marketing, is the Web 2.0 concept. The name was invented by Tim O'Reilly in 2004 and contains the concept of the World Wide Web as one platform(Hettler, 2010, p. 5ff). This provides the possibility to share information and to create user generated content, which then encourages even more users to participate. Tagging and content rating are examples of how to participate (Chaffey & Ellis-Chadwick, 2012, p. 33).

2.4.2 Social Media Tools

A social media site is mostly a software application as well. This means, that users have access to different levels and the possibility to store user-generated content, send messages and exchange data. The most important tools are listed below:

- Social networks
  Social networks are mostly on the top of one's mind when it comes to social media. Facebook with its 1.350 million users in December 2014 (Statista.com, 2014)is the most significant social platform for consumer and LinkedIn (332 million users (Statista.com, 2014)) for business audiences. Interaction on Google+ and Twitter is used for both consumers and businesses. However, Facebook represents an important platform for businesses as well.
- Social publishing and news
  This term comprises the online presence of newspapers and magazines. Nearly all have an online presence. Readers have the possibility to comment on articles on these sites, as well as communities and blogs.

- Social commenting in blogs
  A blog can be included into a company's website or used externally to gather information about potential and existing customers.
- Social niche communities
  These communities exist next to the main networks.
- Social customer service
  Companies make increasingly use of social customer services on for instance Facebook and a company's own website to respond quickly to consumer complaints.
- Social knowledge
  Wikipedia is the most known page, where knowledge is gathered and shared. Yahoo! Answers is another example for a social knowledge page (Chaffey & Ellis-Chadwick, 2012, p. 31ff).
- Social bookmarking
  Social bookmarking allows users to save and share websites so that other users can tag and comment on them. Special social bookmarking sites rate links and list the most popular ones. Users can then easily find their interests (Nations, 2014).
- Social streaming
  Social streaming includes podcasting, videos and photos.
- Social search
  Users have the ability to vote for, tag and comment on results of search engines (Chaffey & Ellis-Chadwick, 2012, p. 31ff).
- Social commerce
  Social commerce has the highest significance for the retail sector. It is a part of e-commerce with increasing relevance, because user reviews and ratings can be integrated into a corporation's website. A company's website can also be linked to social networks to increase the understanding of users and website traffic, which can lead to higher sales. Groupon is an example for a coupon service that involves group buying (Chaffey & Ellis-Chadwick, 2012, p. 20). The concept of group buying takes advantage of scale effects with the underlying fact, that a group of people are able to buy products cheaper together than on their own. These deals are offered on various websites (Wittmann et al., 2013, p. 78).

The most popular platform is Facebook, followed by Xing. Interestingly, 9% of these firms used Twitter in the past, but do not use it anymore. Reasons were impropriety for the firms' purposes, no achievement of objectives or poor measurement methods, too much effort for usage (for instance not enough personnel, or time), and no reach of customer group (Wittmann et al., 2013, p. 19). Furthermore, the usage of google+ has risen during the last year. Companies mostly post on Facebook and Twitter. While 43 percent of small enterprises and 53 percent of big enterprises, 71 percent of medium sized enterprises publish posts every day (Wittmann et al., 2013, p. 24).

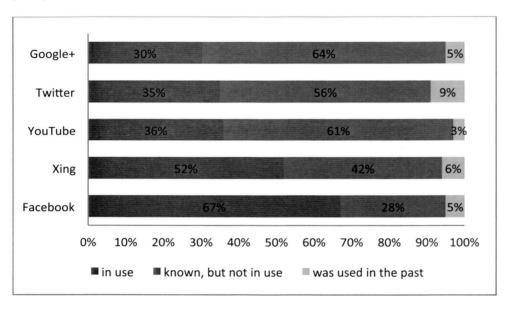

Figure 24: Popularity of Social Media Platforms
Adapted from: (Wittmann et al., 2013, p. 19)

Tool attention

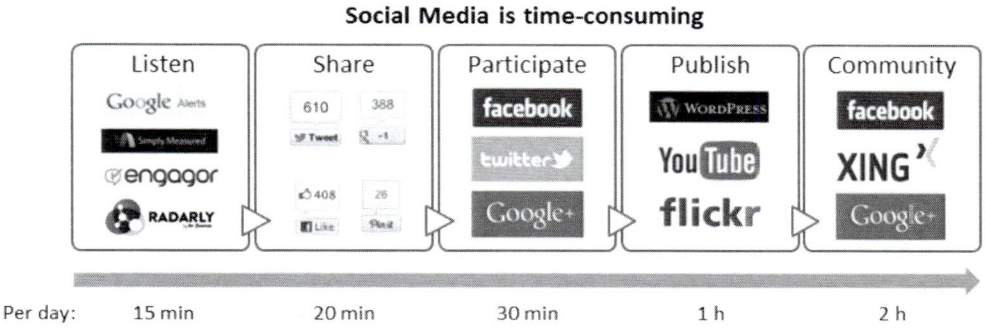

Figure 25: Social Media is time-consuming
Adapted from: (Spriestersbach, 2014)

Companies that first start to use social media should always begin with Listening. This helps to create an understanding of the new environment and its characteristics. Google Alerts, Simply Measured, Engagar and Radarly are social media monitoring tools that capture trends and for instance suggestions of users to different topics and products. Tools like these make it possible to get closer to a company's target group. The first step represents a passive approach. Sharing of information is already a more active approach. This can be done on a firm's website and linked to social media buttons illustrated in Figure 25. The next stage will be the creation of an own account on certain social media platforms, such as Facebook, Twitter or Google+. Participation through posting and sharing helps to establish a dialogue with a company's customers. Publishing own texts, photos and videos on for instance WordPress, YouTube or Flickr is very interactive. These topics then should be integrated into other social media platforms in order to enable customers to share it with friends and comment on them. The establishment of a community within social networks represents the most interactive approach. This can be a Facebook page or group, where special interests are discussed and shared. This stage has the highest effect in terms of customer retention. The figure shows, that social media engagement is very time-consuming, if done properly. If a company choses to create an own community, it also has to take all other steps and the daily time planning into consideration.

2.4.3 Strategy Development

"To successfully exploit the potential of social media, companies need to design experiences that deliver tangible value in return for customers' time, attention, endorsement and data".
(Heller Baird & Parasnis, 2011, p. 30)

As mentioned before, conversations on for instance social media platforms happen mostly between consumers. Users rarely engage with companies just for the feeling to be connected. The quote illustrates, that companies need to create added value in order to get closer to the target group. It also shows the shift from push to pull strategies, which were already mentioned in 2.3. Social media marketing activities are mostly designed by pull principles, because customer wants are addressed directly (Chaffey & Ellis-Chadwick, 2012, p. 432).This shift also needs to be taken into consideration in a company's Customer Relationship Management (CRM). The new approach called Social Customer Relationship Management (SCRM) aims not only at managing customers, but also at getting in a dialogue with them. Heller Baird describes this strategy as being especially important, because of a survey that found out that consumers only interact occasionally with brands. Social media is therefore the main medium to exchange content, pictures, videos and so on between family and friends. In order to create a passion for a brand, the prerequisite is to close the gap between consumer wants and a company's completion. The use of data gained through social media can close this gap. Consequently, a good strategy is needed (Heller Baird & Parasnis, 2011, p. 31). The survey also discovered that customers were mostly only willing to engage with a brand via social media, if he or she has already had a passion for this brand before. This means, that the mere social media participation may not directly result in higher spending or increased loyalty. However, in Heller Baird's view "a recommendation from a friend or family member could make a difference" (Heller Baird & Parasnis, 2011, p. 35). This recommendation can be expressed directly, via 're-tweeting' a company's message on Twitter or 'liking' a company on Facebook. Companies should make use of this finding by designing social media strategies that touch customers emotionally to encourage interaction and sharing of experiences with others.

Situation Review

The first step should always be to discover the most relevant values customers have, so that it is easier to develop campaigns, which motivate users to act. Motivations could be offered in form of incentives, if people share content with friends in order to catch the viral benefits (Heller Baird & Parasnis, 2011, p. 34ff). Since every customer is driven by different motivations, users need to be clustered in order to respond appropriately.

'Wave 7' is a survey conducted by Universal McCann in 2013, where over one billion participants from 72 countries were asked about their social media behavior. One key finding was that "even the most superficial social media activity is driven by a human need" (Parker, 2013, p. 34). Social behavior is mostly sustained either by learning, relationship, diversion, progression or recognition, which represent the five basic needs.

Table 6: Human needs that explain social behavior

Needs	Learning	Relationship	Diversion	Progression	Recognition
Examples	Explore Keep up to date Seek opinion Learn	Belong Stay in touch Share knowledge	Be creative Have fun Escape	Build a career Make money Develop skills	Express yourself Earn respect Change opinions Self-promotion

Adapted from: (Parker, 2013, p. 36)

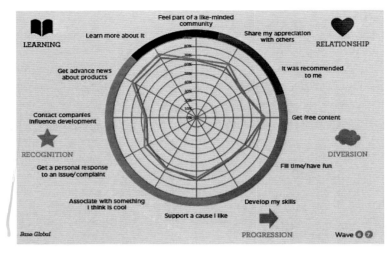

Figure 26: „Please tell us why you joined a brand community."
Adapted from: (Parker, 2013, p. 37)

- Learning helps to get to know customers better, because teaching product features also reveals consumers' needs, which drives sales.
- Relationship is the key to drive recommendation. Brands that help people are more recommended to others.
- Diversion is the key driver for establishing desirability.
- Progression drives people to spend more time with a brand, since they have the feeling that the own skills will be developed by doing so.
- Recognition is needed to create loyal customers. For instance, if a company reacts on a customer's complaint, he or she feels valued.

Figure 26 illustrates, that learning, recognition and relationship are values with growing importance and therefore reasons for connecting with brands via social media. Parker found out, that customers value brands that focus on meeting those needs. After having found the needs, the main struggle is to connect these with a company's brand objectives. It needs to be done in order to communicate successfully to customers in a brand likely manner. This 'value exchange' can drive sales and build strong brand preference (Parker, 2013, p. 39ff).

Next to an analysis of customer needs, a company should also review its internal resources. The extent to which a firm engages in social media is strongly related to its budget. Figure 25 showed that social media engagement is time consuming and requires skilled workers. Gattiker suggests using a 'maturity model' in order to identify a company's current position. He also notes that a company's maturity also depends on its skills in terms of usage of different tools. It can be for instance a newcomer to a blog, but has already gained a lot of experience with its Facebook page. Furthermore, it may be the case that employees are on a higher experience level when it comes to social media usage than a company itself. This know-how must be integrated (Gattiker, 2013, p. 5ff).

After analyzing customer needs and a company's internal resources, a social media monitoring should be done. However, only few companies have already established a sufficient monitoring. It should include information about the popularity of the own brand, as well as competitor's brands (from a marketing viewpoint). A firm's reputation and trend monitoring should be comprised as well in order to get an overall view of the current situation (Wittmann et al., 2013, p. 40).

Goal Setting

The part of goal setting is important, since the purpose of social media engagement for the own company requires tailored content and actions. There are various motivations to engage in social media, each purpose requiring different performances. Possible aims could be the use of social media as a marketing channel, the improvement of a company's CRM or increased customer support (Gattiker, 2013, p. 4). In Rossmann's opinion, social media is used the most efficiently in the early buying decision process, because it is a good tool to activate and reactivate customers (Rossmann, 2013, p. 48). An additional goal should be the regular update of content throughout all platforms, since poor social media engagement will have an impact on a brand's reputation. Messages and texts should always be up-to-date and relevant to the customer group a company intends to target (Heller Baird & Parasnis, 2011, p. 34ff). Furthermore, employees need to support a firm's social media strategy, because it could have a positive impact on the results. The strategy also needs to be sustainable and integrated into a company's processes. The wording of released texts should always be conforming to corporate governance. A firm should think about establishing internal social media guidelines to increase the efficiency of processes (Spriestersbach, 2014). Consequently, goal setting must be done before the formulation of a precise strategy.

Strategy Formulation

> *"Success lies in understanding that in a social media world, everything communicates and communications affect everything. Silence, especially, can prove to be a brand's most damaging strategy."*
> (Argenti & Barnes, 2009, p. 63)

One study of Ibi research with 539 companies participating, found out, that over 80 percent of companies do not have a written social media strategy document. 37 percent however, plan to establish a plan. The most important aspects a document should contain were aims, benefits for the target group, communication with customers and the choice of the preferred social media platforms. Issues, such as impact measurement and budget planning were equally important, while only one out of six companies planned to establish a social media guideline. As already said before, a social media guideline will help to determine a clear communication in conformance with a brand's visual appearance. It furthermore gives guidance on how to deal with secret data and lists employees responsibilities (Wittmann et al., 2013, p. 32ff). Establishing a social media document and complying with the strategy is crucial since customers "can gain trust in a brand quite rapidly but it can be destroyed rapidly too" (Woodcock et al., 2011, p. 51).

Since social media is mostly led by consumers' wishes, the strategy development requires a change in a company's mindset. To give up control over messaging can be quite challenging for marketers. This is however the only way to communicate effectively with potential and existing customers (Chaffey & Ellis-Chadwick, 2012, p. 31). The communication method needs to be determined. It is advantageous to use content marketing instead of advertising, since it increases the relevance to customers. Content marketing will differentiate brands from others, because it is perceived as being credible. Users will more likely interact with companies that appear honest and give consumers added value. This also includes a transparent communication (Rossmann, 2013, p. 17).

Most companies first establish a social media presence on platforms such as Facebook, Twitter, Xing, LinkedIn or YouTube in order to interact with users and to increase reach. The selection should be based on outcomes of the situation analysis, since a pure presence is not enough to gain new customers. A strategy should be to listen to users' needs and respond on one to one basis. This then can create a dialogue. If it is too difficult to communicate on one to one basis, the integration of digital opinion leaders into a brand's strategy can be helpful. These users, for instance bloggers, have many followers and therefore reach a lot of potential customers. It is crucial to establish a personal and intensive relationship with these digital leaders. Positive customer communication, also in terms of answering to customer complaints, increases positive word-of-mouth. As discussed in section 'Goal setting', employees should be integrated into the social media strategy. Through doing so, personnel can be gained as brand ambassadors. Another strategy with great potential is to enable customer participation in product development, testing, and marketing. User integration can be done through many ways, for instance through a competition on Facebook, where users can develop an own product. This can highly increase innovation potential. Crowd sourcing could also be part of this strategy.

A further strategy requires the availability of software in order to establish own social media channels. This has the advantage of easy return on social media measurement, but the disadvantage of high complexity (Rossmann, 2013, p. 15ff).

Additionally, Chaffey and Ellis-Chadwick suggest the use of 12 questions that help to define a social media strategy:

- Who are our target audience?
- What are the content preferences of our target audience?
- Which content types should have priority?
- Strategic business goals for social network presences?
- How to differentiate the social channel from other communication channels?
- How to integrate social channels?
- Content frequency and editorial calendar?
- Sourcing content?
- How to manage publication and interaction?
- Software for managing the publishing process?
- Tracking the business impact of social network activity?
- How to optimize the social presence? (Chaffey & Ellis-Chadwick, 2012, p. 234ff)

In Howard's opinion, a social media strategy should comprise seven main activities: the monitoring of all platforms, engagement and interactivity, creating and gathering content, analyzing and reporting outcomes, governance, research, and crisis management (Howard, Mangold, & Johnston, 2014).

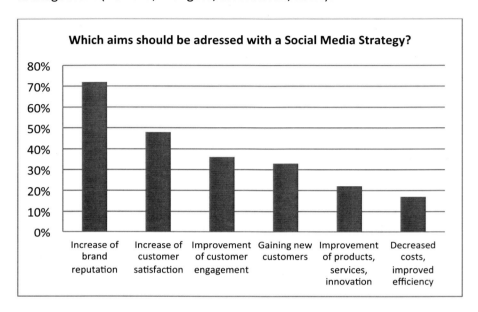

Figure 27: Social Media Strategy aims of companies
Adapted from: (Rossmann, 2013, p. 20)

Figure 27 illustrates aims which companies set with their social media strategy. According to the study conducted by University of St.Gallen in 2013, only 33 percent of participants see the acquisition of new customers as their main strategy. Brand reputation and customer satisfaction are seen as being more important. They have the purpose to increase word-of-mouth and reach and can indirectly lead to customer acquisition as well (Rossmann, 2013, p. 20).

Social Media engagement is mainly done via campaigns. This is the reason why this paragraph will be discussed further in 2.5 Social Media Campaigns.

Resource Allocation & Monitoring

As already discussed, resource allocation and monitoring should be a crucial part not only in social media, but in every department. This issue will also be discussed in 2.4. 'Measuring a return on social media'.

2.5 Social Media Campaigns

> *"Make campaigns, not posts.*
> *Campaigns work better than one-hit wonders."*
> Dana Howard, Social media marketing manager Murray State University
> (Howard et al., 2014, p. 664)

Campaigns can contain various posts and all kind of different actions around one topic, such as promotions, photo contests and the creation of an own hashtag. This helps to establish a top of the mind theme and is more efficient than a single post (Howard et al., 2014, p. 664). A campaign makes users experiences more fluent. Customer experience should be seamless across social media and other channels (Heller Baird & Parasnis, 2011, p. 36).

The AIDA-model describes the way of a customer's first contact (**A**ttention) with a company, the development of **I**nterest and the rise of buying **D**esire to the actual purchasing process (**A**ction). Since Loyalty is of high importance as well, it can be added as an additional phase to the model (Wittmann et al., 2013, p. 56ff). Blum states, that Interest is also named Involvement, since in social media it is crucial to engage with users in order to keep their interest alive. A plan is needed to determine all activities within a specific period of time in order to implement a campaign successfully (Blum, 2014, p. 75). The phases of Attention and Interest/ Involvement are most important for social media; Desire and Loyalty increase in relevance. Social networks are relevant for all five phases, while especially blogs are important for gaining Attention and for increasing reach. If a company engages in e-commerce, an engagement on rating platforms can be advantageous. Such platforms can be important for the Action phase as well. Blogs are additionally a good tool for the Interest, Desire and Loyalty phase next to social networks (Wittmann et al., 2013, p. 56ff). Social media marketing activities should be supported by other digital marketing channels, such as search engine optimization (Blum, 2014, p. 81).

As said before, social media engagement should be done within campaigns, especially for the purpose of promoting an event. This requires a written-out plan with sections for pre-event promos, the day-of promo and content, and post- and wrap-up content. Howard suggests to establish an "own hashtag tracking program by creating a hashtag and then developing pre-event promotions to familiarize people with the hashtag" (Howard et al., 2014, p. 659). All promotion pieces, such as prints, images and signs need to be developed at this time as well. The timing when to post content should be scheduled. However, flexibility is needed in order to react to consumers' issues, which makes constant monitoring inevitable. This is especially important for Facebook and Twitter engagement, since users expect quick responses (Howard et al., 2014).

2.5.1 Measuring a Return on Social Media

"Marketers are under constant pressure to measure everything they do. The result is often a default to tactics that are more easily and accurately measureable, regardless of their effectiveness. This is especially true in social media marketing which often requires qualitative measurement rather than quantitative metrics that are more familiar to online marketers".
(Fisher, 2009, p. 190)

Many companies struggle when it comes to the Return on Social Media determination, often called ROI – Return on Investment. It shows the profit in dependence to the invested budget, employees and time. Fisher states, that marketer are often not able to adopt social media tactics due to an 'inability to measure ROI'. Since most of the conversations between consumers don't take place on a company's website, the traditional approach on measuring online advertisement in quantitative numbers is not valid anymore. As the quote outlines, qualitative measurements might be the better tool, but this data harder to assess (Fisher, 2009, p. 190). In fact, there are various guidelines on how to determine a ROI in social media, none of them having proved to be the ultimate solution yet. Some ideas are discussed below.

In Jacob Morgan's view, a social business consultant, the inability to calculate a ROI has nothing to do with social media itself, but more with the fact that companies do not know the value of their customers. Being able to look at quantifiable numbers starts with understanding what a customer exactly means to a company. Questions that need to be addressed are for instance:

- How much is a customer worth?
- How much does the average customer spend per transaction?
- Is a customer more likely to purchase a product after some sort of social media interaction?
- How much is it worth to convert an unhappy customer to a happy customer?
- On average how many people does a happy customer tell about a product or service?
- How much can an unhappy customer hurt you? (Morgan, 2009)

Morgan suggests establishing a framework in order to estimate rough numbers to get an overall idea of customer value to a company, because it gives guidance to determine the Return on Investment.

Fisher even asks whether a ROI determination is needed, since in her opinion, social media is centered around consumers, and not on money or brands. However, in order to see a firm's effectiveness, some key figures should be calculated. She represents a method developed by Jeremiah Owyang that requires the establishment of a clear strategy first – since only goals can be measured. Afterwards, a measurement system should be built even before the launch as part of the process. Attributes, which require measurement are listed below and combined with elements that were established by Alexander Rossmann, a marketing professor at St.Gallen University.

- Attention: time on website
- Reach: fans, follower, clicks, views, impressions
- Interaction: clicks, comments, likes, shares
- Conversation Index: ratio between blog posts and comments
- Velocity: distance/ time on how fast the message will be spread
- Sentiment: tone, opinion (positive, negative, neutral posts)
- Qualitative: what did they say?
- Impacts: what did they do? (especially influencers)
- Social monitoring: is good for analyzing competitors and general sentiments of communications. Customer journeys can be illustrated through monitor-

ing with the help of cookies and other tracing models (Rossmann, 2013, p. 22).

As discussed before, most companies are not able to measure a return on social media in figures. The missing link to monetary success factors represents the major disadvantage of such models. Metrics need to be professionalized in order to increase suitability.

3 Discussion

After having considered all the facts, the primary set research question *"do Social Media Campaigns have a significant impact on gaining new customers?"* cannot be answered with yes or no. Since social media is mainly about conversations and exchange of pictures, videos, etc. between friends and family, it is not easy for firms to participate in this communication. Only a small amount of consumers interact regularly with companies via social media. Therefore, campaigns need to be well established in order to motivate other users to engage as well. Social media plays an important role in creating long-term relationships with consumers and in transporting emotions. Hence, it is not about gaining new customers in the first way – this will be a positive side-effect if happy customers convert into brand ambassadors and spread positive word-of-mouth. This and recommendation of friends have much more power than plain advertising. Many companies see brand reputation and customer satisfaction as their main goals they strive to achieve.

(1) Relevance of Social Media to companies?
It is a prerequisite for companies to be part of the digital marketing sphere in order to survive in the fast changing digital environment. Over 3.025 billion people are nowadays active internet users ("We Are Social's Digital Statshot 003," 2014), most of them exchange thoughts and opinions about topics that are related to a company's business. Firms need to participate in order to be part of this dialogue and influence brand awareness and reputation, since companies are experiencing a shift of power, as they are increasingly losing control over their organization's reputation and messaging.
If done properly, firms can benefit from social media marketing. Main advantages are the interactivity and possibility to send individualized messages, as well as inte-

grating a user into e.g. product development or assessment. This helps to build strong customer ties and users can be as close to brands as never before. Another strength of social media lies in the early phase of a purchase decision, when consumers need to be mobilized and are receptive for emotionalized products or brands.

Main obstacles that companies face are the complexity of digital marketing and the question which channels to use in order to serve potential and existing customers best. Time intensity of social media engagement, loss of control over communication due to change to pull strategies and responding to changes in technology are further challenges. IT plays nowadays a significant role in determining a company's success, as dysfunctional IT management can jeopardize advantages. However, many firms are still in an early stage to discover the potential of IT. ITracy is a skill that all managers need in today's information economy. Since only few companies monitor their social media activities due to inadequate experience and too much effort, social media strategies need to be carefully established.

(2) How to set up an appropriate strategy?
The smartphone has become "an ever present companion" with all different types of media, calling for companies that are always up to date and ready for quick responses. Since Internet communication strategies have mainly shifted from push to pull, marketers need to redefine their communication strategies in order to be relevant for customers.

Social behavior is mostly sustained either by learning, relationship, diversion, progression or recognition, which represent the five basic human needs. A study found out, that learning, recognition and relationship are values with growing importance and therefore reasons for connecting with brands via social media. Customers value brands that focus on meeting those needs – value exchange can enhance sales and drive strong brand preference.

Most social media strategies have potential for improvement. They should be focused on the long-term and also consider the available budget. Marketers are often not able to adopt social media tactics due to an inability to measure ROI'.

(3) How to analyze impact?
The question whether there exists an appropriate tool for a return on social media determination can be answered with no. There are lots of theories about different measurement tools, but one single best solution has not been found yet. Problems

often arise due to inappropriate quality of a firm's social media strategy and integration into its processes.

4 Conclusion

The adoption of technology is a prerequisite for successful marketing management. A shift from Internet to digital marketing is needed in order to include all available technologies. Only then companies can keep up with and stay ahead of further technological development.

Social media has already an influence on relevant purchase decisions and especially an impact on brand awareness and product selection and assessment. However, knowledge, skills and competencies within the field of social media in companies have a great potential for improvement and innovation - most probably because companies are struggling to link social media activities directly to financial profit. It is hard to assess profitability of social media investments. The engagement will increase once a suitable tool will be developed, which needs to include both quantitative and qualitative methods. There hasn't been a best tool for measuring a return on social media established yet; hence it will evolve since it is getting more and more important for marketers to justify social media investments. An enhancement of quality in a firm's social media strategy, for instance through an overall integration into all company's internal processes, will support these efforts.

As the world gets more and more digital, social media tools will be available at any time and almost at any place. This demands quick answers of companies due to customers' expectations and enables direct communications between brands and their target audience on a daily basis. Consequently, social media marketing will still increase in relevance as a key strategy in a company's communication mix.

Enhancing Emotional Involvement with Video-Marketing

Jonathan Schrempf/Jochen Strähle

Abstract

Purpose - The purpose of this paper is to elaborate if video marketing enhance emotional involvement. Therefore a literature research is done in two parts. Firstly there is a review on the development of marketing communication and video marketing. In the second part of the review the focus is set on emotions itself, how emotional involvement is generated and how emotions influence consumption behavior.

Design/methodology/approach- Literature Discussion

Findings – The key finding of this paper is that videos can enhance emotions through their multi-sensory character in an efficient way. Furthermore there could be identified that especially viral videos create emotional enhancement and meet the direct marketing approach.

Research limitations/implications- The findings of the paper are mainly focused on video advertising even there are other forms of video marketing. Furthermore the paper faces a limitation regarding the effect of emotions within videos, because the lack of empirical evidence.

Keywords – Video- marketing, emotions, involvement, viral videos, video advertisement, psychological processes

Paper type – Research paper

1 Introduction

Often Video marketing is directly associated with TV advertising. And most people are annoyed from all the TV ads. But at the same time looking in social networks there is an increasing number of campaigns people share because they like it. Such ambivalent developments make it interesting to take a closer look on how video marketing is affecting people.

"The power of sight, sound and motion combined with engagement opportunity creates a powerful emotional connection with consumers." *Sam Smith- Tube Mogul* (Mackenzie, 2014, p. 67)

Quotes like this imply that video marketing is one of the most effective marketing communication tool existing. But is this really true? How do videos affect us? Through the technological development within the last 20 years we face more and more video marketing: for example in TV, within social media channels, in video blogs, on web pages, at video walls on streets, on screens in stores and so on. With these developments and the increasing global networking people today are faced with an overload of information and stimulus satiation. But how does video marketing affect people in this environment? Therefore the central research question of this paper is: Can video marketing enhance emotional involvement?

To answer this question a literature review is conducted to evaluate the development of marketing communication and to display the trends of video communication. In the next step the importance of emotions, the rule of psychological processes within the consumption behavior and their impact on sales are analyzed. Based on these literature findings it will be discussed, if videos can enhance emotional involvement and in which forms such an emotional involvement can be fostered.

2 Literatur Review

2.1 Marketing communication

2.1.1 Define Marketing communication

Video- marketing is a form of communication with people. Therefore firstly the term marketing communication has to be classified and defined.

Successful marketing should be managed and coordinated in an effective way. The combination of all marketing activities is clustered mostly within the 4P model: "product", "price", "promotion" and "place", which was introduced by McCarthy. The 4P model illustrate, that all marketing activities have to suit to the whole marketing mix of the company, to do effective marketing. The promotion part of marketing includes all activities in which a company communicates with its stakeholders. Therefore the term "promotion" as it is used in the 4P model and the term "communication" can be seen equally (Scharf, Schubert, & Hehn, 2012, p. 40).

Marketing communication has different orientations. Communication can have the information and promotion aspect that is used to persuade people into product purchase and give them product based rational information. Secondly there is the process and imagery orientation. Here communication activities are used to influence the different stages of the purchasing process by aiming on the customers experience emphasizing emotional massages and product imagery. Communication here is used to develop feelings for the brand and the target group. Another orientation is the integration. This means that all communication resources have to be used in an effective and balanced way to give customers a clear view on the brands proposition. The fourth is the relational orientation. Communication can be seen as hard to build up relationships to the stakeholders of the organization. Communication should create mutual values, mutual meanings and increase the organizations recognition. Therefore different communication needs and styles of the different stakeholders have to be considered (Fill, 2009, p. 15).

Taking all these orientations into account, marketing communication can be defined as "Management process through which an organization engages with its various audiences." or within another definition it is "the process whereby marketers inform, educate, persuade, remind and reinforce consumers. It is designed to influence buyers and other stakeholders"(Hollensen, 2010, p. 272).

The communication model helps to understand the way communication works. In the model it is shown, that a source, which is mostly a company, transmits messages. The different orientations of the communication are reflected within these different messages and tools and build up the communication mix. Tools are: Advertising, public relations, sponsorship, personal selling, publicity, product placement, event marketing, trade fairs, Internet marketing, internal communication and much more. The message is led through some medium to the receiver. Also video is one of these mediums. The objective of the send message by the respective medium is to capture the consumer's attention in an effective way to generate a purchase. To complete the communication loop the feedback on the communication activity has to be tracked. This can be or example purchase data, product awareness and brand loyalty. In this way the communication activities should be improved and developed continuously (Solomon, Marshall, & Stuart, 2012, p. 377).

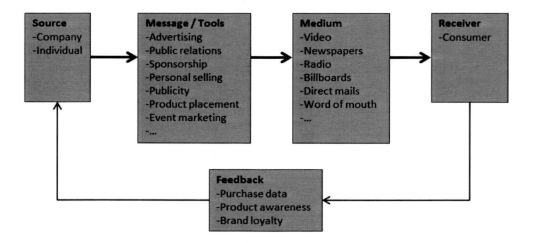

Figure 28: Communication model
Adapted from: (Solomon et al., 2012, p. 377)

Equal which tool and medium is used, efficient marketing communication has to be planned. Therefore a feedback loop of marketing communication can be established, where the marketing needs are firstly analyzed and planned. It is important to develop the right rational, emotional and psychological message to address the right target group with the communication activity. With the right planned communication tool then in the next step the stakeholders should be motivated to act in the way the organization has planned it. In the last step measures should be adopted to control the impact of the respective communication activity. Out of these measures activities can be adopted and next steps can be planned more precisely. But often especially the measurement, how a respective marketing campaign increased sales, is not that easy, because it is difficult to say which activity of the communication mix caused which result (Busch, 2007, p. 9).

2.1.2 Marketing communication in the 21th century

In the last two decades marketing communication has changed extremely. Globalization and increasing networking can be seen as the key words in this development (Kotler, 2007, p. 52). The key driver for this change was the exponential rise in the development of computer-, information- and telecommunication-technology. Based on the Internet and new software applications it became possible to store, update and analyze huge databases with detailed information. This new possibilities lead to an explosion of information for the customer. Based on this availability of information new sophisticated analytical techniques like analyses of geo-demographics, lifestyle, and media usage were developed. So it became possible to create and develop new market segments (Hollensen, 2010, p. 307).

With the developments based on the invention of the Internet, companies became a bundle of new possibilities to create networks with their stakeholders. Firstly this allows the networking with the customers. The Internet is the basis to build up networks with specific customers, to create long-lasting customer relationships and to connect directly with the customer. This networking with the customer will be discussed later on in this chapter within the direct marketing approach. Secondly there is the networking with marketing partners. The Internet allows the networking with other organizational units within the own company. But it also allows to network with suppliers and to build up strategic alliances. And thirdly the Internet enables the efficient networking with the companies' environment. This goes along with an intensified global networking of knowledge, values and responsibilities.

All these networking activities have the effect that the environment in which companies act, change as fast as never before. This can be seen for example very distinctive in the fashion industry. A fashion trend, which is today totally "in" can be tomorrow completely "out". Such an effect can be caused for example through the communication and networking of customers on social media platforms.

Out of this for companies today it is crucial to have the ability to react on the fast changing business environment and new trends. In this sense adopting the marketing communication activities fast and precisely become to a competitive advantage (Kotler, 2007, p. 52).

Focusing on the topic of this paper especially the networking with the customers has great significance. Direct marketing can be seen here as the key word of the marketing communication development in the 21th century. Direct marketing can be defined as "a communication tool that uses non-personal media to create and sustain a personal and intermediary free communication with customers, potential customers and other significant stakeholders"(Fill, 2009, p. 925). Direct marketing means, going away from standardized messages, which target broad mass markets. The trend today is to target customers specifically with messages, which are adapted to the specific needs of the customer. In direct marketing the aim is to create direct connections to selected customers to obtain direct response and create enduring customer relationships. This is also known as one-to-one marketing. Direct marketing has several advantages for customers and buyers. Direct marketing give consumers the advantage to become information and offers that are tailored to their needs and shopping behaviors. Furthermore it gives consumers the possibility to directly interact with the seller and order immediately. In fact direct marketing makes shopping for the consumer easier and more comfortable. For the sellers direct marketing is a powerful tool to build up customer relationships and target their offers better to the needs and wants of the consumers. It enables sellers to reach the right customers at the right time in a cost efficient way (Hollensen, 2010, p. 305).

The following table summarizes the key elements of the new marketing communication approach in the 21th century. All aspects underline the significance of networking between the company and consumer.

Table 7 Traditional and new marketing communication

Traditional marketing communication approach	New marketing communication approach
Sales and product based thinking	Market and customer oriented thinking
Usage of mass- marketing	Focusing the marketing activities on exactly defined segments and individuals
Product and sales is key	Customer satisfaction and customer usage is key
Sales and communication as one- way road	Create customer relationship with interrelated communication
Always search for new customers	Maintain existing customers and create long term relationship
Serve all customers on each price	Focus on profitable customers, stop unprofitable customer relationships
Communication with mass media	Direct communication with customer and more selective communication with new media
Standardized offer	Customized offer

Adapted from: (Kotler, 2007, p. 71)

2.1.3 Video marketing as communication medium

As shown in the communication model in chapter 2.1.1 there are various forms in which medium the messages can be communicated to consumers. Looking on the spread of the advertising spending in different mediums the importance of TV and Internet within the German advertising market becomes clear. These two mediums are also the main mediums for video advertising.

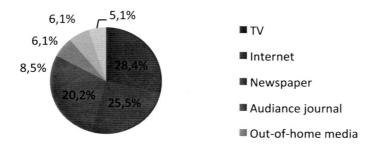

Figure 29: Spread of advertising spending in Germany 2013
Adapted from: (Bundesverband Digitale Wirschaft e.V., 2014)

The importance of videos is based on the dynamic form of this medium. The combination out of pictures, movement, sound and text enables various possibilities to speak to consumers in an emotional and appealing way. With this combination videos can create experiences, which help to emotionalize brands. Therefore in the following the different forms of video advertising are outlined.

Television is the traditional medium of video marketing. It is a traditional medium to reach the mass market. TV has with an average watching time of 205 minutes per day in Germany the highest media usage rate can be still be seen as the mean medium to reach a broad customer base (Meffert, Burmann, & Kirchgeorg, 2015, p. 591). However TV advertising has two significant weaknesses. The first is the increasing fragmentation of audience. This means that consumers are zapping into other channels to avoid watching advertisements. Only 23% of people watching TV also watch TV ads (Hollensen, 2010, p. 284). The second weakness is the high costs of TV advertising. The production of a successful video ad is expansive but the much higher cost is the airtime at the TV channels. Depending on the length of the advertisement and the time when it is aired there has to be paid several thousand euros for view seconds advertising time in a year (ARD, 2014).

As shown in the diagram, with 25,5 % the spread of advertising spending's the internet is the second important medium of advertising. Even this percentage does not only reflect video advertising, online videos in its different forms give video marketing new leverage.

Based on the development and spread of broadband internet connections it became possible to watch videos in the internet. The internet opens up new and different ways to show video commercials. Videos or ads can be integrated in web-pages as unstoppable loops and also the content of the ads can be adapted to the web-page content. In this way it is much more focused on the interest of the consumer. However the classical 30 second TV ads are not suitable for online videos. Therefore new content needs to be developed (Fill, 2009, p. 776).

So a key benefit of web videos is that they can be much more customized compared to the traditional TV ads. This also goes along with the direct marketing trend. Focus within the customizing is set on the right placement of videos. There is developed more and more software to manage where which video is streamed for which consumer. In this way it is determined where video space should be located, based on the consuming behaviors and interests of the consumer. By programmed buying ad space is then bought automatically and the ad is placed at the respective page. In this way the value of videos with their high effect on audience, behavior and engagement are used in a much more customized and effective way than in traditional video advertising.

Video channels are another important way to do video marketing besides the placement of videos on webpages as banners or pop-ups. In video channels like YouTube, Clipfish but also on media libraries of TV channels more often video advertising is run as pre-roll on the online video the user wants to see. These ads can be adapted to the content of the video the usurer is interested in. In this way a custom made TV style content can be created. Also here it becomes clear that digital videos can be more precise in target audiences compared to the classical TV advertising. Furthermore watching these ads is unavoidable, because there is no possibility to zap if the consumer want to watch the video stream (Mackenzie, 2014, p. 65).

The internet gives the possibility to adopt the content of a webpage to the individual user. This adoption is also named rich media. Within the rich media approach information which is given from the consumer by browsing on the webpage or using the search functions is analyzed and used to adopt the messages to the consumer. In this way video ads can be placed in a way the suit much better to the emotional setting of the consumer. More emotions means also creating a stronger branding message (Fill, 2009, p. 776). Using rich media advertisement within videos show significant higher brand favorability, brand awareness and purchase intent compared to the normal placement of picture advertising formats. Rich media can ensure to set the right first advertising exposure to the audience group. (Spalding, Cole, & Fayer, 2009) However the majority of websites are still build up on visual appearance, easy navigation and making the webpage more appealing with the appropriate colors, and fonts. But the success of a webpage relay mainly on the content. Therefore it is important to place the right content which is appropriate to the consumer on the webpage to do successful marketing (Scott, 2010, p. 111).

By the flood of information today, consumers become more and more resistant and more sensible how they are influenced from advertising. Especially young consumers can be only reached difficultly by traditional mass media. There is the trend that consumers prefer more and more trustful and personal recommendations as source of information. The integration of video marketing into social media platforms become here an increasing importance. Trying to use networking of consumers for marketing activities is the so called viral marketing approach. Viral Marketing can be seen as the word of mouth in the internet. Companies can use viral videos as marketing instrument in the way that people speak, like and spread the videos like a message that is infectious and passed along to friends and cause a multiplier effect (Stenger, 2012, p. 43).

By posting videos on social media platforms, people discover new content, interests and information by peer to peer communication. Social media and the usage of mobile devices changed the way of media and video consumption. So Facebook introduced for example the video auto play function, which activates videos automatically by scrolling over it. By clicking on the video the user can hear and see the video in the expanded screen. Such inventions are a completely new style of receiving an ad. Short video clips are consumed by masses as a kind of "snack" (Mackenzie, 2014, p. 67). This has the impact that online and viral videos differ from regular TV spots in content, length and brand communication(Stenger, 2012, p. 43).

A difficulty, especially on social media videos, is the controlling of online videos. Maybe video ads are linked on pages the publishing company don't want to be associated with. So for example advertisements can be placed or posted directly besides communications from political parties or even besides illegal page content. To minimize things like this, Facebook for example, invented an opted out function which allows companies to control their advertising better (Fill, 2009, p. 776).

Video marketing also occurs in the form of branded entertainment. This is also widely known as product placement within videos. By placing products and brands within movies, TV shows or series the brand or product become an element of a film and its storyline. This is a good way to connect emotions, behavior, lifestyles with the brand or product (Fill, 2009, p. 923).

Also in the digital out of home sector videos play an increasing importance. Within this category means all video screens, which are installed on public places. Everybody knows the screens at the airport, in train stations, in busses, in supermarkets, schools, fast-food restaurant and so on. By showing videos on theses screens much more attention and activation is caused than if there is a static advertisement. Because the location of these screens is fixed, such screens allow also an adoption of the content to the respective situation of the viewer (Meffert et al., 2015, p. 619).

Looking at the whole video advertising market it can be said, that it is a strongly growing segment and videos gain in importance. Pricewaterhouse Cooper's estimate that the spending's in the Australian online video advertising market rise from $155 million in 2013 to $718 million in 2018. This is still a relatively small amount compared to the spending's of $3,8 billion in TV advertising but the growth rate speak for the increasing importance of online video marketing. Traditional TV advertising still speaks to an audience of masses but it becomes more and more inefficient and much more money has to be spend to reach the same amount of people compared to other forms of video marketing (Mackenzie, 2014, p. 64).

2.2 Emotions and Involvement in Marketing

2.2.1 Emotions

To understand how videos can enhance emotional involvement there has to be taken a closer look on what emotions are and how they are generated.

Emotions are still a big research topic in neurological science. That's also why there existing a lot of different definitions, researches and studies. In this chapter there should be created an understanding of the effect emotions have on our behavior. It is not the aim to draw a complete scientific picture of the state of the art of emotions.

Emotions can be defined as: "Psychological processes which are accompanied by physiological phenomena. They describe object or situation oriented conditions which are recognized conscious or unconscious and go along with the respective behavior" (Sigg, 2009, p. 24). Another more practice oriented definition delivers Häusel with his Limbic model: "Emotions are complex physically and neuronal processes. The feelings on which we identify emotions are only the visible top of the iceberg. In this way emotions can have impact on us without our consciousness recognizes it" (Häusel, 2009, p. 24). Both definitions show, that emotions are the result out of complex processes in the human brain. Furthermore it becomes clear that emotions have an impact on our feelings and behavior in two levels- conscious and subconscious.

The human brain can be structured roughly into three zones: the neocortex, the interbrain and the brainstem. In the old neurological science there was the thought that these three zones have also specific and clearly separated competences, structured into reason, emotion and instinct. Today in the neurological science it is known that emotions are mainly processed in the limbic system which can be seen as a functional part of whole brain but mainly located in the interbrain and neocortex (Häusel, 2009, p. 15). Sensory imputs for example from video ads can be directly transmitted to the limbic system as the emotional center but they can be also transmitted indirectly to the neocortex where complex thoughts occur (Peacock, Purvis, & Hazlett, 2011, p. 578).

After the understanding what emotions are and where they are generated it is interesting to know which emotions exist. The psychological concept of emotions is extensively covered and there exist a lot of different systems, which all categorize and identify different emotions. According to Scherer emotions exist out of five components. 1. The cognitive component, which is responsible for the positive or negative evaluation of a stimuli. 2. The neuro-physiological component, which determines the emotional excitement of a stimuli. 3. The motivational component, which describes the disposition to act. 4. The expressive component, which determines the external effects. 5. The emotional component which determines reflection and control (Busch, 2007, p. 22).

In the Limbic model by Häusel emotions are categorized within another system. The model class emotions into three main categories: Dominance, stimulant and balance. In each of these categories there exists a positive reward-system and a negative avoidance- system. With this model there can be crated a value scheme in which all emotions can be categorized (Häusel, 2009, p. 24). This can be seen in the following figure.

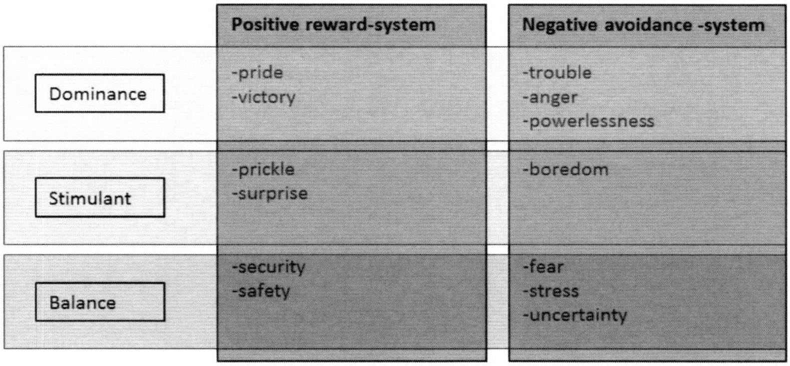

	Positive reward-system	Negative avoidance -system
Dominance	-pride -victory	-trouble -anger -powerlessness
Stimulant	-prickle -surprise	-boredom
Balance	-security -safety	-fear -stress -uncertainty

Figure 30: Emotional system of the Limbic model
Adapted from: (Häusel, 2009, p. 27)

Especially in videos emotions are caused by stimuli of the human senses. In accordance to the shown emotional model there can be categorized different recipients, who are attracted by different senses. All of the now listed senses can cause emotions in each of these 6 categories of the emotional system depending on the personality of the recipient. Shapes, colors and motion are emotional messages to the brain. Each color, shape and motions is associated mostly subconscious with different emotional associations. Secondly sounds equal if it is only a noise or if it is music cause emotions. Not at least also smells, taste and haptic cause emotions. If there are messages communicated over different senses at the same time this cause a multisensory enhancement which multiply the single impressions and emotions up to ten times (Häusel, 2009, p. 77).

Often the knowledge out of neuroscience and psychology is not used to create adds. The bases of using this knowledge, is the measurement when and how emotions occur regarding to different add content. As already mentioned in the definition, there are subconscious emotion and conscious emotions. These two levels of emotions have different types of reactions. While unconscious emotions can be seen in physiological and spontaneous reactions conscious reactions can be seen in spontaneous and prompted reactions. To capture these different reactions on emotions also different measures are needed. Subconscious emotions can be measured by automatic and symbolic methods. Conscious emotions can be also measured by symbolic and the self-report methods. Which kind of measure of emotions should be used, always depend on what you want to know. There is a difference in measurement if you want to know emotional peaks (physiological measure), if you want a mental map (symbolic measure) or examine a brand story (self-reported)(Micu & Plummer, 2010, p. 140). Within the physiological measures for example eye movement, facial expressions or muscle activity can be tracked as indicators for emotions (Teixeira, Wedel, & Pieters, 2012, p. 145)

2.2.2 Psychological processes within consumption behavior

After the emotions itself were analyzed it has to be explained why and which psychological processes affect the consumption behavior. Therefore the Stimulus-Organic-Response Model is seen as a core model within literature. The knowledge about processes like they are described in the SOR- Model allow to plan and implement marketing activities in an effective way (Kroeber-Riel & Gröppel-Klein, 2013, p. 51).

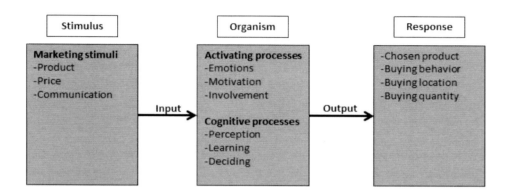

Figure 31: Stimulus-Organism-Response Model
Adapted from: (Scharf et al., 2012, p. 60)

The whole process starts with the perception of marketing stimuli. Perception is defined as: "The way people select recognize and interpret information's from the outside world" (Solomon et al., 2012, p. 162). Marketing stimuli like products, a good price or communication activities like videos are notices from the sensory receptors, which are eyes, ears, nose, moth and skin. The extent on which people react on this stimulus and how strong mental processes are activated depend on the paid attention to the stimulus (Solomon et al., 2012, p. 162).

The psychological processes within the Organism part of the SOR-Model can be distinguished into activating and cognitive processes. Activating processes rely on parts, which are responsible for human behavior. Cognitive processes are processes, which are more responsible for the perception, learning and decision process. Both processes run normally parallel at the same time. Depended which part of the process is more dominant it is called activating or cognitive process.

The third part of the SOR-Model is the response. This can be seen as the result our output of all processes within the organism. The response can be seen and tract directly, because it is the direct human action, for example the purchase of a certain product or service (Kroeber-Riel & Gröppel-Klein, 2013, p. 51).

Regarding to the topic of this paper in the following there will be a closer look on the Organism part of the SOR-Model.

Consumers make decisions out of an interplay between activating and cognitive processes. Taking an advertisement as an exemplary stimulus, this means, that if rational arguments or emotional situations in advertising tab into personal values, the emotional part of the brain is stimulated. The stronger the emotional bond, the more important they become in the decision making process. Emotions can be seen as the "gatekeepers" for further processes. This implies that there has to be an emotional reaction before further cognitive processes take place (Peacock et al., 2011, p. 579).

Besides the rule of emotions, which was already discusses in the previous chapter involvement plays a significant rule within the activating process. Involvement can be defined as motivation to record, process and save information based on emotions and reason (Sigg, 2009, p. 21). Involvement has 3 levels. The first level is the degree of involvement. This varies in context to the experience, the values, the expectations, the reason for the purchase intention and also the nature of stimulus. Involvement can be seen as the reaction on an external stimulus like a video advertising campaign. The second level is the intensity of involvement, which implicates the personal relevance of the stimulus and also the duration of involvement. The third level of involvement is the outcomes and consequences which are identified in the SOR- Model as Response (Fill, 2009, p. 174).

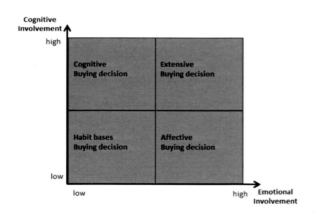

Figure 32: FCB grid
Adapted from: (Sigg, 2009, p. 23)

Looking on the buying decisions the importance and strength of cognitive and emotional involvement can vary. This relation is shown in the FCB grid above which was introduced by Vaughn in 1980. Cognitive buying decisions are highly rational buying behaviors. Products are mainly bought out of rational information. Habit based buying decisions are all routine buying decisions and are a kind of automated. Affective buying decisions are mainly based on emotional effects. This is also known as the impulsive buying decision. Extensive buying decisions are mostly purchases, which are perceived with high risk. Therefore they have a high cognitive involvement and the perceived risk can be reduced by high emotional involvement (Sigg, 2009, p. 22).

Based on the FCB model there can be taken a look on emotions in advertising. Emotions in advertising have the aim to increase the involvement to influence or even change attitudes. Often the target group has already an imagination of the brand within their minds, because consumer view advertising in context of associations in their memory. Emotions can be used here to build up a higher level of awareness and brand strength. Depending on the product and kind of buying decision emotions can here be more important than the rational message (Fill, 2009, p. 487).

However the usage of the knowledge about the psychological processes within the consumption behavior can be seen critical. In the TV advertising market there is still a predominance of the information processing model. This model is mainly a rational information based persuasion model. Important factors like the emotional content and creativity of an advertisement do not play an important rule. Core assumptions of the IP model are: Any ad must communicate a clear message of a product or service and the success of an ad is mainly indicated by the recall of the message. The reason for this is, that in the evaluation of advertising campaigns often only hard values like: product awareness, creating a relationship and creating a unique selling proposition are in focus. Soft values like emotional involvement are often seen as less important. As a result of this, there is little empirical evidence that advertising can also work very successful without rational informational message. But the traditional IP model has forthcoming from psychology. Visuals, sound, symbols, music, gestures, context and environment are central elements in communication and it is obvious that also advertising that contains no message, no proposition or no consumer benefit can by highly effective. Therefore new methodologies needs to be developed which can evaluate advertising with the new knowledge about neurological science (Heath & Feldwick, 2008).

2.2.3 Emotions affect sales

In the previous chapter it was shown, that different psychological processes like emotions and involvement influence the human consumption behavior. Even there are different theories regarding the rule of emotions within the consumption processes, it can be said that emotions affect sales.

Most purchase decisions are done subconsciously and are in this way always emotional. A complete rational consumption behavior can be seen as an illusion because the whole world only become value and meaning with emotions. Emotions are significant to evaluate products and services. This implicates the product interest itself, the quality expectations, the brand decision, the product design preferences and much more. Each product or service runs through a long subconscious evaluation process. Within literature there are differences regarding the share of subconscious within purchase decisions. According to Häusel and the Limbic model there is a share from 70 to 80 percent. This indicates that emotions are a highly relevant factor within the evaluation process of products. That emotions are a main driver in the subconscious evaluation process seems to be evident. But even conscious or explicit rational decisions are highly influenced by emotions. The reason for this is, that also behind rational evaluation and decision processes, there is an emotional construct which can't be noticed from humans. That's why also in rational assumed purchase decisions emotions play an important rule. Because of this it is important to know the emotional systems of customers. This enables to boost positive emotions which increase sales. A company should do everything to evoke emotions which activate the wish within consumers for having the respective product or service (Häusel, 2009, p. 19).

Today most purchase decisions of consumer goods are not done anymore, because the product or service is really needed. Consumption today can be more and more classified as an act of affective experience. That is also a reason why emotions within the selling process get more and more important even for factual and functional elements. With an increasing emotional appeal for consumer goods a positive emotional shopping environment is created. This leads also to a less critical evaluation of the product content itself (Raab & Unger, 2005, p. 236).

Marketing communication is one of the key tools in marketing to push sales. As purchase decisions are done highly emotional it is of high importance to use also the right emotions within the communication activities to create an increased purchase intention. There are several factors which influence the emotional involvement for video advertising. So for example there is a difference how women and men react on emotions within advertising. While women react on the whole emotional package men tend more to react on emotional moments. This becomes clear on a study which was done at a video ad of a car, where a couple comes home from hospital with the baby at the back seat. While women reacted highly positive on the emotional situation in the ad where the parents come home with their baby, men noticed that the baby was not correctly belted in the car seat and where less emotional involved. This example shows obviously how depended the emotional involvement is from the recipient. Also the frame and environment in which advertising is shown is highly relevant for the strength of emotional involvement. In shows or series at the high end of the emotional scale the same ad has a much higher effect on the created purchase intention than if the same ad is shown in a less emotional program or show. Even these are only two examples of emotions in video advertising it become obvious: The stronger and more powerful emotions are communicated to consumers the higher is the buying intent (Lafayette, 2014).

Positive emotions lead also to a higher brand recall than negative emotions or even the absence of emotions. Consumers can better remember brands if they are related with positive emotions (Peacock et al., 2011, p. 583). Positive emotions in relation with products and services also create confidence, satisfaction and risk minimization for customers. In this way positive emotions are the basis to create loyal and profitable customers (Raab & Unger, 2005, p. 237). Being in the mind of customers and having a loyal customer base is an important basis for sales success.

Emotions have a high impact on the evaluation of products as stated above. This is directly linked to the willingness to pay or simple the prices of products. If there are linked a lot of emotions to simple products the price acceptance is much higher. If there are same products, humans are willing to pay more for the product which is more emotional for them. On the example of mineral water the effect of emotions on the prices becomes evident. Food chemist prove that in respective living areas normal tab water has the same or even better quality than bought mineral water. 0,75 liters of such tab water cost around 0,12 cent. But most people buy branded mineral water in the supermarket where one bottle cost 80 cent. This is around 650 times more. Having dinner in the restaurant people buy a bottle San Pellegrino or Apollinaris to their glass of wine for around 7 euro. So the price is around 6000 times higher for water with the same quality. But in fact people buy with a bottle San Pellegino not a bottle of water. They buy a kind of life style, a moment of pleasure and a kind of status. This is nothing else than buying emotions which are packed into a perfect branded product. With this simple example it can be seen easily that emotions can increase the willingness to pay tremendously (Häusel, 2009, p. 10).

This paper has not the aim to show each single effect of emotions on sales of products and services. But it was shown that emotions have a significant impact on different factors. Emotions are highly relevant to build up interest, to increase demand and sales, to create brand awareness and loyal customers and to create acceptance of higher prices.

3 Discussion

3.1 Video marketing enhance emotional involvement

Out of the literature review it becomes clear, that the video marketing format is an effective way to create emotions. It was shown that emotions are created by different stimuli from the environment in which humans interact. As a logical consequence it can be said, that the more stimuli there are, the more emotions are produced in the human brain. Videos are a medium which work with multisensory stimuli. Videos combine pictures, shapes, colors, movements, sounds and texts. These combinations of stimuli speak to different senses of humans and make videos to a highly dynamic and emotion boosting media format.

In a world with a daily flooding of information it is not easy to attract people with marketing communication activities in an effective way. Firstly people have to notice a marketing activity in this information flooding. But even if they notice such an activity it is not said, that it cause emotions in a form that influence their behavior or lead to an action. Referring to the media consumption trend videos can be identified as a format that is highly attractive to people today. Through the development of the internet and new hardware technologies like tablets and smartphones the online video consumption today is higher than never before. The combination of activated senses in videos leads to higher attention even the overall amount of information is increasing. Therefore videos can be identified as a media format which speaks to consumers in an appealing, attractive and emotional way.

Within the literature review it was also shown, that emotions have a significant impact in the purchasing process. In this way emotions directly affect sales. Within the Stimulus- Organic- Response Model the importance of emotions and psychological processes within the organism where shown. Stimuli are the entering point of the purchase process to create emotions. The more stimuli there is entered the better or higher there is also the response. If videos are a good way to create stimuli and emotions they are out of this model also an effective way to increase the response. The different responses of positive emotions also where shown: Build up interest for product or service, create brand awareness, create acceptance of higher prices, create loyal customers and in this way increase demand and sales.

The importance of involvement is reflected within the SOR Model. Getting the consumer connected to the product or service is very important to generate effective response. The degree and intensity of this involvement has a direct impact on the purchase decision. It was shown that emotions are highly relevant to create this motivation to record, process and save information. With videos there can be created high emotional involvement and through this rational factors get less important. It can be said the higher the emotional involvement, the more important they become in the decision making process.

It was shown that videos can create emotional involvement. And it was shown that emotional involvement is highly relevant for customer responses. However it is important to develop the right emotional, psychological and rational message to address the right target group with the video marketing activities. But especially in this important topic for creating effective video marketing nearly no literature and empiric studies are available. There is no empirical evidence how videos have to been designed to create specific emotions. There is also rare evidence which elements of a video cause which emotional result. Thinking at the billions of euros which companies spend each year into video communication activities this lack of knowledge is highly interesting. Emotions within videos seem still to be a big black box, even the importance of emotions within the consumption process is shown by neurological science. How videos cause and create which emotions seems to be an interesting field of further scientific research.

The communication model indicates that each communication activity should be tracked in its results and impacts for example on the sales data or product awareness. By such a tracking communication activities can be improved and developed continuously. But through the lack of deep scientific knowledge these feedback loop can be seen as a critical point of video marketing activities.

3.2 Trends to enhance emotional involvement with video marketing

In the previous discussion it was shown that videos are a good medium to create emotional involvement. Know it should be discussed in which forms videos can be used as an appropriate marketing format to create emotions.

Video marketing is mostly directly associated with TV advertising. Looking into the literature or asking people regarding video marketing the first intention is TV advertising. The reason for this may be that it is still the most important communication medium for consumer goods. But new developments lead to question this medium more and more. TV advertising is very expansive and it is questionable if it is cost efficient. Furthermore through the flood off information and advertising more and more people avoid watching TV ads and increasing trend to zap can be considered as another weakness.

While TV advertising as traditional mass media communication is still the most important communication medium, on the other side there is the direct marketing trend. Instead of targeting broad masses with standardized messages direct marketing means to speak individualized to customers and to adopt messages to customer needs. The question is if it these trend suits to video marketing, because videos are expansive to produce and difficult to adapt to customers individually?

With the Internet as medium for video marketing it become possible to do much more focused video marketing. The Internet is the basis to build up networks with specific customers and enables companies to directly connect with customers. Automated Internet analytic tools enable to adopt the content on webpages, which are shown to the consumer. In this way the video banner or video ad, which is shown to the consumer can be adapted to his or her interests. With this rich media approach video marketing can be done much more individualized and the individual consumer can be emotionalized much better.

The Internet is the basis to do direct marketing and enables also in video marketing to build up networks with specific customers, to create long-lasting customer relationships and to connect directly with the customer. "Viral" is the key word for this networking in the Internet. Viral videos give companies the possibility to influence activities and trends within social media platforms. Viral videos lead to a much higher emotional involvement than traditional TV ads. Facing the flood of advertising companies can use viral videos as marketing tool to influence the way people speak like and spread their campaigns. This word of mouth of the Internet can cause a emotional hype. Friends tell friends that this is cool and up to date. By these recommendation and posting video campaigns are not felt as boring advertisement anymore.

But the question is which emotions can cause such a viral effect and how videos need to be designed to become a successful viral video. The importance and relevance of the viral effect is stated in the literature but there were found no empirical researches how video marketing has to be designed to become viral. This seems once again to be a big black box.

There were found 3 main reasons for videos, which become viral. This cannot be seen as an empirical study or result but it can give an indication of emotional categories from viral videos.

A first reason and probably the most important one, why videos becoming viral, is because people simple feel that it is cool. The difficulty for a company here is to find exactly the tool to activate this emotional "cool" in a broad community. With their cash desk sinfonia EDEKA reached exactly this. Cashiers playing a Christmas song with the cash desk jingle within a view weeks this video reached over 19 million views. In this way broad brand awareness can be created.

Figure 33: EDEKA Cash desk sinfonia
Adapted from: (EDEKA, 2014)

The second reason, how videos becoming viral, is because there are stars within the video campaign which are at the moment in within the society. This is nothing really new and also often used within TV advertising campaigns but it seems to work. Example for this is the Magical Holiday music video from H&M with Lady Gaga and Tony Bennett.

Figure 34: H&M Magical Holidays
Adapted from: (Hennes & Mauritz, 2014)

A third reason for videos becoming viral is because people have the same specific values. A good example for this is the outdoor company Vaude. In their free ski videos they do not directly advertise their products. Instead they show values like freedom and nature experience, which are values who wear these products have.

Figure 35 Vaude Freeski
Adapted from: (*Dreamlines*, 2014)

Not at least because of their cost efficiency viral videos are highly interesting for companies. The production of a successful video is expansive but if the video become viral the cost efficiency is much higher than in TV advertising because the video is spread by the community and no airtime has to be paid.

Not at least the digital out of home segment can be seen as a new trend in doing emotional video marketing. Especially in the fashion industry with virtual shopping windows there can be created much more emotional involvement and attention in comparison to a shopping window with traditional visual merchandising. Instead of static mannequins there can be shown for example videos from fashion shows which demonstrate the real lifestyle of a brand. Also in store with displays and the usage of tablets the regular sales process can be much more emotionalized for example by showing the customer videos from producing a high quality product. But also here a question, which is not answered by literature or empirical studies . Which Emotions should be provoked to push sales?

4 Conclusion

Concluding it can be said: Yes, video marketing can enhance emotional involvement. Through the combination out of picture, movement, color and sound, videos are a multisensory medium, which cause high emotional involvement within the recipients. With this multisensory approach video marketing is a strong tool to face the information and sensory overload today.

It has been shown that emotions play a significant role within the purchase and decision process. Not only subconscious decisions, also the conscious decisions are highly influenced by emotions. Only with the emotional evaluation products and services become a value. In this way high emotional involvement can increase the acceptance of higher prices, create loyal customers and increase sales.

Especially online video marketing seems to be a new powerful way to enhance emotional involvement. In comparison to the traditional TV advertising as mass media, within online video marketing the direct marketing approach can be established. With rich media technology videos can be located on web pages, individual adapted to the consumers' interests. Viral videos can be identified as the word of mouth of the Internet and imply high emotional involvement. By enhancing such a networking environment between customers and companies, problems of traditional TV advertising like zapping, high costs and reaching the right target group are faced.

A limitation of this paper is, that there is little empirical evidence how and in which way videos create emotions. Also there is no literature where it is analyzed in which way videos have to be designed to create specific emotions. Even there could be shown that videos enhance emotional involvement, the emotional part within video marketing is still a black box where further research needs to be conducted. Another limitation of the paper is the focus on video advertising even there are numerous other forms of video marketing.

The paper has shown that it is correct what Sam Smith states in his quote: "The power of sight, sound and motion combined with engagement opportunity creates a powerful emotional connection with consumers." But the paper has also shown that emotions within video marketing are still a unexplored area.

The Purchase Phase - Converting Customers into Shoppers

Impact of Payment Methods on the Buying Decision- How does the Degree of Transparency of a Payment Method influence the Buying Decision in Fashion Business?

Anne Riegger/Jochen Strähle

Abstract

Purpose- This research paper deals with the question how the degree of transparency of a payment method influences the buying decision in fashion business. Therefore, consumer behavior and the decision-making process in fashion business are reviewed. Furthermore, the impact different degrees of payment transparency have on consumer behavior in general are compiled and evaluated.

Design/methodology/approach- Literature Discussion

Findings- It is assumed that the degree of transparency of a payment method has an impact on consumption in fashion business. Transparency relates positively to the pain of paying, which functions as a financial self-regulation tool by sending out signals about the conceivable consequences of spending money. Hence, the less transparent a payment is, the higher the willingness to spend will be. Moreover, it is assumed that transparency not only has an impact on consumption in fashion business, but the effect is also reinforced by consumer behavior.

Research limitations/implications- It is to consider, that consumption behavior also depends on personality and other influencing factors. Therefore, fashion consumption behavior neither relies on a pure decision efficiency perspective, nor a pure and ideal hedonic perspective. However, since fashion consumption is emotionally driven, it tends to be more on the hedonic side.

Keywords: Consumer Behavior, Fashion Business, Transparency of a Payment Method, Willingness to spend, Pain of Paying

Payper type- Research Paper

1 Introduction

Shopping for fashion is fun. At least until you have to queue up at the register. This is where most consumers start dealing with the payment process. The transaction is supposed to be an unemotional matter, in which money is exchanged for goods. However, most consumers feel some emotions when parting with their hard earned money. While waiting in line, they think about which payment method they should use to pay for their purchases. They debate whether they have enough cash in their wallet, or whether using a debit or a credit card would be better in this case.

It is somewhat strange that when using a card-based payment system, the payment often doesn't feel as painful as when using cash. You do not immediately notice the outflow of money. With some payment methods, the payment is more salient than with others. Thus, paying with different payment methods evokes different feelings.

The impact a payment method has on the consumer relates noticeably to the degree of transparency the payment method features.

This paper deals with the question how the degree of transparency of a payment method impacts the buying decision in fashion business.

To begin with, consumption behavior and the decision-making process are analyzed. Thereupon, various payment methods commonly used in fashion business are presented. Also, the term *transparency of payment method* is defined and different payment methods are classified in their degree of transparency and utilization. Not to forget, the impact the degree of transparency of a payment method has on consumer behavior is evaluated. Finally, resulting from the above, implications for the fashion business are presented.

2 Fashion Consumption and the Decision-Making Process in Fashion Business

The world of fashion is very exciting. It affects almost everyone since we are all fashion consumers. Everybody searches for apparel, wears clothes and purchases them at some point in time (Yurchisin & Johnson, 2010). The consumer behavior and the decision making process in fashion business are described in the following.

2.1 Fashion Consumption

The first step in order to grasp consumer behavior in fashion is to understand what consumption is and what constitutes the consumption behavior in fashion.

The term consumption can be defined as

> "*the process involved when individuals or groups select, purchase, use, or dispose of products, services, ideas, or experiences to satisfy needs or desires*" (Solomon & Rabolt, 2004b, p. 23).

The definition above shows that consumption can't be reduced to a single behavior but in fact is an ongoing process. Consumption includes more than the of money for goods or services, e.g. it includes using and eventually disposing the product (Yurchisin & Johnson, 2010).

Another important fact about consumption is that it can also occur without purchasing. In context of fashion, consumption could also be window-shopping at apparel stores or reading fashion magazines. Moreover, consumption fulfills the consumer's need of creating and expressing an identity. Consumers can use products to create their own identity and communicate this identity to others who are familiar with the product's meaning. However, this need cannot always be satisfied by consumption (Yurchisin & Johnson, 2010).

Each consumption activity can be classified as normative- or non-normative behavior. Normative consumer behavior follows traditional and well-known rules of a society (Yurchisin & Johnson, 2010). Norms could be considered as informal rules that describe what is wrong and what is right, what is acceptable and what is unacceptable (Solomon & Rabolt, 2004b).

Consumption norms are consumption related behaviors that are appropriate in a given culture. For instance, Black Friday Shopping in the United States. Individuals who are not familiar with this consumption norm might not understand why consumers in the United States get up at 4 o'clock in the morning to go shopping. However, for people who are familiar with the tradition this seems quite normal to do so (Yurchisin & Johnson, 2010).

Normative consumption is not always rational (Yurchisin & Johnson, 2010). In some cultures, especially women go shopping to improve their mood. In many of these cases, they buy items that they haven't planned to buy (Minahan & Beverland, 2005).

Non-normative consumer behavior on the other hand

"is consumer misconduct in the acquisition, usage or disposition of goods and services" (Callen & Ownbey, 2003, p. 99).

The described behavior seems to be unnatural to people and may in some cases be illegal, economically unhealthy, or unethical. Shoplifting for example is considered as non-normative consumer behavior (Yurchisin & Johnson, 2010).

2.2 Decision-Making

Making the right decision is not always easy. Since there are many options, especially in fashion, consumers have to make buying decisions. A consumer making a decision is trying to solve a problem. In this context, a problem can be described as the deviation between a desired and an ideal state (Rath, Bay, Petrizzi, & Gill, 2008).

Since purchase decisions differ from each other, there are several perspectives on decision-making. The rational perspective is logically based (Rath et al., 2008) and usually applied with high involvement purchases (Solomon & Rabolt, 2004b). Involvement is

"a construct linked to the interaction between an individual and an object and refers to the relative strength of the consumers' cognitive structure related to a focal object" (O'Cass, 2000, p. 548).

Consumers can be involved with a product, the consumption of a product and the purchase decision (O'Cass, 2000). Also, the involvement can be either cognitive or emotional.

In the traditional decision-making model, the consumer carefully searches for information on the product, weighs the pros and the cons, and eventually makes an informed decision. This process (which will be described further in the following) is elaborate and therefore not applied for all decisions. It is not a correct portrayal for many buying decisions (Olshavsky & Granbois, 1979). In more recent literature Solomon, Bamossy and Askegaard pick up this statement to show that consumers do not always go through this complex process (Solomon, Bamossy, & Askegaard, 199). However, if consumers would do so, they would spend a great time of their lives making decisions. Therefore, decision makers possess a range of strategies. The effort required to make a decision is evaluated and then the best suiting strategy is applied. This is called constructive processing (Solomon & Rabolt, 2004b).

Some decisions are made under low involvement conditions. Many of these decisions are a learned responses to environmental factors and specific stimuli, as when consumers buy something on impulse that is promoted in a special way (Solomon & Rabolt, 2004b). Actions like these are collectively called the behavioral perspective. Consumers engage in impulse buying when thy feel the need to buy something immediately without concerning the consequences (Yurchisin & Johnson, 2010). Here, the decision is rather driven by emotions than by rational thinking. Fashion and related products, such as accessories and shoes, are one of the top categories to be bought on impulse (Nguyen Thi Tuyet Mai, Kwon Jung, Lants, & Loeb, 2003). The impulse purchase can be triggered by store design or product placement (Rath et al., 2008).

Finally, there is the experiential perspective. The consumer is highly involved in the decision, however, the selection made cannot be explained on a rational level (Solomon & Rabolt, 2004b). For example, in traditional approaches, it is not entirely possible to explain a person's choice for fashion, music or art. There is usually no single quality as the determining factor. Instead, the totality of the product is stressed (Solomon & Rabolt, 2004b). The Gestalt psychology can among others explain this perspective, as *"it considers the overall experience, not just a particular point or the "how" of the situation"* (Rath et al., 2008, p. 289).

In order to characterize the decision-making process, the amount of effort that a consumer puts into a decision should be considered. Consumer behaviorists employ the terms routine, limited and extensive to describe the level of effort consumers put into a decision. Each category is naturally relative to the personality of the individual (Rath et al., 2008).

Decisions made with extended problem solving are very similar to the traditional decision-making model in which the consumer goes through an elaborate system. The process is usually initiated by the intention of carrying a low degree of risk with the decision. Therefore, the consumer tries to collect as much information about the product as possible and compares the alternatives. Commonly, attributes of one brand at a time are considered and eventually the consumer perceives how the brand characteristics form into a set of desired features (Solomon et al., 1999).

Limited problem solving is the simplest type of decision-making. Consumers are not as involved in the decision as in extended problem solving. Instead of carefully searching for information, buyers use simple decision rules to selects among alternatives. Those simple decision rules are considered to be cognitive shortcuts which enable the consumer to use general guidelines (Solomon & Rabolt, 2004b). The purchase timeline in this case is periodic (Rath et al., 2008).

In contrast to extended and limited problem solving, habitual decision-making is done with little to no conscious effort. Some buying decisions are so habitual that the consumer is not conscious about them. Those decisions are driven by automaticity and performed without any conscious control. At first sight, this seems to be dangerous, however this type of decision-making is quite efficient. Habitual decision-making allows the purchaser to minimize his or her resources spent on everyday buying decisions (Solomon & Rabolt, 2004b).

Based on the explanations above, purchasing of apparel is often an impulsive decision, which means that the emotional involvement is higher than the cognitive involvement (Homburg & Krohmer, 2009). Also, most fashion purchases can be classified as limited problem solving. Reasons are that consumer's involvement in fashion purchases is comparatively high, the frequency of purchasing is compared to others goods, such as food, rather low, and the effort put in the search for information is, depending on the product, moderate to large.

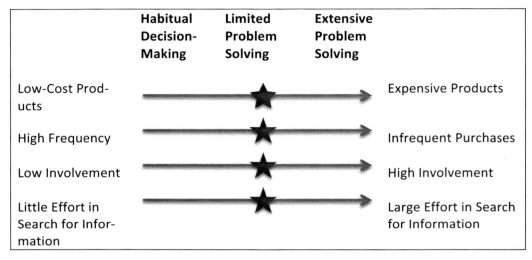

Figure 36: Classification of Fashion Purchases in the Buying Type Model

There are five basic steps; problem recognition, information search, evaluation of alternatives, product choice and the outcome, which consumers go through in the traditional decision-making model (Solomon et al., 1999).

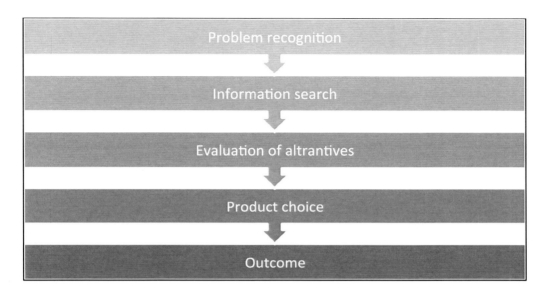

Figure 37: Steps in Consumer Decision-Making
Adapted from: (Solomon et al., 1999)

At first, the consumer has to recognize the problem and identify the lack of something. It occurs when

"the consumer's desired state of affairs departs sufficiently from the actual state of affairs to place the consumer in a state of unrest so that he or she begins thinking of ways to resolve the problem" (Dunne, Lusch, & Carver, 2013, p. 117).

The problem can arise in two ways, either someone needs something (need recognition) or on the other hand, someone wants something (opportunity recognition). In both ways, the gap between the ideal and the current situation is noticeable. The need for fashion items is often created by opportunity recognition simply by exposing the product to the consumer. Problem recognition often occurs naturally, opportunity recognition on the other hand is mostly triggered by marketers (Solomon & Rabolt, 2004b).

For the fashion industry, the planned obsolescence of apparel products is necessary to survive. Marketers need consumers to believe that what they bought last years is no longer adequate to wear this year. Therefore, the fashion industry creates problems for consumers; they create a discrepancy between the actual state and the ideal state (Yurchisin & Johnson, 2010).

Since the problem is now identified, ways to solve it have to be found at this stage. The effort put into the information search differs depending on what is bought and the involvement connected to the purchase (Rath et al., 2008). Information sources can be divided into internal and external sources. Everyone has certain knowledge as a result of prior experience. During the purchase decision, consumers scan their memory and search internally for information. Usually, the internal search is supplemented by an external search (Solomon & Rabolt, 2004b). Fashion-conscious consumers can use different sources to search for information externally, e.g. fashion shows, magazines etc. Surprisingly, the amount of external search is in many cases rather low. However, when it comes to the information search for apparel products, this is less surprising. Fashion items are often symbolic items, therefore the decision is self-expressive and wrong decisions may be seen as having social consequences (Solomon & Rabolt, 2004b). Most purchase decisions entail a perceived risk, which is defined as

"the risk a customer believes exists in the purchase of a good or service from a specific retailer, whether or not a risk actually exists" (Rath et al., 2008, p. 279).

There are 5 risk areas: functional, monetary, physical, psychological and social (Rath et al., 2008).

A large amount of the effort during the decision-making process goes into the **evaluation of the alternatives**. The choice is not easy, since in some cases there are hundreds of alternatives, e.g. there are a lot of fashion brands. Consequently, consumers have to decide what criteria are important for them to narrow the choice down. The evoked set consists of all alternatives actively considered during the decision-making process. The inept set on the other hand, contains the alternatives that are not relevant for the purchase decision. Those alternatives considered in the actual buying decision are referred to as the inert set (Solomon & Rabolt, 2004b).

In order to select the best alternative, the key points that differentiate the products have to be evaluated. Those key points are called determinant attributes. Studies found the main decision criteria used by fashion consumers: Appropriateness (personal style), economy (usefulness), attractiveness (aesthetics), quality, image, country of origin and material (fiber and fabric) (Solomon & Rabolt, 2004b). Generally, consumers select the alternative that made the greatest impression. This alternative shows the biggest gap between the consumer's current and ideal situation (Rath et al., 2008).

Decision rules are frequently used tools to support the decision. Non-compensatory Decision Rules are the simplest form of decision rules. Consumers simply eliminate all options that don't meet their standards. Non-compensatory decision rules are primarily chosen if consumers aren't familiar with the product category and are not motivated to process complex information. Often, the brand name is the most important attribute. The most important attributes of the alternatives are compared and eventually one product is chosen (Solomon & Rabolt, 2004b). When compensatory decision rules are applied, the rating of the product is made by a variety of criteria. The whole product is looked at (Yurchisin & Johnson, 2010).

To simplify decisions, consumers use mental shortcuts. Especially in the case of limited problem solving, heuristics are often used to speed up the decision-making process (Solomon & Rabolt, 2004b). Commonly used heuristics in fashion are the price (the consumer tends to believe that a higher price stands for higher quality), the brand name and the country of origin (Yurchisin & Johnson, 2010, p.70) .

Decision-making among apparel consumers is influenced by a number of factors. The decision-making is done individually, however, people with similar characteristics are likely to behave in a comparable way. Those characteristics can be of demographic nature, such as gender and age. Also psychographic factors, such as lifestyle, that tie personality characteristics to consumer behavior have an impact on the buying decision. Moreover, the culture consumers live in and their financial situation influences their buying behavior (Yurchisin & Johnson, 2010, p.104).

In summary, consumption, especially when it comes to fashion and fashion related products such as accessories and shoes, is not always driven by rational thoughts. Emotions play a big role in fashion consumer behavior and the actual decision-making. Often, the purchase of apparel is considered as limited problem solving. The consumer in this case doesn't go through the traditional decision making model but instead uses mental shortcuts to make a decision. Determinant attributes and heuristics support this process.

3 Overview of Payment Methods used in Fashion Business

Consumers in fashion business today have the opportunity to choose among a continually increasing number of payment methods. In addition to traditional methods such as cash or even checks, the use of plastic payment methods like credit- and debit cards strongly increased over the past years (Soman, 2001).

In the following, payment methods commonly used for transactions in fashion business are depicted.

3.1 Cash

Cash is the most traditional form of payment. It is frequently used in the retail industry. Although there are many sophisticated payment methods, cash is still predominant in Germany's retail. However, a trend towards cashless payment systems is recognizable (EHI Retail Institute, 2014a).

Since cash is very well known, further explanations are not necessary.

3.2 Cashless Payment Systems

Cashless payment systems, also referred to as electronic money transfer systems (EMTS), utilize

> "web based technology, card based information or radio frequency identification (RFID) devices, (...) to direct instructions" (Khan, 2011, p. 14).

In order to gain market share, card based systems have to be acknowledged by three parties: banks need to issue the cards, retailers need to accept the cards and last but not least, customers need to use them (Mann, 2002). Card based systems can adopt several forms and have access to accumulated or borrowed funds at the customer's bank account (Khan, 2011).

Figure 38: Payment Service Providers

The figure above illustrates some of the most relevant payment service providers.

Although, hotels in the United States issued the first credit cards at the beginning of the 20th century (Khan, 2011), most credit and debit cards today are issued by banks and therefore are considered as bank customer cards.

Today's market leaders of the credit card industry, Visa and MasterCard, established in the 1960's and eliminated most of their competition (Khan, 2011). Physically, a Credit Card is simply a piece of plastic with a magnetic stripe applied on the back-side. From the cardholder's perspective however,

> "a credit card account represents an established credit line against which payments are deferred through creation of a loan from the sponsoring financial institution"
> (Khan, 2011, p. 15).

Credit card is a generic term used for various payment cards. It is to differentiate between "real" credit cards (which are described in this section) and other cards falling colloquially under the term credit card, such as delayed debit cards and smart cards (Deutsche Bank AG, 2014).

To begin with, one can differentiate among three types of credit cards: bank cards, travel and entertainment cards and proprietary cards.

As the name already implies, bank cards are issued by the bank based on the customer's credit ranking (Khan, 2011). They come with the logos of payment service providers such as Visa or MasterCard on them. Private companies on the other hand issue travel and entertainment cards. American Express and Diners Club are examples of those cards. Proprietary cards are also issued by private entities and are limited in negotiability. For instance, chain stores such as Sears or online retailers like Amazon may issue their own credit cards. Hence, they perform as the billing and collection agency. In all cases, an Internet connection is necessary for transaction (Khan, 2011).

Most credit cards offer four features: payment, drawing money out of an ATM, granting credit and extended benefits such as insurance (Balzer, 2012).

The number of credit card transactions (the study takes all kind of credit cards into account) in Germany is steadily growing. In 2010, about 482 million transactions were made with credit cards. In 2013, only three years later, credit cards accounted for about 715 million transactions (Deutsche Bundesbank, 2014b).

Physically a Debit card is also a piece of plastic with a magnetic stripe on the back. This stripe includes information about the account number and also information that is necessary to verify transactions (Mann, 2002).

Debit cards have two main functions, as they act as transaction medium and access liquidity. They subtract money from the customer's account and transfer it to the retailer's (Khan, 2011, p.20). The fund is withdrawn from the customer's account, without further actions by the cardholder, in one to two days (Mann, 2002). In order that a transaction can take place, some kind of Internet connection is required. The retailer only accepts the debit card for payment if the issuer of the card can verify that the amount of money will be withdrawn from the cardholder's account (Mann, 2002).

Over the last few years, debit cards in Germany developed into multi functional cards. Through the cooperation of several systems on one card (e.g. maestro and EC), those cards can be used domestically as well as internationally. The chip applied on the card can include additional information and functions, such as a smart card function.

For instance, Deutsche Bank offers a card that includes a smart card function, an electronic cash function and also maestro services. With cards like this, customers are able to pay cashless worldwide, wherever maestro cards are accepted (Deutsche Bank AG, 2014).

The number of transactions with debit cards in Germany continually increases. In 2013, debit cards made 2.95 billion transactions (Deutsche Bundesbank, 2014a).

Oftentimes, debit cards come decorated with the same logos as credit cards from payment service providers such as MasterCard and Visa (Runnemark, Hedman, & Xiao, 2014).

Pure Smart cards require a specific amount of money to be transferred onto them. Those cards usually do not have access to the customer's bank account but only to the amount stored on the card (Khan, 2011). Smart cards are not commonly used to pay with in fashion retail and therefore are not further explained.

3.2.1 Payment Systems in E-Commerce

Common payment methods in e-commerce are purchasing on account, PayPal, credit and debit card (EHI Retail Institute, 2014b).

Purchasing on account is still frequently chosen with online purchases (EHI Retail Institute, 2014b). As a recent study shows, customers rate this payment method as one of the top methods in almost all categories among e-commerce payment methods. Customers believe that purchasing on account is the most secure online payment method and that their personal data is safe with this method (Weinfurtner, Wittmann, Stahl, Wittmann, & Pur, 2013).

PayPal is an online payment system. Companies, as well as private customers can either receive or make payments with their e-mail address only. PayPal is known to be a secure and convenient online payment system. In 2002, it was acquired by eBay.

More than 15 million people in Germany already trust PayPal. Furthermore, statistics show that it is a common way to pay for online purchases (EHI Retail Institute, 2014b). Many online stores in the fashion sector offer PayPal as a payment method.

For instance, Zara online shop offers paying with PayPal among other payment modes (Zara, 2010).

PayPal also offers mobile payments (Bielski, 2010). With mobile devices, the company tries to establish itself in the brick and mortar business. PayPal App customers can check-in into a store and the cashier can recognize them on the basis of their profile picture, which pops-up on the register display. This payment method relies on Beacons (Kling, 2013). The payment can be made without holding any device in hands (Pakalski, 2013). However, this payment method is still in its pilot phase and is getting tested in some Cafes in Berlin (Richtscheid, 2013). Hence, it will not be explained further.

3.2.2 Mobile Payment Systems based on NFC Technology

Most recent developments concerning payment methods are based on NFC (near field communication) technology. Khan defines wireless mobile payment as a

"transaction processing in which the payer uses mobile communication techniques in conjunction with mobile devices for initiation, authorization, and confirmation of an exchange of financial value in return for goods and services" (Khan, 2011, p. 15).

Smart phones are already used on a daily basis by a growing number of customers. Being able to use them also to pay for purchases in store would be a major breakthrough in terms of customer convenience (Lerner, 2013). A study by KPMG and ECC Köln found that already in 2010, more than 20% of the respondents knew about NFC based payment systems, more than 5% had already used it at that time and almost 35% would like to try it in the future (KPMG & ECC, 2010).

The credit card industry also supports mobile payments. They push the United States' retail to upgrade more payment terminals with NFC technology so that mobile payments will be more widespread in the future (Hamblen, 2012).

The European retail is prepared for mobile payments as Visa launched its first contactless payment terminals already in 2007. By today, there are about 1.5 million of those Visa terminals around Europe and they are all ready to take mobile payments (VisaEurope, 2014).

Apple Pay and Google Wallet are two examples of payment systems that already rely on near field communication (NFC)(Maycott, 2014).

Both of them are already quite popular in the United States. Those payment methods enhance the convenience of payments. Moreover, they also enhance the security (Maycott, 2014).

With Apple Pay, the customer's credit card data is tokenized and saved on a secure a chip, which is located in the phone (Maycott, 2014). Apple Pay is already accepted by a large number of retailers around the United States. There are also many apparel retailers and departments stores among those. For instance, Aeropostale, American Eagle Outfitters, Bloomingdale's, Macy's and Nike (Apple, 2014).

The customer is able to recognize NFC payment terminals by the symbols presented below.

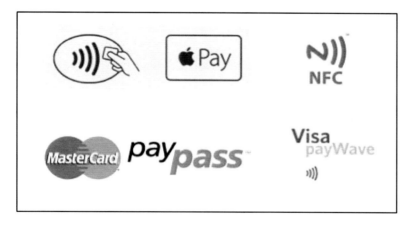

Figure 39: NFC Symbols

4 Transparency of a Payment Method and its Impact on the Buying Decision

Business and economic literature suggest that a transaction is an unemotional matter in which a specific amount of money is exchanged for a product or a service.

However, parting with money is far more than the plain exchange of money for goods or services. Most consumers feel some kind of pain when parting with their money. The term *pain of paying* was formed by Zellmayer to describe the emotions of customers while parting with money (Soman, 2003). The pain felt when making a payment depends not only on the amount spent, but it also depends on the way the payment is made, the payment method. This implies that the payment method could have an impact on the buying decision (Soman, 2003).

A study by Soman found that consumers experienced different levels of pain depending on the payment method they used (Soman, 2001). For instance, the study shows that consumers who are paying by card based payment methods tend to feel less pain when parting with their money than cash payers (Soman, 2001).

Times when cash was by far the predominant payment method are long ago. Nowadays consumers can choose among a lot of different payment methods, as explained above. In many parts of the world, even plastic payment methods such as debit and credit cards are getting outdated at this point in time. For instance, with mobile payments relying on near field communication, the world moves towards a more sophisticated payment system.

Payment methods differ among each other in many points. The perceived degree of transparency of a payment is one of them. It is assumed that the perceived transparency of the payment relates notably to the perceived pain of paying experienced with different payment methods when parting with money (Soman, 2003). Therefore, it is assumed that the perceived transparency of a payment method has an impact on the spending and consumption behavior.

In general, researchers focus on four theories to explain how payment methods have an impact on consumption behavior and purchase decision-making: Prospective and retro-prospective mental accounting, pain of paying and transparency of a payment (Khan, 2011). This paper focuses on the effect the perceived transparency has on the buying decision. Therefore, the focus is put on this topic and other aspects, such as mental accounting might not be considered in detail.

4.1 What is Transparency of a Payment Method?

The term transparency of a payment method is defined as

> *"the relative salience of the payment, both in terms of physical form and the amount, relative to paying by cash"* (Soman, 2003, p. 175).

In this definition cash is considered as the benchmark since it is the most transparent form of payment. When paying cash, the payment is very salient. It is easy for the consumer to see that money is being spent and also how much money is being spent (Soman, 2003).

The term transparency of a payment method describes how noticeable the payment for the consumer is. On the one hand, the physical form of the payment is included in this definition. The physical form expresses what payment method is used, since it differs among the various payment methods. The physical forms of cash payments are either coins or bills. With cashless payment methods the physical forms can either consist of a piece of plastic with a magnetic stripe on the back, as it is the case with card based payment methods like debit or credit cards. On the other hand, the physical form can be nonexistent as in online shopping for instance. Looking at online payments made by PayPal, there is no physical form of the payment recognizable. Mobile payments using near field communication also do not show a physical form of the payment method. However, in this case, one could argue that the phone, which is used to make the transaction, could be seen as the physical form of the payment.

In addition to the physical form, the definition above also includes the amount of money being spent. The salience of the payment in terms of the amount that is spent differs depending on the payment method chosen. With cash payments, the amount being spent is clearly visible since the customer has to count the coins and the bills before handing them to the cashier. Payments made by cashless payment methods such as card based payment methods are less salient. Reasons are that the amount is not as visible since it only appears on a screen and the customer then has to approve the payment by either a signature or a pin code.

4.2 Classification of Payment Methods in the Degree of Transparency and Utilization

The figure below illustrates the classification of payment methods in their degree of transparency and utilization. The degree of transparency of each payment method is classified according to the definition of transparency of a payment above. Statistics were used to classify the degree of utilization. Therefore, there is a geographic focus on the German market.

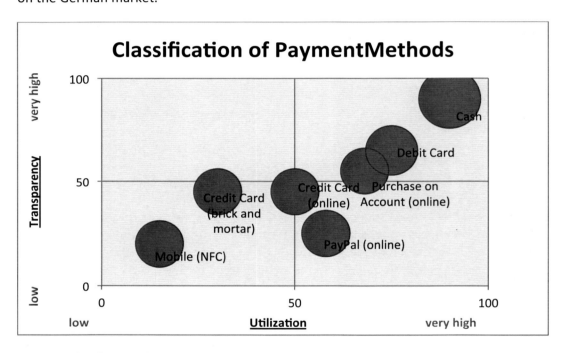

Figure 40: Classification of Payment Methods

4.2.1 Cash

Degree of transparency

Cash is even considered as the benchmark since it is the most transparent form of payment. When using cash, the payment is very salient for the consumer. The buyer sees exactly how much money he or she is spending. The salience of the form, as well as the amount is very high. The relative timing of money outflow and purchase is concurrent. Those factors lead to a high transparency (Soman, 2003).

Degree of utilization

A recent statistic (only considers the German market) shows that the share of cash payments declines. However, it is with a share of 54.4% still the most used payment method (EHI Retail Institute, 2014a). Therefor, the degree of utilization is classified as very high.

Moving from cash towards card based payment methods, the salience of the payment and with it the transparency weakens.

4.2.2 Debit Card

Degree of transparency

The salience of the payment in terms of the physical form and also in terms of the amount is considered to be medium. The actual outflow of money from the customer's account happens shorty after the purchase is done. Hence, the transparency resulting of those factors is classified as medium (Soman, 2003).

Degree of utilization

A statistic shows that the use of cards on which money is deducted shortly after the purchase is quite high. Payments with cards like this accounted in 2013 for approximately 30% of all retail sales in Germany (EHI Retail Institute, 2014a). However, there are no statistics available that show the mere use of debit cards. Since debit cards show similar features to the cards describes in the statistic (EC-Cash and Electronic Direct Debit), it is assumed that the degree if utilization is quite alike and can be classified as medium to high.

4.2.3 Credit Card

Degree of transparency

The salience of the payment in terms of the physical form and the amount is obviously weaker than it is with cash. It is pretty similar to the salience of a debit card, however the actual outflow of money occurs significantly after the purchase was made (Soman, 2003). Therefore, the transparency of the payment is classified to be a bit lower compared to debit cards.

Degree of utilization

Considering Germany's whole retail business, credit cards accounted for 5.4% of total sales in 2013 (EHI Retail Institute, 2014a). This number seems to be low, however it needs be taken into account that it includes all retail industries with both, online and brick and mortar businesses. When considering online retailing only, it is noticeable that the use of credit cards declined over the past years. In 2012, credit cards had a market share of about 20% in online payment methods. One year later, the market share of credit cards reduced to approximately 15% (EHI Retail Institute, 2014c). All in all, the degree of utilization of credit cards can be classified as medium to high.

4.2.4 Purchase on account

Degree of transparency

With online purchases made on account, the physical form of the payment does not exist. However, the amount is rather salient since the customer has to transfer it actively. Usually, the timing of the payment is delayed after the time of purchase (Soman, 2003). From this, it follows that the transparency of purchasing on account is on a medium to a low level.

Degree of utilization

Taking the numbers of Germany's whole retail business into account, purchasing on account only is of marginal importance. This payment method only accounts for less than 3% of all sales (EHI Retail Institute, 2014a). Nevertheless, in online retailing purchasing on account shows the highest market share (25.4% in 2013) among online payment methods (EHI Retail Institute, 2014c). Hence, the degree of utilization of purchasing on account can be classified as medium to high.

4.2.5 PayPal

Degree of transparency

Payments are made by typing in the e-mail address and a password. Hence, the payment is not salient in physical form. Also the amount is not as salient as with purchasing on account, because the customer doesn't have to transfer the money actively. Thus, the transparency of this payment method is low; it is even lower than the payment transparency of credit cards.

With the PayPal App, with which customers can check-in at stores or restaurants, the actual payment process moves to the background, and a great customer experience moves up front (Richtscheid, 2013). This leads to a further reduction of the salience of the payment and with it a reduction of the transparency.

Degree of utilization

A recent study shows that PayPal has a great acceptance on the German payment market. It is actually the second most used payment method in online shopping with a market share of almost 20% in 2013 (EHI Retail Institute, 2014c). The development over the past years shows a rapid growth, in 2011 PayPal only had a market share of about 13% (EHI Retail Institute, 2014c). It is assumed, that this payment method is still gaining market share.

Supposedly, PayPal not only establishes its payment service in an online environment, but also tries to enter the brick and mortar business. However, paying in an offline environment with the PayPal App in Germany is still tested in the pilot phase (Richtscheid, 2013). Therefore, the degree of utilization is still very low. However, in online shopping it is a common way of payment. All in all, PayPal's degree of utilization can be classified as medium.

4.2.6 Mobile Payment based on NFC technology

Degree of transparency

The salience of the form as well as of the amount is even lower with mobile payments (Soman, 2003). As explained above, making the payment is simple. The customer merely needs to hold his or her phone close to a NFC device (Maycott, 2014). It is difficult for the consumer to see how much money he or she actually spent, since the salience of the payment in terms of the amount is very low. Consequently, the transparency of mobile payments can be classified as very low. They can almost be classified as opaque.

Degree of utilization

In fact, Visa launched its first contactless terminals in stores around Europe already in 2007 (VisaEurope, 2014). However, NFC based payments are still rare around here. A study shows that more than 40% of the interviewed retailers believe that payment based on NFC will be relevant for their business within the next 1-3 years (EHI Retail Institute, 2011). Therefore, the degree of utilization can be considered as very low, however the technology has a great potential to grow.

Germany is after the United Kingdom the country within the E.U. that has the most cashless payment transactions (EZB, 2013).

4.3 Impact of Transparency of a Payment Method on Consumer Behavior and the Buying Decision

There are several theories explaining how the payment method influences consumer behavior and the buying decision. One theory describing the relationship between the payment method and the buying decision deals with the perceived transparency of the payment. In the following, it is presented how and in what way the perceived transparency of the payment has an impact on the consumption behavior.

The perceived degree of transparency of a payment differs among various payment methods (Soman, 2003). As described above, cash is the most transparent form of payment. When paying cash, the payment is very salient for the consumer, in both, the physical form and the amount. Moving from cash over card-based payment methods to more abstract and sophisticated payment methods, such as mobile payments, the degree of transparency continually weakens.

There are multiple studies and experiments, which proof that the degree of transparency of a payment impacts consumption behavior.

For instance, a study by Soman aimed at demonstrating that different levels of transparency of a payment method have an impact on consumption behavior. Therefore, participants of the study were instructed to photocopy all articles they find relevant to a certain topic. For this purpose, a two-condition experiment was set up. Half of the participants were given prepaid cards to pay for the photocopies, the other half were given coins to pay for it. Findings were, that participants spend more money on photocopying in the card condition than in the cash condition. As a conclusion, the study proofed that perceived transparency of the payment has an impact on the consumption behavior (Soman, 2003).

Another study, also by Soman, had two goals. First, the study's purpose was to show that consumers paying with less transparent payment mechanisms tend to buy more non-essential products than consumers paying for their purchases with highly transparent payment methods. The second goal of the study was to proof that payment transparency doesn't affect the purchase behavior of essential products. Results could support both statements. The less transparent the payment method was, the more money consumers would spend. However, this applied only to non-essential products (Soman, 2003).

Prelec and Simester came to quite similar results: Respondents would be willing to spend a lot more for the same product when advised to use a credit card rather than when advised to use cash (Prelec & Simester, 2001). Again, the results of the study could be explained by the transparency of the payment method.

Furthermore, Moore and Taylor conducted a survey to describe the willingness to pay for products by payment conditions (A. Moore & Taylor, 2011). Within the survey, they distinguished between cash payments, credit card payments and two kinds of debit card payments. The statistical analysis showed that consumer's willingness to spend was much higher with card-based payment methods than with cash payments (A. Moore & Taylor, 2011). Besides, when it came to enforcing financial self-

pain of paying does not only depend on the amount spent, but also on the payment method used (Soman, 2003).

As classified above, divers payment methods feature different levels of transparency. The less transparent the payment is, the less pain is experienced. It is natural that consumers try to avoid the pain of paying, or at least try to keep it at a low level. Consequently, the consumption and spending behavior is influenced. Reduced transparency naturally leads to increased consumption (Soman, 2003).

The psychological pain of paying experienced when parting with money functions as a controlling and observing mechanism by sending out immediate signals about conceivable consequences of spending money (Khan, 2011). In this case, pain could be considered as

> *"the degree of annoyance experienced with the parting of money"* (Khan, 2011, p. 25).

By functioning as a self-regulation tool, the pain of paying undermines the pleasure resulting from consumption (Prelec & Loewenstein, 1998).

Hedonic efficiency and decision efficiency play an important role regarding the pain of paying. On the one hand, the pain of paying is an important tool for consumer's the self-regulation. On the other hand, it is hedonically costly. From a hedonic point of view, the ideal situation would be one in which the payment would be strongly coupled to consumption. The payment would induce thoughts about the benefits. Consequently, the pain of payment would be eased by thoughts of the benefits resulting from the purchase. Moreover, in this ideal situation, the consumption would be decoupled from the payment, so it wouldn't evoke thoughts about the payment. (Prelec & Loewenstein, 1998)

Coupling of payments is a concept that describes to which degree the consumer relates the payment to the purchase, and vice versa (Prelec & Loewenstein, 1998, p.4). It differs among payment methods. Some payment methods weaken coupling, whereas others strengthen it. Card-based payment methods, such as credit cards, seem to weaken coupling. Cash payments on the other hand show tight coupling between the payment and the purchase (Prelec & Loewenstein, 1998).

Considering the situation from an efficiency perspective, it is essential for the consumer to be aware of the payment. Consumers need to know how much they spent. Hence, a tension between the decision efficiency and the hedonic efficiency is resulting from this (Prelec & Loewenstein, 1998).

All in all, the transparency of a payment method influences consumption behavior. However, it could be said that the impact is rather indirect. The transparency of a payment relates positively to the pain of paying, which serves as a psychological self-regulation tool. Also it is interesting to note that the less transparent a payment is, the weaker it is coupled to consumption and therefore the value transferred is dulled.

Concluding, the less transparent a payment is, the less pain of paying is experienced and therefore, the willingness to spend and the consumption in total might be higher.

The explanations above show that especially card-based payment methods lead consumers to overspend. It is assumed that even less transparent payment methods, such as mobile payments, would further increase consumption. However, there are no studies available at this point in time to verify that assumption.

Moreover, there are other theories trying to explain the cause of overspending with card-based payment methods, and especially with credit cards. Despite the perceived degree of transparency, Feinberg's credit card effect tries to explain the overspending with credit cards. The experiment's goal was to examine the willingness to spend for unbranded items (dress, tent, sweater, etc.) (Khan, 2011). Half of the participants looked at the catalogue with these products in the presence of a credit card stimulus, the other half in the absence of any stimuli (Feinberg, 1986). The participants within the credit card condition were willing to pay about 50%-200% relative to the estimates of the control group (Feinberg, 1986). Feinberg justified the results with two theoretical explanations: classical conditioning and a weapons effect. Classical conditioning occurs when

> "a conditioned stimulus (CS) is paired with an unconditioned stimulus (US) invokes an unconditioned response (UR) until the CS produces the same or a similar response – conditioned response (CR)- by itself" (Shimp & Moody, 2000, p. 19).

Referred to the situation, an artificial stimulus is paired with a natural stimulus. The credit card logo is related to spending and therefore has an impact on spending. Spending money as a reaction can be eventually triggered by the artificial stimulus, the credit card logo. The second explanation is curious as it suggests that the credit card logo encourages aggressive behavior. Perhaps, this refers to risk type behavior (Khan, 2011).

Replications of the study did not come to the same results. Shimp and Moody found that the credit card logo has no noticeable effect on spending behavior (Shimp & Moody, 2000).

The explanations above point out, that the effect of a credit card logo on the spending behavior is not clear. Therefore, the effect of transparency of a payment on consumption is even more relevant.

5   Implications for the Fashion Business

It is to determine, whether the transparency of a payment method has an impact on consumption behavior in fashion business or not. Inferring from the above, the payment transparency might actually influence the purchase behavior and the buying decision in fashion business. Studies found that the perceived degree of transparency of a payment method has an impact on consumption. The less transparent a payment is, the greater the willingness to spend will be.

However, this only applies to non-essential products (Soman, 2003, p.181-182). Fashion products can be classified as non-essential. For most consumers, buying apparel is more of a want, than a need. Needs derive from instincts and are innate drives which everyone is born with (Rath et al., 2008). For instance, basic needs are food, water, sleep, and warmth. Clothes could also be seen as needs in some cases. They could be considered as needs, if their primary purpose was to protect the body from environmental influences, such as cold weather. However, this is not the case with most fashion purchases. Usually, consumers buy fashion because they want to. Even though wants are not necessities, they can enhance one's live. Wants are rather driven by desires than by instincts, since they are not required for survival. Hence, consumer's wants are for the most part resulting from psychological and social forces (Rath et al., 2008). This is why fashion is a non-essential good and therefore the consumption behavior is influenced by the transparency of the payment as described above.

Moreover, it is assumed that fashion consumption is not only influenced by transparency but the effect is even reinforced by typical consumer behavior in fashion business. The purchase of fashion items is often an impulsive decision. The emotional involvement is higher than the cognitive (Homburg & Krohmer, 2009). Typically, the consumer doesn't go through the traditional decision-making model but instead uses mental shortcuts to make a decision.

The payment process is also far more than the mere exchange of money for goods. Most consumers feel some kind of pain when parting with their money (Soman, 2003). In a decision efficiency perspective, the pain of paying functions as a financial self-regulation tool by sending out signals about conceivable consequences. The more transparent a payment is, the more pain of paying is experienced and therefore, the more signals are sent out.

However, since fashion consumption is often more driven by emotions and hedonics, the consumption behavior converges towards a hedonic perspective. From a hedonic point of view, the ideal situation would be one in which the payment would be strongly coupled to consumption, so it would induce thoughts about the benefits resulting from the purchase. The pain of paying would be eased by the notion of the benefits resulting from consumption. Moreover, in this ideal situation, the consumption would be decoupled from the payment, so it wouldn't evoke thoughts about the payment (Prelec & Loewenstein, 1998).

It is to consider, that consumption behavior also depends on personality and other influencing factors. Therefore, fashion consumption behavior neither relies on a pure decision efficiency perspective, nor a pure and ideal hedonic perspective. However, since fashion consumption is emotionally driven, it tends to be more on the hedonic side. The hedonic approach supports the effect of transparency of a payment method.

Driving Excitement through Click and Collect

Claudia Will/Jochen Strähle

Abstract

Purpose – This seminar paper will illustrate how a fashion retailer can emotionalize the process of click and collect.

Research approach – A literature research about click and collect, consumer's behavior in today's retail environment and the major factors of influence on consumer's emotions is conducted. For the literature research, books and articles of learned journals and of major databases provided by the library of Reutlingen University were used.

Findings – Click and collect should be transformed into a unique shopping experience in order to drive excitement and to provide an added value.

Research limitations/implications – This paper mainly analyzes the in-store part of click and collect, meaning the pick up process of the customer. It does not analyze how emotions in the online environment can be created.

Keywords – Emotions, multichannel retailing, click and collect, customer's buying behavior, influence of store environment, influence of sales personnel.

Paper type – Research paper

1 Introduction

In today's world, customers expect retailers to provide an equal amount of products and services. It does not matter where these products and services come from, whether it is from the Internet, a catalogue or a smart phone. Apart from this, customers wish for a seamless shopping experience, meaning that they can shift effortlessly from a digital to a physical channel whenever they like. They want to have the possibility to return or exchange articles in-store, even if the article has been ordered via the online shop. Plus, customers wish to annul or change orders in any channel, no matter which channel has been used to initiate the transaction (Heinemann & Schwarzl, 2010)

Thus, every fourth of the 100 biggest fashion retailers in Germany has introduced the process of click and collect in the German market, meaning that the customers can order products online and pick them up in the store (Rösch, 2014). Moreover, some retailers even include a click and collect lounge within their store that is reserved only for in-store pick-ups. Consequently, click and collect customers are treated on a special service level that differs from the level for offline customers who merely go into the store to buy an article (Mahar, Salzarulo, & Daniel Wright, 2012). However, when compared to the European market, German shoppers rarely use click and collect and do not consider it relevant.

But how come that Germans do not consider click and collect relevant? One reason could be the geographical and infrastructural frame conditions that already allow a fast and relatively cheap shipping of packages in Germany (Schramm-Klein, Wagner, Neus, Swoboda, & Foscht, 2014b). However, a reason that seems rather possible is the fact that click and collect is still a very unemotional process in Germany (Haupt, 2014a). Yet, it is important to mention that the process of click and collect is not a closed book. The British, for example, are considered the world's most frequent users of click and collect and show that click and collect is a sales channel with a huge growth potential (Diehl-Wobbe, 2014). Thus, this paper is guided by the research question: *How can a fashion retailer emotionalize the process of click and collect?*

There is a widespread amount of academic literature on multichannel retailing, mostly focusing on multichannel shopping behavior, that is customer's buying behavior towards the several channels offered and the customer's channel choice (R. R. Dholakia, Zhao, & Dholakia, 2005; Goldsmith & Flynn, 2005; Schoenbachler & Gordon, 2002). Apart from this, a lot of academic literature focuses on the advantages of multichannel retailing and on successful implementation of a multichannel strategy (Bagge, 2007; Berman & Thelen, 2004; J. Zhang et al., 2010b). Also, academic research has deeply examined socio-demographic and psychographic attributes of multichannel shoppers who switch between channels in the buying process (Verhoef, Neslin, & Vroomen, 2007). Moreover, academic literature provides a comprehensive insight into possible future developments of multichannel retailing (Heinemann, 2013b; Heinemann & Schwarzl, 2010).

However, there is no clear distinction between "multichannel", "omnichannel" and "cross-channel" in literature, as these attributes are mostly used synonymously by authors. All of theses attributes describe the same approach (meaning a consistent and customer-focused connection of distribution channels), yet include different strategic approaches (Schramm-Klein et al., 2014). Click and collect is also known as "order online pick up in-store"(Chatterjee, 2010, p. 431) and "in-store pick up" (Berman & Thelen, 2004). However, the process of click and collect is so far mainly discussed in specialist journals (Davis, 2014; Hackenberg, 2013; Haupt, 2014a) and the reason why people order online and pick their order up in-store is not directly explored (Chatterjee, 2010).

Yet, research has investigated the phenomenon of customers using different channels for researching and purchasing (Verhoef et al., 2007c), as well as the significant differences between online and offline shopping (Eroglu, Machleit, & Davis, 2003; Grewal, Iyer, & Levy, 2004).

Finally, though there is widespread literature about measuring customers' emotional responses to shopping experiences as well as responses to shopping environments (Donovan & Rossiter, 1982b; Foxall & Greenley, 1999; Machleit & Eroglu, 2000) there is no literature available about how to emotionalize the process of click and collect so far.

The structure of this paper is as follows: First, today's retail environment is described and a differentiation between multichannel retailing and omnichannel retailing is provided. This should serve as a base to understand click and collect as an integral part of omnichannel retailing and to understand the process of click and collect itself. Then, this paper will describe customers' buying behavior. In this context, the paper will shortly the buying decision-making process and customers' behavior in today's multichannel environment. Chapter 4 gives an overview of emotions in fashion retail and how consumer's emotions can be influenced via different factors. These factors include the store environment, music, scents and the sales personnel. Plus, emotions in the online environment will shortly be described. This chapter serves as a base to derive measures on the topic of how to emotionalize the shopping process in general. The discussion part of this paper combines the literature about click and collect and the literature about emotions in order to provide recommendations on how the process of click and collect can be emotionalized and thus can be improved. The last chapter deals with the limitations of this paper and the fields of research that can be interesting for future research.

2 The New Retail Environment

2.1 Difference between Multichannel and Omnichannel Retailing

Many dismiss omnichannel retailing as merely a new way of defining multichannel retailing, which has been around for more than one decade. However, there is a distinct difference: Multichannel retailing in general refers to the manifold ways a customer can purchase something (Hobkirk, 2013). Moreover, "The practice of trading using two or more methods of distribution concurrently is known as multichannel retailing" (L. R. Poloian, 2013). Consequently, while there are still some firms operating only online or offline, more and more companies turn into multichannel firms. Also, multichannel firms provide bigger exposure and reach to the customer's market (Frambach, Roest, & Krishnan, 2007). Also, several studies show that customers using multiple channels spend more money compared to customers using single channels (Berman & Thelen, 2004). However, the channels of multichannel retailing are several separate channels, which are not integrated (Tritsch, 2014). As a result, this approach fails to include customers who want synergy and service through all channels, who see the retail brand as a unity and who now demand a combination of the multiple channels (Driscoll, 2013). Retailers that do not integrate their channels might miss the chance of profit-maximizing opportunities (Chatterjee, 2010). Thus, "Multichannel retailing has evolved into omnichannel retailing (...)" (Dickenson, 2013, p. 28).

Omnichannel retailing refers to an approach that is completely integrated across the entire retail operation. This retail operation provides a smooth response to the consumer experience via all existing shopping channels, whether on smartphones, tablets, computers, on television, in a retailer's shop or in catalogue. Moreover, omnichannel retailing gives the customer the possibility to experience the brand itself, and not one of multiple channels within a brand. Plus, omnichannel retailing provides a wider product choice, due to the reason that the online store normally offers an extended assortment (Driscoll, 2013). Apart from this, omnichannel retailing gives the customer the possibility to shop at any time, at any place and to switch between several channels (for example: order online, pick up in store) (Tritsch, 2014).

To sum up, "Omnichannel retailing is the optimal practice of aligning merchandising, logistics, technologies, and all other functions fully in order to serve customers consistently well across all selling options" (L. R. Poloian, 2013).

As already mentioned in the beginning, there is no clear distinction between the terms "multichannel", "omnichannel" and "cross-channel" in literature. In order to ensure accurate citation, the author will be using the terms used in the academic literature, though some of these terms mean omnichannel retailing.

2.2 Click and Collect as an Integral Part of Omnichannel Retailing

Giving the customer the ability to pick up his order in-store can be done by two different approaches: First, the *site-to-store* practice, meaning that a retailer does not fulfill a customer's online order with inventory from the store but transports the ordered items from the warehouse to a nearby store for pickup. The customer does not have to pay for this shipment, but might have to wait several days until the order is ready for pickup. The second possibility is the *immediate in-store pickup*, meaning that retailers use their inventory on hand to satisfy pickup orders. Consequently, products bought online may be ready for pickup relatively fast (Mahar et al., 2012). However, this paper will mainly focus on the *site-to-store* practice, meaning click and collect.

In comparison with a multichannel retailer, a cross-channel retailer that offers "order online pick up in store" service provides an extra channel. Consequently, the customer can initiate the purchase transaction in one channel and finish it in another channel (e.g. collect the item in-store). This gives the customer the possibility to take advantages of the benefits of each channel (e.g. being able to look for information about a product on the internet during brand choice and collect the item in-store), while not having to pay additional costs (e.g. travel costs for gaining information about different brands, shipping charges when ordering via the online store), inherent in each channel (Chatterjee, 2010).

Click and collect offers several advantages, such as the possibility of generating additional sales when the customer picks up the order, the possibility to bring the traffic from the company's website back to the store and the possibility to offer alternative products if the ordered item has to be returned (Schramm-Klein et al., 2014). Moreover, many multichannel retailers give the customer the possibility to return online-ordered items in-store, which is not only beneficial for reducing costs for return handling, but also offers an added value to the customers (Forrester Research, 2005).

In a pure online store, the process of returning an item that has been ordered online and the process of obtaining refunds is a rather tedious one. Customers sometimes have to pay for returns, pack the item and bring it to a post office (Grewal et al., 2004). In contrast to that, click and collect can have a positive impact on a retailer's performance by leading to unplanned purchasing by customers (Chatterjee, 2010).

However, if a customer does not pick up his click and collect order, retailers might face problems as the ordered items are normally reserved for the customer for 7 to 14 days. If the customer does not pick up his order, the ordered item is dead capital for the retailer, because he cannot sell it until it is sent back. As already mentioned, there is a new retail environment, meaning a shift from multichannel to omnichannel retailing. Click and collect is an integral part of the latter, because people who order via click and collect use two different, yet connected, channels to get their order delivered. Customers using click and collect visit a fashion shop's website as well as a fashion shop's physical retail environment. As a result, the customer is supposed to get the best of both channels: A convenient order in an online environment and a professional consultation in the physical store (Zimmer, 2014).

3 Buying Behavior

3.1 The Buying Decision-Making Process

(L. R. Poloian, 2013) defines six steps in the decision making process that normally lead customers to buy goods or services:

1. Stimulus. The decision of a customer to buy is not without cause. A stimulus can come in several forms, either from the external surroundings or from within.

2. Problem awareness. A customer's need or want that is unfilled demands to be satisfied.

3. Information search. The customer is searching for facts and figures to accelerate the decision-making process. Collecting information or advertisement material, get information from opinion leaders or looking up information online are activities done by the customer at this stage.

4. Evaluation of alternatives. At this point, the customer studies the received information and ranks choices accordingly.

5. Purchase. The customer has made his decision for one particular product or service and the transaction is done.

6. Postpurchase behavior. The experience of shopping should satisfy the customer. If not, the customer will not repeat the purchase.

These six steps are based on the Consumer Decision Process model by Blackwell, Miniard & Engel, which includes similar stages and illustrates "a roadmap of consumers' minds, that marketers and managers can use to help guide product mix, communication, and sales strategies" (Blackwell, Miniard, & Engel, 2001, p. 71).

With these steps in mind, it is important to also mention the purchase decision process. The process of selecting a distinctive retail store implies that consumer characteristics as well as purchase characteristics need to match the store characteristics. A consumer might consider different aspects to assess which store meets his needs, related to the type of purchase (Blackwell et al., 2001).

3.2 Customers' Behavior in a Multichannel Environment

For multichannel retailers, it is of particular importance to know their customers' behavior and to understand the reasons, especially the shopping motives that lead to this behavior. Doing so is the only possibility to make sure that there is an adequate deployment of resources in the management of the distinct channels. Consequently, retailers can plainly identify customer groups and can take better care of them (Schröder & Zaharia, 2008). Moreover, if multichannel retailers understood what leads customers to purchase from one or multiple channels, marketers could better forecast the probability of attracting new customers with innovative channels and also the probability of cannibalizing existing sales (Schoenbachler & Gordon, 2002). Thus, multichannel retailers have to track customers in an efficient way and need to understand the several types of multichannel patterns based on the customer's shopping experience (Hsiao, Ju Rebecca Yen, & Li, 2012).

(Hsiao et al., 2012) discovered in a study about consumer value in multichannel shopping that pragmatism is the most significant value that customers chase in a multichannel environment. This suggests that pragmatic customers are rather willing to use a multichannel environment in order to manage their money, effort and time wisely. Plus, the study shows that multichannel shoppers achieve shopping enjoyment through gathering special knowledge, which arises from looking at the different product assortments that a retailer offers. Consequently, customers regard multichannel shopping a provider of information to efficiently increase their product-relevant knowledge. Furthermore, customers "treat [multichannel shopping] as an experiential process that satisfies their inner pleasure during the knowledge-acquiring process" (Hsiao et al., 2012).

Apart from this, (Schröder & Zaharia, 2008) discovered in their study about multichannel customer behavior and shopping motives "that five theory- based shopping motives could be established: convenience orientation, recreational orientation, independence orientation, delivery-related risk aversion, and product- and payment-related risk aversion"(Schröder & Zaharia, 2008). Moreover, they discovered in their study that the majority of customers stay in the same channel when it comes to information and purchasing purposes. As for customers who divide the purchasing process over two channels, the prevalent pattern is that customers look for information online and purchase their product in-store (Schröder & Zaharia, 2008). Consequently, "Multi-channel users, who seek information from the online-shop and then make their purchase in the chain stores, are clearly linking independence of information from the online-shop with the reduction in product- and payment-related risk associated with a purchase in a chain store, which allows them to examine and check the products" (Schröder & Zaharia, 2008). This behavior, meaning searching for information in one channel and buying in another channel, has also been discovered by (Balasubramanian, Raghunathan, & Mahajan, 2005).

Actually, this behavior is equivalent to click and collect, meaning ordering instead of researching online and purchasing offline in-store. But how come that customers mainly show this behavior in a multichannel environment?

First, consumers consider "convenience" and the possibility to "search for the lowest price" reliable elements that have an influence on their online purchases (Gajanan & Basuroy, 2007). Moreover, consumers perceive online shopping beneficial regarding selection, easy and extensive information access and regarding privacy. This is due to the fact that online shoppers are enabled to view, compare and purchase products of which they might be hesitant to buy in-store (Ahuja, Gupta, & Raman, 2003). Plus, "Websites have the potential advantage of presenting an almost limitless inventory, since the size of the 'showroom' has no inherent constraints" (Browne, Durrett, & Wetherbe, 2004, p. 244). However, when a consumer decides to order online, he has to pay the transportation charges and the waiting time costs until the product has been delivered. In contrast to online shopping stands the traditional retailer that pays most of the shipping costs and waiting time costs. Besides, a traditional retailer offers customers a physical accessibility and a direct product possession. Yet, consumers need to incur more physical and monetary effort and time to get to the retail store, find the product's physical location and wait at the checkout line. Online shopping, however, lessens the physical and monetary effort to get to the retail store, but consumers must pay shipping charges to get the order delivered. Thus, a customer's decision on a specific channel during ordering, payment and delivery phase of the purchase transaction process is reliant on compromises they make concerning waiting time and effort required to complete each phase in the channel, and differs over shopping occasion (Chatterjee, 2010).

4 Emotions in Fashion Retail

4.1 Influencing Customers' Emotions via Store Environment

"Studying the effect of the environment on human behavior has its roots in Psychology. In his stimulus-response psychology theory, Skinner (1935) was the first to suggest a link between the environment and behavior" (Kawaf & Tagg, 2012, p. 162).

When it comes to marketing research, Kotler (1973) pointed out the significance of atmospherics as a marketing tool. He defined atmospherics as follows: "We shall use the term atmospherics to describe the conscious designing of space to create certain effects in buyers. More specifically, atmospherics is the effort to design buying environments to produce specific emotional effects in the buyer that enhances his purchase probability. [...] Atmosphere is always present as a quality of the surrounding space. Atmosphere is apprehended through the sense" (Kotler, 1973, p. 50).

Also, when it comes to the influence of the environment on a customer, a model that is referred to very often is the model of Mehrabian and Russell (1974) (see figure 1).

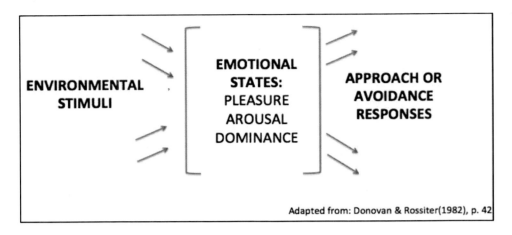

Figure 43: The Mehrabian Russell Model

It implicates that environmental stimuli (S) result in an emotional reaction (O), which, in turn, leads to a customer's response (R), based on the (S–O–R) paradigm (Mehrabian & Russell, 1974). The (S-O-R) paradigm "suggests that when a person is exposed to external stimuli, 'inner organism changes' precede behavioural responses" (Kawaf & Tagg, 2012, p. 163).

Moreover, "Mehrabian and Russell propose that three basic emotional states mediate approach-avoidance behaviors in environmental situations. These emotional responses, known by the acronym PAD are Pleasure – Displeasure; Arousal – Nonarousal; Dominance – Submissiveness" (Donovan & Rossiter, 1982b). Thus, "Behavior toward and within an environment can be classified as either approach or avoidance behavior. Approach behaviors relate to a willingness or desire to move towards, stay in, explore, interact supportively in, perform well in, and return to the environment. Avoidance behaviors relate to the opposites of the above: deteriorated performance and dissatisfaction; feelings of anxiety or boredom; unfriendliness to others; and desire to leave the environment and not to return"(Donovan & Rossiter, 1982b). As a result, this approach to environmental psychology appears to be very important to the interests of service providers as designing and managing the physical and social contexts, where buying and consumption occur, is part of their remit (Foxall & Greenley, 1999).

As a customer, who uses click and collect, has to visit the retailer's store to pick up his order, a retailer should be especially interested in how this pick up location should be designed to generate an approach behavior which leads to the positive results mentioned before. Consequently, this model should be kept in mind.

In a study about perceived retail environment and its influence on consumer's emotional experience, Andreu, Bigné, Chumpitaz, & Swaen (2006) found out that positive perceptions of a retail atmosphere can have several positive effects on the following factors: First, there is an influence on the positive emotions that a customer experiences while shopping. Second, there is an influence on a customer's repatronage intention and lastly, there is an influence on a customer's desire to stay longer at the point of sale. As a result, these findings demonstrate the significance of the physical retail environment in keeping customers. Thus, it is indispensable for retailers to recognize the shopping experience conveyed by their retail environments if these retailers want to design and position the distinct channels as value-rich unities (Andreu et al., 2006).

Two further aspects, that seem important in the context of a customer's perception of a retail environment, are crowding and negative emotions when waiting at the checkout line. When it comes to crowding in a retail environment, "Research has shown that an increase in perceived crowding in a retail store (created from either human or spatial density) can decrease the level of satisfaction that shoppers have with the store" (Machleit, Eroglu, & Mantel, 2000, p. 29). Furthermore, "Perceived crowding is a psychological state that occurs when a person's demand for space exceeds the supply" (Stokols, 1972). When it comes to waiting at the checkout line, it is important to mention that waiting in general is considered a useless loss of time (van Riel, Semeijn, Ribbink, & Bomert-Peters, 2012). Plus, a study has shown that "negative emotional response to the wait as well as store image exert a strong positive effect on satisfaction. [...] A well managed, attractive and equitably perceived waiting environment, that provides sufficient distraction to the waiting customer, can positively contribute to overall satisfaction" (van Riel et al., 2012, p. 158).

These findings should be kept in mind when thinking of the emotional aspect of a customer picking up his order in a retail environment.

4.2 The Influence of Music And Scents

As already noted, "Atmosphere is apprehended through the sense" (Kotler, 1973, p. 50). Thus, this section will have a closer look on other sensual variables.

Beside atmospherics, marketing academics have also examined the significance of appealing to several visual, aural and olfactory elements. Music is considered a significant element in creating an in-store experience and linking straightly to the customer's emotions. However, the music has to "fit", which is a complex and evolving concept. Thus, the music has to match further in-store and brand marketing factors, regardless of the store's strategy (Morrison & Beverland, 2003). Coming back to the Mehrabian Russell model, "Findings indicated that liking of music has a major effect on consumers' evaluations (pleasure, arousal, service quality and merchandise quality), while the music characteristics (specifically slow pop or fast classical) have an additional effect on pleasure and service quality" (Sweeney & Wyber, 2002, p. 51). Moreover, studies that have taken tempo as a variable suggest that slow-tempo music leads to customers slowing down, which in turn leads to customers to stay longer in the store and purchase more than when fast-tempo music is audible (Andersson, Kristensson, Wästlund, & Gustafsson, 2012).

In research, olfactory stimuli have not gained as much consideration as other sensual stimuli, such as visuals. However, smell assuredly seems to be influential in stimulating associations and memories. Though these might be subjective and personal, there seems to be a broad consensus that smell might be a value-adding element of the shopping experience. Yet, retailers need to be careful concerning the aroma and the location where the aroma will be used. While fresh scents are associated with cleanness and seem to be appropriate, strong and food related smells should be avoided (Ward, Davies, & Kooijman, 2007).

4.3 The Influence of Sales Personnel

Sales personnel in a retail environment are sources of information. Customer reliance on the advice of sales personnel when buying clothing is the classical idea of the retail clothing shopping experience (Goldsmith & Flynn, 2005). Moreover, customers can obtain two different benefits when interacting with sales personnel (M. Kim & Stoel, 2005). The first benefit is the functional benefit, which stands for a customer's wish to get support from sales personnel in order to facilitate satisfying the customer's needs (E. Meyer, 1990). The second benefit involves the social aspect of retail stores (M. Kim & Stoel, 2005). In a study on relationships between customers and sales personnel, Beatty, Mayer, Coleman, Reynolds, & Lee (1996) have shown that sales personnel plays an important role in forming a long-lasting relationship between sales personnel and customers. Plus, research suggests that the most influential element on a customer's retail satisfaction is the satisfaction of a customer with a store's sales personnel (Westbrook, 1981). Apart from this, research has shown that sales person's appearance influences customer's positive emotions. Also, research has shown that professional looking appearance of sales personnel play a crucial role on customers' emotions and store image (J.-E. Kim, Ju, & Johnson, 2009).

4.4 Emotions in The Online Environment

Some people really like shopping and enjoy the visual stimulus, sounds and smells. They take pleasure in the interaction with shop assistants and mingling with people. Plus, they enjoy the social interaction with their friends and family members during shopping. Even though online retailers try to create a pleasant shopping experience, many people still consider this experience rather sterile compared to an experience in a traditional store (Grewal et al., 2004). Furthermore, the "store" environment in an online shop misses some elements of traditional retail atmospherics (e.g. several sensory stimuli), but provides some others (e.g. flexibility when it comes to time and space). In an online shop, the whole environment is shortened to a computer screen. Thus, the traditional store designer's competency to stimulate all senses of a customer via an endless composition of ambient, architectural, social and aesthetic components then has to be curbed to a predominantly visual stimuli via a computer screen (Eroglu, Machleit, & Davis, 2001). Coming back to the social component in a traditional store, selling fashion online is a crucial change in this social experience. Furthermore, the lack of adjuvant sales personnel can challenge this this experience, particularly when it comes to fashion products of that are of heterogeneous quality. This stresses the significance of contemporary technologies in ensuring the prospering of the shopping environment for fashion online shops. Consequently, the social dimension of a fashion shopping experience might be achieved through technology (Kawaf & Tagg, 2012).

5 Discussion

Coming back to the research question *"How can a fashion retailer emotionalize the click and collect process?"* it is important to point out that there is no patent remedy to emotionalize the process of click and collect. However, having a look at the current weak points of click and collect and the possibilities of how to enhance emotions in retail in general can at least give hints for fashion retailers on how to bring emotions into the process and thus foster the process of click and collect.

In order to finally give recommendations and find answers to the research question mentioned before, it is important to shortly recall the most important facts presented so far. First of all, this paper has shown that there is a difference between multichannel retailing and omnichannel retailing and that click and collect is an integral part of the latter. Plus, advantages for the retailer as well as for the customer have been discussed. When it comes to the customer buying behavior, it is important to mention that a prevalent behavior is "searching online" and "purchasing offline" in channel switching and that customers expect channels to be seamlessly connected.

The second part of this paper has focused on emotions in fashion retail and has shown that the store environment can have a significant influence on a customer's emotions. Furthermore, this paper has illustrated that crowding in retail environment as well as waiting for long at the checkout line can affect emotions negatively. Other factors of influence presented are music, scents and the store personnel. Finally, this paper has shown that the online environment lacks some components, such as sensory appeals and helpful sales staff.

Coming back to the beginning of this paper, where the new retail environment has been described, it is important to also highlight the crucial role of physical stores in an omnichannel environment. Despite the huge growth of innovative channels (e.g. electronic commerce and mobile commerce), it is undeniable that people still enjoy to go shopping as a leisure activity. Consequently, the function, format and location of traditional physical stores need to be re-evaluated. These physical stores should belong to an integrated omnichannel system that offers distinctive service and experience that leads to a preference of customers over the price-driven, e-commerce competition. As a result, fashion shops should not consider e-commerce as a threat, but as a supportive act of their physical channel. Plus, building a unique physical retail proposition via exceptional service, engaging environment and motivated sales personnel can give the customers an incentive to visit and purchase from a store (Aubrey & Judge, 2012b) and consequently make use of click and collect. These implications for physical stores are important to keep in mind, because from the author's point of view, the biggest potential to emotionalize the process of click and collect lies in making it a unique (physical) in-store experience which customers truly enjoy and which makes them feel special. Furthermore, this point of view derives from the fact that research has shown that creating emotional atmosphere in the online environment is still a difficult task (Eroglu et al., 2001). Thus, as the emotional aspect in the online environment is difficult to enhance, the in-store experience as part of click and collect should be emotionalized even more. However, how can these emotions be created?

The literature research part of this paper has shown that the store environment is a crucial factor of influence on a customer's emotions. As Andreu et al. (2006) have pointed out, positive perceptions of a retail environment can influence the positive emotions, the desire to stay and the repatronage intentions of a customer. Thus, from a retailer perspective, it would truly make sense to create a pleasant environment for the pick-up location of click and collect orders. This suggestion is also supported when having a look at the Mehrabian Russell model, which stresses the impact of the environment on a customer's behavior. In the beginning, Mahar et. Al (2012) mentioned that some retailers include a separate click and collect lounge within their stores and that customers picking up their orders enjoy a special service level. Therefore, the first suggestion for a fashion retailer is to have a close look on the pick-up location. Is it merely an information desk, where customers can ask for information, complain about something and get their click and collect orders without any advice from the sales staff? Or is it a separate, pleasant area with an employee solely responsible for click and collect orders? From the author's point of view, the latter version is the better, as the separate click and collect lounge could not only influence the customers positive emotions when designed in a pleasant and appealing way, but could also convey a feeling of exclusiveness. Other factors that speak for a separate click and collect lounge are the influences on negative emotions mentioned by Machleit et al. (2000) and van Riel et al. (2012), which could be eliminated when having a separate lounge. While Machleit et al. (2000) argued that a rise in perceived crowding in-store can reduce a customer's satisfaction, van Riel et al., (2012) pointed out that longtime waiting at the checkout line can lead to a negative emotional response. Thus, these factors speak for a separate click and collect lounge as well, as a separate lounge could mean that customers could "escape" from the crowding in the retail store when "entering" the click and collect lounge. Plus, a separate cashier desk within the click and collect lounge that is "reserved" for customers and their click and collect purchases could decrease the waiting time for a customer in-store and, again, convey a feeling of being special.

In the context of creating a pleasant environment for a separate click and collect lounge music as well as scents have been investigated in academic literature. According to Morrison & Beverland (2003) music is considered a significant element in creating an in-store experience. Moreover, the implications that "slow pop" and "fast classical" music can affect customer's pleasure (Sweeney & Wyber, 2002) and that slow-tempo music leads to customers slowing down (Andersson et al., 2012) speak for a well-considered selection of music in a click and collect lounge. Plus, Andersson et al. (2012) imply that slow-tempo music also leads to customer staying longer in the store and purchase more. This finding promotes one major opportunity of click and collect in the beginning, which is that click and collect can lead to additional sales. Consequently, slow-tempo music in a separate click and collect lounge could (at least in theory) go hand in hand with the potential of additional sales of click and collect itself.

Turning now to the olfactory factors in the context of an environment, research has shown that these stimuli have not gained much consideration (Ward et al., 2007). Thus, recommending specific types of aroma for a click and collect lounge does not seem appropriate for now, but indicates that there is still a huge potential for future research.

Another major aspect that needs to be considered when emotionalizing the process of click and collect is the sales personnel.

This is due to the fact that click and collect only makes sense when combined with consultation, exceptional service and a direct dialog with the customer. This means that click and collect needs to provide an added value, because offering free shipping is simply not enough (Hackenberg, 2013). This added value understandably has to be provided by the sales personnel, among others. Hence, also the sales personnel can contribute to emotionalizing click and collect. Having a look at the literature, Westbrook (1981) suggests that a customer's satisfaction with a store's sales personnel is the most influential element on a customer's retail satisfaction. Plus, research has pointed out that that a sales person's appearance influences customer's positive emotions (J.-E. Kim et al., 2009). Consequently, it is obvious that a retailer who offers click and collect also needs qualified sales personnel which is able to give fashion advice to the customer, offer additional matching items to the ordered items and consequently foster additional sales (Zimmer, 2014). In order to do so, sales personnel should be aware of the item ordered and provide some extra items that match the ordered item (Zimmer, 2014). By doing so, a retailer can provide the added value mentioned before. Plus, having a look at the buying decision-making process mentioned previously, it is important to point out again that in the fourth phase (evaluation of alternatives) the customer studies the received information (L. R. Poloian, 2013). Thus, this stresses the importance of service, professional consultation and dialog between customer and sales personnel even more, as the sales personnel could give advice especially when the consumer is in the phase just mentioned. The sales personnel in a click and collect lounge could provide additional information about the item ordered by the customer and make it easier for him to make a decision. Yet it is especially this lack of service and dialogs that lead to the unpopularity of click and collect in the German market, as most sales assistants merely deliver the closed package that includes the order and say goodbye to the customer (Haupt, 2014a). In addition, Zimmer (2014) emphasizes that the sales personnel does not know what a customer ordered via click and collect, while Rösch (2014) points out that sometimes sales personnel is simply not aware of the multichannel technology offered by a company. As a result, in today's omnichannel world, it is essential for fashion retailers to educate their store personnel about the available omnichannel technologies in order to provide the best service experience possible for a customer. A retailer offering omnichannel options can only benefit from these options (e.g. by generating higher revenues) when the sales personnel is aware of these options. If a customer is aware of these options and the sales personnel is not, a customer might be dissatisfied with the sales person due to the lack of knowledge, which in turn, according to Westbrook (1981), would lead to an retail dissatisfaction of the consumer.

In the context of the exceptional service mentioned before queues also the *immediate in-store pick up* aspects mentioned by Mahar et al. (2012) meaning that a retailer uses the inventory on hand to satisfy orders. Consequently, a major aspect for retailers is to have a complete logistical coherency concerning the stock in order to have the right product at the right place in a short time. As a result, real time visibility of stock through all the channels is a prerequisite to fulfill customer's orders as fast as possible (Aubrey & Judge, 2012b). Therefore, a complete coherency regarding the stock can drive emotions in click and collect as well, as these technological advances give the customers the possibility to get their orders delivered very quickly, which in turn could lead to a higher customer satisfaction. By doing so, bad examples such as delivery delays for click and collect orders could be prevented.

Another major weak point of click and collect is that most retailers offering click and collect still focus on their old-established processes (Zimmer, 2014). However, research has shown that nowadays multichannel customers not only expect a seamless shopping experience (Heinemann & Schwarzl, 2010) but also have grown accustomed to fast product deliveries from the online pure players. As a result, driving emotions in click and collect implies not only the logistical coherency concerning stock mentioned before, but also to re-think the logistical process itself, in order to reduce waiting times for customers. By doing so, retailers could especially catch up spontaneous shoppers, who want to have their product right away (Zimmer, 2014).

6 Conclusion

In a typical customer's mind, click and collect seems primarily to be connected to free shipping and a store's long opening hours. Yet, these advantages are rather pragmatic ones. This implies that neither the consumer nor the fashion retailers have an understanding of the potential added value of click and collect so far. However, this paper has shown that there is a high potential for fashion retailers to emotionalize the process of click and collect. The research part of this paper has shown that a customer's emotions can be influenced in several ways, especially via the store environment. This paper therefore suggest to integrate a separate click and collect lounge into the retail environment, giving the customer a feeling of being special and "escape" from a crowded retail environment and check out faster.

Moreover, this separate lounge should be designed in a pleasant way in order to make the customer feel comfortable and relaxed. Furthermore, there should be sales personnel solely responsible for the separate click and collect lounge in order to assure an adequate personal consultation. Another major point in emotionalizing click and collect is that the sales personnel not only has to be aware of several omni-channel possibilities of the retailer, but also of the unique benefits offered by click and collect. The store personnel can be considered the "heart" of the store, as they are in direct contact with the consumers and are one of the major factors of influence when consumers make a buying decision. Consequently, when a retailer wants to emotionalize and benefit from click and collect, he first of all has to teach the sales personnel about the benefits and define concrete actions, such as checking what the customer has ordered in order to provide an added value via personal consultation. Additionally, this paper has shown that sales personnel should be able to give professional fashion advice and recommend additional items on the base of the item ordered by the customer in order to foster additional sales. Plus, literature suggests that logistical processes should be re-thought, e.g. in order to give the customer the possibility for real time visibility of the stock. When doing so, a consumer can not only pick up an item much faster but also customers' spontaneous shopping intentions can be satisfied.

To sum up, click and collect should not be considered merely a means of saving shipping charges, but should evoke an emotional connection between the customer and the fashion retailer. The customer should think of click and collect as a real added value, like a "VIP shopping treatment", and should look forward to having a professional consultation with a sales person in a pleasant shopping environment. By creating a unique click and collect in-store experience, a fashion retailer could give customers incentives to enjoy the convenience of online shopping and the professional consultation of sales personnel. Thus, it should be every fashion retailer's aim to enhance the process of click and collect and to recognize the benefits both for himself and for the customer.

7   Limitations and Further Research

This paper has primarily analyzed the in-store experience of click and collect and has shown that a customer's emotions can be influenced in several ways. Plus, this paper has shown potentials of making the in-store experience of click and collect a unique one. However, this paper did not analyze the online part of click and collect, meaning that it has not explored to what extent the online environment can influence the likelihood of a customer to make use of click and collect. Moreover, this paper did not explore how the online experience of click and collect can be emotionalized. This is due to the fact that the real added value of click and collect is experienced in-store, meaning a professional consultation of sales personnel and a pleasant shopping environment. Thus, further research concerning click and collect could focus on the online experience in the context of click and collect and explore the main reasons for customers choosing click and collect.

Plus, in nowadays omnichannel environment, store concepts like House of Fraser's "Buy and Collect" store and their impact on customer's buying behavior could be explored. The "Buy and Collect" store "does not stock merchandise but instead features iPads, computers and interactive screens where customers can order products which are then delivered the following day to either the customer's home or to the store for collection"(Harrison, 2011). Consequently, some retailers might make use of this store concept as well and research could investigate whether consumers really consider this concept an added value or return to traditional retail formats with "physical" merchandise. In this context, it would not only be interesting to investigate what consumers really perceive as an added value, but also to explore to what extend click and collect really leads to additional sales.

Another interesting field of research could be ways how retailers can improve their internal processes in order to integrate click and collect seamlessly to their overall omnichannel strategy. In this context, empirical studies among fashion retailers could investigate whether the retailers and their store personnel really make use of the benefits that click and collect offers or whether they still use it as a marketing gimmick.

The Post-Purchase Phase - Transforming Shoppers to Lovers

Loyalty Programs for Fashion Retailers- An emotional perspective

Franziska Greiner/Jochen Strähle

Abstract

Purpose – The purpose of this paper is to analyse the main elements of successful customer loyalty programs in general and emotional components of the buying process in order to determine loyalty programs for fashion retailers. This paper aims to close this gap.

Design/methodology/approach – This study clarifies customer loyalty programs current status in fashion retail, and provides possible suggestions about how to improve customer loyalty programs in fashion retail.

Findings – The results of this study indicate that loyalty program in fashion retail require considerable non-monetary benefits such as sense of exclusive membership and enhanced status to distinguish from competitors customer loyalty programs.

Research limitations/implications – Only theoretical literature and models were evaluated in this study. Addressing this could be a good direction for future research, specifically with its comparison with stand-alone and multi-partner programs.

Keywords – Customer loyalty program, customer satisfaction, customer loyalty, relationship marketing, customer behaviour, emotionality, fashion retailing

Paper type – Research paper

1 Introduction

Nowadays, more than ever, retailers are being challenged to create loyalty among customers. In order to achieve year over year same-store sales and profit growth, retailers' attention has shifted to services and became more aware and responsive to changes in the marketplace (Gable, Fiorito, & Topol, 2008). Customer loyalty programs have emerged as perhaps the most popular formalized relationship marketing approach and playing an increasingly important role in companies' customer relationship efforts. These customer loyalty programs are used by companies to create, develop, and maintain valuable customer relationships (Lacey, 2009) (J. Zhang & Breugelmans, 2012). Loyalty programs are promotion, which offer some reward or benefit to customers based on their history of purchase. However, it can be questioned whether these programs foster loyalty. They are generally used and are essential promotional tools (Sayman & J. Hoch, 2014). Customer loyalty programs are widespread across a variety of industries, such as retailing, travel, and financial services and have achieved high participation rates among consumers (J. Zhang & Breugelmans, 2012). The main reasons that companies introduce loyalty programs are to gain additional customers, increase the share-of-wallet (SOW) from existing ones, or discourage switching to other marketers, among other things (Sayman & J. Hoch, 2014).

Consumer choice is a process that is determined through various aspects. For this reason, researcher examinants how durable preference schemes emerge and why certain customers are loyal to one firm and others defect to other companies or switch between brands. Thus, companies are in constant search of tools that have the ability to build loyal customers. Based on the overall expectations that the membership in customer loyalty programs will encourage customers to stay with one brand, retail chain, or product. The number of customer loyalty programs in business and consumer markets is growing steadily, along with the number of consumers joining these programs (Kreis & Mafael, 2014).

In the past, one of the main targets of marketing campaigns have been to increase customer loyalty to a product or service. These targets were driven by the perception that more loyal customers will do more repeat business and will develop a larger tolerance to price increases and therefore are more profitable to the firm. Despite, this is not always the case. A very loyal customer may also be an individual who repeatedly calls customer service with questions and is constantly hunting for the best price on a product, taking advantage of every rebate and sale offer. Eventually, such a customer could be costing the company money rather than providing a source of profits. An important part of customer relationship management is identifying the different types of customers and then developing specific strategies for interacting with each customer. Examples of such strategies are, developing better relationships with profitable customers, locating and appealing new customers who will be profitable, and finding appropriate strategies for unprofitable customers (Kumar & Reinartz, 2012).

The average number of memberships per household in the U.S. is 18. Of these 18 programs, however, on average only 8.4 were actively used. As a consequence, not every member seems to value the programs offerings, while companies invest large amounts of money to make their customer loyalty program more attractive to customer retention (Kreis & Mafael, 2014).

1.1 Research question and purpose

Most of the trading chains and different stores in Europe and USA have their own customer loyalty programs in use or are part of a multi-partner program. The structures of the programs differ from each other. There exist lots of information and research material about the domestic (Germany) and international (European, USA) customer loyalty programs in general.

The aim of this paper is to clarify the role of loyalty programs for fashion retailers and understand psychological needs of customers in the selling context. Fashion retailers can achieve a true understanding of customer needs and shopping behaviour variables. In order to strengthen the customer's commitment in different fashion retail stores, it is important to clarify customers' opinions, expectations and development suggestions for existing customer loyalty programs.

This study concentrates to clarify customer loyalty programs current status in the fashion retail market, to analyse shortly other industries' position in loyalty programs, and to provide possible suggestions about how to improve the customer loyalty program in fashion retail in the future. By understanding the similarities and differences of the industries and the customers' expectations and ideas for development of the customer loyalty program towards meeting customer's needs.

Delimitations in the theoretical part of this study are made in customer relationship management and consumer behaviour. Only basis of customer relationship management, customers' expectations, and customer satisfaction are covered in this study, because these themes are relevant and important for the customer loyalty. Customer commitment, customer loyalty and customer loyalty programs are discussed more in detail in the theoretical part, because these results are mostly related to the study topic. Also specific features of fashion retailing are pointed out, in order to understand the needs for increasing the loyalty among fashion retail customers.

There is no research that considers consumers' emotional values in the fashion retail context. Therefore, the contribution of this study is to help retailers to understand what benefits or needs shoppers may seek to satisfy and achieve their interaction with customer loyalty programs. If the relationship is built successfully, it is capable of generating particular positive emotions, thus creating positive outcomes for both parties.

This study aims to find answers to following two main research questions:

1. What is the current status of customer loyalty programs?

2. How to create a unique shopping experience and enhance loyalty programs through emotionality in fashion retail?

With the first research question the current status of customer loyalty programs is described. Current status is analysed by using the theoretical literature. The overall picture about the current status of customer loyalty programs will lead the study to the next question about how the customer loyalty program could be enhanced through emotionality in fashion retail. By answering these two research questions this study provides important information about the status of customer loyalty programs for fashion retailers, and suggests identified development areas for customer loyalty programs for the future perspective.

1.2 Literature Review

In order to answer the research questions mentioned before, a literature review has been done. The framework of this study is organized around theoretical base from different existing sources, such as books, articles, studies and websites. The theoretical base is related to customer relationship management, customer's expectations, customer satisfaction, customer commitment and customer loyalty. All these theoretic substances are strongly related to the research objective of this study, because the aim of the study is to clarify customers' expectations, satisfaction, commitment and loyalty towards customer loyalty program in fashion retail. Also general information about customer loyalty programs is provided in the theory part, because it is important to understand the basics of the loyalty program and to receive an understandable picture about the current situation of customer loyalty programs.

This literature review includes 8 books, 29 articles in journals, and 4 articles in magazines. Articles in journals as well as articles in magazines have been found via databases provided by the library of Reutlingen University. The keywords that have been used for searching were:

- Customer loyalty programs, loyalty program membership, relationship marketing, fashion retailer, sense of community, purchase behaviour, buying behaviour, emotionality, S-O-R Modell, emotions in fashion retail

2 Theoretical background to loyalty programs

For a better understanding of how satisfaction, customer loyalty (behaviour loyalty and attitudinal loyalty) and customer experience affect customer loyalty programs. Therefore, the three determinants will be described, before analysing customer loyalty programs in general.

2.1 Customer Satisfaction

Satisfaction is a person's feelings of pleasure or disappointment resulting from comparing his or her perception and expectation (Kotler, 2012b). Buttle (2009) agreed that satisfaction is a pleasurable fulfilment response while dissatisfaction is unpleasurable fulfilment response. Satisfaction may be defined as the perception of pleasurable accomplishment of a service, which can be assessed as the sum of the satisfactions with various attributes of a product or service. Moreover, determinants of customer satisfaction are ease of obtaining information, attribute level performance prior experience and search time in choosing the service (Thomas, 2013). Individual customers have different motivations for shopping like daily routine, learning about new products, or enjoyment of bargaining. These differences mean that they will derive satisfaction from diverse aspects of the shopping experience (Clottey, Collier, & Stodnick, 2008).

2.2 Customer Loyalty

Past literature pointed out, that there are several definitions of customer loyalty. Customer's loyalty is a customer's affection to a brand, store, manufacturer, service provider or other entity based on favourable attitudes and behavioural responses such as repeat purchase (Baran, 2008). The customer loyalty is evident in different ways including a commitment to re-buy or patronize a preferred product or service. Customer loyalty may be considered as being either behavioural or attitudinal. The behavioural approach is that customers are loyal as long as they continue to buy and use a good or service. The problem with relying on terms of behaviour loyalty is that there may be many reasons for repeat patronage other than loyalty, among them lack of other choices, habit, low income, convenience, etc. (Egan, 2011). Thomas (2013) agreed, those mere repurchases may be indicative of inertia and not loyalty. However, behavioural measures do not provide any insight into the consumer's attitude towards buying a particular brand; all that behavioural loyalty can reveal is that consumer has purchased a brand on multiple occasions as mentioned before (Härtel & Russell-Bennett, 2010).

In contrast to behaviour loyalty, attitudinal loyalty focuses on the customer's attitude towards the brand, not their behaviour. Furthermore, customers feel a sense of belonging or commitment to the good or service. Attitudinal loyalty includes attitudinal preferences, commitment towards the brand and intention to purchase the brand. Consumers can hold, positive, negative or ambivalent attitudes towards repurchasing a brand (Härtel & Russell-Bennett, 2010; Thomas, 2013). According to

Härtel & Russell-Bennett (2010) they define attitudinal brand loyalty as a consumer's affective and cognitive evaluation of repurchasing a brand.

Research has developed many assets of customer loyalty, such as making it a trend for retailers to follow, as well as establish and maintaining a loyal customer base. Loyal customers are important benefits to companies; they make proportionally more purchases at their 'first choice' store than customers who switch, and they are more willing to spend a larger amount compared to less loyal customers. In addition, companies that adopt loyal customer base are able to cut down operational and marketing cost. Therefore, companies should pay more attention to customer loyalty, as the financial performance of the organization is normally driven by the increase of customer loyalty (Yuen & Chan, 2010).

2.3 Creating customer experience

When asking for an answer does satisfaction equal loyalty? Supposing that there are many occasions when customers are satisfied but not loyal. Hence, the answer to this question is "no". Loyalty is relationship-based and focuses on the overall customer experience (Gable et al., 2008). Creating superior customer experience is a central matter in retail management and most managers recognize that enhancing customer experience is important for customer satisfaction, loyalty, and ultimately the firm's profitability (Kumar, Pozza, & Ganesh, 2013). Therefore to provide good positive customer experience, it is important to understand the factors that create customer experience, how to measure it and how it affects customer satisfaction and loyalty in different service settings ("Phil" Klaus & Maklan, 2012).

For many retailers one of the most popular tools used to enhance customer experience, satisfaction and loyalty is a loyalty program (Gable et al., 2008). Firms in various industries around the world have adopted programs that offer incentives, rewards, and benefits for enhanced customer loyalty (Lin & Bennett, 2014).

2.4 Loyalty Programs

A loyalty program is defined as an organized marketing activity that offers a firm's customers additional incentives, rewards or benefits to persuade them to be more loyal (Jun Kang, Alejandro, & Groza, 2015)(Jun Kang et al., 2015). The steady acceptance of such programs reflects acceptance of the relationship marketing idea, which can be seen as a paradigm shift from transaction-based marketing to customer retention and relationship management. The fundamental motivation for loyalty programs is usually based on the idea that: first, the amount to retain a customer is far less than the amount of acquiring a new one and secondly, the Pareto rule which suggests that 80 per cent of revenue comes from 20 per cent of customers. Therefore it seems reasonable to invest in retaining the company's most valuable customers (Lin & Bennett, 2014).

Loyalty programs are designed to improve customer's satisfaction and commitment due to a variety of marketing initiatives, that positively influence consumers' attitudes and behaviours toward the brand or company (Henderson, Beck, & Palmatier, 2011).

2.4.1 Differentiation between loyalty programs

There are three dimensions of loyalty programs: program type, target group and the performance orientation of programs distinguish them.

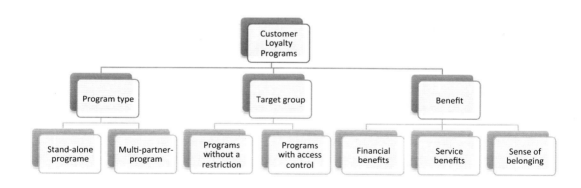

Figure 44: Definition of Customer Loyalty Programs
Adapted from:

The program types are differentiated between stand-alone programs and multi-partner programs. Stand-alone-programs are characterized, that the performances are related to the company that simultaneously operates the loyalty program. In contrast to stand-alone programs, several partner retailers apply a multi-partner program. There is a central and independent operator of the loyalty program (e.g. Payback (Aßmann & Schildhauer, 2008). In this case, the consumer's loyalty to the program does not necessarily involve loyalty toward each of the partner retailers. Indeed the consumer distributes his expenditure and points redemption among the different partners. Companies benefit from using multi-partner programs for their customers that bring in complementary stores. The greater the synergy among the stores participating in the program, the greater the number of opportunities for using the program and the more each business will directly or indirectly profit from it (Frisou & Yildiz, 2011). Loyalty program structure elements may include also rules of entry, number of firms included in the program, and usually some kind of benefits for program members.

2.4.2 Perceived Benefits of Loyalty Programs

The major aim of a loyalty program is to provide added value to customers with the purpose of building customer retention. As previously noted, to build customer loyalty the program should be recognized as beneficial to customers. The perceived benefits of loyalty programs are defined as the value(s) that the program provides for members. Hence, a critical key of the success of a loyalty program is whether a consumer can perceive and identify the benefits of membership and appreciate receiving rewards (Zakaria et al., 2014).

Over the years, the benefits associated with participation in loyalty programs have been classified in different ways. For example, in early research, O'Brien and Jones (1995) suggested that five elements determined the values of a loyalty program: cash value, choice of redemption options, aspirational value, relevance, and convenience (O'Brien & Jones, 1995). Afterwards, several researchers categorized the benefits into two categories: hard benefits or soft benefits (Gable et al., 2008; Lacey, 2009). Hard benefits are generally economic, e.g. providing special discounts, coupons, gifts or rebates for past purchases or generate savings for the customer on future purchases.

The soft benefits were emotionally oriented elements, they are exclusive member benefits that go beyond a financial component. These benefits focus on special conveniences or information that facilitates the business transaction between customers and retailers e.g. preferential treatment, restricted check-in counters for loyalty cardholders, special communications, special invitations, exclusive "after-hours" shopping times, which were thought to give customers a sense of recognition and importance. Hard benefits may be easier for customers to evaluate but on the other hand, soft benefits serve as an emotional tie that binds the customer to the retailer (Gable et al., 2008; H.-Y. Kim, Lee, Choi, Wu, & Johnson, 2013).

Furthermore, the attractiveness of a loyalty programme is influenced by three categories: economic (e.g., discounts), psychological (e.g., sense of community), and sociological (e.g., prestige or recognition, exclusive treatment) (J. Zhang & Breugelmans, 2012). Sociological benefits are captured from a loyalty program's association with social status, social class, or a specific social group, whereas psychological benefits involve a person's basic human need to feel a sense of belonging and acceptance (H.-Y. Kim et al., 2013).

Finally, Mimouni-Chaabane and Volle's (2010) classification of benefits is utilitarian, hedonic, and symbolic. The first category, utilitarian, relate to financial advantages. The second category, hedonic benefits, derives from exploration and entertainment. Consumers often enjoy receiving incentives because it provides enjoyment, inspiration, and emotion. Apparel retail loyalty programs may provide exploratory benefits through trend information on new styles for the coming season and trying on new styles before others (e.g. magazines or personal invitations) (Mimouni-Chaabane & Volle, 2010) (H.-Y. Kim et al., 2013). Loyalty programs attract consumers because of the pleasure associated with collecting and redeeming points. In this case, customers act like players and experience a feeling of entertainment (Mimouni-Chaabane & Volle, 2010). In the context of fashion retailer loyalty programs, entertainment can be also provided through special promotions, including fashion shows and other entertaining events (e.g. shopping parties, designer preview event) (H.-Y. Kim et al., 2013).

The final category, symbolic benefits, are the benefits that are linked to customers' need for social approval and sense of worth. Symbolic benefits are extrinsic and intangible values of a program that can fulfil consumers' needs for recognition, personal expression, self-esteem, and social approval. Symbolic benefits are embodied by two constructs: recognition and social benefits. Participants in loyalty programs may receive special treatment, extra attention, or personalized services. These benefits allow participants to feel differentiated from other customers. As a consequence, the programs enhance awareness of social benefits, such that members consider themselves part of an exclusive group of privileged customers, identify with that group, and share values associated with the brand (Mimouni-Chaabane & Volle, 2010). Consumers can achieve a sense of community when they derive benefits from participation in loyalty programs, such as a feeling of belonging, influence, a shared emotional connection, and fulfilment (H.-Y. Kim et al., 2013) (Rosenbaum, Ostrom, & Kuntze, 2005).

2.4.3 Program Loyalty

Program loyalty is described as a highly positive attitude toward the loyalty program. Several researchers have proposed that there is a connection between the benefits of a loyalty program and consumers' program loyalty. For example, the more economic and noneconomic benefits a customer associated with a loyalty program, the higher the possibility of the customer enrolling in the program. Additionally, if customers perceive a certain loyalty program to be more attractive than competing programs, it is reasonable that they will be more likely to join and actively participate in that program (H.-Y. Kim et al., 2013).

2.4.4 Examples for successful loyalty programs

Nearly all retailers depend in repeat business from customers to survive and aim to develop favourable attitudes among shoppers who may influence others to consider shopping at their stores. Some retailers have attempted to achieve improved sales goals by targeting selected groups of consumers. Consciously shunning the mass market, they appeal to more lucrative, up-scale and conscious customers who appreciate, desire and require both merchandise quality and assortment as well as personal service. Retailers employing this approach include Neiman Marcus, Saks Fifth Avenue, Chanel, Hermes, Tiffany's and Nordstroms. They have employed these strategies and have adopted programs designed to foster customer relationships and maintain an on going dialogue with their customers to determine their preferences (Gable et al., 2008).

For example, Saks Fifth Avenue, a New York–based apparel retailer, is known for its customer relationship management–based loyalty program, SAKSFIRST. This program provides five different reward tiers, ranging from a $1,000 tier (Classic) up to a $25,000 tier (Diamond), based on customers' spending per year. At the end of each year, the retailer grants each member a discount coupon for store merchandise. Preferred members also receive special coupons and exclusive offers linked to the retailer's strategic partners, such as Ritz-Carlton Hotels and British Airways. The SAKSFIRST program consists of not only rewarding loyal customers but also gaining critical intelligence about how customers think and perform. Membership information is used among other things for strategic decision-making about store locations to recruiting for focus groups to assist in promotion and merchandising decisions (H.-Y. Kim et al., 2013).

Another example is the German most successful multi-partner program Payback. It enables consumers to collect points with hundreds of companies offline and online. More than 24 million active customers are using the program and taking advantage of its benefits in Germany. The program incorporates a wide range of retail and online partners, so it enjoys a far higher level of awareness than a stand-alone programme. Two-thirds of all households in Germany enjoy all benefits of a Payback card. According to a survey carried out by a German market research institution, Payback is the most popular German bonus program with the highest level of customer satisfaction (Emnid, 2012). There are good reasons for this success. As a program connecting various industries, Payback offers its users added value for their daily shopping activities. PAYBACK partners include well-known brand names such as Aral, Galeria Kaufhof, real,-, dm-drogerie markt and WMF. Redemption of points is possible at the PAYBACK rewards shop or directly at particular points of sale. Shopping vouchers and cash are other options. In addition, members can change points into miles for frequent flyer programmes (Lufthansa Miles & More) or donate points to non-profit organizations like UNICEF ("Payback The Multi Partner Loyalty Program Marketing Essay," 2013) ("payback.net," 2015).

Further example is the Esprit Fiends Card. Esprit offers its customers four different types of loyalty cards, namely the Friends Card, the Gold Card, the Platinum Card and the Esprit Visa Card. The last is an ordinary credit card, which can be acquired for an annual fee. Upgrading from the Friends card to the Gold- and Platinum Card takes place automatically when a certain amount of "e-points" in a certain period of time is gathered. An upgrade brings additional benefits to the customer. They are both monetary and non-monetary. With the friends card customers get 3% bonus on every purchase they make (offline and online) back in the form of valuable e-points. For example the purchase is 200 €, then customers receive 600 e-points credited to the Esprit Friends account - 600 points correspond 6,00 €. Esprit sends an automatically generated voucher with the value of the current e-points balance to customers and they can redeem the voucher within the next 12 month. After reaching 900 e-points within 12 months, Esprit sends automatically the new, exclusive Esprit Friends Gold Card. Customers can enjoy more benefits: two vouchers for free alteration service, surprises (for example, on your birthday) and more experiences (invitations to exclusive Esprit event). With the next tier the Platinum Card customers have even more benefits: free alteration service at Esprit Stores, free Esprit Friends Platinum Service, professional shopping advice by personal appointment, newsletter about products and promotions selected specially for customers, exclusive offers only for Esprit Friends Platinum customers ("Esprit-friends.com," 2015).

3   Trends and Developments in Consumer Behaviour

Current worldwide trends impact the consumer behaviour. Consumers increasingly demand for integrated marketing channels and for corporate-responsible images of firms. They spend a considerable time reserved for shopping making online researches and comparing products. It makes it harder for retailers to differentiate their products and services from those of their competitors in a way that attracts attention and influences purchase decisions (Kumar & Reinartz, 2012). In addition, emotional shopping is becoming more and more important when going shopping.

The retail fashion industry is not stable or static, but is distinguished by a continuously changing environment whereby retailers continuously adapt their products, services and images to meet the demands of the consumer market. Fashion retailers are constantly trying to improve market position by re-evaluating their product and service provision and investing in new innovative marketing strategies in-store and online via multi-channel activities (Donnell, Hutchinson, & Reid, 2012).

3.1 Emotional components in Consumer Behaviour

Within the context of retailing and relationship marketing, a loyalty program must be seen through consumers' eyes, given that its objective is to build and maintain relationship with customers. In order to maintain a relationship and in order to expand the relationship emotionally, new commitments must be established. The implementation of relationship marketing will be influenced by the perceptions of customers about the efforts made by the companies. The benefits that customers can obtain from loyalty programs may focus on an increase in confidence, the reduction of risk; functional and social benefits as well adaptability. The functional benefits include time savings, convenience, making the best purchase decision, while the social benefits include how pleasant and comfortable the relationships is (Marzo-Navarro, Pedraja-Iglesias, & Pilar Rivera-Torres, 2004).

3.2 Shopping Motivations for Consumers

Loyalty programs will be most effective when retailers have understood the needs (motivations) of the consumer. Fashion consumption is inherently linked to one's self image, thus loyalty programs which build relationships through targeted communication are more likely to have more loyal participants (Ashman & Vazquez, 2012). Shopping motivations can help indicate what the loyalty program needs to stay competitive among competitors. Shopping motivations can be utilitarian or hedonic. Recognized hedonic shopping motivations include enjoyment, whereas utilitarian motives are ease of use and usefulness. Hedonic motivations to shop include adventure, social, gratification, idea, role and value shopping. Consumers with high levels of fashion innovativeness are driven by adventure and idea motives and less concerned with value. Motivations are also linked to customer's evaluation of loyalty program elements (Ashman & Vazquez, 2012).

3.3 Individual and Group Influences on Consumer Behaviour

Every purchase is made on personal needs and wants. Classic psychological theories attempt to categorize and explain human complexities. They include need determination, physiological and psychological bases of behaviour and personality. Into two broad categories are human needs divided: biogenic and psychogenic. Biogenic needs are physiological needs for food, warmth and shelter. Psychogenic needs stem from the socialization process involve intangibles such as status, acquisition, or love. The two types affect behaviour. According to James Bayton the psychogenic needs provide more insight regarding human behaviour.

- Affectional – The need to love and beloved.
- Ego-bolstering – The need to build ourselves up in own thoughts or in the eyes of others; to develop self-esteem or desire status.
- Ego-defensive – The need to protect ourselves and our weak ego.

For advertising campaigns are these psychogenic needs often the basis. Perfume and cosmetic ads often play on affectional needs. Insurance, personal, and health care products on ego-defensive needs. Designer apparel and luxury automobiles on ego-bolstering needs (L. G. Poloian, 2013) (Bayton, n.d.).

Shopping is a part of self-expressions, considering personality types are helpful to retailers. Humans with certain types of personalities respond to in buying situations in particular ways. It means for fashion retailers, that personality differences influence shopping behaviour, customer choices, and willingness to spend. The more knowledge retailers can gather about potential customers, the better their chances of success will be. Attitudes are also created by our interaction with others. Friends and family, peers and professionals influence the behaviour, some to a greater degree than others. A self-image is refined from both external and internal influences. In addition reference groups guide the decision-making process, these reference groups are social or professional involvement with which a person identifies (L. G. Poloian, 2013). In addition, an important shopping factor involves shopping with others versus alone. Some evidence submit that shopping with peers increases the impulse to purchase while the presence of family members decrease it. If impulsiveness is socially acceptable within the group, buyers are more likely to do so. Family members may arouse feelings of responsibility and affect shopping behaviour. This also builds on the cohesiveness of the group and how affected the shopper is to social influence and desires to comply with social norms. Retailer may be able to influence how shoppers shop (Flint, 2014).

At this point, customers seek facts and figures to pass forward the decision-making process. During this step the buyer is looking for reading materials, talking to opinion leaders, phoning friends, seeking out advertising materials or going online to compare shops and learning about the product. Each information source preforms a different function in influencing the buying decision (Kotler, 2012b; L. G. Poloian, 2013).

3.4.3 Evaluation of Alternatives

The next phase of the process is studying the information collected and ranking choices appropriately. Marketers need to know about alternative evaluation, that is, how consumers process information to choose among alternative brands. Unfortunately, consumers do not use a simple evaluation process in all buying situations. However, several evaluation processes are at work. In some cases, shoppers use careful calculations and logical thinking. At other times, the same shopper does little or no evaluation. In contrast they buy on impulse and rely on intuition. Occasionally consumers make buying decisions on their own, another time they turn to friends, online reviews or salespeople for buying advice (Kotler & Armstrong, 2014).

3.4.4 Purchase decision

Mostly, the shopper's purchase decision will be to buy the most preferred brand, but two aspects can come between the purchase intention and the purchase decision. The first aspect is the 'attitudes of others'. If someone close to you thinks that you should buy the lowest-priced car, then the chances of you buying a more expensive car are reduced. The second aspect is 'unexpected situational factors'. The shopper may form a buying intention based on factors such as expected income, expected price and expected product benefits. Despite, unexpected events may change the buying intention. Hence, preferences and even buying intentions do not always result in an actual purchase choice (Kotler, 2012b).

3.4.5 Post-purchase behaviour

The stage of the buyer decision process in which consumers take further action after the purchase is based on their satisfaction or dissatisfaction. The marketer's job does not end with the purchase. After the purchase is made, consumers will either

portant determinant of consumer intention. Moreover, loyalty programs can only be measured from the consumer's viewpoint by separating information quality, system quality, and service quality. Previous studies have shown that the design of loyalty programs plays a key role in influencing consumer's emotional states, such as excitement and enjoyment. In line with this argument, it is expected that consumer perception of loyalty programs will predict consumer's positive and negative emotions. Retailers often focus on enhancing customer satisfaction through customer loyalty programs. Research generally supports the idea that customer satisfaction is an antecedent of customer loyalty. Satisfied customers are affected to be more willing to be engaged in cross- and up-buying of a retailers' or brands' product, and also express higher repurchase intention, and actual repurchase.

3.6 Stimuli and characteristics affecting consumer behaviour

Numerous factors have an impact on the final decision of consumers. Within the process of decision-making, the consumer's psychology, and thus the motivation, perception, learning and memory play a crucial role. Besides, there are further external stimuli and consumer characteristics that may affect the final purchase decision. In addition, the situation in which a decision is undertaken may play a role. Kotler et al. (2012) distinguish between three study dimensions of consumer behaviour, namely "culture, social groups and individual". These dimensions can be analysed individually even through each one impacts the others. Marketers attempt to gain as much information as possible about the influencing stimuli and characteristics to find out what marketing stimuli work best for their target group (Kotler, 2012b).

Marketers attempt to gain as much information as possible about the influencing stimuli and characteristics to find out what marketing stimuli work best for their target group (Kotler & Armstrong, 2014). Kotler et al (2012) developed on basis the S-O-R model a more detailed version that splits up the purchasing process in greater detail.

program. Expanding social rewards offers can build retailer or company loyalty. Most successful loyalty programs include pleasure providing, rather than functional, rewards to evoke pleasant association. Favourable feelings and emotions also match the hedonic element of consumers' behaviour, which boosts retail or company loyalty. Through a loyalty program, a company or retailer can express an attractive core identity; the loyalty program can be seen as an instrument to communicate the company's core values and defining characteristics. Balancing financial and social benefits is another important measure of loyalty programs' effectiveness for building company or retail loyalty. Managers should make social benefits more visible, because of their direct, positive influence on consumers' behaviour.

4.1 Interactive experience

Customer loyalty programs are important and beneficial strategies to attract attention of the consumers. Thus, they need to be innovative to keep up with fashion's varying seasonal changes and trends. One example could be an interactive loyalty program app for mobile phones. With this app loyalty program members can check out special offers, fashion campaigns and read feeds. Companies and retailers could use this app to build a closer relationship with their loyal customers and communicate their expertise on trends. Furthermore, retailers also can engage with customers on a personal level by displaying merchandise through images and video, based on the customer's fashion preferences. With the app, members can connect to their accounts without any cards in hand. Such a mobile app also provides new opportunities for marketing. Loyalty program members could also earn loyalty points for connecting to their social media sites. For example, just by "liking" the Loyalty program Facebook page through the app, the customer earns 10 points. It could be also interesting to inform customers via the app alert promotions and offers immediately, based on customer location. Furthermore, an interactive website additional to the app where loyalty card members have access to an exclusive platform of videos, campaigns, interviews with opinion leaders and styling advices. Members can check out fashionable styles and helpful suggestions on wardrobe that go accordingly to previous purchases made by the member. With this approach a company or retailer could achieve a smart connection making customers buying products as an emotional experience. With such platforms users can enhance and share their shopping activities while providing retailers an insight to customers shopping behaviour. The app and website allows the customer to discover new stores, browse fashion retailer's catalogues online and develop a community of fashion shoppers. Nowadays, shoppers are demanding more interactive experience. Loyalty programs must pursue a strategy of integrating the physical experience of shopping with the interactive and social experience online. However, apps and interactive websites need to provide incentives and entertainment to keep customers engaged.

4.2 Multi-partner program

Due to the great success of the multi-partner program Payback, it could be also considerable for fashion retailer and brands to set up a multi-partner program in fashion retail. Multi-partner programs enable consumers to collect points from various different companies offline and online with just a single card. With a multi-partner program in fashion retail, shoppers enjoy an even more rewarding shopping experience ("payback.net," 2015). Consumers will experience enhanced possibilities to earn points quickly and to convert them into attractive rewards. It would offer members better deals on their purchases; purchase redemption at all partners of the multi-partner program. This approach puts more control in the hands of customers; they can redeem the earned points by choosing any retailer or brand. A negative outcome could be increased program loyalty than loyalty towards a company.

4.3 Status

The retail markets is all about service; fashion companies prefer to be identified as classic, exclusive and sophisticated retailer and use this image as a tool that is reflected in their customer loyalty programs. The luxury industry often uses approaches such as special events, after-sales services and complimentary services on different service tiers. Different tiers could be a fact that loyal customers are willing to spend more money if they feel important and are trying to reach the next level.

4.4 Communication

In terms of staff understanding and commitment with a loyalty program. The benefits of the loyalty program should been fully communicated to the customer by the sales personnel. The sales personnels' daily contact with potential customers can be used as an entry point to get new consumers into the loyalty program involved. Sales assistants can educate and train consumers to use the loyalty program, so that it becomes an integrated part of the buying- and selling process of the company. Especially during promotion times, customers are much more likely to subscribe to a loyalty program as during the time without. To get more customers in the loyalty program enrolled is one of the considerable advantages a company can get. There are more people in the loyalty program a retailer or brand can communicate with, build closer relationships and learn about their buying behaviour

One opportunity is leveraging loyalty card member's insight to better understand how the consumers engage with the brand or retailer. Innovations such as Burberry Customer 1-2-1, an opt-in tool enabling sales associates to create and view customer profiles on iPads in-store, displays preferences and on/offline transaction history. It enables the retail associates to share a more personal, seamless and channel-agnostic experience with the customer (Manley, 2014).

5 Conclusion and Limitation

The purpose of this study was to investigate how loyalty programs in fashion retail can be emotionalized. The results of this study indicate that loyalty programs in fashion retail require considerable non-monetary benefits such as sense of exclusive membership and enhanced status to distinguish from competitors' customer loyalty programs. As the large body of customer loyalty data shows that a loyalty program that induce customer motives with exclusive benefit structures could lead to higher customer involvement and higher recognition for customer loyalty programs. As a guideline for companies is to tailor their loyalty programs to the needs of their customers, to activate more participant and build stronger emotional approach towards the company.

There are some limitations of this study, which must be recognised. An empirical study was not investigated in this study. Addressing this could be a good direction for future research, specifically with its comparison with monetary benefits and non-monetary benefits or stand-alone loyalty programs versus multi-partner programs. Moreover only theoretical literature and models were evaluated in this study. In order to give a more holistic picture more loyalty programs need to be tested including recommendation sources as other consumers and marketers. Another interesting topic could be the characterization of the fashion retail consumer.

Integrated Marketing Communication in Fashion: Converting Customers into Promoters?

Julia Wiedemann/Jochen Strähle

Abstract

Purpose – The purpose of this paper is to analyze the importance of Word-of-Mouth for fashion companies and to answer the research questions if fashion companies should integrate their customers actively in their marketing communication and if so, how can they approach the conversion of their customers into promoters?

Design/methodology/approach – A critical literature review is conducted to develop a thorough understanding and to infer practical implications.

Findings – The integration of the customer into the marketing mix is inevitable in today's marketplace. Customers are heavily influencing the fashion industry especially the transmission of trends. Thereof, a redefinition and proactive integration of the customer as promoter is necessary.

Research limitations/implications – Further methodology optimization can be achieved through an increased scope of the literature review and the integration of an empirical study to strengthen validity of the results.

Keywords – Word-of-Mouth, electronic Word-of-Mouth, Fashion, Viral Marketing, Consumer Generated Media

Paper type – Research paper

1 The Customer as Promoter an Introduction

Traditional marketing communication is characterized by a one-way, non-personal, paid-for communication that targets the audience through mass media. Thereby, the intention is to inform, persuade and remind customers (Berthon et al., 2008, p. 24).
In the 21st century which is characterized by a continuously changing media environment one can doubt that persuading through mass media is the key to success.
Customers are overwhelmed day by day with a bulk of information and it can be stated that traditional above-the-line communication is obsolete and has lost its effectiveness (Kirby & Marsden, 2007, p. xviii). This fact contributes to a selective and defensive attitude against commercial advertising. The sensory overload of customers triggers a natural scepticism which opens the door for non-traditional marketing (Bakanauskas & Bičiūnaitė, 2011, p. 7). Even if the phenomenon Word-of-Mouth (WOM) is not a recent field of research (De Bruyn & Lilien, 2008, p. 152), the growing importance in today's era of Web 2.0 is remarkable. The bidirectional interaction between brands and customers enables the customer to actively shape the market development and to influence the purchase behaviour of others twenty-four-seven. This interconnection accelerates the diffusion of positive and negative Word-of-Mouth on a different level (De Bruyn & Lilien, 2008, p. 151). Especially in the fashion context new communication disciplines are the rising stars. Social Media platforms and blogs have been quickly adapted and used by opinion leaders such as normal customers. These virtual platforms are places for discussions and posts about brands, products or services. Thereby, the company's intention towards customer-driven interventions in the marketing communication is not considered. Hence, the evolution of Web 2.0 was accompanied by shifting powers in the marketing communication. Fashion customers are actively engaging in brand activities, they are forming brand communities, they are deciding about the diffusion of trends and innovations and about the success or failure of brands (Brannon, 2010, p. 47). If fashion companies can steer and influence Word-of-Mouth in the right direction the success of a company can be leveraged (De Bruyn & Lilien, 2008, p. 151).

As an interpersonal communication, WOM is non-controllable and companies are scared of its effects. This uncontrollability leads to a dread in the marketing departments. Many marketers try to circumvent modern communication disciplines which are encouraging customers to engage in WOM communication. If the integration of new marketing disciplines cannot be avoided, their implementation is often half-hearted, not consequent and with a huge lack of know-how. Therefore, the purpose of this paper is to, first of all, answer the question if companies, especially in the fashion industry, should integrate the customer actively into their marketing communication and, secondly, to answer the question how fashion companies can best approach the conversion of their customers into promoters? To fulfil the purpose of this paper WOM Communication is explained by highlighting the evolution from WOM to electronic WOM. Furthermore, the underlying motives are presented which are driving customers to engage in WOM activities. Then, this knowledge is applied to examine WOM in the fashion retail context. Subsequently, modern communication disciplines are presented and Viral Marketing such as Consumer Generated Media are described in detail. The effectiveness and efficiency of WOM communication is evaluated to finally answer the research questions and to develop practical implications. In conclusion, limitations and restrictions such as the current relevance and possibilities for further investigation are analysed.

2 Status Quo in Literature

2.1 The Power of Word-of-Mouth Communication

2.1.1 Methodology

Embedded in the seminar fashion chain management this research paper is analysing the topic "The customer as promoter?" in the fashion context. Based on this broad topic two research questions are formulated to clarify the research purpose:

- *Research Question 1:* Should fashion companies integrate the customer actively into their marketing communication?
- *Research Question 2*: If so, how can fashion companies approach the conversion of their customers into promoters?

The structure of this paper has the purpose to answer the research questions and to guide the reader through the elaboration.

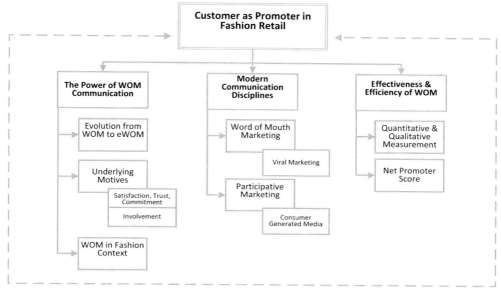

Figure 48: Structure of Research Paper

A critical literature review is conducted to develop a thorough understanding of the state of the art. The research is conducted using GoogleScholar and EBSCO. Thereby, emphasis is put on scientific primary and secondary literature. The chronology of literature revealed that the discussed topic has been of academic importance mainly between 2000 and 2009. This importance is a result of the evolution of Web 2.0 which triggered new fields of research. Nevertheless, the topic is still of great importance for academics and especially for practitioners who need to think about the rising opportunities and threats hidden behind the "customer as a promoter". The main purpose is to transfer the gained knowledge and to develop practical implication for the fashion industry. As this research paper is narrowed down, the aim is to go deep rather than wide. For that reason paragraph 2.5 is covering two selected new communication disciplines. The reason for choosing these disciplines, Viral Marketing and Consumer Generated Media, for a detailed examination is given due to their current relevance in literature and their valence in the fashion context.

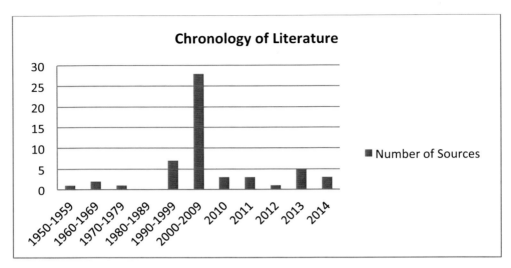

Figure 49: Chronology of Literature

2.2 Evolution from WOM to eWOM

Since the early 1950's the phenomenon Word-of-Mouth has been discussed in literature and can be defined as an "informal, person to person communication between a perceived non-commercial communicator and a receiver regarding a brand, a product, an organization or a service"(Walker, 2001, p. 63). Communication is a two-way process in which participants exchange information, ideas, feelings and news. The classic communication process, which is composed of a sender who is encoding information within a message that is intended for the receiver or audience, who decodes the message, is no longer applicable due to vast evolution of the Internet. With the exponential increase of electronic peer-to-peer referrals today's communication is revolutionized. Communication in the era of Web 2.0 is characterized by two-way dialogues and interactive conversation between customers and brands (Hamid, 2011, p. 273). Thereby, marketing communication incorporates all processes to communicate within the company and between the company and its environment. Aim is to provide and implement a market and customer-oriented corporate governance (Tropp, 2007, p. 1101). In the past marketing communication has been structured on the basis of three functions: Self-image function (to determine the company's image), marketing function (to market products or services) and dialogue function (to communicate with stakeholders). Due to the media evolution this function-oriented approach was extended with a fourth dimension: the media function. This dimension incorporates the increased use of Social Media in the context of new communication strategies such as Viral Marketing, Brand Community Marketing or Consumer Generated Media. Hence, the media function of marketing communication covers the indirect sociality and the generation of publicity and is realized through the institutionalization of communication platforms for market oriented unilateral or bilateral communication processes (Tropp, 2007, p. 1106). In this context not only the communication process has changed but also the definition of WOM and its attributes in the digital social environment. Word-of-Mouth can occur physically or digitally and scholars identified WOM as a persuasive alternative to the traditional communication tools. Thereby, the Internet facilitates customers the access to unbiased advices from others and provides the opportunity to create own consumption or brand related referrals by engaging in electronic Word-of-Mouth (eWOM). Electronic Word-of-Mouth is defined as "the positive or negative statement made by a potential, actual or former customer about a product or a company, which is made available to a multitude of people and institutions on the Internet" (Strauss, 2000, p. 235). Companies need to know the differences between traditional Word-of-Mouth and electronic Word-of-Mouth in order to develop strategies to manage these important components of the marketing mix. The differences are not selective but both, eWOM and WOM, are characterized by special attributes explained in the following. While traditional WOM is temporary and vanishes as soon as it is uttered (Buttle, 1998, pp. 242–243), the electronic counterpart is long-term available and is accessible for all participants in the virtual world. Moreover, the speed at which eWOM accelerates in cyberspace is much higher and reaches a greater audience (Wolny & Mueller, 2013, p. 565). EWOM is electronically mediated and no face-to-face communication is taken place. This lack of personal contact leads to anonymity and the trustworthiness of the electronic message is often questionable. Additionally, the fact that the referral can be produced by a company paid person, who promotes the brand or organisation in the Internet, is not contributing to its credibility (Breazeale, 2009, pp. 635–636). As the electronic referrals are unsolicited they are not automatically attracting the audience's interest. Unsolicited means that advices or messages are sent to an audience which is not necessarily searching for exactly that kind of information (De Bruyn & Lilien, 2008, p. 152). Furthermore, a difference in availability exists between traditional and electronic WOM. Within the electronic environment geographical boundaries are not existent (Wolny & Mueller, 2013, p. 565). In short "Internet WOM stands for a customer's boundless dialogue with a potentially unlimited number of other Internet users" (Helm, 2000, p. 3). Regarding this differences some authors postulate a so called "web advantage" (Cakim, 2010). Highlighting these differences of eWOM and WOM clarifies that even if both are reaching the same goal, the sharing of information, they are not a similar phenomenon (Breazeale, 2009, p. 637). Since WOM and eWOM have a major impact on customers perception and are not always positive for companies, it is tremendously important to recognize the relevance of this phenomenon and to develop proactive management strategies to benefit from the positive effects (De Bruyn & Lilien, 2008, p. 152).

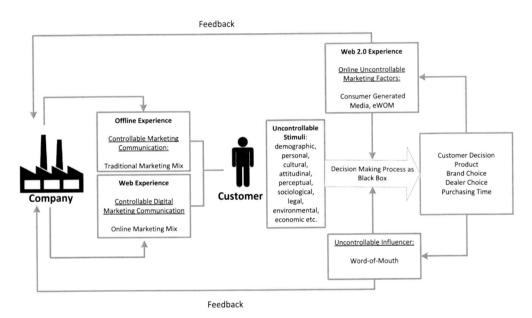

Figure 50: Factors Influencing the Customer in Nowadays Marketing Environment

2.3 Underlying Motives for Word-of-Mouth Communication

Academics identified strong dependences between the informal interpersonal information exchange and the purchase decision (Arndt, 1967, p. 295) and stated that WOM can be characterized as the "most effective form of communication influencing customers"(Yang, Hu, Winer, Assael, & Chen, 2012, p. 1; Katz & Lazarsfeld, 1955 cit. De Bruyn & Lilien, 2008). Moreover, WOM is a crucial indicator for customer expectation (Ziethaml, Berry, & Parasuraman, 1993, p. 9) and influences the pre-purchase attitudes (Ziethaml et al., 1993, p. 9) as well as the perception of post-purchase performance (Fitzgerald Bone, 1992, p. 582). WOM may be positive (PWOM), such as recommendations, or negative (NWOM), like advising against a product. Concluding, WOM is a tremendously important informal input in the purchase decision making process (Helm, 2000, p. 159). The Nielsen Global Survey of Trust in Advertising from 2013 polled 29.000 customers in 58 countries to answer the question to what extent they trust in different forms of advertising. Thereby, Word-of-Mouth has been identified as the most influential one "[…] as 84 percent said […] this source was the most trustworthy" (Nielsen Company, 2013). Hence, it is crucial for marketers to understand the motivational factors which are driving Word-of-Mouth communication. Whereas, the consequences of Word-of-Mouth have been studied in-depth there has been less attention to the antecedents of WOM. To understand the motivation of people to share and talk about certain products or brands rather than about others or why the word spreads faster in some contexts is crucial to develop efficient marketing tactics.

2.3.1 Customer Satisfaction, Trust and Commitment

Widely acknowledged, the individual degree of satisfaction or dissatisfaction with consumption experience is one of the key antecedents of product related Word-of-Mouth (Anderson, Fornell, & Mazvancheryl, 2004, p. 7). "Satisfaction can be defined as an evaluation of an emotion in response to the ownership and/or usage of a product or service"(Lang & Hyde, 2013, p. 4). Several researchers proofed a significant influence of satisfaction or dissatisfaction on the WOM production (Anderson, 1998; T. J. Brown, Barry, Dacin, & Gunst, 2005). Thereby, satisfaction influences the likelihood of engaging in WOM-activities such as the quantity of referrals (Wangenheim & Bayón, 2007, p. 235). Nevertheless, Anderson's (1998) indicated that satisfaction is important but not the single cause triggering the production of PWOM or

NWOM. Within one of his conducted studies he validated that even if customers are neutral pertaining to a certain issue "WOM is still produced at about 80 per cent of the maximum level" (East, 2008, p. 253). Concluding, it is unilateral to take customer satisfaction as the single motivational factor to explain the production of WOM (Anderson, 1998, p. 15). Diverse studies examined that customer commitment is an additional antecedent of WOM (Walker, 2001) or a mediator of the relationship between WOM and customer satisfaction (T. J. Brown et al., 2005). Customer commitment is "[…] the desire to maintain a relationship with a particular brand […]" (Henke, 2013, p. 4). This is mainly developed when customers are satisfied, have trust in a brand, and connect the brand's self-image to their personal one. The difference between commitment for a brand and customer satisfaction is that customer satisfaction is more backward-looking, whereas the commitment to a brand is more future-oriented and forward-looking. Customers who commit to a brand or an organisation are more actively engaged in WOM communication compared to those who are only satisfied (Wolny & Mueller, 2013, p. 566). Nor do customers make referrals if they don't feel attached to the product (Kumar, Petersen, & Leone, 2007, p. 146). Especially emotional or affective commitment to brands encourage WOM activities (Wolny & Mueller, 2013, p. 567). Both commitment and trust are described in literature as additional motivational drivers influencing WOM but they are highly context related and not universal applicable across product categories (Lang & Hyde, 2013, p. 11).

Summing up, customer satisfaction, commitment and trust are important pre-amplifiers for the formation of WOM (Lang & Hyde, 2013, p. 4). This presented approach, which reduces the appearance of WOM on trust, satisfaction and commitment, enables marketing practitioners to derivate basic practical actions and implications. However, it should be noted that no fundamental understanding of the underlying psychological motives inducing WOM activities is given.

2.3.2 Involvement Construct

Even if customers are having equalized levels of satisfaction the WOM activities among them varies in quantity and volume (Anderson, 1998, p. 15). Satisfaction and Dissatisfaction does not explain *why* and *when* customers engage or not engage in WOM. Therefore, it can be inferred that customer-specific characteristics and dispositions are crucial for the participation in WOM-communication. These personal variables have moderating effects on the satisfaction-WOM-link (Wangenheim & Bayón, 2007, p. 236). In the following a broader view is adapted to present a holistic answer why customers engage in WOM activities. Aspects of customer psychology and situational influences are considered to extend the previous knowledge. Up to date only a few studies analysed these underlying motives in detail (Sundaram, Mitra, & Webster, 1998, p. 527). For a holistic explanation of the motivational antecedents of WOM communication mainly involvement theories are applied (Thorsten Hennig-Thurau, Gwinner, Walsh, & Gremler, 2004, p. 40). Arising from the field of socio-psychology the involvement construct is transferred to customer psychology to explain general customer traits (Rodríguez-Santos, González-Fernández, & Cervantes-Blanco, 2013, p. 1107). Involvement is defined as "the state of motivation or 'excitation' of an individual derived from a perception of a stimulus as being of personal relevance" (Rodríguez-Santos et al., 2013, p. 1107). The construct involvement itself is multifaceted and the most long-standing motivational construct discussed in literature (Wolny & Mueller, 2013, p. 565). While examining literature covering involvement theories in the context of WOM communication there is some controversy regarding the underlying identifiable dimensions (Wangenheim & Bayón, 2007, pp. 235–236). Differentiating involvement in situational involvement and enduring involvement is consensus in literature. This timely differentiation is important for strategic planning and a successful implementation of marketing policies (Rodríguez-Santos et al., 2013, p. 1108). Situational involvement occurs while the customer is evaluating the product itself or having a short-term involvement when acquiring and using a low involvement product. Permanent involvement relates to a more general attitude towards a product or brand. Thereby, this long-lasting involvement occurs because the individual classifies the product or brand as highly personal relevant (Wolny & Mueller, 2013, p. 565). Over five decades ago Dichter (1966) identified four different motivational categories that dispose customers to positively talk about products or services: Product Involvement, Self-Involvement, Other involvement and Message Involvement (Dichter, 1966, p. 148).

- *Product Involvement* is the level of personal relevance customers see in a product, or the personal relevance of a product (Thorsten Hennig-Thurau et al., 2004, p. 41; Wolny & Mueller, 2013, p. 567).
- *Self-Involvement* or self-confirmation is generally the need to share consumption experience with the aim to enhance one's self image among others in society (Dichter, 1966, p. 149).

- *Other Involvement* includes the senders motivation to give the WOM receiver positive advices through WOM. This motivational factor arises from the basic human need to be helpful and to give advices (Smith, Coyle, Lightfoot, & Scott, 2007, p. 395).
- *Message Involvement* refers to WOM induced by advertisements or public relations (Thorsten Hennig-Thurau et al., 2004, p. 567).

Engel, Blackwell and Miniard (1993) extended and modified Dichter's motivational typology by renaming the four motivational categories and adding one category labelled *dissonance reduction* to explain the formation of NWOM. *Dissonance reduction* can be defined as the reduction of cognitive dissonance occurring in the post purchase phase (Thorsten Hennig-Thurau et al., 2004, p. 40). In 1998 Sundaram, Mitra and Webster investigated within one study the relation between consumption experiences and WOM production. Taking findings from customer behaviour, cognitive psychology and sociology studies into account, the authors deduced "that consumption experiences and motivations are closely related in the process of WOM transmissions"(Sundaram et al., 1998, p. 527). This connection between consumption experiences, in other words customer satisfaction or dissatisfaction, and the motivational factors underlying WOM communication are crucial for a holistic understanding of WOM. Moreover, they carried out a comprehensive study and extended the former studies in this field of research. Therefore, this study is the basis for following assumptions. For engaging in PWOM communication Sundaram et al. (1998) identified 4 major motives which equate to some extent to the motivational categories of Dichter's typology presented above. *Altruism* equates to Other Involvement, *Self-Enhancement* equates to Self-Involvement and the motive *Product Involvement* is in both studies included. In addition to these three motivational factors, Sundaram et al incorporated the motive *Helping the Company*. This motive includes the intention of the WOM-sender to help the company rather than the receiver. Taking the motives for NWOM into consideration, Sundaram et al. identified different underlying motivations in comparison to PWOM production except for the motive *Altruism*. Besides, *Altruism* the motives *Anxiety Reduction*, *Vengeance* and *Advice Seeking* were identified. *Anxiety Reduction* stands for the sender's motivation to reduce anger and frustration through NWOM. *Vengeance* means that the sender of NWOM takes revenge on the company due to dissatisfying experiences with the company. The motive *Advice Seeking* includes the intention of the customer to share negative experience and to obtain problem solving advices from others (Sundaram et al., 1998, pp. 528–530). The following overview illustrates the relation between WOM-activities, customer satisfaction, customer commitment and the direct influencer involvement. Thereby, the concept of Sundaram et al. is applied due to its high level of detail and its coherent derivation.

Summing up, all presented studies covering involvement in the context of WOM communication are incorporating basically the same idea. The difference is that some are covering motives for PWOM only and some for PWOM and NWOM. Regardless of the level of detail it is widely accepted in literature that the degree of personal involvement has a direct influence on WOM activities. As a result of the mentioned significant differences between traditional WOM and eWOM the above illustrated typology has to be revised and further extended (Thorsten Hennig-Thurau et al., 2004, p. 40). In recent researches the electronic context was incorporated and additional motives that are influencing especially the engagement in eWOM were identified. Thereby, literature suggests that the need for social interaction, the desire for economic incentives, altruism and self-enhancement are the primary motivators leading to eWOM behaviour" (Thorsten Hennig-Thurau et al., 2004).

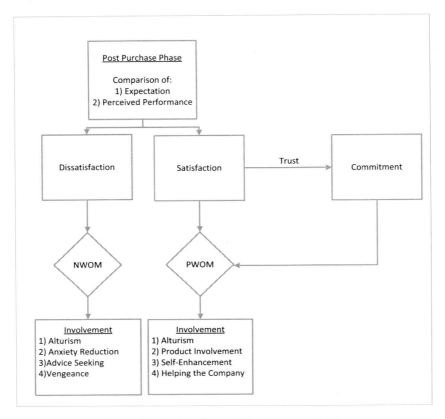

Figure 51: Antecedents Affecting Traditional WOM Communication

2.4 Word-of-Mouth in the Fashion Context

Traditional marketing channels are important for fashion advertising, but the rise of electronic communication in social networks changed the diffusion process of trends such as the whole interaction between brands and customers (Posner, 2011, p. 30). "Fashion has been classified as high involvement, which refers to products that are either expensive, rarely bought, linked to personal identity, or carry high risks (social or otherwise)" (Wolny & Mueller, 2013, p. 563). Usually, fashion involvement has the character of enduring involvement because the customer relates the product to one's self-image and therefore it is highly personal relevant (Wolny & Mueller, 2013,

p. 566). The concept of fashion involvement incorporates five dimensions of fashion adoption-related behaviours:

- Fashion innovativeness and time of purchase
- Fashion interpersonal communication
- Fashion interest
- Fashion knowledgeability
- Fashion awareness (Tigert, Ring, & King, 1976, p. 47).

Within society a wide difference in terms of the characteristic feature fashion involvement is identifiable. Especially, high fashion involved customers are of great importance for the formation and diffusion of fashion trends (Tigert et al., 1976, p. 51). Trends transmit through Word-of-Mouth among personal networks and the Internet fastens the spread and the reach of buzz. In fashion the customer orients oneself more and more towards non-traditional media. Fashion leaders, early adopters and celebrities are co-creating the image of fashion brands. Instead of just wearing and perpetuating the latest trends they personalize them and decide whether a brand is in or out. Representing oneself with self-selected styles and to create a desired self-image has become more and more important. Web 2.0 has opened up a new channel to express ones identity and to show fashion preferences. Because fashion has the unique ability to be used as a vehicle for social connection and communication, it is proposed in literature to consider marketing tactics such as Viral Marketing, Social Media Marketing or to support Consumer Generated Media (Posner, 2011, p. 30). Recapitulating, the Internet has given the fashion industry a whole new dimension to advertise its products, to market brands and to influence the purchase behaviour of customers. Therefore, academics suggest the consideration of modern communication disciplines in the marketing mix.

2.5 Modern Communication Disciplines

2.5.1 Viral Marketing

New personal communication technologies, the increased marketing literacy among customers, the advertising clutter, the media fragmentation and ad blocking technologies have dramatically changed the strategies and tactics of marketing communication (Kirby & Marsden, 2007, p. xx). "The new media environment has further complicated marketers' perennial challenge to build effective and efficient marketing communication programs" (Keller, 2003, p. 219). These enormous changes have shifted the powers in the external marketing environment, nowadays the customer dominates the marketplace (Keller, 2003, p. 178). Due to the changing media landscape a re-evaluation of the marketing communication a strategy is inevitable (Keller, 2003, p. 219). The urge of the customer to present oneself in the virtual world opens up new possibilities for companies to broaden and deepen their knowledge about their customers (Tropp, 2014, p. 201). Besides the traditional communication strategies the so called modern communication disciplines are decisive for a successful marketing mix. The principal of dictatorial advertising is replaced by high qualitative communication content. Participative Marketing Communication (PMC), Guerrilla Marketing (GM), Word-of-Mouth Marketing (WOMM), Viral Marketing (VM), Social Media Marketing (SMM) and Utility Marketing (UM) stand out against the traditional communication disciplines by incorporating the communication criteria selectivity, reflexivity and contextuality in a goal-oriented manner. Thereby, experience-oriented approaches with surprising and captivating content are created to evoke the desired output (Tropp, 2007, p. 1110). Within this paper Consumer Generated Media and Viral Marketing are examined and discussed in detail.

Word-of-Mouth Marketing (WOMM) can be defined as the type of marketing that encourages and promotes natural inter-personal communication through many different tactics. The Word-of-Mouth Marketing Association (WOMMA) describes WOMM as "Giving people a reason to talk about your products and services, and making it easier for that conversation to take place. It is the art and science of building active, mutually beneficial customer-to-customer and customer-to-marketer communications" ("An Introduction to Word of Mouth Marketing.," 2008 cit. Meiners, Schwarting, & Seeberger, 2010, p. 82). According to this definition Word-of-Mouth marketing is the generic term to that. Tactics such as Viral Marketing, Buzz Marketing or Social Media Marketing are subordinated (Tropp, 2014, p. 540).

> Viral Marketing can be understood as a communication and distribution concept that relies on customers to transmit digital products via electronic mail to other potential customers in their social sphere and to animate these contacts to also transmit the products. (Helm, 2000, p. 159)

Thereby, the underlying concept of Viral Marketing is derived from Darwin's theory of evolution and popularized by Dawkins' in the 1976. Dawkin transferred the basic idea of self-running gene replication and spread from biological theory or evolutionism to social theory. With the term "meme" he introduced an analogy to the term "gene" in the Darwinian evolution theory (Williams, 2002, pp. 162–163). Memetic is based on the postulation of so called "memes", which are "self-replicating ideas moving through time and space without further effort from the source" (Gelb, 1997, p. 57). In other words, memes can be skills, habits, ideas, stories, inventions, trends or any concept which ensures its self-replication by appearing in several different formats. Thereby, self-replication of memes stands for their passing along from person to person by imitation (Brannon, 2010, p. 64). Considering the theory of evolution, memes in the marketing context are like genes in the theory of evolution. They have to compete for free space in human's memories to get passed or copied. Blackwell (1999) stated that marketers have to adapt Darwin's idea of the "Survival of the Fittest".

> Self-replication is not easy to be achieved and memes need [...] to fit the environment of the brain and [need to have] a better fit than the multitude of other idea, utterances and theories that compete for brain space. More specifically, in advertising, the advertiser is attempting to create new combinations (mutations) of ideas that they hope will fit – be adapted to- the target market. However, only the fittest will survive. (Blackmore, 1999, p. cited by; Williams, 2002, p. 163)

The term Viral Marketing arises from the similarity between the dissemination process of memes and the spread of viral infections. Viral Marketing incorporates systematic strategies, tactics and measures to specifically trigger Word-of-Mouth (Langner, 2009, p. 24). This marketing discipline uses the connectivity amongst individuals to capture attention and to create buzz (Posner, 2011, p. 30). Building on the power of Word-of-Mouth in social networks Viral Marketing campaigns involve individuals who know each other and individuals who do not know each other (Brannon, 2010, p. 64). The aim of Viral Marketing campaigns is to trigger a snowball effect or to create a meme. Thereby, the connection between Viral Marketing and Word-of-Mouth marketing is one of cause and effect. Viral Marketing creates awareness and buzz by using attention getting and captivating marketing tools. Positive Word-of-Mouth is theoretically the desired output which in turn contributes to higher profitability and new customers (Ferguson, 2008b, p. 178). The following figure illustrates the possible reach which can be achieved through Viral Marketing campaigns if a multiplier effect occurs. Assumed that one customer forwards the Viral Marketing campaign to five other customers and these are sending the message to five others, 125 potentially new customers are reached. On the next level 625 and then 3.125 new customers are addressed (Langner, 2009, pp. 15–16).

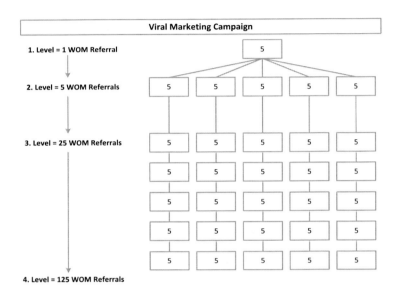

Figure 52: Multiplier Effect in the Transmission of Viral Marketing Campaigns

Adapted from: (Langner, 2009, p. 16)

To evoke an epidemic-like propagation of marketing messages the composition of society has to be considered. Gladwell (2001) stated in his book "The tipping point" that in the beginning of the diffusion process the desired message is forwarded by a few key individuals or carriers (Gladwell, 2001 cit. Brannon, 2010, p. 64) Therefore, he subdivided society in connectors, mavens and salesmen to explain who is influencing the diffusion of WOM or trends. Connectors are decisive for the diffusion of Viral Marketing campaigns because they know many people and connect different social networks. Market mavens, or so called information specialists, are people who are more likely to share their knowledge with general public due to underlying altruistic motives. Salesmen or persuaders are the third decisive group in the transmission process. They boost or weaken the viral campaign (Langner, 2009, pp. 21–23; Mourdoukoutas & Siomkos, 2009, p. 7). This perception of society shows companies which customers they have to contact directly while implementing a Viral Marketing campaign. The contact between the firm and the "normal audience" is therefore just indirect and mavens, connectors and salesmen are functioning as intermediaries. Nonetheless, it is inevitable to create high qualitative, memorable and context related messages to trigger viral infections in the market place (Helm, 2000, p. 159). The viral campaign content can be presented in several ways:

- *Viral Clip*: Video specially produced for the Internet.
- *Spoof:* Imitation or humoristic parody of an existent viral clip.
- *Ad game:* Online game gratis downloadable in the Internet.
- *Websites:* Internet pages especially provided for viral campaigns.
- *"Share" and "Sent to"- Buttons:* Into Social Media or traditional website integrated buttons. When pressing the button the content is shared or forwarded.
- *Content of Consumer Generated Media, Guerrilla Marketing or other modern communication disciplines:* These contents are highly relevant, eccentric, captivating and therefore triggering viral campaigns (Tropp, 2014, p. 556).

Managing Viral Marketing

The three key objectives of Viral Marketing are to increase brand awareness, to gain customer related information and to initiate purchase actions. The core idea of Viral Marketing is that the customer spreads the virus situational and not out of a long-lasting customer-brand relationship. Thereby, referrals can be either passive or active. Active referrals are initiated by the customer. Concluding, the customer is actively willing to forward the marketing message. Passive referrals are often hidden and the referral is usually automatic but not cognitively recognized by the customer (Langner, 2009, p. 34). This difference in customers' required activity level, active referral or passive referral, leads to a classification of Viral Marketing strategies. Two different strategies, the low involvement strategy and the high involvement strategy are identified by Helm (2000). The low involvement strategy is often based on the mentioned passive referral which is induced simply by the use of the promoted service or product. The high involvement strategy actively engages the customer in the creation of brand awareness. Whether the low or high involvement strategy is adapted is a question of desired output (Helm, 2000, pp. 159–160). Regardless of the strategic decision the first crux for firms is to design the viral campaign content. Companies have to decide whether they choose a value-added or incentive-oriented content. Value-added campaigns try to maximize the entertainment and amusement of the customer while spreading or sharing the campaign. This playful approach differs extremely from the incentive-oriented campaign. Choosing the incentive-oriented approach the firm links the use of the viral campaign content to a reward that the customer has to deliver. Aim of this approach is to achieve concrete marketing goals such as the accumulation of customer data. The chosen tactic depends on the company's marketing strategy such as the desired output (Langner, 2009, pp. 86–87). However, all viral campaigns have to be pragmatic, free of charge, utile, novel and valid (Tropp, 2014, p. 555). Managing the seeding of viral campaigns is decisive for their success. Seeding is the target group oriented transmission of the viral campaign. The seeding process can be either passive (basic) or active (extended) (Tropp, 2014, p. 556). Passive seeding focuses on the authentic contact with the target audience; hereby existing customers are used as carriers for the campaign content. The active seeding aims to speed up the transmission of viral campaigns and multiple viral elements are applied. The defined goal is to address as quickly as possible as many people as possible. Active seeding tries to reach this aim by using traditional mass media but this can diminish the authenticity of the viral campaign (Langner, 2009, p. 87).

As the literature review highlights, considerable advantages can be achieved through Viral Marketing: the transmission of new products is fastened, buzz is generated, awareness is enhanced and customers can be tied to brands. To achieve all these positive outcomes companies have to create viral campaigns which "connect at the front end of [firms'] customer strategy, open a doorway into customer data collection, and then connect on the back end to engage [the firms] most valuable segments" (Ferguson, 2008b, p. 181). As several authors state Viral Marketing campaigns can be a worthwhile marketing tactic if critical success factors are considered:

- Firms need to clearly identify the target audience to best address the campaign and to create high quality content (Bakanauskas & Bičiūnaitė, 2011, p. 10)
- The campaign has to be value-adding for the customer or incentive based (Langner, 2009, p. 87).

- The message provided by the company has to fulfil the following requirements: stickiness, simplicity, unexpectedness, concreteness, credibility, emotionally involving (Brannon, 2010, p. 64).
- The simplicity of transmission is the prerequisite for an efficient viral effect (Langner, 2009, p. 87).
- The first individuals who should spread the virus have to be chosen carefully (Helm, 2000, p. 181).
- The company has to provide the physical and virtual resources which are necessary for the diffusion of the viral campaign (Langner, 2009, p. 87).
- Viral Marketing campaigns are primary useful for creating brand awareness. The direct influence on profitability should not be the superficial aim (Ferguson, 2008b, p. 181).
- When customers are spreading the virus it does not automatically mean that the customer is loyal. Therefore, companies have to integrate emotional binding elements into their viral campaigns to boost the affective commitment (Ferguson, 2008b, p. 182).
- Companies have to bow out from the idea of being in control. Viral Marketing can be guided but not controlled (Hamid, 2011, p. 266).

Recapitulating the examined communication discipline Viral Marketing is subordinated to the generic term Word-of-Mouth Marketing. The strategic purpose is the creation of reception relevance thus the customer is conducting desired subsequent actions in social networks. Embedded in the theory of memes, Viral Marketing campaigns are seeded by companies and indirectly passed along by the audience via Internet like epidemics. The relation between WOM and Viral Marketing is thereby one of cause and effect. Viral Marketing can be an efficient tool to trigger WOM and to increase brand awareness. Considering the fashion industry, Viral Marketing can be perfectly based on the power of brand communities. If created and implemented carefully the viral campaign can evoke an exclusive "sender" feeling which expresses itself in the attitude of being "in the know". Whether or not a correlation between Viral Marketing, WOM and profitability increase exists, is discussed in paragraph 2.6 Effectiveness and Efficiency of Word-of-Mouth.

2.5.2 Consumer Generated Media

Participative Marketing Communication can be seen as an evolution of Social Media Marketing and is defined as a marketing communication discipline that explicitly integrates target subjects in the interpretation of a brand and the realisation of the communicative output. The wording Participative and Participatory Marketing can be applied synonymous. Considering the quality of the communication, this discipline tends to incorporate an equated level of attention arousal, receptions relevance and aims to trigger a subsequent action (Tropp, 2014, p. 452). Within the concept of Participative marketing the customer is transformed into a prosumer (Tropp, 2007, p. 1111). Highlighting the role of Participative Marketing within the process of marketing evolution, the following figure is given.

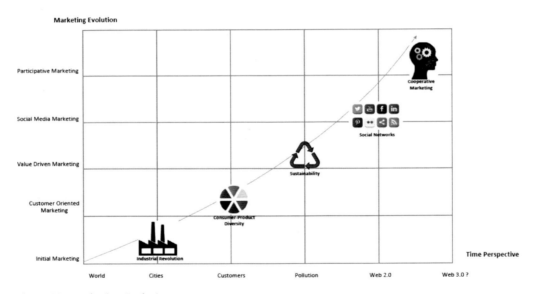

Figure 53: Marketing Evolution

Participative Marketing Communication can be realized in form of Consumer Generated Media (CGM) (Tropp, 2007, p. 1111). While reviewing the literature no consistent terminology is identifiable. To simplify the further investigation the term Consumer Generated Media is utilised only in accordance with Dickey and Lewis

(2009). CGM is created and driven by customers and can be a useful information source for firms and customers, a socialization attribute or a customer resource. The aim of this marketing tactic is to involve customers in the development of the communication policy of a product or brand. The structural and interactive features of CGM have a huge potential to build a relationship between customers and brands, hence effective commitment can be evoked (Dickey & Lewis, 2009, p. 182). The most common types of CGM are:

- *Blogs:* Regularly updated web pages with publication in an informal or conversational spelling style usually driven by individuals or small groups of individuals.
- *Message boards and forums:* Online platforms for holding discussion in form of posted messages.
- *Review or rating sites:* Websites on which product, brand or service experiences can be shared and assessed.
- *Platforms for direct company feedback:* Web applications run by the company to encourage and ease the contact between customer and company. Enables direct feedback.
- *Third party websites:* Websites on which persons or groups besides the two primarily involved in a situation (customer and brand) actively engage in generating comments.
- *Moblogs:* Acronym combining the terms "mobile" and "blog". Moblogs are mobile enabled blogs.
- *Vlogs/Videos:* Acronym combining "video" and "blog". Blog that consist of video clips.
- *Podcasts:* Digital media files, always a series of such files, available on the Internet for downloading to a portable media devices (Dickey & Lewis, 2009, p. 182).

Generally, academics identified three underlying motives for customers to engage in the creation of Consumer Generated Media: *Intrinsic enjoyment* (customers create advertisement for the creation itself), *Self-promotion* (customers create advertisement to promote themselves and to create a self-image linked with the brand, product or service) and *Change perceptions* (aim is to change the perception of the brand, product or service in society) (Berthon, Pitt, & Campbell, 2008, p. 10). Besides, these underlying motives, economic or personal relevant incentives offered by the company can trigger CGM. Moreover, the customer's ability, the availability of relevant CGM sites such as the ease to identify these platforms or webpages are decisive factors for the adoption of CGM. Furthermore, these elements are crucial for the likelihood of customers to post their experience or preferences to products, brands or services. CGM can on the one hand create a sense of belongingness, community thinking and group identification and on the other hand can be intensified through brand communities (Dickey & Lewis, 2009, p. 182).

> A brand community is a specialized, non-geographically bound community, based on a structured set of social relationships among admires of a brand. It is specialized because at its centre is a branded good or service. Like other communities, it is marked by shared consciousness, rituals and traditions, and a sense of moral responsibility. Each of these qualities is, however, situated within a commercial and mass-mediated ethos, and has its own particular expression. Brand communities are participants in the brand's larger social construction and play a vital role in the brand's ultimate legacy. (Muniz Jr. & O'Guinn, 2001, p. 412)

Brand communities are composed of highly involved customers. Remarkable is the trust and high credibility among the brand community members. These facts contribute to the facilitation of Consumer Generated Media within Brand Communities. Therefore, a brand community can function as an ambassador and mouthpiece (Dickey & Lewis, 2009, p. 182; Tropp, 2014, p. 462). As Figure 54 highlights, WOM and eWOM can be triggered by CGM. The potential of CGM is obvious and therefore "Managers may be better off viewing the customer-generated advertising phenomenon as a Word-of-Mouth problem rather than a conventional advertising dilemma" (Berthon et al., 2008, p. 25). Such as WOM, CGM can be high volatile and is not easy controllable but the credibility, authenticity as well as the unconventionality of CGM is unique. Primary objective of firms should be to create an supporting environment where the customer can spread the word and engage actively in CGM to market the brand, product or service in the desired way (Berthon et al., 2008). Consumer Generated Media can be fertilised by the company, for example initiated through economic or other personal relevant incentives or unfertilised, in other words non-sponsored. The following figure illustrates, summarizes and systematizes Participative Marketing Communication (Tropp, 2014, p. 459).

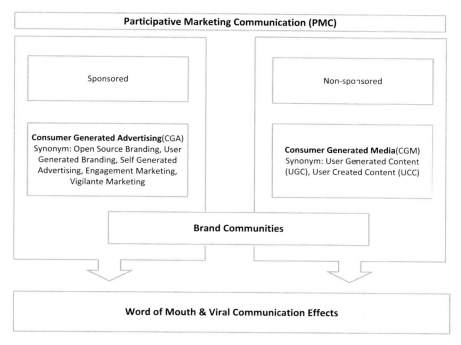

Figure 54: Participative Marketing Communication

Managing Consumer Generated Media

For developing tactics how to deal with Consumer Generated media, the variety and valence of attitudes has to be considered. In this case variety means the range of consumer generated content (customers' attitudes polarity). Valence stands for the quality of CGM. Considering both characteristics of CGM, managerial actions can be inferred. Referring to Berthon et al (2009), four different strategies can be adapted when managing CGM:

- *Disapprove:* The firm's attitude towards CGM is negative and the behaviour is passive. Actions can vary from ignorance to reluctant tolerance. While not taking any actions the company is not overreacting but can be labelled as being unqualified in the confrontation with its customers.
- *Repel:* The company's attitude towards CGM is negative and the behaviour is active. Thereby, the company aims to minimize CGM by actively denounc-

ing the consumer created content. This strategy involves the danger of being classified as an unsympathetic non customer-oriented brand.

- *Applaud:* The firm's attitude towards CGM is positive but the behaviour is passive. In this case companies are verbally expressing their preferences but no action easing and facilitating CGM is implemented. The missing commitment is not encouraging customers and the full potential is not exhausted.
- *Facilitate:* The company's attitude towards CGM is positive and the behaviour is active. Verbal commitment and active facilitation of CGM is creating ideal conditions for customers to participate in the marketing communication. Facilitation can vary from providing platforms to the direct encouragement of customers. While exploiting all positive aspects of CGM this strategy is very time consuming and if not guided in the right way the firm can be confronted with the loss of control (Berthon et al., 2008, pp. 16–19).

Arising from the top management's attitude towards CGM, these strategies are depending in the situational context. Therefore, the following visualization illustrates the four different strategies presented above in a situational context considering the variance and valence of attitudes among the customers (Berthon et al., 2008, p. 19).

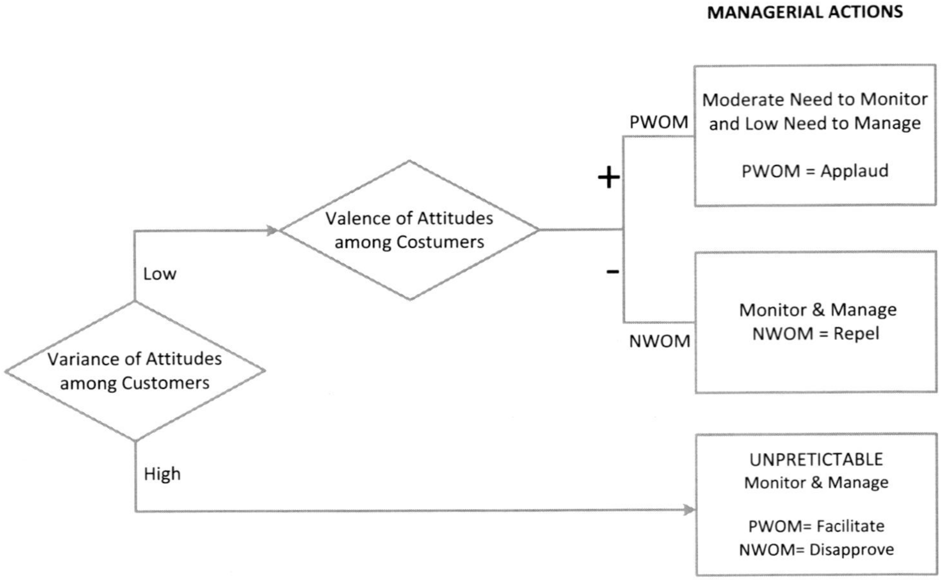

Figure 55: Situational Related CGM-Management

Recapitulating, the strategy of engaging the customer actively in the marketing communication of products, brands or services can be an effective and efficient marketing tactic. Consumer Generated Media cannot be switched off; hence top management has to strategically incorporate Participative Marketing Communication within the marketing mix (Dickey & Lewis, 2009, p. 183). Especially in fashion retail, Consumer Generated Media can have a significant impact on the marketing communication. Used as a vehicle for social interactions and communication, fashion has a unique ability to be the content of Consumer Generated Media. Intrinsic enjoyment, self promotion such as a changing perception can be ideally realised through CGM in the fashion context. Moreover, fashion customers rely more and more on the trends submitted through opinion leaders and innovators in the virtual world. A huge opportunity, to provoke CGM for fashion companies is the so called product seeding. Through submitting next season's products to influential individuals, who are wearing the new designs, trends are spread and buzz is created (Brannon, 2010, p. 64; Hamid, 2011, pp. 265–269; Posner, 2011, p. 30).

2.6 Effectiveness and Efficiency of Word-of-Mouth

2.6.1 Quantitative and Qualitative Measurement

Word-of-Mouth communication, as an interpersonal exchange process, is quite difficult to monitor. It is widely acknowledged that WOM can have a significant impact on generating momentum for a company, brand or product. The relevance of WOM for marketers is even higher due to the fact that it is costless, it takes its effects immediately when spreading through the cyberspace and it is highly credible (Keiningham, Aksoy, Cooil, Andreassen, & Williams, 2008, p. 81). Quantifying and measuring the efficiency and effectiveness of WOM releasing marketing campaigns is a serious issue for academic researchers and practitioners. It is undeniable that WOM builds brand awareness but the direct influence on profitability is debatable (Ferguson, 2008b, p. 179). Furthermore, it is not scientifically proven that WOM communication has a long-lasting effect that creates brand loyalty (Ferguson, 2008, p. 181). Academic researchers developed different methods to measure WOM, buzz or Viral Marketing effectiveness (Smith et al., 2007, p. 387). Traditional WOM and its effects can be hardly measured in a cost-effective manner, whereas, the performance measurement of online marketing campaigns can either be conducted by using qualitative or quantitative measurements. Quantitatively performance can be measured through web server inquiries. Thereby, the server determines the number of transmitted files from the server to a client and the requests done by the client. Through retrievals and queries the usage pattern of a viral campaign can be identified and conclusions can be drawn from these usage patterns. The qualitative performance measurement is based on the evaluation and analysis of the WOM or CGM content. Combining the quantitative and the qualitative measurement techniques a broad overview of the effectiveness of marketing campaigns that trigger WOM can be generated (Langner, 2009, p. 100). Nonetheless, this performance measurement and evaluation does not make a statement whether or not WOM communication directly affects the profitability of a firm.

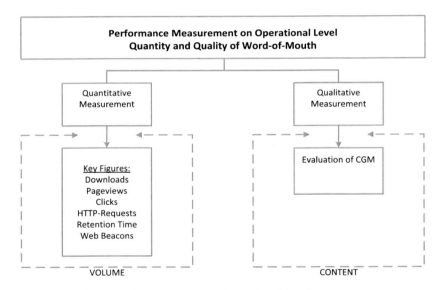

Figure 56: Performance Measurement on Operational Level
Adapted from: (Langner, 2009, p. 93)

Net Promoter Score

The Net Promoter Score (NPS) was introduced in 2003 by Reichheld in the Harvard Business Review (Reichheld, 2003). The concept of the NPS changed the status quo by introducing a new loyalty metric: the Net Promoter Score. Promoted nowadays as a powerful management philosophy "the Net Promoter Score, or NPS®, is a straightforward metric that helps companies and every employee understand and be accountable for how they engage with customers" ("Net Promoter Score," n.d.). Adapted by many companies due to its simplicity, the basic idea behind the Net Promoter Score is to measure the loyalty between a provider (company) and its customer. Reichheld postulates a strong correlation between customer loyalty, further growth and Word-of-Mouth recommendation. As a consequence hereof, the NPS can confess companies' future development and profitability (Reichheld, 2003).

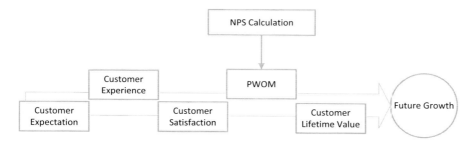

Figure 57: Net Promoter Score in Customer Purchase Decision Making Process
Adapted from: (Greve, 2010, p. 42)

The NPS is calculated by asking in a customer survey *the* single question: "How likely is it that you would recommend [company X] to a friend or colleague?" ("Net Promoter Score," n.d.) Using a zero- to- ten scale, whereby 10 means "extremely likely", Reichheld identified three logical clusters of customers. Customers answering nine or ten have the highest rate of likelihood to recommend and are called "promoters" The cluster of "passively satisfied" answered with a seven or an eight, whereby the third group "the detractors" is most unlikely to recommend and scored from zero to six (Reichheld, 2003). The NPS is then calculated by subtracting the percentage of Detractors from the percentage of Promoters ("Net Promoter Score," n.d.). The Net Promoter score is critically discussed due to its claim of being the best predictor of growth (Grisaffe, 2007; Keiningham et al., 2008). Reviewing the literature little statistical evidence can be identified that NPS is the most reliable single indicator of a company's ability to grow. Keiningham et al. (2008) prove that no correlation between the indicator NPS and the future growth of a company is identifiable due to a Pearson correlation of 0,484. (Keiningham et al., 2008, p. 83). Moreover Keiningham et al. negated the correlation between the intention for recommendation, PWOM, and the change in share-of-wallet (Keiningham et al., 2008, p. 86). Reichheld also claimed that the NPS is better than the metric customer satisfaction but the scientific lack of relation between WOM, loyalty and profitability disprove this claim (Grisaffe, 2007, p. 40). Furthermore it is not possible to equate customer loyalty attitudes (likelihood to recommend) with customer loyalty behaviour (purchase) (Keiningham et al., 2008, p. 87). The main problem hereby is that the referral intentions remain just intentions. Customer loyalty does not make any statement about the value or the spending behaviour of customers, thereof it is not possible to infer the future growth potential (Kumar et al., 2007, p. 140). These presented arguments are only extracts of the debate that compass the Net Promoter Score.

Summing up, the NPS is not the ultimate tool for measuring WOM effectiveness, efficiency and its direct influence on the profitability. Up to date no simple solution exists which can predict WOM's influences on the future growth of a company. This debate shows that a single metric is not suitable to give an holistic explanation and to guide strategic decisions efficiently (Grisaffe, 2007, p. 40). The NPS, as a single diagnostic measure, can be relevant in giving broad insights but due to the complexity of Word-of-Mouth communication, its underlying motives and its effects, an examination based on multiple metrics is necessary even if multiple metrics are more complex, time and cost consuming. NPS is just "paring something complex down to a single number or a single metric" (Keiningham et al., 2008, p. 88). Concluding, there has been little success predicting brand or company performance based on WOM communication data (East, 2008, p. 269).

3 Discussion and Practical Implications in the Fashion Context

As an overall strategic issue the management of marketing communication has an major impact on the firm as a whole. The increased individualization in society, which is accompanied by the multi-optionality, causes new challenges for companies and brands. The general information overload in society requires new marketing communication strategies and approaches focusing not primarily on the criterion of quantity, such as the frequency of contact, but on the quality of the content. Designing and implementing a successful marketing mix to leverage the brands equity are affairs of great moment. Companies' ultimate ambition should be to create enthusiasm that contributes to customer loyalty. Therefore, firms have to listen to and comprehend their customers, they have to build strong ties to their customers, and they need to see customer loyalty as a growth opportunity. The implication of the transformed media landscapes remain, first and foremost, the redefinition of the relationship between the company and the customer as well as of roles in this relationship. Nowadays, the company is not a pure "producer" but rather a "service provider" who has to fulfil the needs and wants of his customers. This paradigm shift induces a change of thinking. On that basis, firms have to accept that marketing messages are not just received by the customer; they are modified, developed, and transmitted. This circumstance forces companies to develop strategies to deal with participating customers. Integrated Marketing Communication (IMC), the set of all marketing communication activities used by firms to communicate with the target market, need to proactively incorporate new communication disciplines such as Word-of-Mouth Marketing, Participative Marketing, Viral Marketing, Guerrilla Marketing, and Social Media Marketing et cetera. Thereby a reasonable and balanced combination has to be implemented. Recapitulating the first research question, if companies should integrate their customers actively into their marketing communication, the assumption is that this question can be answered with an explicit yes.

Especially in the hypercompetitive fashion industry, retailers and brands can use high qualitative integrated marketing communication as an instrument for creating a unique selling proposition and to differentiate from contenders. As mentioned in 2.4 Word-of-Mouth in the Fashion Context, fashion itself as a high involvement product category, is very likely to be subject of WOM communication and the willingness of fashion involved customers to invest in promoting the company or brand is quite high. With the increasing importance of peer-to-peer referrals in the fashion industry, especially Consumer Generated Media has the ability to change and shape a fashion brand's marketing and its perception in society. Thereof, particular attention should be paid to the customers' influence on the brand's image. As indicated so far, the confrontation with the modern marketing communication disciplines is inevitable for marketers. Companies cannot control the whole WOM communication process, instead of negating the power of customers in today's marketplace they should jettison their old mental models and open up, as well as share, resources with users. The customer of today is a crucial player in the marketing process and firms have to apply methods which influence and shape the public discussion in a way that correspond to the company's image and contribute to the overall performance. Therefore, the following practical implications are answering the second research question how fashion companies best approach the conversion of their customer into promoters is:

3.1 The Customer as Focal Point

- Anticipate the perspective of Customer Based Brand Equity to provide a strategic orientation towards the customer.
- Get to know the target audience before thinking about new marketing strategies and tactics. Not every customer base is ready for its new role in the marketing mix. Develop Integrated Marketing Communication in accordance to the target audience and their abilities.
- Brand Communities have to be treated as valuable amplifiers for your brand's image. Encourage community building through the supply of platforms where customers can meet each other and share their experience.
- The customer as an active player in the marketing communication is inevitable. Accept the uncontrollability and try to guide your customer base by using incentives or psychological tricks. Engage in two way dialogues to create strong ties. The emotional connection can be intensified by including experience positioning whereby multi-sensory, authentic and personal relevant content is transmitted.
- Provide your customer "added value" through exclusivity, membership, excitement or personal relevance.

3.2 Company Internal Redefinition of Strategies

- Clearly define the role of new marketing communication disciplines in your marketing mix. Communicate the changes in your marketing policy within your company. Anticipate the approach, that your customer is a tremendously important influencer in the market place.
- The redefinition and reorientation of marketing communication programs have to be done consequently. Define strategies, implement tactics and monitor the accomplishment. Invest in your new marketing program and focus on marketing tactics matching your company's image. Covering all communication disciplines often causes inefficiency and half-hearted execution.

- Modern marketing communication disciplines can add value to your marketing communication but they do not replace your traditional marketing. Even if the diffusion of fashion trends is heavily influenced by modern communication disciplines, do not neglect above-the-line communication. Try to combine and integrate your marketing tactics to a balanced marketing program.
- Develop products that meet customers' requirements and provide relevant information to your customer. You need to know customers' desires as well as their needs and wants. This understanding can be achieved through the implementation of a customer feedback loop. Using the given feedback to adapt and revise strategies can lead to higher customer satisfaction.
- Shift the focus from pure profitability increase to the enhancement of brand awareness and customer satisfaction. The ROI is hardly measurable when using modern communication disciplines as the discussion that surrounds the Net Promoter Score showed. A holistic examination is necessary to understand the importance of Word-of-Mouth for the company's image.

3.3 Design and Operational Implementation of Marketing Communication

- Create relevant content through traditional media that can function as an important input for WOM amplification. Thereby, the content can be amusing, creative or outrageous. Above all, the chosen content should encourage customers to think and talk about your company.
- Monitor the effects of your marketing communication, scan the Internet and listen to traditional Word-of-Mouth. Respond to NWOM to uncover the possibilities for continuous improvement and to prevent shit storms.
- Put emphasis on high qualitative content instead of quantity.

In accordance to the statement "the strongest brands will be those to which customers become so attached and passionate that they, in effect, become evangelists or missionaries and attempt to share their beliefs and spread the word about the brand"(Keller, 2003, p. 133), fashion companies and retailers should restructure and redefine their marketing mix to exploit all opportunities given. Succeeding in today's marketplace is not as easy as it was before the rise of Web 2.0. Therefore, it is a need to differentiate from contenders through the marketing communication and to consider the given practical implications.

4 Conclusion and Limitations

In summary, today's problematic of fashion companies do not lie in the decision whether they *want* their customers integrated into their marketing communication *or not*. Web 2.0 has given today's customers the free admission for participating in the marketplace and shaping the brand's image without needing the permission of the company. On the assumption that the target audience is "ready" for their transformation into promoters, this research paper pleads for the development of integrated marketing programs which are actively engaging the customer into the marketing communication of a firm. Despite summarizing and interpreting the literature that surrounds the topic Word-of-Mouth, the gained knowledge has been transferred to the fashion context. The results of this research paper can assist fashion brands to understand the influence of the customer in today's marketplace and to revise and implement new marketing communication programs. Thereby fashion companies should target a combination strategy between the traditional and the modern marketing approaches to realise a homogenous and successful brand image. Key success factor is a well elaborated integrated marketing approach in accordance to the customer base.

As the scope of this research paper is narrowed down, the findings need to be interpreted as an insight but not as a holistic examination. Considering all literature covering the topic of Word-of-Mouth has not been possible, thereof, the findings of this paper should be seen as a motivation to continue working. Approaches for further methodology optimisation are to increase the scope of the literature review and to integrate an empirical study to strengthen reliability, objectiveness and the validity of the here presented practical implications. The integration of an empirical study would enhance the understanding and the relevance of this topic in practices. Furthermore, an empirical survey could test the here given practical implications. As this research paper is presenting two modern communication disciplines, Viral Marketing and Customer Generated Media; the investigation of other disciplines in the fashion context would be a starting point for further analysis. Nonetheless, this research paper highlights the importance of the customer's role in the marketing communication and argues in favour of customer integration into the marketing mix. In the continuously changing and hypercompetitive fashion environment, companies have to develop marketing tactics to be one step ahead.

Special Issues for the Sustainable Customer

The Sustainable Fashion Oxymoron- Want vs Act!

Timo Brandt/Jochen Strähle

Abstract

Purpose – This paper is to show what sustainable fashion is and how it has developed in recent years. Also the paper discusses which factors are important in order to be sustainable. Above all, it's about customers who show a lot interest in sustainable fashion. Child labor, working conditions, poor quality and poisonous substances are strictly rejected by these consumers. Amazingly, fashion companies that repeatedly hit the headlines with bad properties are very successful. It's about the sustainable oxymoron, the act and want of the consumer.

Design/methodology/approach – The research design is a literature study. Books and articles built the foundation of the topic.

Findings – It is difficult for fashion to be sustainable. The reasons for that are the consumption, not much transparency in textile chains, fast fashion and much more. It's almost impossible for a product to achieve the 100 percent sustainability. On one hand the consumer want to have sustainable products, on the other hand they purchase for newness and cheap clothes. It has become clear, that they buy in a conflict.

Research limitations/implications – One limitation of this research paper is that there is no empiric data of consumers conflict buying. Also it is difficult to find real information on the company's sustainable behavior. Naturally they only present positive sustainable reports. For future researches it would be helpful to understand the topic "oxymoron of fashion" and sustainability better through the empiric foundation of customer's real behavior on sustainable products and concern's real sustainable producing.

Keywords – sustainable, consumer conflict behavior, textile chain, fast fashion, slow fashion

Paper type – Research paper

1 Introduction

We live in a time, were we get confronted with a lot of current and important topics in magazines, internet and television every day. Maybe there are often positive ones, but mainly the attention is on negative topics. Fashion and the appendant industry was and is always a present and debatable issue. In a time, where people get more and more in touch with environment themes fashion is under criticism. The words sustainable, green, ethical and so on are titles getting popular in reports and marketing campaigns about fashion. A lot of books and research papers handle sustainability but only a few authors are dealing with the contrariness of sustainability and fashion. The topic "The Sustainable Fashion Oxymoron- Want vs Act" is followed by the question whether sustainable fashion in itself is an oxymoron. Is it possible that fashion is sustainable? Both, consumer and fashion manufacturers must take responsibility and think about life settings if sustainable fashion should be the way to go. High consumption of people, not much transparency of textile chains as well as savings in production and quality do not contribute to a sustainable behavior. There is a demand for organic textiles. Why is this demand not complied with offers? Or is the demand just by a little group of people, wanting to bring more sustainability in people's minds? Or do people want to be sustainable but act differently? Consumer's behavior is also an important topic of this paper. Furthermore it will also show how the buying behavior has changed in the last years and that there is a conflict in consumption of people. How could the future purchase behavior be positive for environment, animals and people? This question will be clarified also.

2 Literature Review

2.1 The Sustainable Fashion

The critical mindset of people to the industrial society already started in the 60's. The concerns of people were consumption and there was cultural criticism that especially turned against the large-scale technologies and industrialism. These facts were the basis of the eco movement. People had a new philosophies of life at that time. There were also a lot of new movements in the 70s and 80s.

Many political issues were discussed by people in different groups, criticized and publicized. It grouped many people and in their everyday life the new eco attitude was reflected. Humility, asceticism and renunciation of consumption were important to those people. The eco movement was popular at the end of the 70's. People wanted to demonstrate with their eco-look against current fashion. They did not want to look fashionable, because their intention was to draw attention to the bad influence of fashion industry. They believed that is only possible with the typical eco-look. The sustainable wardrobes had to be practical and comfortable. The designs were simple and without details such as decorative stitching's. This facts bring us to a huge problem nowadays. The consumers often associate sustainability with the sloppy look of the past time. Thus eco clothing has a negative image. Nowadays, it is hard for designer and producers to build up a new and positive image of eco clothing (Werner & Kirsten, 2010, pp. 10–11). In 1991 the fashion company Esprit launched a new line which was called Ecollection. Currently labels are using the eco aspect for better marketing strategies as well (English, 2013, p. 182).

Terms should be clarified. Often the word combination green fashion is being used in a confusing manner because there are so many synonyms. It is also called eco fashion, sustainable fashion, ethical fashion, slow fashion, responsible fashion, style with substance and so on. There are many more words for it, often invented by journalist and experts. But all together they mean the same thing. All the terms have on conforming quality: they define fashion as something which is well considered. In the United States they often use green or eco-fashion. In Europe it´s often called slow fashion. In the UK they use ethical fashion (Eagan, 2014, p. 22). In a research paper "Clothes That Connect", Kate Fletcher (2007) arguments that in order for eco-fashion to be sustainable, its apparel must now be fashionably chic as well as environmentally correct. The author and American academic Theresa Winge assumes that eco-fashion isn´t about political topics and stereotyped people anymore. Nowadays sustainable fashion gets famous through the influence of celebrities. People like George Clooney, Annie Leibovitz, Lindsey Lohan and Julia Roberts support sustainable fashion and use it as an aesthetic life choice. That means they use their status to show the importance of ecological correct clothes by showing sustainable fashion on the red carpet and also in fashion magazines (2008b, p. 513). However if someone ever tried to adopt an eco-conscious lifestyle, he knows such ambition requires great discipline and commitment.

So in fact, the process requires a cultural change much further than the action of any single person. The complete vastness and associated expenses of addressing a sustainable lifestyle, such as fixing energy-efficient windows and solar panels, might seem impossible for the lower middle class. The fashion industry is under criticism because they do not have many positive characteristics regarding the environment. Others have to settle for newness in fashion and constant growth of consumption. New products have to be presented continually. Humans, animals and local and global environment are getting ill of the fashion industry. Furthermore there is an exploitation of human rights regarding child labor issues and sweatshops. The World Health Organization evaluates that dangerous number of people are getting poisoned every year. They estimate that about three million people are affected especially in developing countries (Minney, Watson, Siegel, & Firth, 2011, p. 22). Accordingly the world and the apparel industry are dealing with ecological and human rights. They are recognizing and scrutinizing these two topics. The editor Graydon Garter from the Vanity Fair magazine confirmed in the first environmentally zoom on issue that "Green Is the New Black" in 2006 (Winge, 2008, p. 513). The word "green" is often used for metaphorically pro-environment (Shrum, McCarty, & Lowrey, 1995, p. 72). Also other famous fashion magazines have shown celebrity activists who pursue ecofashion in their "green" lifestyle. Consequently famous fashion designer such as Giorgio Armani, Stella McCartney, Oscar de la Renta, Betsey Johnson and Todd Oldman have started to produce eco fashions for boutiques, runways, mass markets and mostly for celebrities. There is a huge demand for a "green" lifestyle, but it's hard to live for the average person, also because of the more expensive products (Winge, 2008, p. 513).

More than 70 definitions of the word sustainability exist in literature (Pearce, Markandya, & Barbier, 1989)(Holmberg, 1992). Different academic fields and disciplines have their individual definitions and points of view, but all together agree that it is important to consider the future of the earth. Thus, there are ways for people to protect the earth while satisfying different stakeholder needs. Lots of expert circles want to find another word to replace sustainability, because of its deeper significances. The most extensively cited definition was given 25 years ago by the famous Bruntland report (WCED, 1987).

Bruntland defines sustainability as "[...] development that meets the needs of the present without compromising the ability of future generations to meet their own needs" (WCED, 1987).

The idea of sustainability came along and people felt for it. Also because the principle behind sustainable development was perfectly admirable and suitable for poor countries. In contrary Wood illustrates in *Designers, Visionaries and Other Stories* (Chapter 5):

> Before we knew where we were, we had stretched the original idea of 'sustainable development' and were talking about 'sustainable products', 'sustainable approaches' and 'sustainable housing'. By now, the ice was getting thinner, and we were dressed for skating, rather than for swimming. Politically, the idea of sustainable development created the idea that there was a common agenda or consensus. (Wood, 2007, p. 99)

Furthermore the question is how experts should use 70 definitions of sustainability in the fashion industry? Which of these terms are make us think about how we create und consume apparels? There is the "Milking Stool Model" with tree legs and a seat, which easily shows the complexity of sustainability. The first leg symbolizes people, the second leg shows profit and the third leg the planet, which all facilitate the seat characterizing the sustainable stage. For this metaphor a more sustainable fashion industry must be as good as they can to achieve and support all three legs. To make this clear, an example from the fashion industry: Let's take a t-Shirt, which was produced with organic cotton garments symbolizing the third leg (planet). But what if it is produced by a child, leg one (people). Or if it is flown around the globe to European markets, leg two (profit). Now there is the question of sustainability. Is the t-shirt sustainable? Maybe it is. But it could also be said that the t-Shirt isn´t sustainable. It depends on the 70 definitions. Which one do we choose (Gwilt & Rissanen, 2011, p. 20)? There is another combination of words which is used by companies. "Fashion with consciousness" or "ethical fashion" which can be defined as following: Fashionable clothes that combine sweatshop-free labor conditions and fair trade morals. It's important that clothes don't harm the environment or influence workers badly.

Furthermore the apparel has to be biodegradable and made out of organic cotton (Joergens, 2006, p. 361). More and more the fashion industry is considering about organic cotton.

Organic cotton is grown according to established standards. This cultivation takes place in controlled and organic agricultural systems. It is important that no toxic and non-degradable chemical and synthetic pesticides and fertilizers are used. Since

1990 organic cotton is sold. There was a high demand at the beginning of the 90s. The trend was towards eco clothing. In 1990 there were just 1000 fields on which organic cotton was planted. In 1994 however, 25,000 fields were registered. Then unfortunately, there was a decrease in demand in the following years. However, further strategies were developed in the garment industry. So the demand increased again in early of the year 2000 (Fichter & Clausen, 2013, p. 256).

2.2 Sustainable Fashion is an Oxymoron

Autor Kate Flechtner says that "Fashion is eating itself". Fashion items reinforce inequalities, prey workers, fuel resource use, increased environmental impact and produce waste. These are only a few facts which have a negative impact. Also the sector places escalating emotional, physical and psychological stresses on everyone involved, from producers and designers to consumers (Chapman & Gant, 2007, p. 119). Fashion is no longer only a product, which is necessary. It is a must-buy product the consumers need for identifying and expressing themselves. It presents a whole lifestyle (Solomon, Bamossy, Askegaard, & Hogg, 2010, p. 577).

> In the collective cultural consciousness, fashion is consumption, materialism, commercialization and marketing. It is buying high street and high end. It is watching, shopping, purchasing (Fletcher, 2013, p. 139).

Pressures such as the drive to consume faster and cheaper, the ever present demand for newness and the constant reformulation of identity damage us as individuals and collectively as a society. We are alienated, dissatisfied, depressed, anorexic and more cynical than ever before The challenge of sustainability is slowly bringing a shift in the awareness of consumers, chiefs of industry and designer.

Fashion is always renovating itself. Small companies producing shareable clothes turn to alternative models of social activism and aesthetic modernization. For examples huge companies are announcing plans to go carbon neutral and are presenting Fairtrade cotton and recycled polyester product lines. Thus, it is up to each customer to steer this change towards sustainability and demand a new type of fashion created more on transformative actions and less on consumptive ones. Consumption as it is nowadays has to change quickly. A lot of people are realizing that, but in fact this is not enough. Consequently the key problem is the passion of consumption. The difficult issue is that there is no real detailed solution that replaces quantity with quality. This means shifting from global to local and from consuming to making. Also it's important to stop the consumption of natural resources and start appreciating the natural world. It's vital to have small and big steps to create a sustainable life. Each new step initiates a rethink and may lead to an improved lifestyle which have positive aspects to environment. The business with clothes is extremely problematic. The producing, selling, wearing, and disposal of textiles has a negative effect on the environment. Latest data suggest the fashion and textile sector is among the most environmentally damaging, compared to the chemical industry. Fast changing trends and low prices contribute to consumers buying more and more often than they actually need. In big fashion companies like Primark, Walmart and Tesco is a trend to higher volumes and falling prices. They take advantage of the high consumption of people and so people buy as much as they never did before. The output of clothing has increased in recent years while prices have fallen (Chapman & Gant, 2007, pp. 119–121). Nowadays there are a lot of research papers and literature in general which deal with the topic sustainability. There are many tools that help us to understand this topic. They are used to show the difficulty of this topic but in fact nobody really cares about the information. Especially designers are not interest in this huge topic, unfortunately. They should show interest because they are directly in connection with consumers. If they only produced sustainable, people would buy it. There is so much overproduction which maybe helps the sales, but not the environment (Gwilt & Rissanen, 2011, p. 22). To make the sustainable fashion oxymoron clear, there is an example for a better understanding. The material cotton is biodegradable. So it is sustainable in terms of reducing the loads on landfills.

At the same time planting, finishing and consumption of cotton need a high quantity of chemicals and more water.

This shows that fashion can't be a hundred percent sustainable but there are ways to converge sustainability

2.3 Consumer's behavior

The consumer in the modern society is different than in the past. Nowadays people can choose their products, services and activities which define them. Especially the fashion buyer have never had so many choices (Langdown, 2014, p. 33). Thus they can create a social identity with products. With that new identity they communicate with others. So product choices show, who people are (Solomon et al., 2010, p. 577). People buy clothes because they want to be modern and in fashion. In fashion means you belong to the group which spread new trends (Solomon et al., 2010, p. 66). Nowadays consumers are more interested in the way companies produce their clothes. They now demand correct and honest labeling. Also important is the information about fair payment and healthy working conditions. Using this information the consumers buy their clothes assiduously. We choose among different products every day. Our buying choices don't always influence ourselves. Now ethical buying behavior is almost taking accountability for the effect which we examine ourselves. It can make a huge difference to other people, environment, nature and animals how the products are produced (Brinkmann, 2004, p. 130). It's apparent that customers show lot of interest in fair trade products. They are willing to pay more for them, but they need more offers in each product category (Halepete u. a., 2009, p. 144). Consumers are worried about the so called sweatshop clothing production, so the demand for fair trade in the clothing area has increased. Especially the food sector has an increase in fair trade products (D. Shaw, Hogg, Wilson, Shiu, & Hassan, 2006, p. 428). To be ethical means you buy products, which are made without harm of humans, animals or the environment. Ethical consumption is buying things that are produced ethically by companies that act ethically. There are some tips for shoppers who want to act ethically. Consumers should search for local shops which use fair trade and products, that aren't tested on animals. Also they have to try to buy in second hand shops or shops which use recycling clothes (Brinkmann, 2004, p. 130). There is a trend in companies to consider heeding sustainability in their fashion products. They can't achieve the goal because of the main problem, the consumer. People are hungry for new products and the wardrobe has to change as soon as possible.

2.4 The change of the attitude towards life

A new group of people, who also deal with the issue of sustainability, are the so-called LOHAS. This abbreviation stands for Lifestyle Of Health And Sustainability. The focus is still luxury and pleasure, but they reflect on values such as solidarity, social responsibility. Furthermore to them, creativity and initiative are important. This trend came in 2000 from the States. Consumer want to be dressed trendy and contemporary. They are not against the fashion system and all its associated properties.

(Werner & Kirsten, 2010, pp. 10–12) Another group of people, who deal with the topic sustainability are ethical consumers. Their interests lies in political beliefs, engaging themselves in promotion of worldwide human rights, environmental sustainability and animal welfare (Hilton, 2003, p. 317). Companies realized the trend to eco fashion as well. Thus their focus is on marketing campaigns because they can increase their sales. Social and political commentary has become connected with sartorial, design, art and so the demand for sustainable fashion is getting bigger. Clothes people purchase also have to be fashionably stylish as well as environmentally correct today (English, 2013, pp. 182–183). The attitude of many people has changed a lot in the last few years. For example demand for organic products in the food sector has risen sharply. Many discounters offer customers the choice between organic products and the normal range. Consumers often reach for more sustainable products. (Werner & Kirsten, 2010, p. 7) Customers need an ethical alternative to the regular product to make a choice. Choices should be possible to make (Doane & New Economics Foundation., 2001, p. 6). More and more people care about the things they consume. Are the products environmentally friendly and produced under humane conditions? This is observed in the clothing industry as well as in the food sector. But where can you buy fashion that owns this requirement? This question was investigated by students in the field Fashion Journalism / Media Communication AMD Fashion & Design Academy Dusseldorf. Their outcomes have been brought together in a very well researched publication. On more than 100 pages they show the first "Fair Fashion Shopping Guide Dusseldorf" where people can buy sustainable fashion in the fashion city. The magazine in a handy pocket format is available for free in selected stores in the city of Dusseldorf, and directly through the academy. After the successful premiere they want to release more magazine in other cities.

2.5 Consumer's conflict of buying

"It's an obvious truth that the relationship between fashion and high-volume consumption conflicts with sustainability goals" (Fletcher, 2013, p. 139).

Nowadays consumers always want to have something new. The products they purchase must always have the latest design and be fashionable. Also a reason for huge demands for newness is that people express themselves, e.g. through their clothes. They often show a certain status with their clothes. A new version of the old product has to come out again and again. Permanent consumption is guaranteed and the company's pleased by that (Chapman & Gant, 2007, p. 10). It's challenging for people to figure out what to wear every day. Their goal is to select the right style. The outfit tells what the world should think of them and what they think of themselves (Eagan, 2014, p. 13). Consumers play an ambiguous role when commuting between morals and market (Heidbring, Schmidt, & Ahaus, 2011, p. 14). Nobody wants to have products which are involved in child labor reports. A phenomenon is the company Primark for example. Always having the latest trends to cheap prices. Especially young consumers want to spend their pocket money on clothes. Thus if you have 50 Euro to spend per month, you get three outfits from Primark. At that point nobody cares about working conditions in developing countries where the clothes come from. For people it is about having fun and the negative aspects doesn't fit to their consumption (Piatscheck, 2013). So for consumers it is normal to throw away clothes rather than repair it (Fletcher, 2013, p. 140). Customers might think that green products are not as good as the normal products.

There is a study to measure buying purpose in relation to green products from Shrum, McCarty and Lowrey (1995, p. 78). They use the statement "I would switch from my usual brands and buy environmentally safe cleaning products, even if I have to give up some cleaning effectiveness. The hypothesis indicates that green goods are associated with less performance or quality. Thus, consumers think green products offer poor quality.

In the market we have to deal with a lot words, which want to describe sustainable. Companies like to label products as "a sustainable option," "made from sustainable materials," or "produced sustainably." Thus it appears consumers will have a huge influence on the success of new arrangements for sustainability. But the problem is that consumers might not recognize the complexity of the topic. Consequently, we see that there is a problem with transparency. It is important to develop sustainable standards and certifications, which are important to both consumers and marketers to have transparency in their products (Simpson & Radford, 2012, p. 273). An organization which brings some clearness in the difficult topic is the Fair Trade Organization (FTOs). They are dealing with topics like fair pays, safe working conditions, environmental friendly production and so on (Halepete, Littrell, & Park, 2009, p. 143). The more consumers know about the ethical dimensions of goods, the more they're possibly buying those product (Dickson, 2001, p. 98). Organic labels are very confusing for consumers in the textiles sector. The reason for this is as follows. The manufacturers set their own standards. They often only part of the production chain take into account. In 2008 a comprehensive and independent seal of approval was introduced.

Figure 58: GOTS
Adapted from: (Fichter & Clausen, 2013, p. 256)

GOTS stands for Global Organic Textile Standard. This label stands for control of entire production chains. It is one of the most famous labels which clarify the features of a textile product.

Since German development minister Gerd Müller has demanded more transparency in the German textile and clothing industry there is a lot of criticism. There has been groups which actively went up against the plan. Others like representatives from industry, commerce, trade associations, trade unions and development and human rights organizations are happy about the idea and together they worked out a plan of action for the alliance. The minister met with representatives from Adidas, C & A, the Otto Group, Aldi and Tchibo to discuss the feasibility of the so called Textile Alliance. The Membership in the textile alliance is voluntary. However Müller is probably interested in encourage as many players from the German textile and fashion industry as well as the trade sector. For experts the requirements of the action plan including the timetable set for implementation isn't workable and realistic.

A textile symbols which Müller wanted to introduce is off the table because of the many stages of production in textiles and clothing which were not completely controllable. Experts' said that Müller's initiative has now ensure that the Öko-Tex Association presented the label "Made in Green by Oeko-Tex". This certification will replace the previous system of certification Oeko-Tex Standard 100plus (Wollenschläger, 2014a). Hess Natur joins the voluntary alliance for sustainable textiles that the German Development Minister Gerd Müller has initiated. This step was logically and consistently aimed by Hess Natur-chief Marc Sommer. The industry associations have a completely opposite view. Textil+Mode and GermanFashion will not join. They say that a series of demands from the action plan of the minister were not executed, including the required full transparency of supply chains. Also the Confederation of German Employers' Associations (BDA) isn't excited about the plans. In a letter to Müller's ministry, which is published in TextilWirtschaft, states that the activities they wanted weren't practical realism and so they strongly refuse the plan. According to Müller's ideas, companies should take responsibility for processes that are beyond their reach. A lot of criticism of the actions of the industry associations is exercised by the Clean Clothes Campaign (CCC), which demands to participate in the alliance. The action plan was a push to bring transparency in the supply chain for the first time and is geared to international, social and environmental standards.

Experts guess that a scaled-down version of the plan is presented and the problematic points will be rewritten in the next years (Wollenschläger, 2014c). So the huge problem of the topic transparency is that there is no effective standardization for products to confirm a product as organic. It is important labeling and licensing products directly in the manufacturing plant (Mishra & Sharma, 2012, p. 36).

2.6 Demand and supply of sustainable fashion

Demands for eco-friendly products are increasing because the customer is more interest in the environment and in a sustainable lifestyle. So the companies act on that demand and try to serve products and services, which are ecological and sustainable. Also it is a goal for the companies to achieve sustainability in their business commitments (Earthshare, 2012). Nowadays we have limited resources. But there are people, which wants are unlimited. It is important for the companies and designers to use the capabilities resourcefully and produce as few waste as possible.

Thus for firms it is significant to adopt to the green theme and illustrate it to the outside world, such as in marketing campaigns. "Green Marketing" deals with the whole marketing concept. Fabrication, marketing, use disposal of products and services done in a way, which are less harmful to the environment (Mishra & Sharma, 2012, p. 35). Consumers and retailers are increasingly sensitive to sustainable products. This is especially true on issues such as global warming and harmful effects of pollutants. Due to the growing presence of these issues, customers' interest in sustainability increases. Because of these reasons the demand for products, which protect the environment is growing. Consumers feel safe if they buy sustainable products. They buy with a good feeling and companies can benefit from this demand. People are asking for products, which have the property of being recyclable, non-toxic and environment-friendly (Mishra & Sharma, 2012, p. 35). To position green products, it is important to companies to identify their consumers, who are possibly dealing with environmental topics. (Bohlen, Schlegelmilch, & Diamantopoulos, 1993, p. 415). Demand for fair trade and organic cottons are present, but the share of the total amount of cotton sold worldwide is not much (Minney et al., 2011, p. 22).

Sustainability of the fashion industry can be checked through the textile chains. It is important that each step is comprehensible.
From fiber production to the end use of the consumer, different factors play a role, which influence the environmental negatively or positively. It's very difficult and expensive for the producer and also for the retailer to control everything accurately (Piegsa, 2010, p. 3). Through all the channels being sustainable. Is this possible or not? Is there a way to be sustainable in all processes? Faced with everyday demands of commercially driven product designs it becomes hard to visualize how anything mass-produced can be truly benign in environmental terms. Every step has an impact of some sort, whether through resource extraction, production, shipping, retailing, use, disposal, recycling and so on. For some fashion designers the ultimate ambition is to create 100 per cent of sustainability in their work. It is the direction a lot of people want to go. But it should be clear that the term 100 per cent of sustainability is as exclusive as it is inclusive. Perhaps a more useful way to framing this is to consider degrees of sustainability. Then the questions could be: ´How sustainable is my product? ´; or ´How sustainable could it be? ´. Thus an important question is: ´How can we get more sustainable throughout all the processes? ´.

So there is a big need for new ways measuring sustainability, which are inclusive and participation-widening as a means to engage a broader industry populace. In addition new means of gauging and mapping sustainability must be more effective in enabling the deeper complexities of the subject to embrace the diversity of creative approaches that might be developed. It is necessary that sustainable design is not only about checking whether you have used recycling materials or not. Also the topic sustainability is not thorough enough if you use solar cells in the office of the company. Yes, these changes would make things more sustainable. Also any motion towards a more sustainable future should be embraced, but that should not be where it ends. A constant aspiration for improvement and renewal should be preferable. Sustainable designer should require a level of engagement that goes beyond these immediate solutions, delving deeper into the multifaceted issues relating to object creation (Chapman & Gant, 2007, pp. 8–9). The company Hennes and Mauritz is one of the global fashion chains. They start to produce with organic cotton and use fair trade products. Li & Fung, one of the international trading companies, have imposed corporate sustainability strategies for their supply chains. They have committed to this change to control the use of resources of our planet (Bin Shen, Yulan Wang, Chris K.Y. Lo, & Momoko Shum, 2012, p. 235). In practice it looks as following. The latest sustainability report from C&A shows the existing and future sustainability orientation of fashion chains for 2020.

Also they have presented details about their work of the past two years. To update their report immediately, C&A shows the detailed report online. So if there is any change in products or in textile chains they can refresh and expand the report quickly. The German retailer has made process in organic cotton, the extension of the standards on suppliers and the reduction of emissions of environmental degrading substances in the past two years. C&A have 85 Million sales in organic cotton. Next to Hennes & Mauritz they are the world's leading sellers in this area. In fact the company from Düsseldorf has already made 38% of the total cotton sales with organic cotton. Their aim for 2014/2015 is to sell 130 million pieces of organic cotton. The goal for 2020 is to completely avoid hazardous chemicals. They focus on initiatives within supply chains to achieve reform of the textile chain. Thus since October 2014 all C&A leather products have been made from chrome-free tanned leather. For tanning the concern is only using chemicals which base is synthetic or vegetable. After the disaster in Bangladesh the retailer has improved his engagement to safe and better working conditions in supplier's countries. The company attaches great importance to comprehensive audits and trainings as well as working with other companies and international organizations. C&A has 600 suppliers in 40 countries worldwide. These are 200 suppliers less than in the year 2012. The reason for that is that they want to focus on strong and longer partnerships. The main production countries are China, Bangladesh and Kambodscha (Wollenschläger, 2014b, p. 36). A new way to make textile chains more sustainable are the "Take Back" campaigns. For example in the UK the textile company Mark and Spencer has started taking clothes back. That means comforting customers to detach unwanted garments. At the same time they can look and shop for new clothes and get for example a reduction for the new shopping's. Hennes and Mauritz has also started with this new revolution. A negative aspect is that this program supports more consumption. More consumption is not sustainable. The positive side is that consumers start to think more about waste and where it can be disposed. Thus higher waste costs force companies to produce more with recycling garments that are more durable and easier to reuse and recycle (Fletcher, 2013, p. 134).

To create newness, fast fashion has become a normal system for apparel companies. Dresses are being created with shorter lifespans than ever before. The clothes are fast and cheap because of the low-priced fabrics, low payments and worker exploitation (Clark, 2008, p. 428). But fast fashion is really popular by the consumer.

In just a few weeks new trends from the catwalk can be in the shops. Designers command what is trendy, and what is a mess. Fast fashion can be described as follows: Retail strategy has confirming merchandise assortments to existing and upcoming trends as quickly and effectively as possible. Retailers have replaced the traditional designer push model with this new innovation. If retailers use the fast fashion model in the right way, they can be really successful. A famous example is the company ZARA from Spain. ZARA integrated clothing production with retailing in order to react more quickly to changing consumer fondness. To be fast ZARA mainly produces the fashion items in near proximity to its core market while other retailers outsource the whole production to Asia or South America (Sull & Turconi, 2008, pp. 5–7). Zara and Hennes & Mauritz are pioneers of the fast fashion model and both developed it in the 1990s and early 2000s. Mass production brought out a fast-paced consumption and always changing styles (Eagan, 2014, p. 15).

Slow fashion is about caring for the environment. It is dealing with the huge wastefulness and people's lack of concern in relation to ecological issues. The slow process has more sustainable influence on design, production, consumption and use. It's an ethical way to be fashionable. In blogs and articles on the internet fashion industry welcomes the topic "slow fashion" (Clark, 2008, p. 428). Authors Parkins and Craig deal with the topic "slow living" in their correspondent book. For them slow living is a process which is connected with care and attention in daily life experience. Above all, it is about the challenge living in this time in a meaningful, sustainable, thoughtful and pleasurable way (Parkins & Craig, 2006, p. xi). In fact more products with a sustainable character must be developed. Thus there has to be a reorganization of manufacturing structures so that they are conceptually and pragmatically connected with sustainable philosophies (Fletcher, 2013, p. 154). "As we do so, new types of products will emerge whose aesthetics go deeper than shape and surface and which start to embody ethics and to reflect these new sensitivities and understandings" (Fletcher, 2013, p. 154).

3 Discussion

The topic of this research paper was the statement is "The Sustainable Fashion Oxymoron - Want vs. Act". Out of this the question arises: Is sustainable fashion an oxymoron in itself?

When I started the literature research it looked to me as if there hadn't been written much about sustainability and nobody really cared about it. But after a closer examination I saw that there is a lot of interest in this topic - from consumer to companies, from authors to readers, from food to clothes. Sadly the right and final solution of this whole issue is not there yet. A lot of people are discussing about it and pointing out improvements. But I also found that oxymoron, which is present all the time. Consumers know so much about bad working conditions, child labor, chemicals in their clothes and so on.

On the one hand everyone rejects this bad characteristics but on the other hand they consume as fast and much as they can and drool over newness. They buy in stores which are constantly under criticism because of little transparency in their textile chain. People know this but they are conflicted. What should they do? Not consuming anymore and when they need something to wear buy it in a second hand shop? That will not happen and it is not a solution because people will consume anyway. We have to distance from the disposable items. We have so much money to spend and people express themselves through clothes. They show who they are and demonstrate their wealth. People are interest in production of products. Unfortunately not everyone shows this awareness. Like the so called LOHAS, some individuals are forming groups to demonstrate and live a sustainable lifestyle. Especially in the food sector, there is a huge demand for organic products. A lot of discounters offer such products now. Fair trade is a trend which sadly doesn't really hit the fashion industry. Sales of fair trade fashion items are a very small number. Fast fashion business is raising. Companies like Zara are very successful. The newness, the fast realization of trends and many collections per year has made the Spain Company popular. Of course they are not contributing to sustainable products because of their fast textile chains. Zara isn´t interested that much in "green" clothes as for example Hennes und Mauritz, because they pursue another marketing strategy. I think that a lot of firms use the eco-fashion for their advertising campaigns.

The literature research brought to light that more and more celebrities are trying to show and live a sustainable lifestyle. That includes food as well as apparel. Lots of people might think that such a "green" way of life is expensive. I think that is not right. Because who is saying that you are only "green" when you live 100 percent sustainable? Is that even possible? This raises the question what 100 percent sustainable is? Literature gives us 70 definitions already. So you could easily choose the most fitting definition and use it for yourselves. I have noticed that it is very difficult, especially for consumers to buy and live sustainably. When you look on the major cities in Germany, the big textile chains string together. "Cheap", "sale", "reduction" and other words are allurements which let us consuming more and more. A map that shows sustainable business could be very helpful to people, like the one in Düsseldorf. Things like this should really be promoted more to bring more sustainability in to people's minds. The next important point is transparency. It is really difficult to understand where a garment was produced.

Of course there are details, such as "Made in China", visible on apparels label. But the fiber was perhaps colored by children in Bangladesh, sewn by young women for hours without breaks and then finally the label is stitched in China. So it isn't "Made in China". Consequently the company could provide this information on the place of manufacturing. However even this does not really work. Still there are scandals that show under which unworthy conditions people have to work, especially in developing countries. Briefly all people are shocked and they take their friends on a shopping spree the next day – all forgotten. In that moment they forget everything bad they have heard. It's all about the moment. And in that moment people want to consume and child labor and sustainability don't match their new shopping experience. For example if young people have 50 € pocket money, they get three outfits from Primark. So who cares about bad qualities of items and horrible working conditions for employees? Therefore companies communicate a sustainable lifestyle which is confusing to customers. People pay attention to inscriptions like "consciousness", "Go Green", "Better living" and so on. So companies might give consumers a feeling of "doing the right thing" and they persuade themselves that a t-shirt for 2€ is sustainable. And they leave the shop with a good conscience. Furthermore there is a new innovation which might let people think they're doing thinks the right way. For example unused clothes can be brought back to Hennes Mauritz and they use it to make new recycling collections out of the old yarns.

Information how exactly this works out and where recycling takes place are not given by the company. Here we go again, the oxymoron. It lures customers with discounts and vouchers which they get when putting textiles back. Sustainability and driving consumption? It doesn't fit together.

Future researches should concentrate on the customer in relation to sustainable products. Furthermore focus should be on producers and their fast textile chains. Questions in this case could be following: "How can they achieve 100 percent transparency in their chain?" or "Why is the demand for sustainable products not completely filled?"

4 Conclusion

There are some findings which help answering or trying to answer the question of sustainable and fashion altogether. First it was important to clarify what sustainable fashion is. It started in the 1960´s when there was a green movement and lots of political issues were scrutinized and discussed. Then at the end of the 1970´s eco-movement was famous. People were trying to demonstrate against the fashion industry with their clothes. Clothes looked sloppy and not stylish - exactly what the people wanted. But now, decades later the negative aspect of that reveals itself. The image of sustainable clothes is not as good as it should be. The perception of consumers in relation to green fashion is still linked to the old eco look. That's the reason why people still associate green fashion with the look of the 70´s movement and why only little consumption can be made in that department. Also the different words and combinations which deal with the term sustainability are confusing. Consumers don't really know what eco fashion, sustainable fashion, ethical fashion, slow fashion, responsible fashion, style with substance and so on mean. Together, they are all the same. All the terms have on conforming quality: they define fashion as something which is well considered. Author Kate Fletcher says that for eco-fashion to be sustainable, its clothing must now be fashionably chic plus environmentally correct. Another opinion from Theresa Winge is that eco-fashion isn´t about political issues and stereotyped people anymore. Nowadays with the influence of celebrities, sustainable fashion becomes famous. Fashion industry does not have many positive characteristics regarding the environment and they're under criticism. Others have to settle for newness in fashion and constant growth of consumption.

Magazines issue that "Green Is the New Black". So there is a change in the fashion sector. There is a huge demand for a "green" lifestyle but hard it's to life for normal people because products are more expensive. Transparency is a huge topic in sustainability. It can only exist if all steps are traceable in the production. There are some methods to achieve this goal but mainly it is important to develop sustainable standards and certifications, which are essential to both consumers and marketers in order to have transparency in their products. For example German company C&A update their sustainability report immediately and release it online on their website. If there is any variation in the products or in the textile chain they can refresh and expand the report rapidly. A textile symbol which German Minister Gerd Müller wanted to introduce is not a relevant topic anymore.

The many stages of production in textiles and clothing are not completely controllable. What the minister wants is a voluntary alliance where companies can joy in. Firms have to comply with the standards which are given by the alliance. Fair trade products are offered by individual organizations, but the sales are not as high as they should be. Consumers want to be "green" but act contrarily. Demand for fast and cheap clothing is high and is also filled with a lot of offers. Slow fashion is a trend which is mainly followed by a small group of people. It is dealing with huge wastefulness and lack of concern in relation to ecological issues. Also it is to find sustainable fashion solutions which are good for all sectors in textile chains. Hopefully the demand for slow fashion items will rise in the next years. We can protect our nature only by a sustainable thinking and acting. Furthermore we have to care about the people, who are working for our clothes. It cannot be a goal to buy as cheap as possible while have to suffer from this. All together we have to rethink our consumption that reaches alarming proportions.

Information Demand of the Sustainable Consumer

Kristina Gehrke/Jochen Strähle

Abstract

Purpose – The purpose of this paper is to assess the state of the art concerning the information demand of the sustainable consumer focusing on the characterization of the sustainable customer, the demanded information content with regard to fashion products and the expected information frame.

Design/methodology/approach – The research methodology applied for this purpose is a literature review examining academic references.

Findings – Key findings of this paper are that sustainable consumers share certain psychographics such as sustainable knowledge and perceived customer effectiveness. So demanded information content is about general sustainable knowledge and the concrete impact of sustainable purchase behavior. Fashion product attributes demanded are details about production, material and the after-purchase use. Concerning the information frame, consumers expect information to be credible, transparent and comprehensible. Eco-Labels play an important role within the information frame.

Research limitations/implications – Most results in literature were conducted by qualitative research methods, so that further quantitative testing of the results is recommended.

Keywords – information, sustainable consumer, sustainable fashion, consumer behavior, sustainable consumption

Paper type – Research paper

1 The Importance of Information within Sustainable Fashion

The Brundtland Report of 1987 and the Rio Summit of 1992 established the concept of sustainability globally (Drexhage & Murphy, 2010, p. 6). Facing global challenges such as the climate change, poverty and the increasing consumption of resources due to economic growth in developing countries accompanied with increasing resource scarcity, sustainability is becoming more and more important for governments, society and companies. The issue of sustainability is also affecting the textile and fashion industry, regarding its environmental and social problems especially in production and transportation. On the other side customers' awareness of their impact on people and environment by purchasing fashion rises (Beard, 2008, p. 451). This development results in a growing market for sustainable fashion: The number of sold items of fair trade labelled fashion in Germany grew importantly from 850.000 items in 2008 to 3.585.850 items in 2013 (TransFair, 2014b). The graph below shows this positive development.

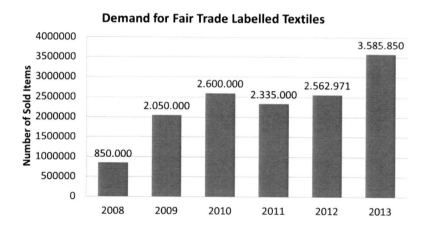

Figure 59: Growing Demand for Fair Trade Labelled Textiles in Germany
Adapted from: (TransFair, 2014a)

So the issue of sustainability is not just a challenge for fashion companies, but also a chance representing a growing market opportunity and an opportunity of differentiation in competition with conventional fashion companies (Ritch & Schröder, 2012).

Within the trend of sustainable fashion consumption information play a major role. Aspects of sustainable clothing such as a fair production or the use of organic material cannot be perceived by consumers unless they are explicitly communicated with the help of information (Rex & Baumann, 2007). Information are leading to consumers' awareness about sustainability issues and they build the knowledge to understand the quite abstract principle of sustainable fashion and its impact. Increased customer awareness and customer knowledge about sustainability are therefore beneficial for the demand for sustainable products (Moisander, Markkula, & Eräranta, 2010 cited by Ritch & Schröder, 2012 ; Shen, Zheng, Chow, & Chow, 2014). On the other hand missing information or hardly available information can be prohibiting factors in purchasing sustainable fashion (Jiyun Kang, Liu, & Kim, 2013). So providing the right information in the right way to consumers is one crucial element to develop a sustainable purchasing behavior (McDonald, Oates, Thyne, Alevizou, & McMorland, 2009).

This paper presents the sustainable consumer's information demand with regard to fashion consumption. The method chosen to give this insight is a literature review providing the state of the art in research concerning this topic. More than 30 academic references are cited. The presentation of the findings starts with a general definition of sustainable development in chapter 2.1. The next chapter presents the theories of communication and cognitive information processing in order to provide a general understanding of consumer behavior for the following more specialized assessment of the information demand. To begin with this assessment the sustainable customer and his information searching behavior are characterized in chapter 2.3.1 as a prerequisite to examine his wishes and needs concerning information. The demanded information content is then presented in chapter 2.3.2 involving general knowledge, positive effects of sustainable purchasing behavior and product attribute information that focus on fashion items. The question how information should be communicated to the customer is pursued in chapter 2.3.3 with the most important topics credibility, transparency and comprehensibility. In chapter 3 all findings are discussed and chapter 4 closes with a conclusion and a recommendation about further research concerning the topic of sustainable consumer's information demand.

2 Literature Review

2.1 The Definition of Sustainable Development

In order to examine the information demand of the sustainable consumer it is important to first clarify the term sustainable development. To briefly explain its meaning the two most common approaches are presented in this chapter. The most known definition of sustainable development is based on the UN document "Our common future" from 1987, better known as the Brundtland Report (Glavič & Lukman, 2007, p. 1884). The UN-Commission describes sustainable development as follows:

> Humanity has the ability to make development sustainable to ensure that it meets the needs of the present without compromising the ability of future generations to meet their own needs. (…) Poverty is not only an evil in itself, but sustainable development requires meeting the basic needs of all and extending to all the opportunity to fulfill their aspirations for a better life. (Drexhage & Murphy, 2010, p. 2)

Baumgärtner and Quaas refer to this description defining that sustainability is based on justice within human-nature relationships, which includes justice between different generations, justice between human beings of the same generation and justice between humans and nature (Baumgärtner & Quaas, 2010).

In order to adapt the principle of sustainable development on business context John Elkington developed a framework, the so called Triple Bottom Line in 1994. It consists of three dimensions regarding social, environmental and economic aspects. Therefore these dimensions are also called the three Ps: People, Planet and Profit (Drexhage & Murphy, 2010 ; Slaper & Hall, 2011). This framework opens up companies' perspectives, compared to the former concentration on economic and monetary indicators, and enables them to install integrated objectives serving sustainable development. Companies should strive for a complementarity of objectives between all three domains, as shown in the figure below.

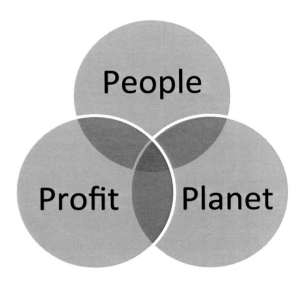

Figure 60: The Triple Bottom Line

Therefore sustainable development can be described as a long term orientated development, which aims to meet the needs of all human beings, including future generations, while respecting the environment and ensuring economic profitability.

2.2 The Theory of Communication and Information Processing

2.2.1 Communication

To set another base for the assessment of the sustainable consumer's information demand the theory of communication and information processing is presented in this chapter. Kotler presents nine elements of the communication process: the sender, the codification of the message, the message and media, the decoding process, the recipient, the recipient's response to the message, the feedback and the disturbance level (Kotler, 2012). The following figure shows the connection of these nine elements as a cyclical process of communication.

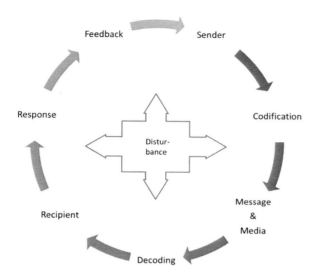

Figure 61: Communication Process

First the sender codifies the message with the help of symbols such as words, illustrations and music, so that the actual message sent is a combination out of these symbols. The message is sent by media, which are described as ways of communication between sender and recipient. In the decoding process the recipient interprets the perceived symbols. Then the recipient reacts on the interpreted message in various ways. The feedback describes the part of the recipient's reaction that is transmitted back to the sender. A very important factor is the unplanned disturbance level that can influence all parts of the communication process (Kotler, 2012). For an effective communication process the message has to be codified in a way that the recipient can decode it. That is why the sender has to be aware about the knowledge and experiences of the recipient, in order to codify the message in a comprehensible way. It is also important for the transmission process that the media applied are used by the recipient (Kotler, 2012).

2.2.2 Information Processing

As mentioned the step of information decoding is crucial in the communication process. The decoding of information is a psychological process within the stimulus-object-response-paradigm, which aims to explain the behavior of consumers including the consumer's consciousness (Rennhak, 2010). Kroeber-Riel et al. define two kinds of psychological processes: cognitive processes and activating processes. Cognitive are the processes of information perceiving, processing and memorizing (Kroeber-Riel, Weinberg, & Gröppel-Klein, 2009). Together with the activating processes, which are characterized through emotions, motivations and attitudes, they determine consumer behavior in complex processes triggered by stimuli, as shown in the figure below.

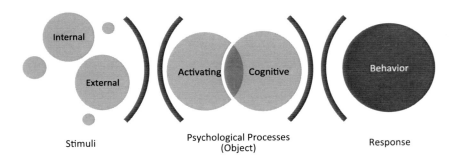

Figure 62: Stimulus-Object-Response-Paradigm

Stimuli

In order to understand this process the relevant characteristics of each step are shortly presented. Regarding the stimuli, Kroeber-Riel et al. examined the role of internal and external stimuli; in this context internal and external information are the focused stimuli. In general consumers prefer internal information, because the majority of purchase decisions are made by habits and with a limited information base. When the consumer has affective purchasing motives he prefers internal information. On the other hand the consumer tends to collect external information when he is rationally motivated. Another factor influencing external information seeking is the individual tendency of each customer to search for information, also described as personal involvement. Besides also the product involvement and situational involvement are important influencing variables. The higher the involvement, the more information is collected. External information can be collected actively or by undesigned adoption. The searching behavior is characterized by an estimation of costs and benefits, so that easily accessible information is favored (Kroeber-Riel et al., 2009). In this context Kroeber-Riel et al. also present the sources for external information seeking of the average customer. Customers mainly use sales conversations, consultation within the circle of friends, magazines, shop windows, advertisement and the internet to get informed. Often sales conversations and consultation of friends are the preferred sources of information as they also serve the human need of social interaction (Kroeber-Riel et al., 2009).

Cognitive Processes

The first part of the cognitive process is the reception of the stimuli, which takes place in the sensory register of the modal model of memory (Kroeber-Riel et al., 2009). The second part of the cognitive process is the perception of information which contains the perception and judgment of information and which takes place in the working memory (Kroeber-Riel et al., 2009). The perception is selected by the attention. Attention can be given consciously, when the customer is searching for information, but it can be also provoked by certain stimuli with a high activation potential (Kroeber-Riel et al., 2009). Activation is defined by Rennhak as the willingness of a person to think, feel and act (Rennhak, 2010,). A stimulus in general possesses a high activation potential when it is emotional and corresponding to the recipient's needs and wishes (Kroeber-Riel et al., 2009). The higher the activation level, the higher is the extent and intensity for information perception (Kroeber-Riel et al., 2009). The information processing is also part of the perception. The "Fluency Theory" describes that if information is presented fluently and repeated, the information will be processed faster (Kroeber-Riel et al., 2009). The judgment results of the newly perceived information, the already stored information and the information processing of both (Kroeber-Riel et al., 2009). The third component of cognitive processes is learning and memorizing, which is located in the long term memory (Kroeber-Riel et al., 2009). Kroeber-Riel et al. state that for example shorter brand names are remembered better than longer names, and associative names better than not associative names. If a scheme for understanding and judging the perceived stimulus already exists in the individual's long term memory, the information is faster processed, judged and better remembered. So information should be communicated in a way that they match to the existent schemes or that they change the consumer's schemes. (Kroeber-Riel et al., 2009)

Activating Processes

Besides the cognitive process the activating process is influencing customer's behavior. Activating processes are characterized by emotions, motivations and attitudes and they are key drivers for human behavior. Activating processes influence cognitive processes, as they are the initiator for information perception. But activating processes are also influenced by cognitive processes (Kroeber-Riel et al., 2009). The definitions of the terms emotion, motivation and attitudes show this connection with cognitive processes: emotion is described as central nervous excitation patterns plus cognitive interpretation, motivation consist of emotion plus cognitive goal orientation and attitude is motivation with cognitive judgment of objects (Kroeber-Riel et al., 2009).

Consumer behavior

As already described above, the response, here the consumer behavior, consist of a complex interaction of activating and cognitive processes. Rennhak resumes that the attitude formed by cognitive and activating processes, influences the consumer behavior together with subjective norms and the specific situation of purchase, which are not included in the stimulus-object-response paradigm. It is the aim of each, especially promotional, communication to provoke a certain behavior. The communication and information processing theories try to explain and to predict the consumer behavior. But often other important influencing variables are not included and therefore the results are less valid (Rennhak, 2010).

2.3 The Information Demand of the Sustainable Consumer

2.3.1 The Sustainable Consumer

Demographic Variables

The first step in assessing the information demand of the sustainable consumer is to examine the target group of the sustainable consumer. A first possibility of target group segmentation is the use of demographic characteristics. In general literature states that sustainable or green customers are rather young, female with a higher income and education level (Chan, 1999 ; Finisterra do Paço & Raposo, 2010, cited by Ritch & Schröder, 2012; Straughan & Roberts, 1999, cited by Rex & Baumann, 2007 ; Tseng & Hung, 2013). But literature agrees that there is a weak coherence between these demographics and a sustainable buying behavior (Akehurst, Carolina Afonso, & Gonçalves, 2012 ; Straughan & Roberts, 1999).

Psychographic Variables

Akehurst et al. substantiated in a quantitative study that rather psychographic variables influence ecological conscious consumer behavior, which is a part of sustainable consumer behavior (Akehurst et al., 2012). Psychographic variables in this context are concerns, attitudes and environmental knowledge (Tseng & Hung, 2013). One important concern described by Hailes, which characterizes the green customer, is the association of purchase with the possibility of environmental preservation, so that green customers are aware about consumption and its environmental impacts (Hailes, 2007, cited by Akehurst, 2012). Chan agrees with that description and stresses that out of this environmental concern they develop a strong self-identity as green consumers (Chan, 1999). Additionally Cervellon and Wernerfelt observed that sustainable customers feel responsible acting as driving forces in order to develop sustainable consumption through word of mouth or educational activities (Cervellon & Wernerfelt, 2012). In their study Akhurst et al. also identified the most important psychographics influencing ecological conscious consumer behavior. They are the Perceived Consumer Effectiveness, "as the belief that each of one's actions as individuals has an important role on preserving environment" (Akehurst et al., 2012, p. 976) and altruism, "as the concern about the welfare of the society and others" (Akehurst et al., 2012, p. 976). Chan agrees with the approach of Perceived Customer Effectiveness describing the heavy green customer as somebody who believes in the ability of environmentally friendly products to help to save resources and to positively influence personal health (Chan, 1999). Paulins and Hillery confirm this approach as well, also taking into consideration the social aspect of sustainability, saying that for these customers consuming in a sustainable way is a basic human psychological need regarding the attitudes of equality and sustainability (Paulins & Hillery, 2009, cited by Shen et al., 2014).

Environmental Knowledge

The third psychographic variable described above is environmental knowledge, again only affecting the environmental part of the holistic concept of sustainability. Environmental knowledge is important in the context of information demand, because information, as one basis, leads to knowledge. Environmental knowledge is defined as "factual information that individuals have about the environment, the ecology of the planet, and the influence of human actions on the environment/ecology" (Arcury & Johnson, 1987). Consumers who possess much environmental knowledge also tend to be more environmentally concerned than consumers with a lower level of environmental knowledge, so that they take environmental attributes of products into concern within the buying process (Kim & Damhorst, 1998, cited by Kang et al., 2013). This thesis is confirmed by Chan stating that green consumers have a good knowledge about green consumption (Chan, 1999). Cervellon and Wernerfelt found out that sustainable customers seek to improve their knowledge over time. They conducted two timely shifted observations of two US American online forums for green fashion. They examined the state and evolvement of customer's knowledge about green fashion in the years 2007-2008 and 2010-2011. The result of this study was that customers, that used these online forums, tend to be more informed and more objective about this topic in the year 2011 than in 2007. They started to use a more specific language and their interests shifted from more environmental concerns to more social issues (Cervellon & Wernerfelt, 2012).

Consumer Behavior

Tseng and Hung found out that there are contradictory results in literature concerning the impact of knowledge on green consumer behavior (Tseng & Hung, 2013). In order to analyze the influence of psychographic variables on consumer behavior, Kang et al. examined the interaction of several psychographic variables, in specific consumer knowledge, perceived consumer effectiveness and perceived personal relevance. The results show that they do influence the consumption of, in this case, environmentally sustainable textiles and apparels only indirectly "through attitude, subjective norm and/or behavioral control" (Kang et al., 2013, p. 449). These results are partially conform with the results of the study by Akhurst presented above, as they both describe the noteworthy influence of perceived customer effectiveness on consumer behavior. But this study also shows that the impact of psychographics on the actual buying behavior is limited as the influence is only indirectly. This leads to the difficulty identifying the sustainable customer with the help of psychographics. A study by McDonald et al. illustrates this problem. Even if customers identified themselves as green customers with correspondent attitudes, concerns and knowledge, they showed an inconsistent and unrelated purchase behavior across different product sectors (McDonald et al., 2009). This study confirms the approach of Peattie, who developed a concept of inconsistent and unrelated purchases that consist of a series of individual and independent purchases (Peattie, 1999, citedy by McDonald et al., 2009). This model neglects the idea of a rationally and systematically acting consumer and hence makes it difficult to identify the sustainable consumer by psychographics or demographics (McDonald et al., 2009 ; Tseng & Hung, 2013).

McDonald et al. propose a concept of

> [...] green or ethical consumption as a process by which individuals make sense of themselves and their relationships with others, and also act within the constraints of the institutions and the norms of society of which they are a part. (McDonald et al., 2009, p. 139)

Consumption as a Process

This concept stands for a more holistic approach of explaining sustainable consumption, which includes external factors such as norms and relationships besides the individual psychographic variables. And it emphasizes that the consumption is a complex process (Horne, 2009). Kroeber-Riel et al. defined the different steps within the process of general consumption. First the consumer realizes a certain problem. Then he/she searches for information and processes this information. After he/she judges on the different alternatives and chooses one of them. The next step would be the decision for purchase and in the end of this process are the consequences of the decision (Kroeber-Riel et al., 2009). The graphic below illustrates this process.

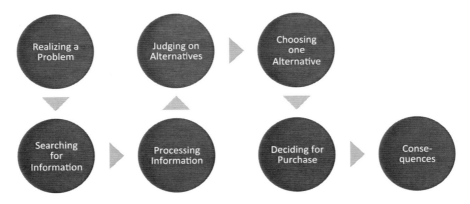

Figure 63: Purchase Decision Making Process

Concretely many factors come into play while purchasing sustainably such as "price, awareness, trust, and the complexity and availability of information, not to mention product availability, social practices and habits, brand reputation and identity" (Horne, 2009, p. 179). Aspects concerning information will be examined further in this paper starting with the information searching behavior of sustainable consumers.

Information Searching Behavior

Information play an important role within the purchase process, as they are the prerequisite for judging on alternatives and hence any decision making as illustrated in the figure. In the context of this paper it is important to understand the information searching behavior and the processing of information. In chapter 2.2 these two steps were explained generally. Adapted to the context of the sustainable consumer behavior the authors agree, that sustainable customers which show a high involvement (e.g. member of online forums about sustainable fashion) are in demand of information and aim to build their knowledge about sustainable consumption (Cervellon & Wernerfelt, 2012 ; Chan, 1999 ; Hendry, Silcox, & Yokoyame, 2007). This result accords with the findings in chapter 2.2, that high involvement has a positive effect on external information search. On the other side Ehrich and Irwin found out that customers with a lower involvement on sustainability tend to avoid knowledge of unethical practices in order to protect themselves emotionally what prevents them from information seeking (Ehrich & Irwin, 2005). This result is also consistent with the theoretic basis presented in chapter 2.2, as customers with a lower involvement seek less external information. A second reason for this result could be also the lower activation level of stimuli that are contrary to the consumer's wishes and needs, as information about unethical practices cause rather negative emotions, such as anger (Ehrich & Irwin, 2005). But Ehrich and Irwin also found out, that the easier available information about sustainability and ethics is, the more customers are willing to consider them together with other product attributes (Ehrich & Irwin, 2005). As an important source of information literature emphasizes the role of the retailer, as customers expect them to communicate aspects of sustainability (Hendry et al., 2007 ; Ritch & Schröder, 2012). Also this result is accordant with the findings of chapter 2.2, where the sources of information with social interaction were ranked first. Trust is an important aspect of any source of information. Ritch and Schröder describe that customers tend to extend a retailer's service orientation toward the customer to a general service orientation toward all stakeholders. A consequence is that customers transfer their trust also to other parts of the business, as they believe that retailers are also responsibly acting in these fields. Then they do not require additional verification information. But when unethical practices are revealed, customers' trust is broken (Ritch & Schröder, 2012). Many authors state that this is already the case, as sustainable customers distrust, especially large, companies thinking that they are mainly profit orientated and that their activities within sustainable development are characterized through green washing (Goworek, Hiller, Fisher, Cooper, & Woodward, 2013 ; Topolansky Barbe, Gonzalez-Triay, & Hensel, 2013).

2.3.2 The Information Content

General Information on Environmental Impact

After having presented characteristics of the sustainable consumer, the recipient of the information, the concrete demanded information content will be examined in this chapter. Basically the information content should be rather relevant to the recipient than offering a high variety. Therefore it should be designed with regard to the recipient's needs (Kallweit, Spreer, & Toporowski, 2014). In chapter 2.3.1 characteristics and needs of sustainable customers were presented. One of it is the environmental knowledge and concern, so that information should support these two characteristics. Cervellon and Wernerfelt found out with their observation of green fashion online forums that consumers tried to understand the whole concept of sustainable fashion. Beside concrete product attributes such as organic materials, they also discussed on the influence of clothing on climate change, pollution and the protection of the environment (Cervellon & Wernerfelt, 2012).

Information Triggering the Perceived Customer Effectiveness

Another important factor influencing consumer behavior as explained in the previous chapter is the Perceived Customer Effectiveness. Literature recommends designing correspondent information. Companies should communicate progresses towards sustainability in a clear way, "providing motivation and a common purpose" (Hendry et al., 2007, p. 52). Many authors state that it is important to explain the environmental impacts to customers and that they can make a difference in the environment by purchasing sustainably.(Akehurst et al., 2012; Kang et al., 2013). Hekkelman found out that information provoking self-reflection, in this context hang tags with a mirror and a picture of a production worker, can give a more concrete idea about the impact of sustainable consumption (Hekkelman, 2014). This kind of information consists of the description of 'collective' benefits, as Topolanksy Barbe et al. describe. Besides the 'collective' benefits, also 'private' benefits exist, which should be even more valuable for the customer than general collective benefits (Topolansky Barbe et al., 2013). Private benefits are perceived health benefits or nutritional values of sustainable products (Topolansky Barbe et al., 2013). Information triggering these perceived private benefits could be the claims "pesticide-free" or "free from genetically modified ingredients" (Topolansky Barbe et al., 2013). Akehurst resumes:

> More than to educate and advise consumers of the environmental problem, the focus of the communications should be on the environmental features, advantages and benefits associated with the product and its real impact on ecological preservation. (Akehurst et al., 2012, p. 983)

Product Attribute Information

Another customer need is the information search within a concrete purchase process, which is also presented in the previous chapter. Within this step, product attribute information is important. Tseng and Hung conducted in-depth-interviews with green product consumers in order to find out their main concerns toward sustainable products (Tseng & Hung, 2013). They structured the results in the three categories tangibles, assurance and reliability. The table below presents the individual contents of each category.

Table 8: Concerns of Green Consumers

tangibles	assurance	reliability
appearances (aesthetics)	environmental impacts of materials	functional performance
eco-labels	recyclability ratio	conformance
labelling of product ingredients	energy conservation rates	durability
user friendliness	recycling packaging materials	

These results are intersectional and not specifically applicable to one product group. Adapted to the fashion branch the important concerns are appearances (aesthetics), labelling of product ingredients and environmental impacts of material, as highlighted in the table above. They are also mentioned by other authors concerning sustainable fashion products. The first important concern is appearances or aesthetics. Especially within sustainable fashion creating a fashionable and aesthetically appealing product is very important (Cervellon & Wernerfelt, 2012). Customers expect sustainable clothing's design and quality equal to conventional clothing's design and quality (Horne, 2009 ; Shen et al., 2014). Cervellon and Wernerfelt found out that that clothing labelled "sustainable" is linked to ecology and environmental preservation in a more broad sense, whereas the label "organic" is more linked to fashion (Cervellon & Wernerfelt, 2012).

The second concern "environmental impacts of material", where a prerequisite is the concern "labelling of product ingredients", has to be widened to "environmental impacts of material and production processes" when it comes to fashion products. Cervellon and Wernerfelt came to the result that green customers wish to gain more knowledge about the green fashion value chain (Cervellon & Wernerfelt, 2012). Within this topic the environmental impact of fashion production, in the shape of CO_2 emissions, environmental pollution and non-biodegradable material, is a major concern (Cervellon & Wernerfelt, 2012). In this context Cervellon and Wernerfelt observed a shift of interest towards social responsibility in the fashion value chain (Cervellon & Wernerfelt, 2012). Rich and Schröder state that social issues are adding complexity to the topic sustainability because of cultural distance between the customer and the workers in the production countries and a low level of customer's knowledge (Ritch & Schröder, 2012). A study that consists of an experiment in a Kuyichi-store testing several hangtags informing about sustainable product attributes, states that the most effective hangtag should include information about "labor conditions in factories, the suppliers' location and sustainable materials" (Hekkelman, 2014) as customers are most concerned about these three aspects. Another important part of the concern "environmental impacts of material" in fashion is the after purchase phase, that includes the usage and disposal of the product (Goworek et al., 2013). Participants of a focus group conducted by Goworek et al. spoke about their need for more information concerning especially the disposal of clothes. They were weakly aware about the possibilities of recycling, because of a lack of information where and how clothes can be recycled (Goworek et al., 2013). Providing information about the recycling process and its impact is important for triggering behavioral change (Ritch & Schröder, 2012 ; Shen et al., 2014). Goworek et al. developed useful information contents for the usage and disposal of fashion such as "Wash at 30°C", "Line dry more often", "Repair more at home", "Keep clothes as long as possible" and "Put clothes in recycling bank" (Goworek et al., 2013, p. 383). These information could be placed on the labelling inside the garment. (Goworek et al., 2013).

Another important product attribute information within the purchase process is the price, as it influences the purchase intention of customers (Horne, 2009 ; Topolansky Barbe et al., 2013). Ritch and Schröder describe that almost all study participants "felt restricted financially in applying sustainability principles to fashion consumption" (Ritch & Schröder, 2012, p. 206). Concerning the meaning of price as a buying restriction or as a proof of sustainable quality literature provides different results. Ritch and Schröder argue that consumers link lower prices to bad working conditions with low salaries. Ethically sourced products, in this case food, were recognized as more expensive. Contrary to this is the identification of the absence of a green price premium as one success factor of a green clothing collection in Switzerland (Meyer, 2001, cited by Rex & Baumann, 2007). Another approach is to add non-monetary values to the traditional pricing information, such as the ecological and energy footprint, greenhouse gas emissions or violations of the principles of sustainability (Hendry et al., 2007).

2.3.3 The Information Frame

Credibility

This chapter deals with the question how the information content should be presented to the sustainable customer in order to provoke a sustainable consumer behavior. For the sustainable customer trust is considered as the most important factor influencing purchase intentions, so that information should support trust (Topolansky Barbe et al., 2013). But many authors describe that sustainable customers distrust companies and companies' information, because they think that companies have mainly commercial interests and do not act ethically (Goworek et al., 2013 ; Horne, 2009 ; Skov, 2012, cited by Cervellon & Wernerfelt, 2012). Another reason for missing trust is the perceived complexity of outsourced fashion production processes; so that customers are unsure whether it is possible to guarantee sustainable production (Cervellon & Wernerfelt, 2012 ; Ritch & Schröder, 2012). Goworek et al. state that reliable information is needed in order to overcome consumer's distrust and to trigger sustainable consumer behavior (Goworek et al., 2013). Cervellon and Wernerfelt found out that improved customer knowledge on sustainable production processes led to a higher level of customer trust in companies (Cervellon & Wernerfelt, 2012). As means to change more information and collaboration between industry and a third party, e.g. government or NGOs, are mentioned (Goworek et al., 2013 ; Visschers et al., 2010). Collaborations between industry and third party organizations are mostly communicated by eco-labels which are described in the text below. Information to create more customer knowledge should be presented factual and informational, with the help of product labels or in-store brochures. Companies should avoid a promotional character of the information, but they should make them easily accessible through a prominent placement (Goworek et al., 2013). This recommendation is conform to the findings in chapter 2.2 stating that customers prefer easily accessible information. Another interesting aspect is that information about sustainable products is perceived more reliable within a sustainable retail environment, such as organic shops in the food sector. (Topolansky Barbe et al., 2013) This result is supported by Kroeber-Riel et al. who also described the positive effect of product environment information on the product and information perception of customers. (Kroeber-Riel et al., 2009)

The Role of Eco-Labels

Eco-labels are instruments to support customers in making sustainable purchase decisions by presenting information on the environmental and social performances of products (Horne, 2009). They are frequently used to position sustainable products so that they play an important role within green marketing (Rex & Baumann, 2007). Horne presents two major characteristics of eco-labels: whether the label is mandatory or voluntary and whether it is certificated independently or not (Horne, 2009). An advantage of eco-labels is that sustainable customers consider them to be a very helpful tool purchasing sustainable products (Topolansky Barbe et al., 2013). A prerequisite is that customers know about the label and its criteria (Topolansky Barbe et al., 2013). This aspect leads to the disadvantages of eco-labels. Many eco-labels have a very low recognition and they are often misinterpreted by customer (Cervellon & Wernerfelt, 2012 ; Visschers et al., 2010). A study by GfK shows that fashion eco labels seem familiar to only 46% of interviewed women and 32% of interviewed men, whereas 80% of women and 79% of men showed interest on sustainable clothes (GfK, 2008). As described above eco-labels are instruments to build consumer's trust. As the most important label criteria of building customer's trust Topolansky Barbe et al. describe the government involvement within the certification process, the clarity of the presented information and the label's reputation, which is strongly positively linked to its longevity (Topolansky Barbe et al., 2013). Eco-labels are trusted more if they are third-party-certificated, because customers think that companies cannot influence the certification process conducted by a third party. (Topolansky Barbe et al., 2013) Horne and Gertz confirm that third party labels are perceived more trustworthy by customers than company certificated labels (Gertz,

2005 ; Horne, 2009). But Topolansky Barbe et al. also name the main problem of eco-labels lowering their credibility: the growing number of different eco-label schemes and information confuse customers and lead to mistrust (Topolansky Barbe et al., 2013). That is why customers ask for a clarification and harmonization of eco-labels around the world (Cervellon & Wernerfelt, 2012).

Transparency

Transparency is another important aspect within the information frame, also supporting the credibility of information. Transparency is mandatory for delivering information on which customers can rely (Cervellon & Wernerfelt, 2012 ; Ritch & Schröder, 2012). Cervellon and Wernerfelt observed that customers demand for clear information especially on production processes and product origin. Customers with high expertise on sustainable fashion expect concrete and measurable information on companies' sustainability activities and their impacts on environment and society. But there is a lack of transparent information provided by retailers or manufacturers which leads to customer frustration (Cervellon & Wernerfelt, 2012). That is why Hendry et al. rank information transparency and openness first in order to communicate sustainability successfully. In consequence customers will develop a better understanding of sustainability and business reality (Hendry et al., 2007). Shen et al. describe the positive impact of providing transparent information to customers on their willingness to purchase sustainable fashion (Shen et al., 2014). Tseng and Hung mention that clear and transparent information raise the convenience in the information seeking process which enables sustainable purchase decisions (Tseng & Hung, 2013). Also for eco-labels clarity and transparency of information are important factors in creating customer's trust and satisfaction (Topolansky Barbe et al., 2013).

Comprehensibility

Comprehensibility of information is important within the step of message decoding. For a successful communication process the customer has to understand the intended content of the perceived message, as already mentioned in chapter 2.2. Within the topic of sustainable consumption complexity has been identified as a prohibiting influence. (McCallum, 2008, cited by Ritch & Schröder, 2012) According to this sustainable customers are more likely to integrate simple provided information in their decision making. (Oates et al., 2008, cited by McDonald et al., 2009) But most companies failed to communicate clear and comprehensible information about sustainability. Customers think that purchasing fashion in a sustainable way is energy and time consuming. They face difficulties in understanding information or the labels. That is why they often think that producing sustainably is a vague issue (Cervellon & Wernerfelt, 2012). Especially eco-labels provoke information overload of customers. Customers feel overwhelmed by information and text to read and they are confused by the increasing number of existing eco-labels (GfK, 2008 ; Horne, 2009). Leverages to change this confusion are the language, the communication design, the use of media and a modification of eco-labels. First the language of information presented should match to customer's knowledge. So fashion business jargon should be translated into more common terms (Cervellon & Wernerfelt, 2012). Beard identified the classical terminology with vocabulary such as "ethical", "fair trade", "organic", "natural", "sweat shop free" as a main cause for customers' confusion. A clear definition of terms ideally by governments is recommended (Beard, 2008). The design of information can trigger attention and facilitate the processing of information (Kroeber-Riel et al., 2009). An important determinant of the communication design should be the personal involvement of the sustainable customer, already mentioned in chapter 2.2 as a factor for the information searching behavior. Kroeber-Riel et al. summarized communication characteristics for highly involved customers and customers with low involvement, presented in the table below (Kroeber-Riel et al., 2009).

Table 9: Communication Characteristics and Involvement

Communication Characteristics	High Involvement	Low Involvement
Communication Aim	to persuade	to please
Content	arguments	identification
Duration	long	short

Instrument	language	picture
Repetition	less	frequent

Kroeber-Riel et al. recommend different communication designs adapted to the degree of personal customer involvement: highly involved customers should receive detailed, persuasive written information in form of arguments with a low repetition level. Customers who show a lower involvement expect shorter information in pictures with frequent repetition in order to identify with the communication content. Fashion companies also should be aware about an effective use of media. The experiment in the Kuyichi-store testing the optimal hangtag for sustainable clothes showed that customers use the hangtag for fast and short information whereas for more detailed information they search on the Kuyichi website at home (Hekkelman, 2014). For eco-labels it is important to be clearly legible, as it allows customers to save time searching for information and finding sustainable products (Shen et al., 2014 ; Topolansky Barbe et al., 2013). Half of respondents in a study conducted by Topolansky Barbe et al. expect eco-labels to assure the environmental friendliness of the product they wish to purchase and not to provide too much additional information. The other half wishes to know more about the labelling criteria and the organization behind (Topolansky Barbe et al., 2013). This difference in the desired amount of information could base on different degrees of customer involvement, which influences the duration of customer's attention as described above.

3 Discussion

3.1 Consistency of results

The findings of the conducted literature review will be discussed in this chapter, starting with the communication and information processing theories in chapter 2.2. There is a large base of literature concerning these topics. The more specialized findings in literature concerning sustainable customer information demand are conform with the theories of communication and information processing: sustainable customers, which are highly involved, are in demand for more external information; easily accessible information are generally preferred; information should match to customer's expectations and knowledge in order to be successfully decoded - to name a few examples of consistent results. So communication and information processing theories provide useful instruments in order to understand consumer behavior and to evaluate communication strategies.

4 Validity of Definition of the Sustainable Customer

Analyzing the sustainable customer literature tends to focus on ecological aspects contrary to the holistic concept of sustainability, presented in chapter 2.1. There is a broad selection about "green customers" and "environmental knowledge" in literature, not covering social or economic aspects of sustainability. Some authors start to include also social aspects in order to define sustainable consumer behavior of fashion customers, e.g. Paulins and Hillery. Cervellon and Wernerfelt observed also a shift of customer's interest from ecological aspects to social aspects of sustainable fashion in four years. These findings lead to the assumption that the meaning of sustainability, from an ecological issue to a more holistic concept, changed over time for customers especially with regard on fashion. A reason for this could be the various scandals of poor working conditions in fashion production that occurred in the past years having their momentary peek with the collapse of the factory Rhana Plaza 2013 in Bangladesh with more than 1.130 dead people (Faigle & Pauly, 2014). This caused an increasing media attention on working conditions in the fashion branch leading to higher customer awareness, so that sustainable fashion customers are paying attention on social and on ecological aspects.

Another issue is the difficulty in identifying the sustainable consumer by demographics or psychographics as commonly stated in literature. A sustainable customer should be somebody who consumes sustainably and not a person who is only concerned about sustainability. And there lays the difficulty: It is feasible to identify specific psychographic elements that show sustainable involvement, such as environmental concern and knowledge, perceived customer effectiveness and altruism as presented in chapter 2.3.1. But it is not possible to reliably filter sustainable customers out of all sustainably concerned persons. Additionally the actual purchase behavior of concerned persons differs from product group to another product group as described by McDonald et al., so that for each product group an own "sustainable customer" may exist. That is also why this paper focuses on the information demand of sustainable fashion customers, in order to be valid for the fashion sector.

4.1 Validity of Assessed Information Content

Though there is no clear characterization of the sustainable customer available in literature, the information demand of sustainable customers presented by literature was conducted reliably. There is not much literature existing concerning the demanded information content of fashion customers, the few results were generated with qualitative studies. The problem of sampling within a target group that is not clearly characterized was solved in various ways. Ritch and Schröder for example used the method of snowball sampling in order to acquire a certain number of participants with similar lifestyles from a pretested reliable small pilot sample (Ritch & Schröder, 2012). Cervellon and Wernerfelt used the method of observing customers in sustainable fashion online communities. With this method it is ensured that the sample consists of customers with at least a high involvement in sustainability and in fashion. Additionally this technique is non-invasive avoiding multiple biases that could occur in interviews (Cervellon & Wernerfelt, 2012). The presented information content is particularly valid for sustainable fashion, as already stated above. Basically sustainable fashion customers, as they are highly involved, showed interest in all aspects of sustainable fashion, such as production, materials, after purchase instructions and the general impact of the fashion industry on environment as described in chapter 2.3.2. Another important aspect is that sustainable customers expect sustainable fashion items to be equal to conventional fashion products in their quality and design, so that also these aspects have to be taken into consideration designing communication and product information. So it is important in order to satisfy customers' information demand not only informing about sustainability issues, but also about more classic product attributes such as quality and design. Additionally the specific effect of the sustainable purchase act is very effective information content in order to provoke a sustainable consumer behavior, as shown in chapter 2.3.1 and 2.3.2. The reason could be that through this specific impact on environment and society, made visible and understandable through information, the quite abstract concept of sustainability becomes clearer to customers and customers are given the possibility to feel better by showing them the positive impact of their action. In consequence the demanded information content is quite broad, so that fashion companies basically can inform their customers on all their sustainability activities and impacts. They should do so with regard on their individual strengths and weaknesses on sustainability in order to highlight their strengths through information.

4.2 Validity of the Assessed Information Frame

In contrary to the relatively broad possible information content, the information frame, describing the way how the information is transmitted to the customers, is critical. Literature describes various problems concerning information transmission, such as missing transparency, resulting low level of consumers' trust in companies, problem of understanding too complex information and confusion on the high number of different eco-labels also described in chapter 2.3.3. Providing more transparent information, especially about fashion production, which is important information content in sustainable fashion, will be a difficult task for most of fashion companies. The reason are the complex sourcing structures in fashion production, that are globally organized, especially in developing countries with weak environment and working laws, encompassing various different actors with often unknown subcontractors. In order to communicate sustainability successfully to the customers and (re-)gaining their trust as a valuable resource, fashion companies have to change their sourcing structures which would be a big and long term challenge: In order to provide really transparent information, fashion companies have firstly to establish a sourcing process that is documented and controlled completely. Not till then they can work on the information content they want to provide to customers. This structural change is the only way to build really transparent information, in order to be sure to not disappoint customers' trust with unreliable information. A more easily implementable improvement is an increased comprehensibility of information. The problem here is that even highly involved customers feel that consuming sustainability is time and energy consuming. Information accessibility and comprehensibility is one aspect within this problem. A solution would be to gain more expertise editing information comprehensibly in fashion companies, as the basic knowledge is available in literature as shown in chapter 2.3.3. A prerequisite for creating clear and understandable information is a detailed knowledge about the recipient as he has to be able and willing to decode the message with his involvement, knowledge and experiential background. So companies should invest in gaining knowledge about their customers (e.g. with market research) which is useful for designing understandable information. This knowledge could be also used for designing appealing products and marketing strategies, so that this investment possesses synergic effects. Eco-labels as another part of the problem in communicating sustainability are widely examined by literature. Third-party certificated eco-labels could be effective instruments in order to provide reliable and clear information about sustainability to customers. The main problem prohibiting this purpose is the steadily growing number of eco-labels, so that customers are unable to know the labels and their meaning. On this point industry, third parties and governments are responsible in creating a clear landscape of relevant fashion eco-labels and communicating their criteria and background to customers, so that they can interpret the labels fast and correctly.

4.3 Assessed Impact of Information on Sustainable Consumer Behavior

Concerning the impact of information and knowledge on consumer behavior, as this should be the aim of communicating certain information, literature shows that it is limited. Besides the information, customers' emotions, already stored knowledge, values, situational specifics etc. influence the communication process and determine consumer behavior, as presented more detailed in chapter 2.2. This could be the explanation for the famous attitude-behavior-gap when it comes to sustainable consumption. So even, if customers are well informed about sustainability and show a high involvement, they do not always show sustainable consumer behavior, as presented in chapter 2.3.1. That is where limits of information are visible. Information are an important prerequisite for sustainable consumer behavior, as they lead to higher awareness and knowledge about sustainability as stated in chapter 1. But also other factors, such as emotional address, product accessibility, and general values etc., are influencing consumer behavior and have to be taken into consideration creating a successful marketing strategy for sustainable fashion products.

5 Conclusion, Limitations and Further Research

5.1 Conclusion

To give a conclusion the findings of this literature review and their evaluation are briefly summarized. The theoretic basis of communication and cognitive information processing were presented in chapter 2.2. An important aspect of communication theory is the individual decoding of the message by the recipient, which determines if the message is interpreted in the intended way. This aspect leads to the examination of the stimulus-object-response-paradigm, which tries to understand this decoding process. This theory gave hints about how information is perceived and processed and that the decoding is a complex process involving also affective processes next to cognitive processes. As other more concrete examinations about information demand of sustainable customers came to consistent results, communication and information processing theory can be seen as helpful instruments in creating effective communication for practical implementation.

In chapter 2.3.1 findings about the characterization of the sustainable customer were presented. Literature agrees that it is difficult identifying the sustainable customer by classic approaches such as demographics or psychographics, because of the attitude-behavior-gap and different purchase behaviors across product sectors. But nevertheless sustainable customers tend to share certain psychographic characteristics, such as environmental concern, environmental knowledge, perceived customer effectiveness and altruism, so that it is possible to asses a homogenous information demand for the product sector fashion on that basis.

Concerning the concrete demanded information content of sustainable fashion customers, literature provided a few results conducted with qualitative studies. Sustainable fashion customers demand for a broad range of information, as presented in chapter 2.3.2. Most important aspects to consider beside classical information about sustainable production, materials and after-purchase are information about product design and quality and positive impacts of sustainable purchasing behavior.

The presented findings end with the assessment of the information frame in chapter 2.3.3. For sustainable consumers information should be credible, transparent and comprehensible in order to be communicated effectively and trustworthy. At the moment they do not feel that information about sustainable fashion is communicated in this way. So it is recommended to implement practical improvements in this area in order to satisfy customers' demand.

5.2 Limitations

The main limitations in literature are the little results concerning the demanded information content of sustainable fashion customers. Besides the low quantity of literature findings, the results are also limited in their structure and quality. Most studies consist of qualitative research methods with an explorative character (Cervellon & Wernerfelt, 2012 ; Kallweit et al., 2014 ; Kang et al., 2013 ; McDonald et al., 2009 ; Topolansky Barbe et al., 2013 ;Tseng & Hung, 2013). The studies were conducted with a small sample, so that the results are not transferable to the population. Also cultural aspects are not examined in order to know if sustainable customer information demand changes in different cultures. Another limitation is the unclear characterization of the sustainable customer in literature making it difficult to build reliable samples in order to examine the sustainable customer's information demand, especially if quantitative studies should be conducted.

The literature review itself is limited in its selection of topics concerning the information demand of the sustainable consumer. It focuses on identifying the sustainable customer and answering the questions what kind of information content is demanded and how the information frame should look like, especially for fashion products. It left out the topic of media, which play a role as information transmitter.

5.3 Further Research

In order to overcome the presented limitations the qualitative results concerning the information demand of sustainable fashion customers should be tested with the help of quantitative studies. Especially for a more and more internationally operating fashion industry intercultural similarities and differences should be examined as well in further research. Another important aspect of further research should be the examination of general customers' information demand concerning sustainable fashion, following the aim of broadening the customer base for sustainable products with the help of information. In contrary to transmitting information to sustainable customers, which are highly involved and thus actively searching for information, providing complex information about sustainability to less involved customers becomes a real challenge. First qualitative studies should be conducted in order explore customers' information demand concerning sustainable fashion products.

List of References

Aagerup, U. (2011). The influence of real women in advertising on mass market fashion brand perception. *Journal of Fashion Marketing and Management: An International Journal, 15*(4), 486–502. doi:10.1108/13612021111169960

Accenture, & GfK. (2010). Non-Food Multichannel-Handel 2015; Vom Krieg der Kanäle zur Multichannel-Synergie. Retrieved from http://www.accenture.com/SiteCollectionDocuments/PDF/Accenture_GFK_Studie_Non-Food-Multichannel-Handel-2015.pdf

Adhami, M. (2013). Using neuromarketing to discover how we really feel about apps. *International Journal of Mobile Marketing, 8*(1), 95–103.

Ahuja, M., Gupta, B., & Raman, P. (2003). An empirical investigation of online consumer purchasing behavior. *Communications of the ACM, 46*(12), 145–151.

Akehurst, G., Carolina Afonso, & Gonçalves, M. (2012). Re-examining green purchase behaviour and the green consumer profile: new evidences. *Management Decision, 50*(5), 972–988. doi:10.1108/00251741211227726

American Marketing Association. (2014, April 8). Statement of Ethics. Retrieved December 21, 2014, from https://archive.ama.org/Archive/AboutAMA/Pages/Statement%20of%20Ethics.aspx

Anderson, E. W. (1998). Customer Satisfaction and Word of Mouth. *Journal of Service Research, 1*(1), 5.

Anderson, E. W., Fornell, C., & Mazvancheryl, S. K. (2004). Customer Satisfaction and Shareholder Value. *Journal of Marketing, 68*(4), 172–185.

Andersson, P. K., Kristensson, P., Wästlund, E., & Gustafsson, A. (2012). Let the music play or not: The influence of background music on consumer behavior. *Journal of Retailing and Consumer Services, 19*(6), 553–560. doi:10.1016/j.jretconser.2012.06.010

Andreu, L., Bigné, E., Chumpitaz, R., & Swaen, V. (2006). How does perceived retail environment influence consumer's emotional experience? evidence from two retail settings. *The International Review of Retail, Distribution and Consumer Research*, *16*(5), 559–578.

An Introduction to Word of Mouth Marketing. (2008). Retrieved November 20, 2014, from http://www.womma.org/events-education/events

Apple. (2014). Apple - Apple Pay. Retrieved December 28, 2014, from https://www.apple.com/apple-pay/

Arcury, T. A., & Johnson, T. P. (1987). Public Environmental Knowledge: A Statewide Survey. *The Journal of Environmental Education*, *18*(4), 31–37. doi:10.1080/00958964.1987.9942746

ARD. (2014). www. ard-werbung.de. Retrieved December 22, 2014, from http://www.ard-werbung.de/tvtarife/

Argenti, P. A., & Barnes, C. M. (2009). *Digital strategies for powerful corporate communications*. McGraw-Hill. Retrieved from http://www.awpagesociety.com/images/uploads/Argenti_Digital_Strategies.pdf

Arndt, J. (1967). Role of Product-Related Conversations in the Diffusion of a New Product. *Journal of Marketing Research*, *4*(3), 291–295.

Ashman, R., & Vazquez, D. (2012). Simulating attachment to pure-play fashion retailers. *International Journal of Retail & Distribution Management*, *40*(12), 975–996. doi:10.1108/09590551211274955

Aubrey, C., & Judge, D. (2012). Re-imagine retail: Why store innovation is key to a brand's growth in the "new normal", digitally-connected and transparent world. *Journal of Brand Strategy*, *1*(1), 31–39.

Bagge, D. (2007). Multi-channel retailing: The route to customer focus. *The European Retail Digest : The Authoritative Guide to Trends and Developments in Retailing across Europe*, *53*, 57–70.

Bakalash, T., & Riemer, H. (2013). Exploring Ad-Elicited Emotional Arousal and Memory for the Ad Using fMRI. *Journal of Advertising*, *42*(4), 275–291. doi:10.1080/00913367.2013.768065

Bakanauskas, A., & Bičiūnaitė, V. (2011). Interaction Model for the Young Fashion Buyers and Brand-Ambassadors., (58), 7–29.

Baker, J., Parasuraman, A., Grewal, D., & Voss, G. B. (2002). The Influence of Multiple Store Environment Cues on Perceived Merchandise Value and Patronage Intentions. *Journal of Marketing*, *66*(2), 120–141.

Balasubramanian, S., Raghunathan, R., & Mahajan, V. (2005). Consumers in a multichannel environment: Product utility, process utility, and channel choice. *Journal of Interactive Marketing*, *19*(2), 12–30. doi:10.1002/dir.20032

Balzer, I. (2012). Funktionen einer Kreditkarte. Retrieved December 28, 2014, from http://www.finance-know-how.de/kreditkarte/funktionen.html

Banister, E. N., & Hogg, M. K. (2004). Negative symbolic consumption and consumers' drive for self-esteem. *European Journal of Marketing*, *38*(7), 850–868. doi:10.1108/03090560410639285

Baran, R. J. (2008). *Principles of customer relationship management* (Student ed). Mason, Ohio: Thomson/South-Western.

Barnes, J. G., & Wright, J. W. (2012). A Framework for Applying Customer Insight and Context to the Development of a Shopping Experience Strategy. In J. Kandampully (Ed.), *Service Management* (pp. 43–65). New York, NY: Springer New York. Retrieved from http://link.springer.com/10.1007/978-1-4614-1554-1_4

Bauer, H. H., & Eckhardt, S. (2010). Integration als Erfolgsfaktor im Multichannel-Retailing. In D. Ahlert, P. Kenning, R. Olbrich, & H. Schröder (Eds.), *Multichannel-Management Jahrbuch Vertriebs- und Handelsmanagement 2010/2011* (pp. 105–122). Frankfurt am Main: Deutscher Fachverlag GmbH.

Baumgärtner, S., & Quaas, M. (2010). Sustainability economics — General versus specific, and conceptual versus practical. *Ecological Economics*, *69*(11), 2056–2059. doi:10.1016/j.ecolecon.2010.06.018

Bayton, J. (n.d.). MOTIVATION, COGNITION, LEARNING—BASIC FACTORS IN CONSUMER BEHAVIOR. *The Journal of Marketing*.

Beard, N. D. (2008). The Branding of Ethical Fashion and the Consumer: A Luxury Niche or Mass-market Reality? *Fashion Theory: The Journal of Dress, Body & Culture, 12*(4), 447–467.

Beatty, S. E., Mayer, M., Coleman, J. E., Reynolds, K. E., & Lee, J. (1996). Customer-Sales Associate Retail Relationships. *Journal of Retailing, 72*(3), 223–247.

Berman, B., & Thelen, S. (2004). A guide to developing and managing a well-integrated multi-channel retail strategy. *International Journal of Retail & Distribution Management, 32*(3), 147–156. doi:10.1108/09590550410524939

Bernecker, M. (2014). *Emotionalisierung von Marken – Haben Sie Kunden oder Fans?*. Retrieved from http://de.slideshare.net/dim/emotionalisierung-von-marken-haben-sie-kunden-oder-fans

Berthon, P., Pitt, L., & Campbell, C. (2008). Ad Lib: When Customers Create the Ad. *California Management Review, 50*(4), 6–30.

Bielski, L. (2010). What's PayPal up to? (cover story). *ABA Banking Journal, 102*(7), 26–29.

Bin Shen, Yulan Wang, Chris K.Y. Lo, & Momoko Shum. (2012). The impact of ethical fashion on consumer purchase behavior. *Journal of Fashion Marketing and Management: An International Journal, 16*(2), 234–245. doi:10.1108/13612021211222842

Bissell, K., & Rask, A. (2010). Real women on real beauty: Self-discrepancy, internalisation of the thin ideal, and perceptions of attractiveness and thinness in Dove's Campaign for Real Beauty. *International Journal of Advertising, 29*(4), 643–668. doi:10.2501/S0265048710201385

Blackmore, S. (1999, February 26). The Forget Meme not Theory. Retrieved November 21, 2014, from http://www.susanblackmore.co.uk/journalism/THESmemes.htm

Blackwell, R. D., Miniard, P. W., & Engel, J. F. (2001). *Consumer Behavior* (9th ed.).

Thomson Learning.

Bloching, B., Otto, A., Luck, L., Kötter, H., Kiene, R., & Franke. (2013, February). Dem Kunden auf der Spur. Retrieved December 21, 2014, from http://www.ece.de/fileadmin/pdf/Studien/Multichannel_-_Studie_Dem_Kunden_auf_der_Spur__Kurzversion_.pdf

Blum, G. (2014). Akquisition und Kundenbindung. In H. Holland (Ed.), *Digitales Dialogmarketing* (pp. 73–96). Wiesbaden: Springer Fachmedien Wiesbaden. Retrieved from http://link.springer.com/10.1007/978-3-658-02541-0_4

Boersma, T. (2010). Warum Web-Exzellenz Schlüsselthema für erfolgreiche Händler ist. In G. Heinemann & A. Haug (Eds.), *Web-Exzellenz im E-Commerce* (pp. 21–41). Wiesbaden: Gabler. Retrieved from http://www.springerlink.com/index/10.1007/978-3-8349-8816-4_2

Bohlen, G., Schlegelmilch, B. B., & Diamantopoulos, A. (1993). Measuring Ecological Concern: A Multi-construct Perspective. *Journal of Marketing Management*, 9(4), 415–430.

Bohl, P. (2012, March). The effects of store atmosphere on shopping behaviour - A literature review. [Monograph]. Retrieved December 23, 2014, from http://portal.uni-corvinus.hu/index.php?id=26979

Bower, A. B. (2001). Highly Attractive Models in Advertising and the Women Who Loathe Them: The Implications of Negative Affect for Spokesperson Effectiveness. *Journal of Advertising*, 30(3), 51–63.

Bower, A. B., & Landreth, S. (2001). Is Beauty Best? Highly Versus Normally Attractive Models in Advertising. *Journal of Advertising*, 30(1), 1–12.

Brannon, E. L. (2010). *Fashion Forecasting*. (3. ed). New York, NY: Fairchild Publications. Retrieved from http://search.ebscohost.com/login.aspx?direct=true&db=cat00207a&AN=reu.333400402&lang=de&site=eds-live&authtype=shib

Breazeale, M. (2009). Word of Mouse. *International Journal of Market Research*, 51(3), 297–318.

Brinkmann, J. (2004). Looking at Consumer Behavior in a Moral Perspective. *Journal of Business Ethics*, *51*(2), 129–141.

Browne, G. J., Durrett, J. R., & Wetherbe, J. C. (2004). Consumer reactions toward clicks and bricks: investigating buying behaviour on-line and at stores. *Behaviour & Information Technology*, *23*(4), 237–245. doi:10.1080/01449290410001685411

Brown, M., Mendoza-Pena, A., & Moriarty, M. (2014). *On Solid Ground: Brick-and-Mortar is the Foundation of Omnichannel Retailing*. ATKearney. Retrieved from http://www.atkearney.com/documents/10192/4683364/On+Solid+Ground.pdf/f96d82ce-e40c-450d-97bb-884b017f4cd7

Brown, T. J., Barry, T. E., Dacin, P. A., & Gunst, R. F. (2005). Spreading the Word: Investigating Antecedents of Consumers' Positive Word-of-Mouth Intentions and Behaviors in a Retailing Context. *Journal of the Academy of Marketing Science*, *33*(2), 123–138.

Bruce, A. (2012). Multi-Channeling der Zukunft – Multi-Channel-Erfolgsfaktoren im wachsenden Markt aus Sicht von Google. In G. Heinemann, M. Schleusener, & S. Zahalria (Eds.), *Modernes Multi-Channeling im Fashion-Handel: Konzepte, Erfolgsfaktoren, Praxisbeispiele* (pp. 50–69). Frankfurt, Main: Dt. Fachverl.

Bruhn, M., & Köhler, R. (2011). *Wie Marken wirken: Impulse aus der Neuroökonomie für die Markenführung*. Vahlen.

Bucik, V., Brenk, K. M., & Vodopivec, B. (n.d.). Emotions Profil Index: Stability and Dimensionality of the Structure, 25 – 45.

Bülbül, C., & Menon, G. (2010). The Power of Emotional Appeals in Advertising. *Journal of Advertising Research*, *50*(2), 169–180.

Bundesverband Digitale Wirschaft e.V. (2014, September 10). OVK Online-Report. Bundesverband Digitale Wirschaft e.V. Retrieved from http://www.ovk.de/ovk-de/online-werbung/daten-fakten/downloads.html

Busch, R. (2007). *Communication policies*. Berlin: Springer.

Buttle, F. A. (1998). Word of mouth: understanding and managing referral marketing. *Journal of Strategic Marketing, 6*(3), 241–254. doi:10.1080/096525498346658

Buvari, R., Dosé, T., & Vonstad, B. (2014, May). A channel approach to fashion.

Caballero, M. J., & Solomon, P. J. (1984). Effects of Model Attractiveness on Sales Response. *Journal of Advertising, 13*(1), 17–33.

Cakim, I. M. (2010). *Implementing Word of Mouth Marketing: Online Strategies to Identify Influencers, Craft Stories, and Draw Customers.* Hoboken, N.J.: Wiley. Retrieved from http://search.ebscohost.com/login.aspx?direct=true&db=nlebk&AN=309024&lang=de&site=eds-live&authtype=shib

C. A. Lindberg, & Stevenson, A. (2010). New Oxford American Dictionary (3rd ed.). Oxford University Press.

Callen, K. S., & Ownbey, S. F. (2003). Associations between demographics and perceptions of unethical consumer behaviour. *International Journal of Consumer Studies, 27*(2), 99.

Carroll, A. B. (1991). The Pyramid of Corporate Social Responsibility: Toward the Moral Management of Organizational Stakeholders. *Business Horizons, 34*(4), 39–48.

Cervellon, M.-C. (2012). Victoria's Dirty Secrets. *Journal of Advertising, 41*(4), 133–145. doi:10.2753/JOA0091-3367410409

Cervellon, M.-C., & Wernerfelt, A.-S. (2012). Knowledge sharing among green fashion communities onlineLessons for the sustainable supply chain. *Journal of Fashion Marketing & Management, 16*(2), 176–192. doi:10.1108/13612021211222860

Chaffey, D., & Ellis-Chadwick, F. (2012). *Digital Marketing: Strategy, Implementation and Practice* (5th ed.). Essex: Pearson Education Limited.

Chang, C. (2008). Chronological Age Versus Cognitive Age for Younger Consumers. *Journal of Advertising, 37*(3), 19–32.

Changjo Yoo, M. P., Jonghee Park, M. P., & MacInnis, D. J. (1998). Effects of Store

Characteristics and In-Store Emotional Experiences on Store Attitude. *Journal of Business Research, 42*(3), 253–263.

Chan, K. (1999). Market Segmentation of Green Consumers in Hong Kong. *Journal of International Consumer Marketing, 12*, 7–24. doi:10.1300/J046v12n02_02

Chapman, J., & Gant, N. (2007). *Designers, Visionaries and Other Stories: A Collection of Sustainable Design Essays*. Earthscan.

Chatterjee, P. (2010). Cause and consequences of "order online pick up in-store" shopping behavior. *The International Review of Retail, Distribution and Consumer Research, 20*(4), 431–448.

Ci, C. (2008). *The Impact of the Abstractness-concreteness of an Ad Copy on Consumers' Responses to a Product: The Moderating Role of Consumers' Regulatory Foci and Types of Product Attribute*. ProQuest.

Ciprian-Marcel, P., Lăcrămioara, R., Ioana, M. A., & Maria, Z. M. (2009). Neuromarketing - getting inside the customer's mind. *Annals of the University of Oradea, Economic Science Series, 18*(4), 804–807.

Clark, H. (2008). SLOW + FASHION--an Oxymoron--or a Promise for the Future…? *Fashion Theory: The Journal of Dress, Body & Culture, 12*(4), 427–446.

Clottey, T. A., Collier, D. A., & Stodnick, M. (2008). Drivers Of Customer LoyaltyIn A Retail Store Environment. *Journal of Service Science, Volume 1*(Number 1).

Cochrane, L. (2014, November 14). The rise of the "inbetweenie" model. *The Guardian*. Retrieved from http://www.theguardian.com/fashion/fashion-blog/2014/nov/14/the-rise-of-the-inbetweenie-model

ComStore. (2014, September 20). QR-Codes in Deutschland populär [Statista]. Retrieved from http://de.statista.com/infografik/618/anteil-der-smartphone-nutzer-die-qr-codes-scannen/

Czinkota, M. R., & Ronkainen, I. A. (2010). *Principles of international marketing / Michael R. Czinkota; Ilkka A. Ronkainen*. Mason, Ohio : Thomson/South-Western, c2010.

Damm, J. (2014, March 6). L+T: Schaufenster mit Augmented Reality. Retrieved from http://www.textilwirtschaft.de/business/LT-Schaufenster-mit-Augmented-Reality_90801.html

DasGupta, N., Journo, M., Loftus, B., & Tardy, O. (2009, January 7). Realizing the Multichannel Promise. Retrieved from https://www.bcgperspectives.com/content/articles/marketing_sales_sales_channels_realizing_multichannel_promise/

Daurer, S., Molitor, D., & Spann, M. (2012). Digitalisierung und Konvergenz von Online- und Offline-Welt: Einfluss der mobilen Internetsuche auf das Kaufverhalten. *Zeitschrift für Betriebswirtschaft*, *82*(S4), 3–23. doi:10.1007/s11573-012-0580-1

Davis, H. (2014). Retailers using stores as part of their online strategy. *Inside Tucson Business*, *23*(36), 6.

De Bruyn, A., & Lilien, G. L. (2008). A multi-stage model of word-of-mouth influence through viral marketing. *International Journal of Research in Marketing*, *25*(2), 151–163. doi:10.1016/j.ijresmar.2008.03.004

De Luce, J. (2001). Silence at the newsstands. *Generations*, *25*(3), 39–43.

Der Handel. (2012, November 23). C&A lässt Onlinekunden Auslieferungsort wählen [Der Handel]. Retrieved from http://www.derhandel.de/news/unternehmen/pages/Multichannel-C%26A-laesst-Onlinekunden-Auslieferungsort-waehlen-9214.html

Deutsche Bank AG. (2014). Deutsche Bank - Deutsche Bank Card. Retrieved December 28, 2014, from https://www.deutsche-bank.de/pfb/content/privatkunden/konto_mit-karte-bezahlen_deutsche-bank-card.html

Deutsche Bundesbank. (2014a, July). Debitkarten - Transaktionen in Deutschland bis 2013 | Statistik. Retrieved December 27, 2014, from http://de.statista.com/statistik/daten/studie/72152/umfrage/transaktionen-mit-debitkarten-in-deutschland-seit-dem-jahr-2007/

Deutsche Bundesbank. (2014b, July). Kreditkarten - Transaktionen in Deutschland bis 2013 | Statistik. Retrieved December 28, 2014, from http://de.statista.com/statistik/daten/studie/6833/umfrage/transaktionen-mit-kreditkarten-in-deutschland/

Dholakia, R. R., Zhao, M., & Dholakia, N. (2005). Multichannel Retailing: A case study of early experience. *Journal of Interactive Marketing*, *19*(2), 63–74.

Dholakia, U. M., Kahn, B. E., Reeves, R., Rindfleisch, A., Stewart, D., & Taylor, E. (2010). Consumer Behavior in a Multichannel, Multimedia Retailing Environment. *Journal of Interactive Marketing*, *24*(2), 86–95. doi:10.1016/j.intmar.2010.02.005

Dichter, E. (1966). How Word-of-Mouth Advertising Works. *Harvard Business Review*, *44*(6), 147.

Dickenson, S. (2013). The Future of Retail. *Home Accents Today*, *28*(3), 28–33.

Dickey, I. J., & Lewis, W. F. (2009). Consumer Generated Media: Evolving Marketing Opportunity for Consumer Engagement. *Society for Marketing Advances Proceedings*, 181–185.

Dickson, M. A. (2001). Utility of No Sweat Labels for Apparel Consumers: Profiling Label Users and Predicting Their Purchases. *Journal of Consumer Affairs*, *35*(1), 96.

Diehl-Wobbe, E. (2014). Britische Onliner auf Rekordkurs, (43), 37.

Dillon-Schalk, L. (2011, June 6). *How to develop a digital strategy*. Retrieved from http://de.slideshare.net/ldillonschalk/mcc11-developing-a-digital-strategy-amp-roadmap

Doane, D., & New Economics Foundation. (2001). *Taking flight: the rapid growth of ethical consumerism : the Ethical Purchasing Index 2001*.

Dong, S., Richards, J., & Feng, L. (2014, November 11). CONSUMERS' AWARENESS OF SUSTAINABLE FASHION: EDDI - Discovery Service der Hochschule Reutlingen. *Marketing Management Journal. Fall2013, Vol. 23 Issue 2, p134-147. 14p*. Retrieved from https://vpn.reutlingen-universi-ty.de/+CSCO+00756767633A2F2F7271662E6F2E726F667062756266672E70627A++/

eds/detail/detail?sid=90974ef4-7145-47c1-924a-6d44d712a0b4%40sessionmgr111&vid=0&hid=104&bdata=Jmxhbmc9ZGUmc2l0ZT1lZHMtbGl2ZQ%3d%3d#db=bth&AN=93686721

Donnell, L., Hutchinson, K., & Reid, A. (2012). Fashion retailing in the new economy: the case of SMEs. *International Journal of Retail & Distribution Management, 40*(12), 906–919. doi:10.1108/09590551211274919

Donovan, R. J., & Rossiter, J. R. (1982). Store Atmosphere: An Environmental Psychology Approach. *Journal of Retailing, 58*(1), 34.

Dorman, A. J. (2013). *Omni-Channel Retail and the New Age Consumer: An Empirical Analysis to Direct-to-Consumer Channel Interaction in the Retail Industry*. Claremont McKenna College. Retrieved from http://scholarship.claremont.edu/cmc_theses/590

Doucé, L., & Janssens, W. (2013). The presence of a pleasant ambient scent in a fashion store: the moderating role of shopping motivation and affect intensity. *Environment and Behavior, 45*(2), 215–238.

Dreamlines: Freeski Preview 2015 | VAUDE. (2014). Retrieved from https://www.youtube.com/watch?v=8obfcT9YN9c&feature=youtube_gdata_player

Drexhage, J., & Murphy, D. (2010). Sustainable Development: From Brundtland to Rio 2012. United Nations. Retrieved from http://www.un.org/wcm/webdav/site/climatechange/shared/gsp/docs/GSP1-6_Background%20on%20Sustainable%20Devt.pdf

Driscoll, M. (2013). Bye-bye, silo retailing, hello, omni-channel. *Value Retail News, 31*(4), 10–14.

Drumwright, M. E., & Murphy, P. E. (2004). How Advertising Practitioners View Ethics. *Journal of Advertising, 33*(2), 7–24.

Dunne, P. M., Lusch, R. F., & Carver, J. R. (2013). *Retailing* (Auflage: 0008). South Western Educ Pub.

Duong Dinh, H. V. (2011). *Corporate social responsibility: Determinanten der Wahr-*

nehmung, Wirkungsprozesse und Konsequenzen. Münster, Wiesbaden.

Eagan, G. (2014). *Wear No Evil: How to Change the World with Your Wardrobe*. Running Press.

Earthshare. (2012). Greening Business. Retrieved from http://www.earthshare.org/greening-business.html

East, R. (2008). *Consumer Behaviour: Applications in Marketing* (1. ed.). Los Angeles: Sage Publications.

ECC Köln. (2014, July 15). Mittelständiger Handel im Fokus - Beratung im Zentrum, Online noch Potenzial. Retrieved from http://www.ecckoeln.de/News/Mittelständischer-Handel-im-Fokus---Beratung-im-Zentrum,-Online-noch-Potenzial

ECC Köln, & hybris GmbH. (2014a). Cross-Channel 2020 - Smart Natives im Fokus. Retrieved from http://www.ecckoeln.de/Downloads/Themen/Zielgruppen/ECCKln_Whitepaper_Cross-Channel2020_SmartNativesimFokus_2014.pdf

ECC Köln, & hybris GmbH. (2014b). Cross-Channel 2020 - Smart Natives im Fokus. Retrieved from http://www.ecckoeln.de/Downloads/Themen/Zielgruppen/ECCKln_Whitepaper_Cross-Channel2020_SmartNativesimFokus_2014.pdf

ECC Köln, & hybris software. (2013). Das Cross-Channel-Verhalten der Konsumten - Herausforderungen und Chancen für den Handel [ECC Köln]. Retrieved from http://www.ecckoeln.de/PDFs/2013/ECC_ManagementSummary_Das_Cross-Channel-Verhalten_der_Konsumenten_2013_D.pdf

Eckstein, A. (2013, February 5). Smartphones im Handel - Interview mit Alice Eckstein. Retrieved from http://www.ifhkoeln.de/News-Presse/Smartphones-im-Handel---Interview-mit-Aline-Eckstein

EDEKA. (2014). EDEKA - Kassensymphonie. Retrieved December 30, 2014, from https://www.youtube.com/watch?v=H965m0Hkk5M

Egan, J. (2011). *Relationship marketing: exploring relational strategies in marketing* (4th ed). New York: Financial Times, Prentice Hall.

EHI Retail Institute. (2011). Mobile Payment per Handy (NFC) im Handel 2011 | Umfrage. Retrieved December 30, 2014, from http://de.statista.com/statistik/daten/studie/239958/umfrage/einsatz-von-mobile-payment-per-handy-nfc-im-handel/

EHI Retail Institute. (2014a, May). Zahlungsarten im Einzelhandel in Deutschland bis 2013 | Statistik. Retrieved December 14, 2014, from http://de.statista.com/statistik/daten/studie/162179/umfrage/zahlungsarten-im-deutschen-einzelhandel-zeitreihe/

EHI Retail Institute. (2014b, September). Beliebtheit von Bezahlverfahren im Online-Handel | Umfrage. Retrieved December 14, 2014, from http://de.statista.com/statistik/daten/studie/20151/umfrage/die-beliebtesten-bezahlverfahren-im-online-handel/

EHI Retail Institute. (2014c, September). Online-Kauf - Nutzung von Zahlungsverfahren 2013 | Umfrage. Retrieved December 4, 2014, from http://de.statista.com/statistik/daten/studie/224827/umfrage/marktanteile-von-zahlungsverfahren-beim-online-handel/

Ehrich, K. R., & Irwin, J. R. (2005). Willful Ignorance in the Request for Product Attribute Information. *Journal of Marketing Research*, 42(3), 266–277. doi:10.1509/jmkr.2005.42.3.266

Ekman, P. (2006). *Darwin and Facial Expression: A Century of Research in Review*. ISHK.

Emnid, T. N. S. (2012). Bonusprogramme in Deutschland. *TNS Emnid Medien-Und Sozialforschung GmbH, Bielefeld*. Retrieved from http://www.payback.net/fileadmin/bilder/pdf/Emnid_Studie_Bonusprogramme_2012.pdf

Engleson, S., & Ganesh, B. (2014). *UPS Pulse of the Online Shopper: A Customer Experience Study*. Retrieved from http://www.comscore.com/ger/Insights/Presentations-and-Whitepapers/2014/UPS-Pulse-of-the-Online-Shopper-A-Customer-Experience-Study

Englis, B. G., Solomon, M. R., & Ashmore, R. D. (1994). Beauty Before the Eyes of Beholders: The Cultural Encoding of Beauty Types in Magazine Advertising and Music Television. *Journal of Advertising*, *23*(2), 49–64.

English, B. (2013). *A cultural history of fashion in the 20th and 21st centuries: from catwalk to sidewalk*. London; New York: Bloomsbury.

Eroglu, S. A., Machleit, K. A., & Davis, L. M. (2001). Atmospheric qualities of online retailing: a conceptual model and implications. *Journal of Business Research*, *54*(2), 177–184.

Eroglu, S. A., Machleit, K. A., & Davis, L. M. (2003). Empirical Testing of a Model of Online Store Atmospherics and Shopper Responses. *Psychology & Marketing*, *20*(2), 139–150.

Esprit-friends.com. (2015, May 1). Retrieved from http://www.esprit-friends.com

Eun Joo Park, Eun Young Kim, & Judith Cardona Forney. (2006). A structural model of fashion-oriented impulse buying behavior. *Journal of Fashion Marketing and Management: An International Journal*, *10*(4), 433–446. doi:10.1108/13612020610701965

Evans, E. D., Rutberg, J., Sather, C., & Turner, C. (1991). Content Analysis of Contemporary Teen Magazines for Adolescent Females. *Youth & Society*, *23*(1), 99–120. doi:10.1177/0044118X91023001005

EZB. (2013, September). Cashless payments - transactions in the EU in 2012, by country | Statistic. Retrieved December 30, 2014, from http://www.statista.com/statistics/276233/eu-member-states-with-the-most-cashless-payment-transactions/

Faigle, P., & Pauly, M. (2014, April 22). Textilindustrie: Die Schande von Rana Plaza. *Die Zeit*. Retrieved from http://www.zeit.de/wirtschaft/2014-04/rana-plaza-jahrestag-hilfsfonds

Fay, M., & Price, C. (1994). Female Body-shape in Print Advertisements and the Increase in Anorexia Nervosa. *European Journal of Marketing*, *28*(12), 5–18. doi:10.1108/03090569410074246

Feiereisen, S., Broderick, A. J., & Douglas, S. P. (2009). The effect and moderation of gender identity congruity: Utilizing "real women" advertising images. *Psychology & Marketing*, *26*(9), 813–843.

Feinberg, R. A. (1986). Credit Cards as Spending Facilitating Stimuli: A Conditioning Interpretation. *Journal of Consumer Research*, *13*(3), 348–356.

Ferguson, R. (2008). Word of mouth and viral marketing: taking the temperature of the hottest trends in marketing. *Journal of Consumer Marketing*, *25*(3), 179–182.

Fichter, K., & Clausen, J. (2013). *Erfolg und Scheitern "grüner" Innovationen : warum einige Nachhaltigkeitsinnovationen am Markt erfolgreich sind und andere nicht* (1st ed.). Marburg: Metropolis-Verlag.

Fill, C. (2009). *Marketing communications: interactivity, communities and content* (5th ed). Harlow, England ; New York: Prentice Hall/Financial Times.

Finisterra do Paço, A. M., & Raposo, M. L. B. (2010). Green consumer market segmentation: empirical findings from Portugal. *International Journal of Consumer Studies*, *34*(4), 429–436. doi:10.1111/j.1470-6431.2010.00869.x

Fiore, A. M., & Kim, J. (2007). An integrative framework capturing experiential and utilitarian shopping experience. *International Journal of Retail & Distribution Management*, *35*(6), 421–442. doi:10.1108/09590550710750313

Fisher, T. (2009). ROI in social media: A look at the arguments. *Journal of Database Marketing & Customer Strategy Management*, *16*(3), 189–195. doi:10.1057/dbm.2009.16

Fitzgerald Bone, P. (1992). Determinants of Word-Of-Mouth Communications During Product Consumption. *Advances in Consumer Research*, *19*(1), 579–583.

Fletcher, K. (2013). *Sustainable Fashion and Textiles: Design Journeys*. Routledge.

Flint, D. J. (2014). *Shopper marketing: profiting from the place where suppliers, brand manufacturers, and retailers connect*. Upper Saddle River, N.J: Pearson Education.

Forrester Research. (2005). *Topic Overview: US Online Retail*.

Fost, M. (2014). Handelsstrukturen von produzierenden Unternehmen. In M. Fost, *E-Commerce-Strategien für produzierende Unternehmen* (pp. 33–51). Wiesbaden: Springer Fachmedien Wiesbaden. Retrieved from http://link.springer.com/10.1007/978-3-658-04988-1_3

Foxall, G. R., & Greenley, G. E. (1999). Consumers' emotional responses to service environments. *Journal of Business Research*, *46*(2), 149–158.

Frambach, R. T., Roest, H. C. A., & Krishnan, T. V. (2007). The impact of consumer Internet experience on channel preference and usage intentions across the different stages of the buying process. *Journal of Interactive Marketing*, *21*(2), 26–41. doi:10.1002/dir.20079

Frisou, J., & Yildiz, H. (2011). Consumer learning as a determinant of a multi-partner loyalty program's effectiveness: A behaviorist and long-term perspective. *Journal of Retailing and Consumer Services*, *18*(1), 81–91. doi:10.1016/j.jretconser.2010.10.002

Fulmer, I. S., & Barry, B. (2009). Managed Hearts and Wallets: Ethical Issues in Emotional Influence By and Within Organizations. *Business Ethics Quarterly*, *19*(2), 155–191.

Gable, M., Fiorito, S. S., & Topol, M. T. (2008). An empirical analysis of the components of retailer customer loyalty programs. *International Journal of Retail & Distribution Management*, *36*(1), 32–49. doi:10.1108/09590550810846983

Gajanan, S., & Basuroy, S. (2007). Multichannel Retailing And Its Implications On Consumer Shopping Behavior. *Journal of Shopping Center Research*, *14*(2), 1–28.

Gallino, S., Moreno, A., & Stamatopoulos, I. (2014, September 10). Channel Integration, Sales Dispersion, and Inventory Management. Retrieved from http://dx.doi.org/10.2139/ssrn.2494516

Gallois, C. (1993). The Language and Communication of Emotion: "Universal, Interpersonal or Intergroup?." *The American Behavioral Scientist*, *36*, 309 ff.

Garcia, J. R., & Saad, G. (2008). Evolutionary neuromarketing: darwinizing the neuroimaging paradigm for consumer behavior. *Journal of Consumer Behaviour*, *7*(4-5), 397–414. doi:10.1002/cb.259

Gattiker, U. E. (2013). *Social Media Audit*. New York, NY: Springer New York. Retrieved from http://link.springer.com/10.1007/978-1-4614-3603-4

Gay, R., Charlesworth, A., & Esen, R. (2007). *Online Marketing: A Customer-Led Approach* (1st ed.). New York, NY: Oxford University Press Inc.

Gelb, B. D. (1997). Creating "Memes" While Creating Advertising. *Journal of Advertising Research*, *37*(6), 57–59.

Geuens, M., De Pelsmacker, P., & Tuan Pham, M. (2014). Do Pleasant Emotional Ads Make Consumers Like Your Brand More? *GfK-Marketing Intelligence Review*, *6*(1), 40–45.

GfK. (2008). Wissen über die Öko-Standards der Textilwirtschaft von Männern und Frauen im Jahr 2008. *TW-Kundenmonitor Socialwear*, 8.

Gladwell, M. (2001). *The tipping point : how little things can make a big difference.* (1. ed.). London: Little, Brown and Company.

Glavič, P., & Lukman, R. (2007). Review of sustainability terms and their definitions. *Journal of Cleaner Production*, *15*(18), 1875–1885. doi:10.1016/j.jclepro.2006.12.006

Goldsmith, R. E., & Flynn, L. R. (2005). Bricks, clicks, and pix: apparel buyers' use of stores, internet, and catalogs compared. *International Journal of Retail & Distribution Management*, *33*(4), 271–283. doi:10.1108/09590550510593202

Goworek, H., Hiller, A., Fisher, T., Cooper, T., & Woodward, S. (2013). Consumers' attitudes towards sustainable fashion: Clothing usage and disposal. In *Sustainability in Fashion and Textiles* (pp. 376–392). Sheffield, UK: Greenleaf Publishing.

Graf, J. (2012, June 21). Fluchtweg Multichannel: Der Deutsche Handel ist der unproduktivste in Europa. Retrieved from http://www.ibusiness.de/aktuell/db/266373jg.html

Gratz, J. E. (1984). The Ethics of Subliminal Communication. *Journal of Business Ethics*, *3*(3), 181–184.

Greenwich Consulting Deutschland GmbH. (2012, February 13). Cross-Channel vs. Multi-Channel. Retrieved from http://www.marketing-boerse.de/Fachartikel/details/1207-Cross-Channel-vs-Multi-Channel/34628

Greve, G. (2010). *Kundenorientierte Unternehmensführung: Konzept und Anwendung des Net Promoter Score in der Praxis*. (E. Benning-Rohnke, Ed.) (1. ed.). Wiesbaden: Gabler.

Grewal, D., Iyer, G. R., & Levy, M. (2004). Internet retailing: enablers, limiters and market consequences. *Journal of Business Research*, *57*(7), 703–713. doi:10.1016/S0148-2963(02)00348-X

Grisaffe, D. B. (2007). Questions About the Ultimate Question: Conceptual Considerations in Evaluating Reichheld's Net Promoter Score (NPS). *Journal of Consumer Satisfaction, Dissatisfaction & Complaining Behavior*, *20*, 36–53.

Grober, U. (2013). *Die Entdeckung der Nachhaltigkeit: Kulturgeschichte eines Begriffs von Ulrich Grober (2013) Broschiert*. Verlag Antje Kunstmann.

Gröppel-Klein, A. (2012). Point-of-Sale-Marketing. In J. Zentes, B. Swoboda, D. Morschett, & H. Schramm-Klein (Eds.), *Handbuch Handel* (pp. 645–669). Wiesbaden: Springer Fachmedien Wiesbaden. Retrieved from http://link.springer.com/10.1007/978-3-8349-3847-3_32

Gründerszene. (2014). Digital Native [Gründerszene.de]. Retrieved from http://www.gruenderszene.de/lexikon/begriffe/digital-native

Gwilt, A., & Rissanen, T. (2011). *Shaping sustainable fashion: changing the way we make and use clothes*. London ; Washington, DC: Earthscan.

Haar, A. (2014, December 10). *Innovationsmotor Digitalisierung - die 10 wichtigsten Erfolgsfaktoren und Handlungsfelder für die Fashionbranche*. Reutlingen.

Hackenberg, A. (2013). Wenn der Postmann fünfmal klingelt. *Textilwirtschaft*, (27a), 16–20.

Hailes, J. (2007). *The New Green Consumer Guide*. London: Simon & Schuster UK.

Halepete, J., Littrell, M., & Park, J. (2009). Personalization of Fair Trade Apparel Consumer Attitudes and Intentions. *Clothing and Textiles Research Journal*, 27(2), 143–160. doi:10.1177/0887302X08326284

Halliwell, E., & Dittmar, H. (2004). Does Size Matter? The Impact of Model's Body Size on Women's Body-Focused Anxiety and Advertising Effectiveness. *Journal of Social & Clinical Psychology*, 23(1), 104–122.

Hamblen, M. (2012, October 23). Mobile wallet adoption could get boost from deadline on retailers to upgrade terminals. Retrieved December 28, 2014, from http://www.computerworld.com/article/2492715/mobile-payments/mobile-wallet-adoption-could-get-boost-from-deadline-on-retailers-to-upgrade-termina.html

Hamid, M. K. A. (2011). *Fashion Branding Unraveled.* (1. ed). New York, NY: Fairchild Publications.

Harrison, N. (2011, October 21). In Pictures: House of Fraser.com, Aberdeen, opens today. Retrieved from http://www.retail-week.com/multichannel/in-pictures-house-of-frasercom-aberdeen-opens-today/5030474.article

Härtel, C. E. J., & Russell-Bennett, R. (2010). Heart versus mind: The functions of emotional and cognitive loyalty. *Australasian Marketing Journal (AMJ)*, 18(1), 1–7. doi:10.1016/j.ausmj.2009.10.003

Haug, K. (2013). Digitale Potenziale für den stationären Handel durch Empfehlungsprozesse, lokale Relevanz und mobile Geräte (SoLoMo). In dgroup, G. Heinemann, K. Haug, & M. Gehrckens (Eds.), *Digitalisierung des Handels mit ePace* (pp. 27–50). Wiesbaden: Springer Fachmedien Wiesbaden. Retrieved from http://link.springer.com/10.1007/978-3-658-01300-4_2

Haupt, D. (2014). Praxismanko click and collect. *Der Handel*, (12), 32.

Häusel, H.-G. (2009). *Emotional Boosting - Die hohe Kunst der Kaufverführung* (Auflage: 1., Auflage 2009). Freiburg, Br.; Berlin; München: Haufe-Lexware.

Häusel, H.-G. (2009). *Emotional boosting: die hohe Kunst der Kaufverführung*. Freiburg, Br.; Berlin; München: Haufe.

Häusel, H.-G. (2013). *Neuromarketing: Erkenntnisse der Hirnforschung für Markenführung, Werbung und Verkauf* (2. Auflage). München: Haufe Verlag.

Havlena, W. J., & Holbrook, M. B. (1986). The Varieties of Consumption Experience: Comparing Two Typologies of Emotion in Consumer Behavior. *Journal of Consumer Research*, *13*(3), 394–404.

Heath, R., & Feldwick, P. (2008). Fifty years using the wrong model of advertising. *International Journal of Market Research*, *50*(1), 29–59.

Heidbring, L., Schmidt, I., & Ahaus, B. (Eds.). (2011). *Die Verantwortung des Konsumenten: über das Verhältnis von Markt, Moral und Konsum*. Frankfurt am Main: Campus Verlag.

Heinemann, G. (2008). *Multi-Channel-Handel: Erfolgsfaktoren und Best Practices*. Wiesbaden: Gabler.

Heinemann, G. (2012). *Modernes Multi-Channeling im Fashion-Handel: Konzepte, Erfolgsfaktoren, Praxisbeispiele*. Frankfurt, Main: Dt. Fachverl.

Heinemann, G. (2013a). Digitale Revolution im Handel – steigende Handelsdynamik und disruptive Veränderung der Handelsstrukturen. In G. Heinemann, dgroup, K. Haug, & M. Gehrckens (Eds.), *Digitalisierung des Handels mit ePace* (pp. 3–26). Wiesbaden: Springer Fachmedien Wiesbaden. Retrieved from http://link.springer.com/10.1007/978-3-658-01300-4_1

Heinemann, G. (2013b). *No-Line-Handel*. Wiesbaden: Springer Fachmedien Wiesbaden. Retrieved from http://link.springer.com/10.1007/978-3-658-00851-2

Heinemann, G. (2014a). *Der neue Online-Handel*. Wiesbaden: Springer Fachmedien Wiesbaden. Retrieved from http://link.springer.com/10.1007/978-3-658-02433-8

Heinemann, G. (2014b). *SoLoMo - Always-on im Handel*. Wiesbaden: Springer Fachmedien Wiesbaden. Retrieved from http://link.springer.com/10.1007/978-3-658-03968-4

Heinemann, G., & Schwarzl, C. (2010). *New online retailing innovation and transformation*. Wiesbaden: Gabler. Retrieved from http://public.eblib.com/choice/publicfullrecord.aspx?p=749066

Heinrich, H., & Flocke, L. (2014). Customer-Journey-Analyse-Ein neuer Ansatz zur Optimierung des (Online-) Marketing-Mix. In H. Holland (Ed.), *Digitales Dialogmarketing* (pp. 825–855). Wiesbaden: Springer Fachmedien Wiesbaden. Retrieved from http://link.springer.com/10.1007/978-3-658-02541-0_34

Hekkelman, H. M. (2014). *Communicating sustainability in fashion*. University of Technology Delft, Delft. Retrieved from http://resolver.tudelft.nl/uuid:9ec21f80-3501-422f-bd81-3d25bf153ad9

Heller Baird, C., & Parasnis, G. (2011). From social media to social customer relationship management. *Strategy & Leadership, 39*(5), 30–37. doi:10.1108/10878571111161507

Helm, S. (2000). Viral Marketing - Establishing Customer Relationships by "Word-of-mouse". *Electronic Markets, 10*(3), 158. doi:10.1080/10196780050177053

Henderson, C. M., Beck, J. T., & Palmatier, R. W. (2011). Review of the theoretical underpinnings of loyalty programs. *Journal of Consumer Psychology, 21*(3), 256–276. doi:10.1016/j.jcps.2011.02.007

Hendry, D., Silcox, L., & Yokoyame, N. (2007). *Communicating Sustainability through Design within Retail Environments*. School of Engineering Karlskrona, Karlskrona, Sweden. Retrieved from http://www.bth.se/fou/cuppsats.nsf/6753b78eb2944e0ac1256608004f0535/27e5e2509ea4ab36c12572ec0058d695?OpenDocument

Henke, L. L. (2013). Breaking Through The Clutter: The Impact of Emotions and Flow on Viral Marketing. *Academy of Marketing Studies Journal, 17*(2), 111–118.

Hennes & Mauritz. (2014). *Lady Gaga & Tony Bennett - H&M Magical Holidays*. Retrieved from https://www.youtube.com/watch?v=cf5K7u8HNhY

Hettler, U. (2010). *Social Media Marketing: Marketing mit Blogs, Sozialen Netzwerken und weiteren Anwendungen des Web 2.0*. München: Oldenbourg Wissenschaftsverlag GmbH.

Hilton, M. (2003). *Consumerism in Twentieth-Century Britain: The Search for a Historical Movement*. Cambridge University Press.

Hobkirk, I. (2013). The Ten-Step Omni-Channel Challenge. *Material Handling and Logistics*, *23*(9), 33–35.

Hollensen, S. (2010). *Relationship Marketing: An Integrative Management Approach*. München: Vahlen, Franz.

Holmberg, J. (1992). *Making Development Sustainable: Redefining Institutions Policy And Economics*. Island Press.

Homburg, C., & Krohmer, H. (2009). *Grundlagen des Marketingmanagements : Einführung in Strategie, Instrumente, Umsetzung und Unternehmensführung; [Bachelor geeignet!] / Christian Homburg; Harley Krohmer*. Wiesbaden : Gabler, 2009.

Horne, R. E. (2009). Limits to labels: The role of eco-labels in the assessment of product sustainability and routes to sustainable consumption. *International Journal of Consumer Studies*, *33*(2), 175–182. doi:10.1111/j.1470-6431.2009.00752.x

Howard, D., Mangold, W. G., & Johnston, T. (2014). Managing your social campaign strategy using Facebook, Twitter, Instagram, YouTube & Pinterest: An interview with Dana Howard, social media marketing manager. *Business Horizons*, *57*(5), 657–665. doi:10.1016/j.bushor.2014.05.001

Hsiao, C., Ju Rebecca Yen, H., & Li, E. Y. (2012). Exploring consumer value of multi-channel shopping: a perspective of means-end theory. *Internet Research*, *22*(3), 318–339. doi:10.1108/10662241211235671

Hsu, H.-Y., & Tsou, H. T. (2011). The effect of website quality on consumer emotional states and repurchases intention. *African Journal of Business Management*, *5*(15), 6194–6199.

Huber, F., Meyer, F., & Weihrauch, A. (2011). Emotion and Identification in Advertising: Me and my cozy security blanket: The role of the "Feeling of care and security" in emotional Advertising. *American Marketing Association*.

Hyman, M. R., & Tansey, R. (1990). The Ethics of Psychoactive Ads. *Journal of Business Ethics*, *9*(2), 105–114.

Innofact AG. (2010, June). Anteil der Befragten im Juni 2010, die die folgenden Aspekte bei Werbung persönlich (sehr) wichtig finden. Retrieved January 4, 2015, from http://de.statista.com/statistik/daten/studie/195838/umfrage/wichtige-eigenschaften-der-werbung-fuer-verbraucher/

Jackson, H. O., & Ross, N. (1997). Fashion advertising Does age, body type or ethnicity influence consumers perceptions. *Journal of Fashion Marketing and Management*, *1*(4), 322.

Jalees, T., & Majid, H. (2009). Impact of "Ideal Models" Being Portrayed by Media on Young Females. *Paradigm (09718907)*, *13*(1), 11–19.

Jiyun Kang, & Haesun Park-Poaps. (2010). Hedonic and utilitarian shopping motivations of fashion leadership. *Journal of Fashion Marketing and Management: An International Journal*, *14*(2), 312–328. doi:10.1108/13612021011046138

Jobber, D. (2010). *Principles and practice of marketing*. London; Singapore: McGraw-Hill.

Joergens, C. (2006). Ethical fashion: myth or future trend? *Journal of Fashion Marketing & Management*, *10*(3), 360–371.

Jörg Aßmann, J. W., & Thomas Schildhauer. (2008). *Kundenkartenprogramme im Customer Relationship Management (CRM) Einsatzmöglichkeiten und Erfolgsfaktoren von Kundenkarten aus Unternehmenssicht*. Göttingen: BusinessVillage.

Kahle, L. R., & Homer, P. M. (1985). Physical Attractiveness of the Celebrity Endorser: A Social Adaptation Perspective. *Journal of Consumer Research*, *11*(4), 954–961.

Kallweit, K., Spreer, P., & Toporowski, W. (2014). Why do customers use self-service information technologies in retail? The mediating effect of perceived service quality. *Journal of Retailing and Consumer Services*, *21*(3), 268–276.

doi:10.1016/j.jretconser.2014.02.002

Kamins, M. A. (1990). An Investigation into the "Match-Up" Hypothesis in Celebrity Advertising: When Beauty May be Only Skin Deep. *Journal of Advertising, 19*(1), 4–13.

Kang, J., Alejandro, T. B., & Groza, M. D. (2015). Customer–company identification and the effectiveness of loyalty programs. *Journal of Business Research, 68*(2), 464–471. doi:10.1016/j.jbusres.2014.06.002

Kang, J., Liu, C., & Kim, S.-H. (2013). Environmentally sustainable textile and apparel consumption: the role of consumer knowledge, perceived consumer effectiveness and perceived personal relevance. *International Journal of Consumer Studies, 37*(4), 442–452. doi:10.1111/ijcs.12013

Karstadt Warenhaus GmbH. (2012, November 16). Karstadt stärkt Online-Geschäft/ Neuer Service bei Karstadt.de: Click&Collect. Retrieved from http://www.presseportal.de/pm/16971/2365261/karstadt-st-rkt-online-gesch-ft-neuer-service-bei-karstadt-de-click-collect

Katz, E., & Lazarsfeld, P. (1955). *Personal influence; the part played by people in the flow of mass communications.* New York: Free Press.

Kawaf, F., & Tagg, S. (2012). Online shopping environments in fashion shopping: An S-O-R based review. *The Marketing Review, 12*(2), 161–180. doi:10.1362/146934712X13366562572476

Keen, C., Wetzels, M., de Ruyter, K., & Feinberg, R. (2004). E-tailers versus retailers. *Journal of Business Research, 57*(7), 685–695. doi:10.1016/S0148-2963(02)00360-0

Keiningham, T. L., Aksoy, L., Cooil, B., Andreassen, T. W., & Williams, L. (2008). A holistic examination of Net Promoter. *Journal of Database Marketing & Customer Strategy Management, 15*(2), 79–90.

Keller, K. L. (2003). *Strategic brand management : building, measuring, and managing brand equity.* (2. ed.). Upper Saddle River, N.J: Prentice Hall.

Khan, J. (2011). *Cash or card: consumer perceptions of payment modes* (Thesis).

Auckland University of Technology. Retrieved from http://aut.researchgateway.ac.nz/handle/10292/3937

Kim, H. (2000). Examination of emotional response to apparel brand advertisements. *Journal of Fashion Marketing and Management*, *4*(4), 303.

Kim, H., Ahn, S.-K., & Forney, J. A. (2014). Shifting paradigms for fashion: from total to global to smart consumer experience. *Fashion and Textiles*, *1*(1). doi:10.1186/s40691-014-0015-4

Kim, H.-S., & Damhorst, M. L. (1998). Environmental Concern and Apparel Consumption. *Clothing and Textiles Research Journal*, *16*(3), 126–133. doi:10.1177/0887302X9801600303

Kim, H.-Y., Lee, J. Y., Choi, D., Wu, J., & Johnson, K. K. P. (2013). Perceived Benefits of Retail Loyalty Programs: Their Effects on Program Loyalty and Customer Loyalty. *Journal of Relationship Marketing*, *12*(2), 95–113. doi:10.1080/15332667.2013.794100

Kim, J. B., Koo, Y., & Chang, D. R. (2009). Integrated Brand Experience Through Sensory Branding and IMC. *Design Management Review*, *20*(3), 72–81. doi:10.1111/j.1948-7169.2009.00024.x

Kim, J.-E., Ju, H. W., & Johnson, K. K. P. (2009). Sales associate's appearance: Links to consumers' emotions, store image, and purchases. *Journal of Retailing and Consumer Services*, *16*(5), 407–413. doi:10.1016/j.jretconser.2009.06.001

Kim, M., & Stoel, L. (2005). Salesperson roles: are online retailers meeting customer expectations? *International Journal of Retail & Distribution Management*, *33*(4), 284–297. doi:10.1108/09590550510593211

Kirby, J., & Marsden, P. (Eds.). (2007). *Connected Marketing : the Viral, Buzz and Word of Mouth Revolution* (1. ed.). Amsterdam [i.a.]: Elsevier. Retrieved from http://search.ebscohost.com/login.aspx?direct=true&db=cat00207a&AN=reu.275138003&lang=de&site=eds-live&authtype=shib

Kling, B. (2013, October 9). Paypal Beacon ermöglicht freihändiges Bezahlen per Bluetooth. Retrieved December 30, 2014, from http://www.zdnet.de/88169099/paypal-beacon-ermoeglicht-freihaendiges-bezahlen-per-bluetooth/

Kolbrück, O. (2014, September 11). Runners Point: Der lange Run zum Mulitchannel. Retrieved from http://etailment.de/thema/player/Runners-Point-Der-lange-Run-zum-Multichannel-2713

Kollmann, T., & Häsel, M. (2006). Cross-channel cooperation: A collaborative approach of integrating online and offline business models. *Cross-Channel-Kooperation: Ein Gemeinschaftlicher Lösungsansatz Der Integration von Online- Und Offline-Geschäftsmodellen*, 69.

Koo, W., & Kim, Y.-K. (2013). Impacts of store environmental cues on store love and loyalty: single-brand apparel retailers. *Journal of International Consumer Marketing*, *25*(2), 94–106. doi:10.1080/08961530.2013.759044

Ko, S., Norum, P., & Hawley, J. M. (2010). Consumer value structures reflected in clothing advertisements. *Journal of Fashion Marketing & Management*, *14*(3), 451.

Kotler, P. (1973). Atmospherics as a Marketing Tool. *Journal of Retailing*, *49*(4), 48–64.

Kotler, P. (2007). *Grundlagen des Marketing*. München [u.a.: Pearson Studium.

Kotler, P. (2012a). *Grundlagen des Marketing*. München [u.a.]: Pearson Studium.

Kotler, P. (Ed.). (2012b). *Marketing management* (2nd ed). Harlow, England ; New York: Pearson.

Kotler, P., & Armstrong, G. (2014). *Principles of marketing*. Harlow [etc.]: Pearson.

Kozar, J. M., & Damhorst, M. L. (2008). Older women's responses to current fashion models. *Journal of Fashion Marketing and Management: An International Journal*, *12*(3), 338–350. doi:10.1108/13612020810889290

KPMG, & ECC. (2010). Kenntnis und Nutzungsintensität einzelner Mobile Payment-Verfahren | 2010. Retrieved December 28, 2014, from http://de.statista.com/statistik/daten/studie/177554/umfrage/kenntnis-undnutzungsintensitaet-einzelner-mobile-payment-verfahren-im-jahr-2010/

Kreis, H., & Mafael, A. (2014). The influence of customer loyalty program design on the relationship between customer motives and value perception. *Journal of Retailing and Consumer Services*, *21*(4), 590–600. doi:10.1016/j.jretconser.2014.04.006

Kroeber-Riel, W., & Gröppel-Klein, A. (2013). *Konsumentenverhalten*. München: Vahlen, Franz.

Kroeber-Riel, W., Weinberg, P., & Gröppel-Klein, A. (2009). *Konsumentenverhalten* (9. ed.). München: Franz Vahlen.

Kumar, V., Petersen, J. A., & Leone, R. P. (2007). How Valuable Is Word of Mouth? *Harvard Business Review*, *85*(10), 139–146.

Kumar, V., Pozza, I. D., & Ganesh, J. (2013). Revisiting the Satisfaction–Loyalty Relationship: Empirical Generalizations and Directions for Future Research. *Journal of Retailing*, *89*(3), 246–262. doi:10.1016/j.jretai.2013.02.001

Kumar, V., & Reinartz, W. (2012). *Customer Relationship Management*. Berlin, Heidelberg: Springer Berlin Heidelberg. Retrieved from http://link.springer.com/10.1007/978-3-642-20110-3

Lacey, R. (2009). Limited influence of loyalty program membership on relational outcomes. *Journal of Consumer Marketing*, *26*(6), 392–402. doi:10.1108/07363760910988210

Lafayette, J. (2014). Strong Emotions Drive Effectiveness of Ads. *Broadcasting & Cable*, *144*(36), 18–18.

Lang, B., & Hyde, K. F. (2013). Word of Mouth: What we Know and What we Have yet to Learn. *Journal of Consumer Satisfaction, Dissatisfaction & Complaining Behavior*, *26*, 1–18.

Langdown, A. (2014). Slow fashion as an alternative to mass production: A fashion practitioner's journey. *Social Business*, *4*(1), 33–43. doi:10.1362/204440814X13948909253785

Langner, S. (2009). *Viral Marketing: Wie Sie Mundpropaganda gezielt auslösen und Gewinn bringend nutzen.* (3. ed.). Wiesbaden: Gabler. Retrieved from http://search.ebscohost.com/login.aspx?direct=true&db=cat00207a&AN=reu.312840470&lang=de&site=eds-live&authtype=shib

Larsen, R. J., & Diener, E. (1987). Invited paper: Affect intensity as an individual difference characteristic: A review. *Journal of Research in Personality*, *21*, 1–39. doi:10.1016/0092-6566(87)90023-7

Lee Yohn, D. (2014, October 17). So Amazon Thinks It Can Do Retail. Retrieved from http://www.forbes.com/sites/deniselyohn/2014/10/17/so-amazon-thinks-it-can-do-retail/

Lerner, T. (2013). Einleitung. In *Mobile Payment* (pp. 1–2). Springer Fachmedien Wiesbaden. Retrieved from http://link.springer.com/chapter/10.1007/978-3-8348-2204-8_1

Lin, Z., & Bennett, D. (2014). Examining retail customer experience and the moderation effect of loyalty programmes. *International Journal of Retail & Distribution Management*, *42*(10), 929–947. doi:10.1108/IJRDM-11-2013-0208

Machleit, K. A., & Eroglu, S. A. (2000). Describing and Measuring Emotional Response to Shopping Experience. *Journal of Business Research*, *49*(2), 101–111.

Machleit, K. A., Eroglu, S. A., & Mantel, S. P. (2000). Perceived retail crowding and shopping satisfaction: what modifies this relationship? *Journal of Consumer Psychology*, *9*(1), 29–42.

Machleit, K. A., & Mantel, S. P. (2001). Emotional response and shopping satisfaction: moderating effects of shopper attributions. *Journal of Business Research*, *54*(2), 97–106.

Mackenzie, E. (2014). beyond the tvc. *B&T Magazine*, *64*(2805), 063–067.

Mahar, S., Salzarulo, P. A., & Daniel Wright, P. (2012). Using online pickup site inclusion policies to manage demand in retail/E-tail organizations. *Computers & Operations Research*, *39*(5), 991–999. doi:10.1016/j.cor.2011.06.011

Manley, S. (2014). Our heritage is not just where we'va been, but the values with which we'll shape the next chapter for Burberry... Retrieved from http://www.bestglobalbrands.com/2014/interviews/burberry-sarah-manley/

Mann, R. J. (2002). Credit Cards and Debit Cards in the United States and Japan. *Vanderbilt Law Review, 55*, 1055.

Mano, H., & Oliver, R. L. (1993). Assessing the Dimensionality and Structure of the Consumption Experience: Evaluation, Feeling, and Satisfaction. *Journal of Consumer Research, 20*(3), 451–466.

Martin, M. C., & Gentry, J. W. (1997). Stuck in the Model Trap: The Effects of Beautiful Models in Ads on Female Pre-Adolescents and Adolescents. *Journal of Advertising, 26*(2), 19–33.

Marzo-Navarro, M., Pedraja-Iglesias, M., & Pilar Rivera-Torres, M. (2004). The benefits of relationship marketing for the consumer and for the fashion retailers. *Journal of Fashion Marketing and Management: An International Journal, 8*(4), 425–436. doi:10.1108/13612020410560018

Maycott, H. O. (2014, November 4). Sorry Walmart -- NFC and Apple Pay Have Already Won. Retrieved December 28, 2014, from http://www.forbes.com/sites/homaycotte/2014/11/04/nfc-apple-pay-already-won/

McCallum, H. (2008). Consumers and the environment. *Consumer Policy Review*, (18), 61–62.

McDonald, S., Oates, C., Thyne, M., Alevizou, P., & McMorland, L.-A. (2009). Comparing sustainable consumption patterns across product sectors. *International Journal of Consumer Studies, 33*(2), 137–145. doi:10.1111/j.1470-6431.2009.00755.x

Meffert, H., Burmann, C., & Kirchgeorg, M. (2015). *Marketing Grundlagen marktorientierter Unternehmensführung Konzepte - Instrumente - Praxisbeispiele*. Wiesbaden: Springer Gabler.

Mehrabian, A. (1996). Pleasure-arousal-dominance: A general framework for describing and measuring individual differences in Temperament. *Current Psychology, 14*(4), 261–292. doi:10.1007/BF02686918

Mehrabian, A., & Russell, J. A. (1974). *An approach to environmental psychology*. MIT Press.

Meiners, N. H., Schwarting, U., & Seeberger, B. (2010). The Renaissance of Word-of-Mouth Marketing: A "New" Standard in Twenty-First Century Marketing Management?! *International Journal of Economic Sciences & Applied Research*, *3*(2), 79–97.

Meyer, A. (2001). What's in it for the customers? Successfully marketing green clothes. *Business Strategy and the Environment*, *10*(5), 317–330. doi:10.1002/bse.302

Meyer, E. (1990). Retail on the rebound. *Direct Marketing*, *53*(1), 7.

Meyer-Waarden, L., Benavent, C., & Castéran, H. (2013). The effects of purchase orientations on perceived loyalty programmes' benefits and loyalty. *International Journal of Retail & Distribution Management*, *41*(3), 201–225. doi:10.1108/09590551311306255

Micu, A. C., & Plummer, J. T. (2010). Measurable Emotions: How Television Ads Really Work. *Journal of Advertising Research*, *50*(2), 137–153.

Mimouni-Chaabane, A., & Volle, P. (2010). Perceived benefits of loyalty programs: Scale development and implications for relational strategies. *Journal of Business Research*, *63*(1), 32–37. doi:10.1016/j.jbusres.2009.01.008

Minahan, S., & Beverland, M. (2005). *Why Women Shop: Secrets Revealed*. Milton, Qld.: John Wiley & Sons.

Minney, S., Watson, E., Siegel, L., & Firth, L. (2011). *Naked fashion: the new sustainable fashion revolution*. Oxford, UK: New Internationalist.

Mishra, P., & Sharma, P. (2012). Green Marketing: Challenges and Opportunities for Business. *Journal of Marketing & Communication*, *8*(1), 35–41.

Mithas, S., & Lucas, H. C. (2010). What is your digital business strategy? *IT Professional*, *12*(6), 4–6.

Moisander, J., Markkula, A., & Eräranta, K. (2010). Construction of consumer choice in the market : challenges for environmental policy. *International Journal of Consumer Studies*, *34*(1), 73–79. doi:10.1111/j.1470-6431.2009.00821.x

Moore, A., & Taylor, M. (2011). Time to Cut Up Those Debit Cards? Effect of Payment Mode on Willingness to Spend. *Journal of Consumer Policy*, *34*(4), 415–422. doi:10.1007/s10603-011-9172-7

Moore, D. J., & Harris, W. D. (1996). Affect Intensity and the Consumer's Attitude toward High Impact Emotional Advertising Appeals. *Journal of Advertising*, *25*(2), 37–50.

Morgan, J. (2009, May 11). Do You Know the Value of Your Customers? Retrieved December 28, 2014, from /opinions/2009/22561/do-you-know-the-value-of-your-customers

Morrison, M., & Beverland, M. (2003). In search of the right in-store music. *Business Horizons*, *46*(6), 77–82.

Morschett, D. (2012). Distanzhandel – Online-Shops und andere Formen. In J. Zentes, B. Swoboda, D. Morschett, & H. Schramm-Klein (Eds.), *Handbuch Handel* (pp. 375–398). Wiesbaden: Springer Fachmedien Wiesbaden. Retrieved from http://link.springer.com/10.1007/978-3-8349-3847-3_19

Mourdoukoutas, P., & Siomkos, G. J. (2009). *The Seven Principles of WOM and Buzz Marketing*. (1. ed.). Berlin; Heidelberg; New York: Springer Berlin Heidelberg. Retrieved from http://search.ebscohost.com/login.aspx?direct=true&db=cat00207a&AN=reu.327011297&lang=de&site=eds-live&authtype=shib

Müller-Lankenau, C. (2007). *Multikanalstrategien im stationären Einzelhandel: eine empirische Untersuchung in der Konsumelektronikbranche*. Eul, Lohmar; Köln.

Muniz Jr., A. M., & O'Guinn, T. C. (2001). Brand Community. *Journal of Consumer Research*, *27*(4), 412–432.

Nadler, S., & Rennhak, C. (2009, 01). Emotional Branding in der Automobilindustrie - ein Schlüssel zum langfristigen Markenerfolg? ESB Business School.

Nations, D. (2014). Social Bookmarking 101 - What is Social Bookmarking and How Can It Help Me? Retrieved December 28, 2014, from http://webtrends.about.com/od/socialbookmarking101/p/aboutsocialtags.htm

Neslin, S. A., & Shankar, V. (2009). Key Issues in Multichannel Customer Management: Current Knowledge and Future Directions. *Journal of Interactive Marketing*, *23*(1), 70–81. doi:10.1016/j.intmar.2008.10.005

New Oxford American dictionary. (2010) (3rd ed). Oxford ; New York: Oxford University Press.

Nguyen Thi Tuyet Mai, Kwon Jung, Lants, G., & Loeb, S. G. (2003). An Exploratory Investigation into Impulse Buying Behavior in a Transitional Economy: A Study of Urban Consumers in Vietnam. *Journal of International Marketing*, *11*(2), 13–35.

Nielsen Company. (2013, September 17). Nielsen Global Survey of Trust in Advertising. Retrieved November 5, 2014, from http://www.nielsen.com/us/en/insights/news/2013/under-the-influence-consumer-trust-in-advertising.html

North, S., & Jason Oliver, J. (2014). A strategic look at how to extend your digital footprint. *Strategic Direction*, *30*(7), 1–3. doi:10.1108/SD-05-2014-0061

Nufer, G., & Wallmeier, M. (2010). Neuromarketing. Retrieved from https://publikationen.uni-tuebingen.de/xmlui/handle/10900/44087

Oates, C., McDonald, S., Alevizou, P., Hwang, K., Young, W., & McMorland, L. (2008). Marketing sustainability: Use of information sources and degrees of voluntary simplicity. *Journal of Marketing Communications*, *14*(5), 351–365. doi:10.1080/13527260701869148

O'Brien, L., & Jones, C. (1995). Do rewards really create loyalty? *Harvard Business Review*, (73), 75–82.

O'Cass, A. (2000). An assessment of consumers product, purchase decision, advertising and consumption involvement in fashion clothing. *Journal of Economic Psychology*, *21*(5), 545–576. doi:10.1016/S0167-4870(00)00018-0

Oliver, R. L. (2010). *Satisfaction: A Behavioral Perspective on the Consumer* (2nd ed.). New York, United States of America: M.E. Sharp.

Olshavsky, R. W., & Granbois, D. H. (1979). Consumer Decision Making- Fact or Fiction? *Journal of Consumer Research*, 6(2), 93–100.

Page, G. (2012). Scientific realism: what "neuromarketing" can and can't tell us about consumers. *International Journal of Market Research*, 54(2), 287. doi:10.2501/IJMR-54-2-287-290

Pakalski, I. (2013, November 26). Bezahlen per Smartphone: Paypal will sich im stationären Handel etablieren - Golem.de. Retrieved December 30, 2014, from http://www.golem.de/news/bezahlen-per-smartphone-paypal-will-sich-im-stationaeren-handel-etablieren-1311-102968.html

Panda, T. K., Panda, T. K., & Mishra, K. (2013). Does Emotional Appeal Work in Advertising? The Rationality Behind Using Emotional Appeal to Create Favorable Brand Attitude. *IUP Journal of Brand Management*, 10(2), 7–23.

Panigrahi, M. S. K. (2013). Seamless Purchase - An Insight into the Issues. *ELK Asia Pacific Journal of Marketing and Retail Management*, 4(4). Retrieved from http://www.elkjournals.com/MasterAdmin/UploadFolder/8.%20SEAMLESS%20PURCHASE%20-%20AN%20INSIGHT%20INTO%20THE%20ISSUES-2/8.%20SEAMLESS%20PURCHASE%20-%20AN%20INSIGHT%20INTO%20THE%20ISSUES-2.pdf

Parker, G. (Ed.). (2013). Wave7: Cracking the Social Code. Retrieved from http://wave.umww.com/

Parkins, W., & Craig, G. (2006). *Slow Living*. Berg.

Paulins, V. A. (2009). *Ethics in the fashion industry*. New York, NY: Fairchild Publications.

Paulins, V. A., & Hillery, J. L. (2009). *Ethics in the fashion industry*. New York: Fairchild, 2009.

Paunksnienė, Ž., & Banytė, J. (2012). Consumer's Emotions in Store Environment:

Why do Emotions arise? *Economics & Management*, *17*(1), 279–288.

payback.net. (2015, April 1). Retrieved from http://www.payback.net/en/about-payback/

Payback The Multi Partner Loyalty Program Marketing Essay. (2013). Retrieved January 3, 2015, from http://www.ukessays.com/essays/marketing/payback-the-multi-partner-loyalty-program-marketing-essay.php

Peacock, J., Purvis, S., & Hazlett, R. L. (2011). Which Broadcast Medium Better Drives Engagement? *Journal of Advertising Research*, *51*(4), 578–585. doi:10.2501/JAR

Pearce, D., Markandya, A., & Barbier, E. B. (1989). *Blueprint 1: For a Green Economy*. London: Earthscan.

Peattie, K. (1999). Trappings versus substance in the greening of marketing planning. *Journal of Strategic Marketing*, *7*(2), 131–148.

Peterson, R. T. (1987). Bulemia and Anorexia in an Advertising Context. *Journal of Business Ethics*, *6*(6), 495–504.

"Phil" Klaus, P., & Maklan, S. (2012). EXQ: a multiple-item scale for assessing service experience. *Journal of Service Management*, *23*(1), 5–33. doi:10.1108/09564231211208952

Piatscheck, N. (2013). Konsum Kinder. (German). *Textilwirtschaft*, (19), 0018.

Piegsa, E. (2010). *Green Fashion: Ökologische Nachhaltigkeit in der Bekleidungsindustrie*. Hamburg: Diplomica Verlag.

Pine, B. J., & Gilmore, J. H. (2011). *The experience economy* (Updated ed). Boston, Mass: Harvard Business Review Press.

Poloian, L. R. (2013). *Retailing Principles - Global, Mulitchannel, and Managerial Viewpoints* (Second Edition). New York: Fairchild.

Polonsky, M. J., & Hyman, M. R. (2007). A Multiple Stakeholder Perspective on Responsibility in Advertising. *Journal of Advertising*, *36*(2), 5–13.

Posner, H. (2011). *Marketing Fashion.* (1. ed.). London: Laurence King.

Prelec, D., & Loewenstein, G. (1998). The Red and the Black: Mental Accounting of Savings and Debt. *Marketing Science, 17*(1), 4–28. doi:10.1287/mksc.17.1.4

Prelec, D., & Simester, D. (2001). Always Leave Home Without It: A Further Investigation of the Credit-Card Effect on Willingness to Pay. *Marketing Letters, 12*(1), 5–12. doi:10.1023/A:1008196717017

Raab, G., & Unger, F. (2005). *Marktpsychologie : Grundlagen und Anwendung / Gerhard Raab; Fritz Unger.* Wiesbaden : Gabler, 2005.

Raithel, S. (2014). Vom Verkäufer zum Touchpoint. *TextilWirtschaft,* (14), 24–25.

Rath, P. M., Bay, S., Petrizzi, R., & Gill, P. (2008). *The Why of the Buy: Consumer Behavior and Fashion Marketing.* New York : Fairchild Books, 2008.

Reichheld, F. (2003, December). The One Number You Need to Grow. Retrieved November 28, 2014, from https://hbr.org/2003/12/the-one-number-you-need-to-grow

Rennhak, C. (2010). Grundlagen moderner Kommunikationspolitik. In *Kommunikationspolitik im 21. Jahrhundert* (pp. 1–22). Stuttgart: Ibidem-Verlag.

Rex, E., & Baumann, H. (2007). Beyond ecolabels: what green marketing can learn from conventional marketing. *Journal of Cleaner Production, 15*(6), 567–576. doi:10.1016/j.jclepro.2006.05.013

Richins, M. L. (1991). Social Comparison and the Idealized Images of Advertising. *Journal of Consumer Research, 18*(1), 71–83.

Richtscheid, C. (2013, November 26). Berlin: PayPal CheckIn Pilot gestartet - PayPal Deutschland Blog. Retrieved December 30, 2014, from https://www.paypal.de/blog/berlin-paypal-checkin-pilot-gestartet/

Ritch, E. L., & Schröder, M. J. (2012). Accessing and affording sustainability: the experience of fashion consumption within young families. *International Journal of Consumer Studies, 36*(2), 203–210. doi:10.1111/j.1470-6431.2011.01088.x

Rittinger, S. (2013). *Cross-Channel Retail Branding Eine verhaltenswissenschaftliche Untersuchung in Deutschland, Frankreich und Großbritannien*. Wiesbaden: Imprint: Springer Gabler.

Rittinger, S. (2014). Erfolgsfaktoren von Multi-Channel-Retailern. In S. Rittinger, *Multi-Channel Retailing* (pp. 13–30). Wiesbaden: Springer Fachmedien Wiesbaden. Retrieved from http://link.springer.com/10.1007/978-3-658-05197-6_5

Robison, J. (2006). Is That a Neuromarketer in Your Brain? *Gallup Management Journal Online*, 1.

Rodríguez-Santos, M., González-Fernández, A., & Cervantes-Blanco, M. (2013). An analysis of the construct "involvement" in consumer behaviour. *Quality & Quantity*, *47*(2), 1105–1123.

Rösch, B. (2014). Kanäle Grande. *Textilwirtschaft-Stores and Systems 2014*, 54–56.

Rosenbaum, M. S., Ostrom, A. L., & Kuntze, R. (2005). Loyalty programs and a sense of community. *Journal of Services Marketing*, *19*(4), 222–233. doi:10.1108/08876040510605253

Rossmann, P. D. A. (Ed.). (2013). Auf der Suche nach dem Return on Social Media: Perspektiven und Grenzen der Erfolgsmessung im Social Web. Universität St.Gallen, Institut für Marketing.

Runnemark, E., Hedman, J., & Xiao, X. (2014). *Do Consumers Pay More Using Debit Cards than Cash? An Experiment*. Retrieved from http://openarchive.cbs.dk/bitstream/handle/10398/8926/Hedman.pdf?sequence=1

Sabini, J., & Silver, M. (2005). Ekman's basic emotions: Why not love and jealousy? *Cognition & Emotion*, *19*(5), 693–712.

Santilli, P. C. (1983). The Informative and Persuasive Functions of Advertising: A Moral Appraisal. *Journal of Business Ethics*, *2*(1), 27–33.

Sashi, C. M. (2012). Customer engagement, buyer-seller relationships, and social media. *Management Decision*, *50*(2), 253–272. doi:10.1108/00251741211203551

Sayman, S., & J. Hoch, S. (2014). Dynamics of price premiums in loyalty programs. *European Journal of Marketing, 48*(3/4), 617–640. doi:10.1108/EJM-11-2011-0650

Scharf, A., Schubert, B., & Hehn, P. (2012). *Marketing: Einführung in Theorie und Praxis*. Stuttgart: Schäffer-Poeschel.

Schoenbachler, D. D., & Gordon, G. L. (2002). Multi-channel shopping: understanding what drives channel choice. *Journal of Consumer Marketing, 19*(1), 42–53. doi:10.1108/07363760210414943

Schramm-Klein, H. (2003). *Multi-Channel-Retailing: verhaltenswissenschaftliche Analyse der Wirkung von Mehrkanalsystemen im Handel*. Dt. Univ.-Verl., Wiesbaden.

Schramm-Klein, H. (2012). Multi Channel Retailing – Erscheinungsformen und Erfolgsfaktoren. In J. Zentes, B. Swoboda, D. Morschett, & H. Schramm-Klein (Eds.), *Handbuch Handel* (pp. 419–437). Wiesbaden: Springer Fachmedien Wiesbaden. Retrieved from http://link.springer.com/10.1007/978-3-8349-3847-3_21

Schramm-Klein, H., Wagner, G., Neus, F., Swoboda, B., & Foscht, T. (2014). *(R)Evolution des Mehrkanalhandels Von Multi-Channel- über Cross-Channel- zu Omni-Channel-Retailing*. Frankfurt am Main: Deutscher Fachverlag.

Schramm-Klein, H., Wagner, G., Steinmann, S., & Morschett, D. (2011). Cross-channel integration – is it valued by customers? *The International Review of Retail, Distribution and Consumer Research, 21*(5), 501–511. doi:10.1080/09593969.2011.618886

Schröder, H., & Zaharia, S. (2008). Linking multi-channel customer behavior with shopping motives: An empirical investigation of a German retailer. *Journal of Retailing and Consumer Services, 15*(6), 452–468. doi:10.1016/j.jretconser.2008.01.001

Schwerdt, Y. (2013, February 26). Multi-Channel, Cross-Channel und Omni-Channel Retailing. Retrieved from http://schwerdtblog.absatzwirtschaft.de/2013/02/26/multi-channel-cross-channel-und-omni-channel-retailing/

Scott, D. M. (2010). *The new rules of marketing and PR: how to use social media, blogs, news releases, online video, & viral marketing to reach buyers directly*. Hoboken, N.J.: John Wiley & Sons.

Shankar, V., Inman, J. J., Mantrala, M., Kelley, E., & Rizley, R. (2011). Innovations in Shopper Marketing: Current Insights and Future Research Issues. *Journal of Retailing, 87*(Supplement 1), S29–S42.

Shannon, C. E., Weaver, W., & Wiener, N. (1950). The Mathematical Theory of Communication. *Physics Today, 3*(9), 31. doi:10.1063/1.3067010

Shapiro, S., & Spence, M. T. (2005). Mind Over Matter? The Inability to Counteract Contrast Effects Despite Conscious Effort. *Psychology & Marketing, 22*(3), 225–245. doi:10.1002/mar.20056

Shaw, C. (2007). *The DNA of customer experience: how emotions drive value*. Basingstoke: Palgrave Macmillan.

Shaw, D., Hogg, G., Wilson, E., Shiu, E., & Hassan, L. (2006). Fashion victim: the impact of fair trade concerns on clothing choice. *Journal of Strategic Marketing, 14*(4), 427–440. doi:10.1080/09652540600956426

Shen, B., Zheng, J.-H., Chow, P.-S., & Chow, K.-Y. (2014). Perception of fashion sustainability in online community. *Journal of the Textile Institute, 105*(9), 971.

Sherman, E., Mathur, A., & Smith, R. B. (1997). Store Environment and Consumer Purchase Behavior: Mediating Role of Consumer Emotions. *Psychology & Marketing, 14*(4), 361–378.

Shimp, T. A., & Moody, M. P. (2000). In Search of a Theoretical Explanation for the Credit Card Effect. *Journal of Business Research, 48*(1), 17–23. doi:10.1016/S0148-2963(98)00071-X

Shrum, L. J., McCarty, J. A., & Lowrey, T. M. (1995). Buyer Characteristics of the Green Consumer and Their Implications for Advertising Strategy. *Journal of Advertising, 24*(2), 71–82.

Sigg, B. (2009). *Emotionen im Marketing: neuroökonomische Erkenntnisse*. Bern; Stuttgart; Wien: Haupt.

Simpson, B. J. K., & Radford, S. K. (2012). Consumer Perceptions of Sustainability: A Free Elicitation Study. *Journal of Nonprofit & Public Sector Marketing, 24*(4), 272–291.

Sirgy, M. J. (1982). Self-Concept in Consumer Behavior: A Critical Review. *Journal of Consumer Research, 9*(3), 287–300.

Skinner, D. B. (1935). The generic nature of the concepts of stimulus and response. *Journal of General Psychology, 12*(1), 40–65.

Skov, L. (2012). Trust and mistrust in the ethics of the fafshion business. Copenhagen Business School.

Slaper, T. F., & Hall, T. J. (2011). The Triple Bottom Line: What Is It and How Does It Work? *Indiana Business Review, 86*(1), 4–8.

Sloboda, R. (2014, November 4). Why You Should Get Excited About Emotional Branding. Retrieved December 16, 2014, from http://www.smashingmagazine.com/2014/04/11/get-excited-about-emotional-branding/

Smith, T., Coyle, J. R., Lightfoot, E., & Scott, A. (2007). Reconsidering Models of Influence: The Relationship between Consumer Social Networks and Word-of-Mouth Effectiveness. *Journal of Advertising Research, 47*(4), 387–397.

Solomon, M. R., Bamossy, G., Askegaard, S., & Hogg, M. K. (2010). *Consumer Behaviour: A European Perspective*. Pearson Education.

Solomon, M. R., Bamossy, G. J., & Askegaard, S. (1999). *Consumer behaviour : a European perspective / Michael Solomon; Gary Bamossy; Søren Askegaard*. New York ; Munich [u.a.] : Prentice Hall Europe, c 1999.

Solomon, M. R., Marshall, G. W., & Stuart, E. W. (2012). *Marketing: real people, real choices*. Boston; London: Pearson.

Solomon, M. R., & Rabolt, N. J. (2004a). *Consumer behavior in fashion / Michael R. Solomon and Nancy J. Rabolt*. Upper Saddle River, N.J. [u.a.] : Prentice Hall, 2004.

Solomon, M. R., & Rabolt, N. J. (2004b). *Consumer behavior in fashion / Michael R. Solomon and Nancy J. Rabolt*. Upper Saddle River, N.J. [u.a.] : Prentice Hall, 2004.

Soman, D. (2001). Effects of Payment Mechanism on Spending Behavior: The Role of Rehearsal and Immediacy of Payments. *Journal of Consumer Research, 27*(4), 460–474.

Soman, D. (2003). The Effect of Payment Transparency on Consumption: Quasi-Experiments from the Field. *Marketing Letters, 14*(3), 173–183.

Sommer, S. (2013, May 22). Der ROPO-Effekt: Die Wechselwirkung zwischen Online und Offline sichtbar machen! Retrieved from http://www.twoqubes.com/blog/2013/05/der-ropo-effekt-die-wechselwirkung-zwischen-online-und-offline-sichtbar-machen/

S-O-R Modell. (2014). In *Wirtschaftslexikon24.com*. Retrieved from http://www.wirtschaftslexikon24.com/d/s-o-r-modell/s-o-r-modell.htm

Spalding, L., Cole, S., & Fayer, A. (2009). How Rich-Media Video Technology Boosts Branding Goals. *Journal of Advertising Research, 49*(3), 285–292.

Spriestersbach, K. (2014). *Erfolgreiche Websites: Online-Marketing, Usability, SEO, SEA*. Bonn: Galileo Press.

Statista.com (Ed.). (2014, December). Führende Social Networks nach Nutzerzahlen weltweit 2014. Statista.

Statistisches Bundesamt. (2014, January). Anzahl der in deutschen Krankenhäusern diagnostizierten Fälle von Anorexie und Bulimie bis 2012. Retrieved January 5, 2015, from http://de.statista.com/statistik/daten/studie/28909/umfrage/in-krankenhaeusern-diagnostizierte-faelle-von-anorexie-und-bulimie/

Stenger, D. (2012). *Virale Markenkommunikation [Elektronische Ressource] : Einstellungs- und Verhaltenswirkungen viraler Videos / von Daniel Stenger*. Wiesbaden : Gabler Verlag, 2012.

Stokols, D. (1972). On the distinction between density and crowding. *Psychological Review, 79*(3), 275–277.

Stout, P. A., & Leckenby, J. D. (1986). Measuring Emotional Response to Advertising. *Journal of Advertising*, *15*(4), 35–42.

Strähle, J. (2013). Script International Marketing. Hochschule Reutlingen.

Strähle, J. D. (2013). *Script Fashion Chain Management*. Hochschule Reutlingen, Fakultät T&D.

Strähle, J., Von der Forst, F., Micarelli, S., & Schmidt, P. (2014, November 26). *Retail Symposium: Digitalisierung - Letzte Rettung für den stattionären Handel?*. Reutlingen.

Strang, R. (2013, November). Retail without boundaries. Retrieved from www.scmr.com

Straughan, R. D., & Roberts, J. A. (1999). Environmental segmentation alternatives: a look at green consumer behavior in the new millennium. *Journal of Consumer Marketing*, *16*(6), 558–575. doi:10.1108/07363769910297506

Strauss, B. (2000). Using New Media for Customer Interaction: A Challenge for Relationship Marketing. In T. Henning-Thurau & U. Hansen (Eds.), *Relationship marketing: gaining competitive advantage through customer satisfaction and customer retention.* (1. ed., pp. 233–253). Berlin; Heidelberg; New York: Springer. Retrieved from http://dx.doi.org/10.1007/978-3-662-09745-8

Sull, D., & Turconi, S. (2008). Fast fashion lessons. *Business Strategy Review*, *19*(2), 4–11.

Sundaram, D. S., Mitra, K., & Webster, C. (1998). Word-of-Mouth Communications: A Motivational Analysis. *Advances in Consumer Research*, *25*(1), 527–531.

Sweeney, J. C., & Wyber, F. (2002). The role of cognitions and emotions in the music-approach-avoidance behavior relationship. *Journal of Services Marketing*, *16*(1), 51–69. doi:10.1108/08876040210419415

Teixeira, T., Wedel, M., & Pieters, R. (2012). Emotion-Induced Engagement in Internet Video Advertisements. *Journal of Marketing Research (JMR)*, *49*(2), 144–159. doi:10.1509/jmr.10.0207

The Net Promoter Score and System - Net Promoter Community. (n.d.). Retrieved November 28, 2014, from http://www.netpromoter.com/why-net-promoter/know/

Theng So, J., Grant Parsons, A., & Yap, S. (2013). Corporate branding, emotional attachment and brand loyalty: the case of luxury fashion branding. *Journal of Fashion Marketing and Management: An International Journal*, *17*(4), 403–423. doi:10.1108/JFMM-03-2013-0032

Thomas, S. (2013). Linking customer loyalty to customer satisfaction and store image: a structural model for retail stores. *DECISION*, *40*(1-2), 15–25. doi:10.1007/s40622-013-0007-z

Thorsten Hennig-Thurau, F., Gwinner, K. P., Walsh, G., & Gremler, D. D. (2004). Electronic Word-of-Mouth via Consumer-Opinion Platforms: What Motivates Consumers to Articulate Themselves on the Internet? *Journal of Interactive Marketing*, *18*(1), 38–52. doi:10.1002/dir.10073

Tigert, D. J., Ring, L. J., & King, C. W. (1976). Fashion Involvement and Buying Behavior: A Methodological Study. *Advances in Consumer Research*, *3*(1), 46–52.

Tiggemann, M., & Polivy, J. (2010). Upward and Downward: Social Comparison Processing of Thin Idealized Media Images. *Psychology of Women Quarterly*, *34*(3), 356–364.

Topolansky Barbe, F. G., Gonzalez-Triay, M. M., & Hensel, A. (2013). Eco-labels in Germany. *Journal of Customer Behaviour*, *12*(4), 341–359. doi:10.1362/147539213X13875568505868

Toth, A. (2014). Das Einkaufserlebnis im Handel. In A. Toth, *Die Beziehung zwischen Einkaufserlebnis und Preiszufriedenheit* (pp. 15–115). Wiesbaden: Springer Fachmedien Wiesbaden. Retrieved from http://link.springer.com/10.1007/978-3-658-04234-9_2

TransFair. (2014a). Absatz von Fairtrade-Textilien in Deutschland bis 2013 | Statistik. Retrieved January 5, 2015, from http://de.statista.com/statistik/daten/studie/171742/umfrage/absatz-von-textilien-mit-fairtrade-siegel-seit-2008/

TransFair. (2014b). *TransFair Jahresbericht 2013/2014*. TransFair e.V. Retrieved from http://de.statista.com/statistik/daten/studie/171742/umfrage/absatz-von-textilien-mit-fairtrade-siegel-seit-2008/

Tritsch, R. (2014). Trends & Technologies In Retail. *Checkout, 40*(10), 58.

Tropp, J. (2007). Marketingkommunikation als Teil der Unternehmenskommunikation. In A. Zerfaß & M. Piwinger (Eds.), *Handbuch Unternehmenskommunikation* (1. ed., pp. 1099–1120). Wiesbaden: Gabler Verlag. Retrieved from http://search.ebscohost.com/login.aspx?direct=true&db=edb&AN=95566090&lang=de&site=eds-live&authtype=shib

Tropp, J. (2014). *Moderne Marketing-Kommunikation System - Prozess - Management*. (2. ed.). Wiesbaden: VS Verlag für Sozialwissenschaften.

Tryon, W. W. (2014). Chapter 5 - Emotion. In W. W. Tryon (Ed.), *Cognitive Neuroscience and Psychotherapy* (pp. 257–288). San Diego: Academic Press. Retrieved from http://www.sciencedirect.com/science/article/pii/B9780124200715000053

Tseng, S.-C., & Hung, S.-W. (2013). A framework identifying the gaps between customers' expectations and their perceptions in green products. *Journal of Cleaner Production, 59*, 174–184. doi:10.1016/j.jclepro.2013.06.050

Van Bruggen, G. H., Antia, K. D., Jap, S. D., Reinartz, W. J., & Pallas, F. (2010). Managing Marketing Channel Multiplicity. *Journal of Service Research, 13*(3), 331–340.

Van Riel, A. C. R., Semeijn, J., Ribbink, D., & Bomert-Peters, Y. (2012). Waiting for service at the checkout: Negative emotional responses, store image and overall satisfaction. *Journal of Service Management, 23*(2), 144–169. doi:10.1108/09564231211226097

Verhoef, P. C., Neslin, S. A., & Vroomen, B. (2007). Multichannel customer management: Understanding the research-shopper phenomenon. *International Journal of Research in Marketing, 24*, 129–148.

Vieira, V. A. (2013). Stimuli–organism-response framework: A meta-analytic review in the store environment. *Journal of Business Research, 66*(9), 1420–1426. doi:10.1016/j.jbusres.2012.05.009

VisaEurope. (2014, September 9). Visa mobile payments coming to Apple's iPhone 6, iPhone 6 Plus and Apple Watch. Retrieved December 28, 2014, from http://www.visaeurope.com/newsroom/news/visa-mobile-payments-coming-to-apple-s-iphone-6-iphone-6-plus-and-apple-watch

Visschers, V., Tobler, C., Cousin, M. E., Brunner, T., Orlow, P., & Siegrist, M. (2010). *Konsumverhalten und Foerderung des umweltverträglichen Konsums: Bericht im Auftrag des Bundesamtes fuer Umwelt BAFU*. Zürich: ETH Zürich. Retrieved from http://www.google.de/url?sa=t&rct=j&q=&esrc=s&source=web&cd=1&ved=0CCMQFjAA&url=http%3A%2F%2Fwww.bafu.admin.ch%2Fprodukte%2F10446%2Findex.html%3Flang%3Dde%26download%3DNHzLpZeg7t%2CInp6I0NTU042I2Z6In1acy4Zn4Z2qZpnO2Yuq2Z6gpJCGeH9%2CgWym162epYbg2c_JjKbNoKSn6A--&ei=W7eeVJ7wMcn0OpWdgMAM&usg=AFQjCNFFMgWBySZRJFvuizjmRTKjaddgUQ&bvm=bv.82001339,d.ZWU

Wade, T. J., Fuller, L., Bresnan, J., Schaefer, S., & Mlynarski, L. (2007). Weight halo effects: Individual differences in personality evaluations and perceived life success of men as a function of weight? *Personality and Individual Differences*, *42*(2), 317–324. doi:10.1016/j.paid.2006.07.011

Walker, L. J. (2001). The Measurement of Word–of–Mouth Communication and an Investigation of Service Quality and Customer Commitment as Potential Antecedents. *Journal of Service Research*, *4*(1), 60.

Walsh, G., Shiu, E., Hassan, L. M., Michaelidou, N., & Beatty, S. E. (2011). Emotions, store-environmental cues, store-choice criteria, and marketing outcomes. *Journal of Business Research*, *64*(7), 737–744. doi:10.1016/j.jbusres.2010.07.008

Wangenheim, F. v., & Bayón, T. (2007). The chain from customer satisfaction via word-of-mouth referrals to new customer acquisition. *Journal of the Academy of Marketing Science*, *35*(2), 233–249.

Ward, P., Davies, B. J., & Kooijman, D. (2007). Olfaction and the retail environment: examining the influence of ambient scent. *Service Business*, *1*(4), 295–316. doi:10.1007/s11628-006-0018-3

WCED. (1987). Our common future. *Brundtland Commission (WCED) Report*. Retrieved from http://search.ebscohost.com/login.aspx?direct=true&db=edsoai&AN=edsoai.757367072&lang=de&site=eds-live&authtype=shib

We Are Social's Digital Statshot 003. (2014, November 12). Retrieved from http://de.slideshare.net/wearesocialsg/we-are-socials-digital-statshot-003

Weber, T. D. (2012). *Visual Merchandising,*. Hochschule Reutlingen.

Wehner, T. (Hrsg. ., & Gentile, G.-C. (Hrsg. . (2012). *Corporate Volunteering*. [s.l.]: Gabler Verlag Springer Fachmedien Wiesbaden GmbH.

Weinfurtner, S., Wittmann, G., Stahl, E., Wittmann, M., & Pur, S. (2013, March). Studie_Erfolgsfaktor_Payment_2013.pdf. Retrieved November 4, 2014, from http://homepages-nw.uni-regensburg.de/~ecl60018/download/Studie_Erfolgsfaktor_Payment_2013.pdf

Werner, K., & Kirsten, D. (2010). *Eco Fashion Top-Labels entdecken die Grüne Mode*. München: Stiebner.

Westbrook, R. A. (1981). Sources of Consumer Satisfaction with Retail Outlets. *Journal of Retailing, 57*(3), 68–85.

Wiehr, H. (2011, March 4). Von Multi- zum Omni-Channel. Retrieved from http://www.channelpartner.de/a/von-multi-zum-omni-channel,2383094

Wilding, R. (2013). Multichannel or omnichannel? *Logistics & Transport Focus, 15*(10), 44–44.

Williams, R. (2002). Memetics: a new paradigm for understanding customer behaviour? *Journal of Marketing Practice: Applied Marketing Science, 20*(3), 162–167.

Willmott, P., & McIntosh, B. (2014, May). Digital strategy | McKinsey & Company. Retrieved December 15, 2014, from http://www.mckinsey.com/insights/business_technology/digital_strategy

Winge, T. M. (2008). "Green Is the New Black": Celebrity Chic and the "Green" Commodity Fetish. *Fashion Theory: The Journal of Dress, Body & Culture, 12*(4), 511–

524. doi:10.2752/175174108X346968

Wirtz, B. W. (2008). *Multi-channel-Marketing: Grundlagen - Instrumente - Prozesse*. Wiesbaden: Gabler.

Wittmann, D. G., Stahl, D. E., Horn, N., Peschl, T., Preis, M., & Bolz, T. (2013, March). Social Media in Deutschland: Daten, Fakten und Status quo. ibi research an der Universität Regensburg GmbH. Retrieved from www.ecommerce-leitfaden.de

Wollenschläger, U. (2014a). Bundesregierung: Textilbündnis statt Siegel. *TextilWirtschaft*, (41), 6.

Wollenschläger, U. (2014b). Drei Säulen der Nachhaltigkeit. *TextilWirtschaft*, (Nr. 46), 36.

Wollenschläger, U. (2014c). Textilbündnis sorgt für heiße Diskussionen. *TextilWirtschaft*, (42), 6.

Wolny, J., & Mueller, C. (2013). Analysis of fashion consumers' motives to engage in electronic word-of-mouth communication through social media platforms. *Journal of Marketing Management*, 29(5/6), 562–583. doi:10.1080/0267257X.2013.778324

Woodcock, N., Green, A., & Starkey, M. (2011). Social CRM as a business strategy. *Journal of Database Marketing & Customer Strategy Management*, 18(1), 50–64. doi:10.1057/dbm.2011.7

Wood, J. (2007). Relative Abundance:Fuller´s Discovery that the Glass Is Always Half Full. In *Designers, Visionaries and Other Stories: A Collection of Sustainable Design Essays*. Earthscan.

World Commission on Environment and Development. (1987). *Our Common Future*. United Nations.

Yang, S., Hu, M. (Mandy), Winer, R. S., Assael, H., & Chen, X. (2012). An Empirical Study of Word-of-Mouth Generation and Consumption. *Marketing Science*, 31(6), 952–963. doi:http://dx.doi.org/10.1287/mksc.1120.0738

Yuen, E. F., & Chan, S. S. (2010). The effect of retail service quality and product quality on customer loyalty. *Journal of Database Marketing & Customer Strategy Management*, *17*(3), 222–240.

Yurchisin, J., & Johnson, K. K. P. (2010). *Fashion and the Consumer*. Oxford; New York: Bloomsbury Academic.

Zaharia, S. (2013). Integrierte Multi-Channel-Geschäftsmodelle ermöglichen Zeitersparnis beim Einkauf. In dgroup, G. Heinemann, K. Haug, & M. Gehrckens (Eds.), *Digitalisierung des Handels mit ePace* (pp. 123–136). Wiesbaden: Springer Fachmedien Wiesbaden. Retrieved from http://link.springer.com/10.1007/978-3-658-01300-4_7

Zakaria, I., Rahman, B. A., Othman, A. K., Yunus, N. A. M., Dzulkipli, M. R., & Osman., M. A. F. (2014). The Relationship between Loyalty Program, Customer Satisfaction and Customer Loyalty in Retail Industry: A Case Study. *Procedia - Social and Behavioral Sciences*, *129*, 23–30. doi:10.1016/j.sbspro.2014.03.643

Zara. (2010). SCHLUSSVERKAUF | ZARA Deutschland. Retrieved December 28, 2014, from http://www.zara.com/de/de/schlussverkauf-c643506.html?

Zentes, J., Foscht, T., & Swoboda, B. (2012). *Handelsmanagement*. München: Vahlen.

Zentes, J., Morschett, D., & Schramm-Klein, H. (2011a). Instore Marketing. In J. Zentes, D. Morschett, & H. Schramm-Klein, *Strategic Retail Management* (pp. 273–295). Wiesbaden: Gabler Verlag. Retrieved from http://www.springerlink.com/index/10.1007/978-3-8349-6740-4_14

Zentes, J., Morschett, D., & Schramm-Klein, H. (2011b). *Strategic retail management text and international cases*. Wiesbaden: Gabler. Retrieved from http://dx.doi.org/10.1007/978-3-8349-6740-4

Zhang, J., & Breugelmans, E. (2012). The impact of an item-based loyalty program on consumer purchase behavior. *Journal of Marketing Research*, *49*(1), 50–65.

Zhang, J., Farris, P. W., Irvin, J. W., Kushwaha, T., Steenburgh, T. J., & Weitz, B. A. (2010a). Crafting Integrated Multichannel Retailing Strategies. *Journal of Interactive Marketing*, *24*(2), 168–180. doi:10.1016/j.intmar.2010.02.002

Zhang, J., Farris, P. W., Irvin, J. W., Kushwaha, T., Steenburgh, T. J., & Weitz, B. A. (2010b). Crafting Integrated Multichannel Retailing Strategies. *Journal of Interactive Marketing*, *24*(2), 168–180. doi:10.1016/j.intmar.2010.02.002

Zhang, Y., Kong, F., Zhong, Y., & Kou, H. (2014). Personality manipulations: Do they modulate facial attractiveness ratings? *Personality and Individual Differences*, *70*, 80–84. doi:10.1016/j.paid.2014.06.033

Ziethaml, V. A., Berry, L. L., & Parasuraman, A. (1993). The Nature and Determinants of Customer Expectations of Service. *Journal of the Academy of Marketing Science*, *21*(1), 1–12. doi:10.1177/0092070393211001

Zimmer, D. (2014). Auf der Suche nach dem Service. *Internet World Business*, (07/2014), 8–11.

Zurawicki, L. (2010). *Neuromarketing: Exploring the Brain of the Consumer*. Berlin, Heidelberg: Springer Berlin Heidelberg.